Official deviance: readings in malfeasance, misfeasance, and other forms of corruption

Jack D. Douglas
University of California at San Diego

John M. Johnson
Arizona State University

J. B. LIPPINCOTT COMPANY
Philadelphia
New York   San Jose   Toronto

2894107

Contents

Contents

part I

Introduction

"I knew no wrong. I did no evil thing . . . I did not diminish the grain measure. I did not diminish the land measure. I did not load the weight of the balances. I did not deflect the index of the scales." Supplication by an official to Osiris in *The Book of The Dead.* / "If a king says, 'What will profit my kingdom?', the high officials will say, 'What will profit our families?', and the lower officials and commoners will say, 'What will profit ourselves?' " Mencius, a disciple of Confucius in ancient China. / "Just as it is impossible not to taste the honey or the poison that finds itself at the tip of the tongue, so it is impossible for a government servant not to eat up at least a bit of the king's revenue. Just as fish moving under water cannot possibly be found out either as drinking or not drinking water, so government workers cannot be found out while taking money for themselves." Kautilya, in the *Arthasastra* of ancient India. / "Except one be able to give the Regent or Provost of a House [at Oxford] a piece of money, ten pounds, twenty pounds, yea a hundred pounds, a yoke of fat

1

oxen, a couple of fine geldings or the like, though he be never so toward a youth, nor have never so much need of maintenance, yet he come not there I warrant you." Philip Stubbes, *Anatomie of Abuses,* 1583. / "The fact is New York politics were always dishonest—long before my time. There never was a time when you couldn't buy the Board of Aldermen." William Marcy Tweed, New York, 1873. / "I am not a crook." Richard M. Nixon, Washington, D.C. 1974.

Government corruption and the usurpation of power have been major concerns of human beings since the beginnings of government. The pervasiveness of corruption and usurpation varies from one society to another and within a single society over time. Public concern rises and falls correspondingly. But the problems and the resulting concerns seem to be an inherent part of the governing process. Indeed, in spite of the vast differences in the societies, and the long periods of time that separate us, it is striking how similar the problems and the public concerns of ancient civilizations are to those of modern technological society. Any American citizen can understand very well the ideas expressed in the diverse statements above, ranging from *The Book of The Dead* in ancient Egypt to Richard Nixon's recent statement.

Members of all modern Western societies differ considerably in their concerns with the problems of corruption and usurpation of power. But all of them are very concerned now compared to earlier periods of their own histories. Americans have probably always been more concerned than most other people, perhaps because of their long-standing skepticism about government. The many and complex forms of official deviance that surfaced in the Watergate scandals have obviously produced a great heightening of this concern, and of the desire to understand such deviance, so that something can be done to prevent it in the future. Sociologists, political scientists, journalists, and other students of deviance and government have shown the same heightened concern.

Sociologists have always been deeply involved in the study of deviance and its relationship to social order, or disorder. They have done vast amounts of research, analysis, and writing on suicide, mental illness, crime, delinquency, and other social ills. Rarely have they been concerned with political corruption, or with official usurpation of power. Political scientists and other students of government, especially journalists, have been deeply involved in the study of political corruption and official power seizure. But rarely have they been concerned with other forms of deviance, and even more rarely have they used or contributed to the theories of deviance developed by sociologists.

This failure of the two disciplines to draw on each other's work in these related fields is almost certainly the result of professional blinders. For the fact is, as will become abundantly clear to the readers of this book, both disciplines have been dealing with remarkably similar phenomena in remarkably similar terms for decades, without realizing it, and without taking advantage of each other's strengths. Sociologists, for example, would be surprised to discover that in 1910 Robert Brooks published a classic work, *Corruption in American Politics and Life,* in which he "rediscovered" certain things Durkheim had already written about. He also discovered certain ideas contained in the very recent labeling theory, proposed by Howard Becker and others. And political scientists and journalists may be surprised by some of the very different ideas about social rules, deviance, and social order that have developed out of the sociology of deviance in recent years. (See Readings 13, 16, and 34.) Bringing together all the evidence, theoretical analysis, and proposed solutions of these major disciplines—journalism, sociology, and political science—should help greatly to increase our understanding of the complex problems of official deviance.

The Complex Meanings of Official Deviance

As Robert Brooks (Reading 1) and Arnold Heidenheimer (Reading 2) have argued in some detail, the generic concept of official (political) corruption has been one of the most complex, problematic, and changeable concepts of political and social science. The term has been used to cover everything from the common-sense idea of "the putrid rot of the body politic," which is obviously grounded in metaphorical allusions to physical decay, to the very abstract and technical-legal definitions of official misfeasance (nonperformance of duty) and official malfeasance (misperformance of duty). The words normally used to deal with the subject are taken directly from common-sense usage, as they should be, if they are to deal with the problems that concern average citizens. Their ambiguities, which include semantic confusion, are a direct result of the complex, problematic, and conflicting nature of our ordinary experience with these matters. Since it is precisely those natural or real world complexities, problems, and conflicts that we want to understand and to correct, it is useful to have common-sense terminology. On the other hand, as social thinkers and social scientists, we want to arrive at some more precise, reliable, and objective understanding of these phenomena; and words in common use can be a tremendous detriment to achieving that goal, unless we analyze them carefully. Part I is intended to clarify the conceptual problems in this area and to show how terms are generally (though not always) used in the succeeding chapters and in the general literature.

We have chosen to use the general term "official deviance" both because it is a direct derivative of the sociology of deviance, and because it helps to avoid two confusions of using the more popular term "political corruption." First, we use the term "official," rather than "political," because everyone today is concerned with the deviance of a much broader spectrum of officials than was the case when the word "corruption" was first used. Many government officials today are not conceived of as political, either by themselves or by the public. Yet, they become involved in many of the same things, are subject to many of the same social concerns, and to many of the same laws about deviance as public figures are. We wish to consider the whole range of problems, so we shall use the broader term. Second, the word "corruption" has come to mean primarily material corruption, or receiving some kind of financial benefit in return for deviant practices. Since most people are more concerned with usurpation of power by officials than with their material corruption, an ordering of concerns we share, we think it best to use a generic term that leaves no doubt about our concern with the gamut of official deviance.

Like most journalists, who have taken a moralistic stand on corruption, except for such rare individuals as Walter Lippmann (see Reading 28), social scientists have not been content to merely analyze what the public thinks about corruption. Probably more than sociologists of deviance and crime, they are strongly oriented toward policy. That is, they have been generally outspoken about what they think the public *should* feel, think, and do about official deviance in its various forms. This will be apparent in almost all of the following essays, sometimes explicitly, but more often implicitly. Part of the reason for this is that the citizens of every major Western nation are in partial disagreement about what should be considered deviant, what the order of seriousness should be and what should be done about it. Conflicting opinion is apparent in highly pluralistic nations like the United States but, although it exists to a lesser degree in more homogeneous nations like Sweden or the Netherlands, it is present even there today. (Reading 34 tries to show that this is a direct result of growing conflicts between certain groups and their governments because government has grown so massively in size and power in recent decades.)

It should be made clear, however, that social scientists have rarely tried to interject their personal values or feelings into the argument. Rather, they have tried to show that official deviance does not necessarily have the bad effects the members think it does and that the moral fervor of people who seek to eradicate all official deviance can have unanticipated consequences which those same people would consider dreadful. Moreover, social scientists have tried to show that our social discord involves great conflict over what acts should be considered deviant. Consequently, moralistic attempts to eradicate the evildoing can lead to greatly increased internal conflict. For both reasons, one of the consistent themes in social science literature (as discussed in Reading 21) is the insistence that citizens should distinguish between different kinds of corruption and should see that they have very different consequences for society, even some very desirable consequences, as defined by the citizens themselves. One such argument is found in the modern literature about political machine corruption (the spoils system, etc.). There is a very large body of literature based on the idea that the distribution of material gains by political machines, in return for personal loyalty, has some very positive "functions" (as Merton calls it in Reading 29) for society, and most people would agree, if they understood the actual operation of most machines. This argument, which was first clearly formulated by such politicians as Boss Tweed (and later clarified by George Washington Plunkitt of Tammany Hall), will be cited over and over again in this book. (See Boss Tweed's formulation of this point in Reading 8.) At the same time, some of the literature (as in Reading 9) has argued that one must distinguish clearly between different kinds of political machines and their effects, because some are socially benign and some are catastrophic for entire social groups. We have tried to include all of the major arguments about these basic points so that readers may decide for themselves what pragmatic position they should take.

The Complex and Changing Forms of Official Deviance

Most members of society tend to take an absolutist or a moralistic view of official deviance. That is, they think their views of what is deviant and what is not are necessarily true, and that everyone else should agree. To the social scientist who studies the many complex forms of official deviance through history and across societies, nothing is clearer than that official deviance does not lend itself to a single definition or viewpoint. In medieval Europe, public offices, including that of tax collector, were commonly sold to the highest bidder. The successful buyer of the office was then able to recoup his expenses, and far more, by levying as great a tax on his portion of the tortured body politic as it would bear, although this was constrained by custom. This remained common practice in Great Britain until the early nineteenth century. Though the burdened taxpayer may not have wholeheartedly endorsed the system, he seems to have accepted it as is the natural way of government. The educated commonly did accept it and, although the Enlightenment *philosophes* were instrumental in producing the changes in public opinion that eventually led Napoleon to introduce sweeping reform, Montesquieu strongly approved the selling of offices on the grounds that it would lead to a better officialdom than would the free choice of appointments by the princes. Such a practice would be universally condemned in the Western world today. The custom was found in the United States as late as the nineteenth century, but at that time it was swept away by the rising tides of the political reform movement, which led to many basic changes in our conceptions of official deviance and our reactions to it. A contract given by the U.S. Secretary of the Treasury Richardson to one John Sanborn to collect delinquent taxes for a 50% fee is now ridiculed as one of the more ludicrous excesses of the age of the Robber Barons. Americans looking at histories of government often think the difference between that age and our own consists simply of ours being more moral, theirs more immoral. They overlook the fact that their own moral standards are implicit in that view. Some students of corruption would insist that this popular viewpoint developed because the average citi-

zen does not know what is really going on behind all the political pronouncements. They would argue that our age may be seen as one of great official
deviance, in our own terms, once this deviance is more fully revealed. Many
government practices, now accepted as perfectly moral, will produce serious
problems that will lead to their eventually being labeled as deviant. The essays
in Part II show how ethical standards and practices have changed in our own
society during the past century. But these essays also show that certain things
have remained unchanged and seem to differ primarily because new labels
have been applied to them. The same can be said, only more so, about
variations among nations and cultures. We have chosen to deal with these
variations only when they have an important bearing on our own situation,
because a full consideration would have changed the focus of our work. But
anyone interested in that literature can find references to most of it in such
works as James Scott's *Comparative Political Corruption.*

Usurpations of Power, Official Violence, Police Corruption, and Regulatory Deviance

Americans have probably been more concerned, even shocked, by the
revelations of federal usurpations of power in recent years than by any form
of material corruption. The Watergate investigations, which revealed everything from violations of civil rights by the CIA and the FBI to payoffs to
the vice-president and cover-ups by the president, have revealed more pervasive usurpations of power at the federal level than at any time since the
Civil War, when Abraham Lincoln suspended such civil rights as habeus
corpus on a massive scale. Earlier violations of this sort, with the possible
exception of the Palmer raids against alien radicals in 1920, were generally
responses to clear threats to the government, such as were apparent during
the Civil War. (We must note, however, that a high percentage of Americans
at that time violently disagreed with the supposed necessity of arresting and
even deporting political figures without due process of law. Although there
was no evidence of presidential complicity in the many murders of political
figures during the Civil War era, the banishment of the Democratic contender
for the governorship of Ohio, was literally kidnapping. The public outcry was
so great that Lincoln later allowed him to return secretly, apparently with the
understanding that he stay out of politics.) The controversy over such usurpations will be intense for many years, perhaps forever. We have tried to present
examples of major viewpoints, but obviously cannot cover the entire spectrum
of views.

For the same reasons, we have had to be very selective in choosing articles
on the many different forms of official deviance. Just as we have emphasized
federal usurpations of power, because these are most clearly seen by people as
endangering the basic institutions of our society, and thus endangering our
basic rights, so we have focused on official violence and police corruption and

usurpations of power. Official violence which goes beyond the law is clearly one of the most important kinds of power usurpation, perhaps the most important. Extralegal violence is basic to any form of tyranny and is destructive of any constitutional democracy. The controversies about official violence and its implications are immense. But there can be little controversy about the need to examine as carefully as possible all the evidence and all the available ideas.

Fortunately, there is much more social science evidence about the pervasive forms of police corruption and usurpations of power by the police. In fact, this is probably the only area in which there have been many valid and reliable studies of official deviance. We have chosen those we think are the best and most representative. The reader can easily go from these to any of the few dozen other such studies, many of which are referred to in the selections.

Our selection of essays concerning regulatory agency corruption and usurpation is restricted by space to the mere tip of the iceberg. Although social scientists have been derelict in researching these problems, and can, in some cases, be accused of conflicts of interest because of their own involvement in regulatory agencies, there are now many good studies by investigative reporters and social critics. These make it obvious that problems of deviance are pervasive in the bureaucracy of government regulatory agencies. Even though the problems of political and police deviance are more individually critical because of the greater power of the organizations, it is clear that the regulatory agencies are riddled with official deviance, simply because they are so much bigger than police agencies at all levels of government. Regulatory agencies are especially powerful in the United States because of the purposeful decentralization of power away from the politicians to the agencies. One might argue that in nations like Great Britain the entrenched position of civil servants gives them similar control. But in the United States, regulatory agencies have both civil service powers *and* the powers to interpret laws. This gives them truly massive authority and creates tremendous problems in making the agencies responsive to the public will. It also creates tremendous temptations for usurpations and corruption. If Big Government continues to grow, it will probably do so in large part because of the proliferation of regulatory agencies and their powers. They would become even more the centers of public controversy over official deviance.

Explanations and Proposed Solutions
For Official Deviance

Many people take a reasonably simple approach to official deviance; that is, they think it can be explained in terms of individual morality and that it can and should be resolved by levying severe penalties. Social scientists and the more analytical journalists like Walter Lippmann (see Reading 28) have almost all found this approach useless or, at best, useful only in isolated instances. Their reasoning is roughly the same as that which refutes the moralistic view of crime. There are social patterns to official deviance, as well as to public concern over such deviance, some of which are found all the time through the Western world. Although severe penalties may curtail some forms of deviance, penalties generally have very problematic relations to deviance, and sometimes they even increase deviance. Many of the readings that follow show the most important patterns of official deviance in American society. These include the patterns of machine politics (both old and new): the pervasive corruption in Eastern and some Midwestern police departments versus the relatively clean departments of the West, the greater corruption of state governments compared to city governments, the relative absense of federal corruption and usurpations between the 1890s and the early 1960s, and so on. Some of the essays in Part VIII show that there are very clear relationships between certain patterns of official deviance and other social patterns. For example, there is widespread agreement among social scientists who have studied machine spoils systems that such political systems developed in direct response to profound demands by citizens which were not, or could not be, met by more legal forms of government action. There is also widespread agreement that these forms of deviance not only helped the people, but also served the social purpose of helping to integrate the society. Some analysts have argued that this is generally true, but only in those situations in which there are some built-in or individually imposed restraints on the spoils, generally in the form of a "balanced machine." Without such restraints, a political machine, especially the kind of huge payoff system of voters that exists in some Western nations today, can create a fiscal hemorrhage. There is also widespread agreement that some forms of corruption, such as bribery in all its forms, can best be understood as a kind of black market system. Whenever there is a significant disparity between what the majority of people want and what they are allowed to get through formal, legitimate, official channels, a black market system will almost inevitably develop to provide the goods, and the bribery of officials will be its necessary lubricant. This argument has some evident, but startling, implications. In particular, it leads to the immediate conclusion that the more government tries to regulate the lives of the people, and the more powerful government becomes, the more official deviance there will be.

Except for the extensive literature in political science, there have been relatively few attempts to explain official deviance. As sociologists become more involved in the study of official deviance, there will probably be further attempts to apply the theories already developed in order to understand many other forms of deviance. It remains to be seen how well they will do the job. At the moment, there is little agreement about how even major patterns, other than the few mentioned here, are best explained. It is small wonder, then, that there is even more disagreement over which solutions we should try. This will be apparent in our concluding readings. We have tried to provide the best major examples of proposed solutions. Anyone who has followed closely the great controversies and legal battles over the proposals to limit campaign contributions and spending, which have gone on since the early part of this century (those in the post-Watergate era being only the latest and most intense), knows that there are no simple solutions to that. Even if we had a simple solution to propose, there would be no political possibility that its application would be simple. We suspect that in this era of Big Government, and massively complex government, official deviance will become an increasingly complex social problem and that citizens will have to struggle continually with all their wisdom to deal with this problem. This work is intended as one contribution to that struggle.

part II

The complex meanings of official deviance

Part II includes two articles which analyze the diverse, problematic, ambiguous, and culturally and temporally variable meanings of corruption. In "The Nature of Political Corruption," by Robert Brooks, first published in 1910, the author shows that scholars have long been aware that the term "corruption" is often used to denote diverse behaviors, that it is often used to refer to many actions besides those which society defines as illegal, and that it is a term with great rhetorical power in everyday politics. Charges of political corruption are standard fare for moralists, writers, journalists, muckrakers, reformers, and all the rest of us who seek to change existing practices. One of the important contributions of Brooks's analysis in Reading 1 is the point that perceptions of corruption are reflexively tied to certain standards of conduct, which are usually left implicit by those who use the term, and that without some definition of "duty," as he calls it, there would be no corruption. Another interesting feature of Brooks's article is that it represents a good example of the very argument it advances. To persuade the reader that corruption is not limited to political institutions, he mentions examples of nonpolitical "corruption," such as divorce and childless marriages. While these may have been valid illustrations of corruption at the turn of the century, there are few Western societies that would so regard them today. This in itself illustrates how our changing moral valuations reflexively constitute our judgments about corruption.

In Reading 2, Arnold Heidenheimer catalogues the varied meanings which are attributed to corruption by the public and by professional scholars. For scholars, reaching a definition of corruption has proved to be an illusive task, just as reaching a broader definition of deviance has proved problematic for sociologists. This in itself suggests to us that the concept is fundamentally problematic, both in the abstract and in terms of concrete perceptions. Heidenheimer points out some of the difficulties involved in both the empirical definitions of corruption and the normative ones, or those which have been public-office centered and those which have been public-interest centered, as well as those which use Western criteria of rationality as opposed to non-Western. These distinctions illuminate for us some of the key definitional problems of understanding all the diverse phenomena termed "corruption" and will make us sensitive to these problems.

1

The nature of
political corruption

Robert C. Brooks

In the whole vocabulary of politics it would be difficult to point
out any single term that is more frequently employed than the
word "corruption." Part orators and writers, journalists, "muck
rakers" and reformers all use it with the utmost freedom, and it
occurs not uncommonly in the less ephemeral pages of political
philosophers and historians. Transactions and conditions of very
different kinds are stigmatised in this way, in many cases doubtless with entire justice; but apparently there is little disposition to
inquire into the essential nature of corruption itself and to discriminate in the use of the word.

Detailed definitions of corrupt practices and bribery are, of
course, to be found in every highly developed legal code, but
these are scarcely broad enough to cover the whole concept as
seen from the viewpoint of political science or ethics. The sanctions of positive law are applied only to those more flagrant
practices which past experience has shown to be so pernicious
that sentiment has crystallised into statutory prohibitions and

Source: Robert C. Brooks, *Corruption in American Politics and Life.* New
York: Dodd, Mead, 1910. pp. 41–54. By permission of the publisher.

adverse judicial decisions. Even within this comparatively limited circle clearness and precision are but imperfectly attained. Popular disgust is frequently expressed at the ineptitude of the law's definitions and the deviousness of the law's procedure, as a result of which prosecutions of notoriously delinquent officials, politicians, and contractors so often and so ignominiously fail in the courts. If once we step outside the circle of legality, however, we find extremely confused, conflicting, and even unfair states of moral opinion regarding corruption. Public anger at some exposed villainy of this sort is apt to be both blind and exacting. Reform movements directed against corrupt abuses are no more free than are regular political organisations from partisan misrepresentation and partisan passion. With all their faults, however, it is largely from such forces and movements that we must expect not only higher standards of public morality, but also a clearer and more comprehensive legislative and judicial treatment of corrupt practices in the future. For this reason it would seem to be desirable, if possible, to formulate some fairly definite concept of corruption, broader than the purely legal view of the subject and applicable in a general way to the protean forms which evil of this sort assumes in practice.

Certain verbal difficulties must first be cleared away. Chief among these, perhaps, is the extreme levity with which the word is bandied about. One word, indeed, is not sufficient, and a number of slang equivalents and other variants must needs be pressed into service: graft, boodle, rake-off, booty, loot, spoils, and so on. With all due recognition of recent achievements in the way of gathering and presenting evidence, it is lamentably apparent that charges of corruption are still very frequently brought forward, by party men and reformers alike, on slight grounds or no grounds at all, and also that in many of these cases no intention exists of pushing either accusation or defence to a point where a thorough threshing-out of the matter at issues is possible. In "practical politics" insinuations of the blackest character are made jestingly, and they are ignored or passed off with a shrug or a smile, provided only that they be not of too pointed or too personal a character. Very serious evils may follow reckless mudslinging of this sort. Even if the charges are looked upon as the natural and harmless exuberances of our current political warfare, their constant repetition tends to blur the whole popular conception of corruption. Insensibly the conviction gains ground that practices which are asserted to be so common can scarcely be wholly bad, since public life goes on without apparent change and private prosperity seems unaffected. If, on the other hand, the current accusations of corruption are to be taken at anything like their face value, it becomes difficult to avoid the pessimism that sees nothing but rottenness in our social arrangements and despairs of all constructive reform with present materials.

A second verbal point that demands attention is the metaphorical character of the word corruption. Even when it is distinctly qualified as political or business or social corruption, the suggestion is subtly conveyed of organic corruption and of everything vile and repugnant to the physical senses which the latter implies. It need not be charged that such implications are purposely cultivated; indeed they are so obvious and common that their use by this time has become a matter of habit. Witness in current writing the frequent juxta-position of the word corruption, used with reference to social phenomena, with such words as slime, filth, sewage, stench, tainted, rottenness, gangrene, pollution, and the frequent comparison of those who are supposed to profit by such corruption to vultures, hyenas, jackals, and so on. Side by side with the levity already criticised we accordingly find a usage which, however exag-gerated and rhetorical it may be, appears to indicate a strong popular feeling against what are deemed to be corrupt practices.

Escape from such confusion can hardly come from the accepted formulas of the dictionaries. Their descriptions of periphrases of corruption are in general much too broad for use in exact discussion. Bribery, indeed, is de-fined with sufficient sharpness by the *Century Dictionary* as

a gift or gratuity bestowed for the purpose of influencing the action or conduct of the receiver; especially money or any valu-able consideration given or promised for the betrayal of a trust or the corrupt performance of an allotted duty, as to a fiduciary agent, a judge, legislator or other public officer, a witness, a voter, etc.

Corruption, however, is by no means synonymous with bribery. The latter is narrower, more direct, less subtle. There can be no bribe-taker without a bribe-giver, but corruption can and frequently does exist even when there are no personal tempters or guilty confederates. A legislator may be approached by a person interested in a certain corporation and may be promised a defi-nite reward for his favourable vote on a measure clearly harmful to the public interest but calculated to benefit the corporation concerned. If the bargain be consummated it is unquestionably a case of bribery, and the action involved is also corrupt. But, if current reports are to be believed, it sometimes hap-pens that legislators, acting wholly on their own initiative and regardless of their duty to the state, vote favourably or unfavourably on pending bills, endeavouring at the same time to profit financially by their action, or by their knowledge of the resultant action of the body to which they belong, by speculation in the open market. In the latter instance they have not been approached by a personal tempter, and the brokers whom they employ to buy or sell may be ignorant of the motives or even of the identity of their patrons. Clearly this is not bribery, but equally clearly it is corrupt. The distinction is perhaps sufficiently important to justify the coinage of the term "*auto-corruption*" to cover cases of the later sort.[1] Corruption in the widest

1. Other illustrations of auto-corruption may be found in speculation by inside officials on the basis of crop reports not yet made public, and in real estate deals based on a knowledge of projected public improvements.

sense of the term would then include both bribery and auto-corruption, and may be defined as *the intentional misperformance or neglect of a recognised duty, or the unwarranted exercise of power,*[2] *with the motive of gaining some advantage more or less directly personal.*

It will be observed that none of the terms of the foregoing definition necessarily confines corruption to the field of politics. This is intentional. Corruption is quite possible elsewhere as in the state. That it has so frequently been discussed as peculiarly political is by no means proof that government is subject to it in a greater degree than other social organisations. One might rather conclude that the earlier discovery and more vigorous denunciation of corruption as a political evil showed greater purgative virtue in the state than in other spheres of human activity. For surely the day is gone by when the clamour of reformers was all for a "business administration" of public affairs. Since that era business has had to look sharply to its own morals—in insurance, in public utilities, in railroads, in corporate finance, and elsewhere. Revelations in these fields have made it plain that much of the impetus to wrong-doing in the political sphere comes originally from business interests. This is not to be taken as in any sense exculpating the public officials concerned; it simply indicates the guilt of the business man as *particeps criminis* with the politician. Moreover business can and does suffer from forms of corruption which are peculiar to itself and which in no way involve political turpitude. Such offenses range all the way from the sale by a clerk of business secrets to a rival concern, and the receipt of presents or gratuitous entertainment from wholesalers by the buyers for retail firms, up to the juggling of financial reports by directors, the mismanagement of physical property by insiders who wish to buy out small stockholders, and the investment of insurance or other trust funds to the private advantage of managerial officers.

Besides business and politics, other spheres of social activity are subject to corrupt influences. Indeed wherever and whenever there is duty to be shirked or improperly performed for motives of more or less immediate advantage evil of this sort may enter in. This is the case with the church, the family, with educational associations, clubs, and so on throughout the whole list of social organizations. To ingratiate himself with wealthy or influential parishioners, for example, a minister may suppress convictions which his duty to God and religion requires him to express. A large proportion of the cases of divorce, marital infidelity, and childless unions reflect the operation of corrupt influences upon our family life. In the struggle for endowments and bequests colleges and universities have at times forgotten some of their high ideals. If corrupt motives play a smaller part in the social organisations just

2. Misperformance and neglect of duty do not clearly include cases of usurpation with corrupt motives; hence the addition of this clause to the definition. Some usurpations may of course be defended as involving high and unselfish motives, and hence free from corruption.

mentioned than in politics or business it is perhaps not so much due to the finer fibre of churchmen, professors, and the like, as to the subjection of the more grossly gainful to other motives in clerical, educational, and similar circles.

While the possibility of corruption is thus seen to be extremely broad, our present concern is chiefly with political corruption. To adjust the definition hazarded above to cover the latter case alone it is necessary only to qualify the word "duty" by the phrase "to the state." Further discussion of the various terms of the definition, thus amended, would seem advisable.

To begin with, corruption is *intentional.* The political duty involved is perceived, but it is neglected or misperformed for reasons narrower than those which the state intends. Failure to meet a recognised duty is not necessarily corrupt; it may be due to simple inefficiency. The corrupt official must know the better and choose the worse; the inefficient does not know any better. In either case the external circumstances may appear to be closely similar, and the immediate results may be equally harmful. No doubt what is often denounced in the United States as corruption is mere official stupidity, particularly in those spheres of administration still filled by amateurs and dominated by the "rotation of office" theory. Thus a purchasing official unfamiliar with his duties may prove the source of large profits to unscrupulous dealers. So far as the official himself is concerned no private advantage may be sought or gained, but the public interest suffers just the same. In another case the official understands the situation thoroughly and takes advantage of it by compelling the dealers to divide with him the amount by which the government is being defrauded, or he may go into business with the aid of office boys or relatives and sell to himself as purchasing agent. The latter are clear cases of bribery and auto-corruption respectively, but so far as immediate results are concerned the state is no worse off than with the official who was merely ignorant or careless. To one not in full possession of the underlying facts all three cases may appear very similar.

Successful corruption, however, tends to become insatiable, and in the long run the state may suffer far more from it and from the spread of the bad moral example which it involves than it can easily suffer from simple inefficiency. On the other hand inefficiency also may spread by imitation, although perhaps more slowly, since it is not immediately profitable, until the whole service of government is weakened. Moreover inefficiency may develop by a very natural process into thoroughgoing corruption. If not too stupid, the incapable official may come to see the advantages which others are deriving from his incapacity and may endeavour to participate in them. Because of his failure to obtain promotion so rapidly as his more efficient fellow-servants, he may be peculiarly liable to the temptation to get on by crooked courses. Practically, therefore, inefficiency and corruption are apt to be very closely connected—a fact which civil service reformers have long recognised. It would also seem that the two are very closely connected in their essential nature, and only a very qualified assent can be given to the doctrine that inefficiency, as commonly understood, is morally blameless. To be so considered the incapable person must be entirely unaware of his inability to measure up to the full requirement of duty. In any other event he is consciously and intentionally ministering to a personal interest, be it love of ease or desire to retain an income which he does not earn, to the neglect of the public duties with which he is intrusted. Now, according to the definition presented above, this attitude is unquestionably corrupt. It is, however, so common on the part of both officeholders and citizens that its corruptness is seldom recognised.

Definitions, concepts and criteria of corruption

Arnold J. Heidenheimer

Any attempt to analyze the concept of corruption must contend with the fact that in English and other languages the word *corruption* has a history of vastly different meanings and connotations. In some eras, for instance the 1900s in the United States, corruption was one of the most frequently employed terms in the political vocabulary. According to a critic contemporary with this period, Robert C. Brooks, party orators, journalists, reformers, political philosophers, and historians "stigmatize[d] in this way transactions and conditions of very different kinds . . . [with] little disposition to inquire into the essential nature of corruption and to discriminate in the use of the word." The only connotation that the many usages of the word *corruption* had in common in this period was that it was somehow the antithesis of *reform, rationality,* and the demands of the public weal.

Thus, even the more thoughtful and objective writers of this earlier era would have been nonplussed had they read Samuel Huntington's judgment in a 1968 publication that "corruption may thus be functional to the maintenance of a political system in the same way that reform is." As is implied in Huntington's usage and elsewhere in the contemporary social science literature, the term *corruption* has developed a more specific meaning with regard to kinds of behavior and a much less polarized meaning with regard to ethical connotations. At times, indeed, it is employed in a context that is almost totally value-free, as in this passage by the economist, Nathaniel Leff:

Corruption is an extra-legal institution used by individuals or groups to gain influence over the actions of the bureaucracy. As such the existence of corruption *per se* indicates only that these groups participate in the decision-making process to a greater extent than would otherwise be the case.

Varieties of Meanings

A careful examination of what past and present writers seem to have intended when they employed the term *corruption* in political contexts reveals an even broader catalog of usages and potential ambiguities. Some reasons for this become more apparent by referring to the *Oxford English Dictionary,* where we find that only one of nine commonly accepted definitions for the term is applicable to political contexts: "Perversion or destruction of integrity in the discharge of public duties by bribery or favour; the use or existence of corrupt practices, especially in a state, public corporation, etc."

The *OED* categorizes the nine meanings of corruption as follows:

1. *Physical*—for example, "The destruction or spoiling of anything, especially by disintegration or by decomposition with its attendant unwholesomeness and loathsomeness; putrefaction."
2. *Moral*—the "political" definition already given comes under this category. Another definition in this category is: "A making or becoming morally corrupt; the fact or condition of being corrupt; moral deterioration or decay; depravity."
3. *The preversion of anything from an original state of purity*—for example, "The perversion of an institution, custom, and so forth from its primitive purity; an instance of this perversion."

The present usage of the term *corruption* in political contexts has obviously been colored by the meanings in the "moral" category, and in earlier times usage was frequently colored by the meanings in the two other categories, especially by those in the third category. Thus the author of a nineteenth-century encyclopedia article entitled "Corruption in Politics" developed his discussion essentially in terms of meanings derived by way of Montesquieu from Aristotle, who, for instance, conceived of *tyranny* as a "corrupted" variant of monarchy.

Contemporary Social Science Definitions

The variety of definitions employed by contemporary social scientists interested in corruption fortunately does not cover as wide a span as those given in the *OED*. Among them we can identify usages that seek to define corruption in terms of one of three kinds of basic models or concepts. The largest group of social science writers follow the *OED* definition and relate their definitions of *corruption* essentially to concepts concerning the duties of the public office. A smaller group develop definitions that are primarily related to demand, supply, and exchange concepts derived from economic theory; while a third group discuss corruption more with regard to the concept of the public interest.

Public-Office-Centered Definitions

Definitions of corruption that relate most essentially to the concept of the public office and to deviations from norms binding upon its incumbents are well illustrated in the work of three authors—David H. Bayley, M. McMullan, and J. S. Nye—who have concerned themselves with the problems of development in various continents. According to Bayley's definition of the word . . . ,

Corruption, while being tied particularly to the act of bribery, is a general term covering misuse of authority as a result of considerations of personal gain, which need not be monetary.

M. McMullan says that

A public official is corrupt if he accepts money or money's worth for doing something that he is under duty to do anyway, that he is under duty not to do, or to exercise a legitimate discretion for improper reasons.

J. S. Nye defines corruption as

. . . behavior which deviates from the normal duties of a public role because of private-regarding (family, close private clique), pecuniary or status gains; or violates rules against the exercise of certain types of private-regarding influence. This includes such behavior as bribery (use of reward to pervert the judgment of a person in a position of trust); nepotism (bestowal of patronage by reason of ascriptive relationship rather than merit); and misappropriation (illegal appropriation of public resources for private-regarding uses).

Market-Centered Definitions

Definitions in terms of the theory of the market have been developed particularly by those authors dealing with earlier Western and contemporary non-Western societies, in which the norms governing public officeholders are not clearly articulated or are nonexistent. Leff's definition, cited earlier, would fall into this category, as would the definitions of Jacob van Klaveren and Robert Tilman. Van Klaveren . . . states that

A corrupt civil servant regards his public office as a business, the income of which he will . . . seek to maximize. The office then becomes a "maximizing unit." The size of his income de-pends . . . upon the market situation and his talents for finding the point of maximal gain on the public's demand curve.

Robert Tilman . . . holds that

Corruption involves a shift from a mandatory pricing model to a free-market model. The centralized allocative mechanism, which is the ideal of modern bureaucracy, may break down in the face of serious disequilibrium between supply and demand. Clients may decide that it is worthwhile to risk the known sanctions and pay the higher costs in order to be assured of receiving the desired benefits. When this happens bureaucracy ceases to be patterned after the mandatory market and takes on characteristics of the free market.

Public-Interest-Centered Definitions

Some writers feel that the first set of definitions is too narrowly conceived and the second set too broadly conceived. They tend to maintain that the embattled concept of "public interest" is not only still useful but necessary to illustrate the essence of concepts like corruption. Carl Friedrich, for instance, contends that

The pattern of corruption can be said to exist whenever a power-holder who is charged with doing certain things, i.e., who is a responsible functionary or officeholder, is by monetary or other rewards not legally provided for induced to take actions which favour whoever provides the rewards and thereby does damage to the public and its interests.[1]

Arnold A. Rogow and H. D. Lasswell . . . maintain that

A corrupt act violates responsibility toward at least one system of public or civil order and is in fact incompatible with (destructive

1. Carl J. Friedrich, "Political Pathology," *Political Quarterly*, 37 (1966), p. 74.

of) any such system. A system of public or civil order exalts common interest over special interest; violations of the common interest for special advantage are corrupt.

Whose Norms Set the Criteria?

The definitions employed in the first and third of the categories just discussed directly raise the question encountered in all normative analysis: Which norms are the ones that will be utilized to distinguish corrupt from noncorrupt acts? If the definitions are public-office-centered, then which statement of the rules and norms governing public officeholders is to be employed? If the definitions are public-interest-centered, then whose evaluation of the public's interest is to be operationalized? Definitions couched in terms of market theory appear to bypass this problem, but in fact they do not. They too imply that somewhere there is an authority that distinguishes between the rules applicable to public officials and those applicable to businessmen operating in the free market, or that there are certain characteristics that distinguish a "black market" from the free market.

Political scientists of an earlier generation tried to deal with the problem of norm setting with reference to the legal rules provided by statute books and court decisions. Thus behavior was judged by James Bryce to be either permissible or corrupt in accordance with the criteria established by legislators and judges:

Corruption may be taken to include those modes of employing money to attain private ends by political means which are criminal or at least illegal, because they induce persons charged with a public duty to transgress that duty and misuse the functions assigned to them.[2]

But most contemporary social scientists would echo the skepticism that Robert Brooks articulated in 1910 . . . as to whether legal definitions alone would suffice:

Definitions of corrupt practices . . . found in every highly developed legal code . . . are scarcely broad enough to cover the whole concept as seen from the viewpoint of political science or ethics. The sanctions of positive law are applied only to those more flagrant practices which past experience has shown to be so pernicious that sentiment has crystallized into statutory prohibitions and adverse judicial decisions. Even within this comparatively limited circle clearness and precision are but imperfectly attained.

The author of the article on "Corruption, Political," in the *Encyclopedia*

2. James Bryce, *Modern Democracies,* II, New York: St. Martin's, 1921, p. 524.

of the Social Sciences agreed that "the question of formal legality . . . is not the essence of the concept." The normative judgments that should be used as criteria, he thought, were the judgments of the elite: "Where the best opinion and morality of the time, examining the intent and setting of an act, judge it to represent a sacrifice of public for private benefit, then it must be held to be corrupt."[3]

The definition suggested by Senturia raises numerous problems, namely those related to the difficulties of identification, operationalization, and uniqueness. Although social scientists often select particular elite groups with reference to status and other criteria, few claim to have developed specific techniques for identifying in any society a sample that would represent "the best opinion of the time." Even if this were accomplished, Senturia's particularistic emphasis would require that this fairly large body of elites serve as a jury for each particular case. Their findings, in effect, would relate only to their society of that particular era.

A consensus of the "best opinion" in a time and place, such as Britain in 1960, could presumably establish criteria beyond which private-regarding behavior would be considered corrupt in the contemporary setting. However, it would then be impossible to compare either the extent or the varieties of political corruption between the situations prevailing of Britain in 1960 and in 1860 because of the uniqueness of the suggested definition. This difficulty would apply equally to attempts to compare, say, bureaucratic corruption in nineteenth-century Russia and twentieth-century Chicago. Another difficulty in relying too much on any one elite opinion is that the incumbent elite may change drastically as the result of revolution or decolonization. Thus, in the course of decolonization, the criteria by which the colonial rulers had punished corruption among native officials and subjects were radically diluted within a short time when the opinion of the postcolonial native politicians de-emphasized many of the taboos that had been attached to private-regarding behavior. Still later, in many African and Asian countries, behavior that was widely accepted by the ruling politicians one month was heavily stigmatized the next month after spartan-minded officers successfully carried through a coup d'état.

Western versus Non-Western Standards

If one does not accept the criteria established by law or the norms of a small elite group as delimiting political corruption, how far can one go in delineating the relevant norms with reference to the standards of a more diverse set of reference groups and codes? At present this problem presents itself most directly for those social scientists who have sought to analyze

3. Joseph J. Senturia, "Corruption, Political," *Encyclopedia of the Social Sciences*, IV. New York: Crowell-Collier-Macmillan, 1930–1935.

corruption in developing countries where mores rooted in two very distinct milieus govern the standards of political and bureaucratic behavior. David H. Bayley . . . has outlined the resultant problem posed for the objective investigator:

It not infrequently happens . . . in developing non-Western societies that existing moral codes do not agree with Western norms as to what kinds of behavior by public servants should be condemned. The Western observer is faced with an uncomfortable choice. He can adhere to the Western definition, in which case he lays himself open to the charge of being censorious and he finds that he is condemning not abhorrent behavior, but normal acceptable operating procedure. On the other hand, he may face up to the fact that corruption, if it requires moral censure, is culturally conditioned. He then argues that an act is corrupt if the surrounding society condemns it. This usage, however, muddies communication, for it may be necessary then to assert in the same breath that an official accepts gratuities but is not corrupt.

Given this alternative, authors like Bayley prefer to build upon the "Western denotative meaning of corruption," even in analyzing non-Western systems. This "imposition" on the rest of the world of Western standards in evaluating behavior may well be, at this stage of research and theory building, a prerequisite to meaningful comparative analysis of political corruption phenomena. In general terms (more with regard to bureaucratic than to electoral corruption) there probably does exist today a broad consensus among Western elites and non-elites as to which kinds of behavior are clearly conceived of as corrupt. This consensus has gradually developed over the past century. But the norms embodied in a definition such as that of Nye, quoted earlier, are surely built upon more than the personal preferences of a small clique of academic political moralizers. It is highly probable that any elite or even mass survey of attitudes in Western countries would result in overwhelming support for the proposition that the kinds of deviations from public rules and the kinds of self-regarding behavior that are included in Nye's definition should be labeled corrupt, and guilty practitioners stigmatized accordingly. Writers such as Bayley admit that this consensus is limited rather than universal, but they argue that the norms expressed by it are the only ones that can possibly be applied cross-culturally and that we should go ahead and do so. In further defense of his strategy, Bayley argues that:

the intelligentsia, and especially top-level civil servants, in most underdeveloped nations are familiar with the Western label "corruption," and they apply it to their own countries. . . . It is not unfair, therefore, to make comparative statements between West and non-West based upon Webster's definition. Such judgments will be readily understood by the nation-building elites in most developing countries.

The complex and changing forms of official deviance

The seven readings that follow document some of the changes and some of the continuities in official deviance in the United States. Taken together, they show that certain things that so outraged the citizenry of earlier decades no longer exist, at least to any significant degree. They also show that many actions which were generally accepted as normal practice some years ago are seen today as unacceptable and morally reprehensible. Walter Goodman tells us, in Reading 3, that most, if not all, of the United States founding fathers routinely sold their official influence to the highest bidders, and some even advertised these services in Washington newspapers. We know this to be different from today, if only because our Congressional leaders do not openly advertise their services. Goodman's reading also shows how the successful reforms of 1853–64 diminished the usual forms of influence-peddling and paved the way for other more innovative and subtle forms. Some of these forms are documented further in Reading 4 by James Dickenson, who tells us about the "cupidity, stupidity, and rascality" of our nineteenth- and twentieth-century Washington politicians.

"Question of Ethics," (Reading 5), first appeared as an aritcle in *Newsweek* during the Wayne Hays-Elizabeth Ray "sex and payroll" scandal of 1976. While a score of elected United States officials have been indicted or convicted in the last two decades, the article correctly argued that, in some respects, there is much less official deviance today as in outright influence-peddling, alcoholism, and absenteeism. In other matters, such as those concerning staffing and nepotism, and the less direct forms of selling influence, corrupt routines are still largely unexamined, tolerated, and carried out, independent of the formal rules which were intended to control them. Some gray areas, such as "perks" (perquisites) and expense-paid travel or "junkets," still exist and are currently being reevaluated. This article, like the two previous ones, ties some of the abuses to Congressional pay scales.

In "Wincanton: The Politics of Corruption" (Reading 6), John Gardiner and David Olson offer an extraordinary case study of corrupt practices and public response to them in one large American city over several decades. This chapter well illustrates the complicated interrelations between official rule violations and other segments of a community: the feelings of ambivalence many Wincanton citizens had; and the temporarily successful efforts to reduce the more blatant corruption of their political institutions. Gardiner and Olson also give many examples of "honest graft" and "dishonest graft" in Wincanton—a distinction we learned about in previous chapters. Wincanton represents the old machine politics which characterized most Eastern and Midwestern cities in the United States at one time or another. The machine system is further documented in Mike Royko's "Daley's Machine in Chicago" (Reading 7). According to Royko, the older form of machine politics, also known as the boss system, still exists in Chicago because Mayor Richard Daley was able to effectively control its major components—service, patronage, and money. While Americans are often accused of forgetting the lessons of their own history, Mayor Daley seems to be an exception; he appears to have learned the lessons of Boss Tweed of New York, and has succeeded where Tweed failed.

The two final readings in this section present Jack Douglas's comparative analyses of the traditional form of machine politics with that of the new Welfare State Machine. In "Mayor John Lindsay and the Revenge of Boss Tweed" (Reading 8), he shows both the striking similarities and the important differences in the official actions of Lindsay and Tweed. While the older forms of machine politics succeeded by utilizing practical services, patronage, and immediate material gains, the newer Welfare State Machine uses these practices less often, using instead tax monies to obtain middle-class voting support, in the form of rent subsidies, free college tuition, pension plans for public employees' unions, etc. Although the older and newer machine politics may differ in form, Douglas argues that they both stem from similar social conditions and problems. Reading 9 further analyzes the new political machine and draws some important implications it has for our times.

3

All honorable men

Walter Goodman

Corruption is no stranger to Washington; it is a famous resident. Nineteenth-century America, with its predilection for low doings in high places, may be thought of as working out an unwholesome heritage from the Mother Country. The facts are familiar; still they provide some perspective on our own follies. The easy morals of Restoration England, displayed in gaudy strokes by the South Sea Bubble, had been imported by the Colonial administration, and been found adaptable to independence. Cynical Alexander Hamilton saw in the English system, "bottomed on corruption," a way of reconciling economic and political interests and of strengthening the state, while John Adams, the Puritan, looked about him and concluded that corruption was the very glue of stable government. There were fortunes to be made in the new country, and government officials were more or less openly

From Walter Goodman. *All Honorable Men: Corruption and Compromise in American Life*. Boston: Little Brown and Co., 1963. Reprinted by permission.

prepared to help high bidders make them. They were not courting disgrace, merely working at their jobs. Even such a personage as Daniel Webster practiced gentlemanly extortion when appropriate, and had none of the compunctions of later officials about putting things in writing. In 1833, when President Jackson was trying to kill the National Bank, Senator Webster sent a now notorious note to Nicholas Biddle, the Bank's president: "Sir: Since I have arrived here, I have had an application to be concerned, professionally, against the Bank, which I have declined, of course, although I believe my retainer has not been renewed or *refreshed*, as usual. If it be wished that my relation to the Bank should be continued, it may be well to send me the usual retainers." In addition to Senator Webster, Mr. Biddle served up refreshments to several dozen other national leaders, including Henry Clay, John C. Calhoun (thereby accounting for three of the five great Senators selected in 1957 to adorn the Senate reception room with their portraits), some cabinet members and three vice presidents of the United States.

It was common practice in the early eighteen-hundreds for Congressmen and members of the Executive to represent private individuals in bringing claims against the government. Some of the more enterprising of them even advertised for customers in Washington newspapers. Their influence was openly for sale, and it was understood by everyone in that rough-and-ready time that they would use it without false humility or any show of subtleness. One legislator, dissatisfied with the way a court-martial was proceeding against a client of his, told a member of the military court: "You expect soon to be promoted, and I give you to understand that your confirmation will not get through the Senate without some difficulty."

The ethical scene in Washington during those years was streaky, and it became worse discolored during the Civil War and in the commercial debauchery of the postwar period, which a committee of lawyers has recently described as a time "of actual fraudulent claims, sale of information, claim chasing, overt sale of influence, improper diversion of public lands, corruption in public office, and wartime contract frauds and favoritism." But a more critical attitude toward official morality was spreading. Behavior which would not have warranted a passing shrug in Walpole's England began to seem downright unacceptable to some mid-nineteenth-century Americans. Speaking of the claims agents in 1853, Andrew Johnson said, "The government and the functionaries of government are beginning to stink in the very nostrils of the nation. . . ." Their odor brought about, between 1853 and 1864, America's first four conflict-of-interest statutes—all of them aimed at ending the practice of officials representing private interests in government matters.

A few blatant symptoms of the moment were thus outlawed, but the body politic was far from cured. Cut off from a modest source of income, the nation's legislators soon found themselves showered with largesse from railroad promoters and speculators in land, from contractors and jobbers, tax-collectors and random operators. The country was opening, and it was a rich time in America for daring men outside of government and for accessible men within. In the eighteen-sixties and 'seventies, railroad manipulators disbursed hundreds of thousands of dollars in bribes year after year. Oakes Ames, the Massachusetts Representative who headed the Union Pacific's railroad-milking Credit Mobilier of America, insured the well-being of his enterprise by placing two hundred shares of the company's stock with his fellow Congressmen where, he explained to associates, "they will do the most good to us." Collis P. Huntington, one of the promoters of the Central Pacific Railroad, which during its heyday paid out thousands in graft for the privilege of bilking the government of millions, complained that the country's legislators were "the hungriest set of men that ever got together." And an unusually objective Congressman of the time likened the House of Representatives to "an auction room where more valuable considerations were disposed of under the speaker's hammer than in any other place on earth."* But the Congress held no monopoly on crookedness. The scandals that developed out of the post-Civil War orgy of speculation, and incidentally gave the Grant Administration the soiled name it must wear through posterity, were notable for the numbers and the assortment of high-placed men implicated in them. "One might search the whole list of Congress, Judiciary and Executive during the twenty-five years 1870–1895," wrote the patrician Henry Adams, "and find little but damaged reputation."

This lusty era provides our history texts with as ill-favored a spectacle of dynamic democracy in action as we have produced, but it was not totally unedifying. Bribery, after all, presupposes a certain respect for law—not for its integrity, to be sure, but for its power. By civilized standards, a bribe is preferable to a blow (as our commercial emissaries are now proving to officials of ethically underdeveloped lands), and when businessmen chose to buy their wealth through "high officials sitting half in sight to share the plunder and to fix things right" rather than club their way to it over the bodies of their fellow citizens, they were paying tribute of a sort to the legal establishment. Not only were they several paces beyond barbarity, but by corrupting the law, they acknowledged that they were its subjects; it stood above them and had to be pacified. This thought may provide small comfort to a bilked nation, but in a poetic sense at least, the bribers were setting themselves up for the judgment which, in fact, came for some of them around the turn of

---

*Here, from Mark Twain's *The Gilded Age,* is the president of the Columbus River Slackwater Navigation Company explaining what happened to a $200,000 appropriation his concern had just obtained from Congress: "A Congressional appropriation costs money. Just reflect, for instance. A majority of the House committee, say $10,000 apiece—$40,000; a majority of the Senate committee, the same each—say $40,000; a little extra to one or two chairmen of one or two such committees, say $10,000 each—$20,000; and there's $100,000 of the money gone, to begin with. Then seven male lobbyists, at $3,000 each—$21,000; one female lobbyist, $10,000; a high moral Congressman or Senator here and there—the high moral ones cost more, because they give tone to a measure—say ten of these at $3,000 each, is $30,000; then a lot of small-fry country members who won't vote for anything whatever without pay. . . ."

the century when the great move westward slowed. The public lands, which had only yesterday been boundless, showed signs of running out, and the nation, recently so free and easy with its wealth, reacted against its own carelessness and apathy by punishing numbers of speculators and their abettors in the capitol. Other scandals lay ahead, particularly during World War I and the postwar period—always a perilous time of slump for a nation's ethical bearing—but never again would public corruption be so easy, so accepted, so widespread. The federal government was becoming too important in the lives of too many people for open rascality to be openly tolerated on the national level.

Yet the stakes kept getting higher. The public lands were exhausted, but public spending had barely begun. With the burgeoning of government services—giving, lending, buying, licensing, allocating, subsidizing—during the depression 'thirties and wartime 'forties, Washington became a mecca for favor-seekers of all kinds, setting their sights now not on the corrupt official exclusively, but on his cousins as well—on the weak man, the insensitive man, the foolish man, the irresponsible man. The areas of their activity shifted; Congress, once the sink and center of favoritism, and not yet a temple of the vestals, became investigator, exposer and denouncer, particularly when the other party held power in the White House. (Politicians, as Robert Moses has remarked, are given to pushing away the ladder by which they rose and pretending "that they reached the apex by some mysterious levitation or reverse gravity directed from above.") There was greater wealth than ever to be found in Washington, but the getting of it called for more refined techniques than our pioneering gold-panners knew or needed.

Through the skein of cynicism we place between ourselves and the actions of our public officials there throbs a highly sensitive set of nerve ends. How else explain our agitated response to the quite modest scandals of our time? The nineteenth century's crude displays of venality are unthinkable today on the national level; now we brood over implications and possibilities, appearances and hypothetical circumstances. We are in the fortunate, but sometimes tricky, position of being able to indulge a very nice set of ethical sensibilities, to concentrate on keeping our officials from possible temptation as well as from outright sin. Tricky, simply because it is much easier to pin down a case of bribery than to judge when an official has too heartily enjoyed too good a meal on somebody else's credit card.

Reformers of other eras, bloodied from their battles with men whose methods were as unrestrained as their greed, might be hard put to understand how we can generate so much indignation over the acceptance of a coat or a night's lodging. Perhaps they would brush it all aside as spurious, with H.L. Mencken's axiom that "Bilge goes with politics." Or they might analyze it as the kind of trivial complaint that afflicts well-to-do ladies who have nothing more serious to worry about. Or, giving ourselves the benefit of the doubt now, perhaps they would admire us for the sterner discipline which we exact from our public servants, for our advance from amputation to prophylaxis. Whether it is that we are more neurotic than we used to be, or higher-minded, or simply that with government so large and so intrusive it is impractical to wink away the easy manners of officialdom, our problems are more subtle than they have ever been, more resistant to solution by statute and, as they depend on choices not easily labeled right or wrong, rather more interesting.

4

How the scandals of history left... mud on the White House steps

James R. Dickenson

In 1876 one of the ways the U.S. Senate celebrated the centennial of American independence was in trying the impeachment of W. W. Belknap, Secretary of War in the Grant Administration, for selling the favors of his office.

In 1926, the 150th anniversary of the Declaration of Independence, the first criminal trial of the Harding Administration's Teapot Dome oil scandal began. Will 1976, the bicentennial year, feature the apparently endless Watergate scandal, which is to Richard Nixon what the Credit Mobilier was to Ulysses S. Grant and Teapot Dome was to Warren G. Harding?

The obverse of the great American experiment in democracy is the cupidity, stupidity, and rascality of some of the leading players in the drama. Credit Mobilier, Teapot Dome, and Watergate are code words for the three most lurid scandals involving

Reprinted from the June 9, 1973 issue of *The National Observer*. Reprinted by permission.

the Presidency in American history, and of them all Watergate may turn out to be the worst.

There are certain similarities in the three scandals, however.

Each was a complex of illegalities and corruption in high office. They are similar in scale and size, involving Cabinet officers and other Presidential intimates. Harding's Secretary of the Interior, for example, is the only Cabinet officer to date to be imprisoned, and his Attorney General was forced to resign after standing trial for bribery.

Credit Mobilier tarred both of Grant's Vice Presidents and eight members of Congress, including James Garfield, later to be President. Events of the Watergate era have resulted in the indictment of Attorney General John Mitchell and Commerce Secretary Maurice Stans and have implicated Nixon's top White House staff.

All three scandals appear to have been the result of the President's bad judgment in placing high trust in men who, for differing reasons, abused their power and offices. All three happened after a landslide Republican Presidential victory and at a time when the nation had been gravely disrupted by war.

There are important differences, however. Watergate differs from the others because it is primarily a pattern of official lawbreaking and abuse of Presidential powers for political ends, specifically to manipulate the 1972 election (although Nixon contends that it was a result partly of his concern over high policy). There is no evidence that anyone high up in the scandal made a dime off it, although some enterprising little bag man somewhere down the line may have ripped off a few of those $100 bills.

Teapot Dome and Credit Mobilier, on the other hand, were examples of good old run-of-the-mill, garden-variety thievery of the sort everyone instantly recognizes and appreciates, although on a breath-taking scale. Even so, there was a difference here; Harding's Ohio Gang probably had some idea that they were going to be in trouble if they got caught, while the Spoilsmen of the Reconstruction viewed their depredations as no more than their rightful share of the Great Barbecue that followed the Civil War.

These differences, of course, reflect the differences in the personalities of the Presidents involved as well as the variations in their historical circumstances. Grant was the great general who was honored and revered for leading the Union to victory over the rebellion and was a personally honest man (in these respects the Eisenhower of his day).

The Gospel of Wealth

As the late Richard Hofstadter noted, however, Grant believed that Providence planned to turn over as much of the globe to the Carnegies and Rockefellers as they could grasp. He subscribed fully to the Gospel of Wealth of the age, the belief that wealth was the reward for virtue and that the wealthy were the custodians of God's treasure. "The good Lord gave me my money," John D. Rockefeller once announced.

Harding was a man of limited intellectual means and sleazy personal morality whose virtues—gentleness, humaneness, affability, and gregarious-ness—were liabilities in Washington and made him the easy victim of un-worthy men. Nixon is a man of good mind, driving ambition, Victorian personal habits, and capacity for hard, sustained work. He also seems to be plagued by a personal insecurity unmatched in Presidents of recent memory at least, a distrust of certain powerful elements in the society he leads that seems sometimes to border on paranoia, and a truly remarkable passion for secrecy.

Although Watergate to a great extent is the result of overzealous efforts to ensure Nixon's re-election, it occurred in the historical context of Cold War diplomacy (Nixon's latest justification is that the men who burglarized and bugged Democratic headquarters originally were hired to trace security leaks that endangered delicate negotiations involving Russia, China, and arms limitations). It also was played against a backdrop of civil dissent over the Vietnam War and was made possible by electronic technology. And it has an impact far greater than its predecessors because it comes at a crucial time of shaken confidence in ourselves and our institutions, a confidence that was just beginning to be revived by the ending of the Vietnam War.

The emergence of oil as a global factor was the setting for Teapot Dome. The scandal involved the secret leasing of the Navy's oil reserves in California and Wyoming by Interior Secretary Albert B. Fall, who was appropriately rewarded by the oil barons, Harry Sinclair of the Mammoth Oil Co. and Edward L. Doheny of the Pan-American Petroleum and Transport Co.

As Prof. Robert K. Murray, Harding's latest and best biographer, notes: "At a time [1921] when oil companies were expanding into world-wide complex operations and the quest for oil was corrupting international confer-ences and shaping foreign policies, it was not surprising that one American official succumbed to the temptation to take personal advantage of the situation."

Thus, national security was an element in the scandal. Opponents of Harding and Fall argued that the naval oil reserves should be left safe in the ground, available for future emergencies. Fall, on the other hand, believed the oil should be refined and ready for use, and Professor Murray argues that "there is reason to believe that in the long run the leases may have been in the national interest. On Dec. 7, 1941, those pipelines, oil facilities, and refined oil then available to the Navy on the West Coast and at Pearl Harbor were partly, at least, a direct outgrowth of the Fall leases of 1921–22."

Working on the Railroad

National security and loss of national confidence were not factors with the Credit Mobilier, but national development—manifest destiny—was. The

Credit Mobilier was a construction and finance company set up to build the Union Pacific Railroad right after the Civil War. The nation was still recovering from the profound wounds of the war and beginning the explosive development—industrialization, urbanization, finance capitalism, and settlement of the continent—that the mobilization for war set in motion.

Ah that was a time! Let historian Allan Nevins describe it. "The war explained much . . . the moral exhaustion which it produced; the waste and jobbery which it bred; its creation of vast new Federal responsibilities. Washington became an irresistible lodestone for crooked men. . . . Moreover the '60s were the decade of the most violent turmoil in American history. The South was ruined. . . . The industrial revolution in the North brought the roughest, most aggressive business elements to the front. As the West was settled with amazing rapidity, a more extensive and influential frontier than ever gave manners a cruder cast. Cities were filling up with immigrant communities. Everywhere tested standards, restraints of public opinion, the cake of custom were broken down."

This was the setting for Credit Mobilier. It was organized by the directors of the Union Pacific, including Oakes Ames, a Republican member of the House of Representatives from Massachusetts, who contracted with themselves to build the railroad from the Missouri River to the Great Salt Lake.

This was a typical arrangement in nineteenth-century railroad construction; there was more money in building railroads than in operating them. To say that the contracts were generous is like stating that the sun rises in the east.

Exorbitant is more like it; it was looting and thievery on a truly impressive scale. One estimate of the profits that went into the pockets of the inner clique puts the figure at close to $25 million, and the preditable result was the impoverishment of the railroad.

This presented a bit of a problem, since the Union Pacific had a Federal subsidy of 10 million acres of public land. To prevent Congress from inquiring too closely into its operations, Ames sold Credit Mobilier stock at a discount to his colleagues in Congress, one of whom, Garfield, was later elected President. And to both of Grant's Vice Presidents, Henry Wilson and Schuyler Colfax.

This didn't work, and when Congress investigated during the election year of 1872, Ames' conduct was "absolutely condemned" by the House, 182 to 36. Immediately after the vote, however, the members of Congress crowded around Ames' desk to assure him that they had voted reluctantly and had confidence in his rectitude. Ames himself appeared to firmly share that confidence.

Like Watergate and Teapot Dome in later years, Credit Mobilier became a catchword for all the corruption of the Grant Administration. At various times his Administration was being investigated by the committees on Interior, War, Navy, and Justice, and the granting of customs-collecting posts was a scandal. So was the operation of the notorious "Whisky Ring," which ultimately involved Gen. Orville E. Babcock, secretary to Grant. And then there was the impeachment—and acquittal—of Belknap, the Secretary of War, for selling trading postships in the Indian Territories.

Grant Called It a Smear

Babcock was tried on charges of using his office to block investigation of the Whisky Ring, so called because it included distillers and Internal Revenue collectors who falsified their records to defraud the Federal Government of whisky taxes. Grant backed Babcock because he believed the investigation and prosecution to be a political smear.

Grant ordered Federal attorneys not to promise immunity to Whisky Ring suspects who might turn state's evidence (Nixon suggested a similar caveat concerning White House aides in his April 17 statement on Watergate), which would have crippled the investigation. After first volunteering to travel to St. Louis to testify at Babcock's trial, Grant finally submitted a deposition in his secretary's behalf, which was instrumental in Babcock's acquittal.

Belknap's selling of the trading postships was known apparently to everyone but Grant, and was exposed by Charles Nordhoff of the New York Herald. Belknap resigned from the Cabinet in an attempt to avoid impeachment on grounds that he was no longer an official, which didn't work. The Senate fell 5 votes short of the two-thirds needed to convict, however.

Fifty years later the cast of characters included Fall; Attorney General Harry Daugherty; Col. Charles R. Forbes, director of the Veterans Bureau; and Jess Smith, operator of the famous "Little Green House" at 1625 K St. in Washington, part brothel, part speakeasy.

As Secretary of the Interior, Fall, a rancher and former U.S. senator from New Mexico, secretly leased the Government oil reserves at Elk Hills, Calif., to Doheny and the Teapot Dome, Wyo., (so called because of a rock formation that marks the area) reserves to Sinclair, without competitive bidding. A Senate investigation disclosed that Doheny's son subsequently gave Fall a black bag containing $100,000 and that Sinclair donated $233,000 in Liberty bonds, $85,000 in cash, and a herd of blooded cattle for the Fall ranch in New Mexico.

The break in the case came when the editor of the New Mexico State Tribune disclosed that Fall had purchased land and made improvements on his ranch totaling more than $150,000. The details of the oil money came out, and Fall was convicted of receiving a bribe, fined $100,000 (which he never paid), and sentenced to a year in jail. The bribers—the oil men—were acquitted.

Teapot Dome became the code word for a pattern of corruption in the Harding Administration. Daugherty and Smith, his protege, sold immunity from prosecution, government appointments, criminal pardons and paroles, and liquor withdrawal permits. "My God how the money rolls in," was the theme song that Smith frequently sang to himself.

But Daugherty was forced to stand trial for his involvement in bribery and attempt to defraud the Government in illegal sale of a German-owned subsidiary to a private syndicate. He was acquitted but forced to resign by Calvin Coolidge, who succeeded to the Presidency on Harding's death in 1923.

Smith shot himself in the head with a pistol as a result of the Veterans Bureau scandal under Colonel Forbes; so did Forbes' legal counsel, Charles Cramer. Before he was caught, Forbes managed to swindle the country out of more than $200 million. Disabled war veterans were deprived of bandages, bedding, and drugs as Forbes condemned them by the carload and warehouse lot at the Veterans Bureau depot at Perryville, Md., and sold them at a fraction of their worth in return for a rake-off. He got two years in the Leavenworth Federal penitentiary for his sins.

Harding knew about this scandal. In February 1923, he confronted Forbes and by one account shook him "as a dog would a rat" and shouted to a frightened Forbes that he was a "dirty, double-crossing bastard." Forbes was sent abroad to resign where he couldn't be closely questioned by the press.

There is no evidence that Harding knew of Fall's Teapot Dome depredations or that he was directly involved in his Administration's web of corruption. The same is true of Grant. The judgment on them is that they were betrayed by their friends. "I have no trouble with my enemies," Harding told William Allen White, the Emporia, Kan., editor, just before the Western trip on which Harding died. "But my damned friends, my God-damn friends, White, they're the ones that keep me walking the floor nights."

As Professor Murray notes, however, "there is no such thing as an innocent bystander in the White House." The charge that, like Harding and Grant, he didn't know what the boys upstairs were doing is the best verdict that Richard Nixon can hope for in Watergate. Like its predecessors the burglary and bugging of the Democratic National Committee offices in the Watergate Hotel has become a catch-phrase for a maze of corruption—political sabotage and espionage, illegal surveillance, accusations of influence peddling, a flood of questionable campaign contributions and political payoffs involving suitcases full of $100 bills—mostly aimed at ensuring Nixon's re-election last year.

As an election scandal it has no precedent. The closest in scope is the election of 1876 in which the Republicans elected Rutherford B. Hayes over Samuel Tilden by switching the electoral votes of Florida, Louisiana, and South Carolina. That was in the context of ending Reconstruction and the Federal occupation of the South, however.

5

Questions of ethics

Almost from the start, Americans have looked upon their elected representatives in Congress in a strangely contradictory way. Entrusted with great power to secure the public good, they are regularly caricatured as scoundrels and scalawags. Back in 1894, Mark Twain set a fashionable tone of cynicism: "It could probably be shown with facts and figures," he wrote, "that there is no distinctly American criminal class except Congress." Yet any new scandal on Capitol Hill inevitably touches off another spasm of public shock and indignation.

In fact, the Wayne Hays-Liz Ray revelations come at a time when Congress is probably cleaner than usual and in the midst of a major transition to a more open, professional and effective body. "For many years the morals of Congress were below those

From David M. Alpern, with Henry Hubbard, James Bishop, Jr., Stephan Lesher, Anthony Marro and John J. Lindsay, "Questions of Ethics," *Newsweek* Magazine, Vol. LXXXVII, No. 24, June 14, 1976, pp.21-22, 25-27. Reprinted by permission.

of the general public," says one of the Capitol's most successful lobbyists. "But there has been great progress in recent years and that isn't true any more."

A younger guard, more scrupulous than its elders, is gradually coming to the fore in both the House and the Senate. "The Hays business is an aberration," claims House committee staffer Ted Jacobs, for years an assistant to public-interest advocate Ralph Nader. "The great majority of congressmen are hard-working, able, dedicated, idealistic—and not concerned with perquisites and power, maybe because they don't have it."

The very quickness with which House leaders moved against Hays, and the number of investigations now being pressed against congressmen are themselves evidence of a new willingness to explore corners that were once kept deliberately dark. Still, as in the world of private business, improprieties continue to exist, from complex conflicts of interest to cheating on expense accounts to showing up soused on the Senate or House floor—or not showing up at all. A survey of the sins to which some Congressional flesh still is heir:

Criminal Charges

Some of the men who make the nation's laws continue to break them, get caught and pay the penalty—although not in significantly larger numbers now than in previous periods of Congressional history. According to a Library of Congress survey, sixteen members of Congress were indicted between 1955 and 1975. Of that group, a dozen were convicted or pleaded guilty on charges ranging from tax evasion to taking kickbacks on defense contracts—a crime that came to light most frequently in the years following World War II.

In the current Congress, Rep. Henry Helstoski, a New Jersey Democrat, was indicted just last week; another member, California Republican Rep. Andrew Hinshaw, has been convicted of bribery; two have confessed to misdemeanors—Democrat James Jones of Oklahoma and Republican George Hansen of Idaho—and five more are under investigation by the Justice Department, the House ethics committee or what remains of the Watergate special prosecutor's office.

Few of the recent cases have involved anything so colorful as Adam Clayton Powell's lavish retreat (with a former Miss Ohio) to the island of Bimini to avoid legal action in New York City. Most of the crimes for which members of Congress have been convicted are mundane, unimaginative matters of trading influence for hard cash. Brooklyn Democrat Frank Brasco was convicted in 1974 of taking a bribe from a local trucking company, allegedly controlled by the Mafia, for which he had helped obtain a Post Office contract. Four months later another Brooklyn Democrat, Rep. Bertram Podell, pleaded guilty to a charge that he had received money for helping a Florida airline win Federal authorization to fly more profitable routes. Like most other white-collar criminals, congressmen spend little time behind bars— Brasco received a sentence of only three months in jail (plus a $10,000 fine) and Podell six months (plus a $5,000 fine). Other Congressional felons include:

Rep. Cornelius Gallagher, A New Jersey Democrat who served two years at Allenwood Federal Penitentiary from 1973–1975 for evading payment of $74,000 in taxes.

Rep. John Dowdy, a Texas Democrat convicted of perjury in 1972 in connection with the investigation of a $25,000 bribe allegedly paid to him by a Maryland construction firm.

Pennsylvania Republican J. Irving Whalley, who pleaded guilty to charges of mail fraud in 1973 after being accused of forcing his staffers to kick back part of their salaries to help him pay personal and business expenses. His sentence was three years' probation and an $11,000 fine.

Maryland's former Democratic Sen. Daniel Brewster, who pleaded no contest to a charge of accepting an illegal gratuity from Spiegel, Inc., the mail-order firm, which had a vital interest in influencing his vote on postal rate bills.

Last week's indictment of Helstoski focused on another area of potential abuse that has received growing attention in recent years: the soliciting and accepting of bribes from aliens in the U.S., on whose behalf a congressman may introduce a special bill authorizing citizenship. Although such special bills rarely became law in the past, they could significantly delay scheduled deportation proceedings. In Helstoski's case, the congressman was also charged with seven counts of conspiracy, obstruction of justice and lying to a Federal grand jury, although Helstoski himself charged that the indictment was "absolutely without any foundation . . . politically motivated" and the result of a five-year effort on the part of U.S. attorney Jonathan L. Goldstein "who is out to get me."

In addition to Helstoski, the ethical-purity unit at Justice is known to be investigating Congressional Democrats Joseph Addabbo of New York and Robert Leggett of California, both of whom have been accused of taking bribes (of less than $10,000 each) from the South Korean Government. Addabbo is the fourth-ranking Democrat on the defense subcommittee of the House Appropriations Committee, Leggett has had various contacts with the Korean Government (which buys considerable amounts of rice grown in his home district) and both men are friends of Korean-born Sue Thompson, 45, a Washington party-giver and $15,000-a-year clerk on the staff of House Speaker Carl Albert. Both men have denied any improprieties. Justice investigators are also looking into allegations that Missouri Democrat William Clay has been illegally padding his payroll—and soliciting kickbacks. Clay denies it.

What happens to congressmen who run afoul of the law? For the most part, not much. The House ethics committee has opened only one investigation of a member; the Justice Department ethics division has not been in business long enough to accumulate a track record, and the electorate has often shown a surprising forgiveness. Rep. Hinshaw, who last February received a one-to-fourteen-year sentence on bribery charges, is appealing his conviction and has filed for re-election. There is certainly precedent for such optimism, including the 1965 re-election of former Democratic Rep. Thomas Lane of Massachusetts—even after he had served four months for tax evasion. But few congressmen have handled the matter with quite the flair of the late Rep. James Michael Curley of Massachusetts. Convicted of mail fraud charges, Curley spent six months in jail and had five brass bands waiting outside to trumpet his release in 1947. He then served out his fourth stint as mayor of Boston—to which post he had been overwhelmingly elected while under indictment.

Conflict of Interest

Below the level of outright criminal corruption there exists a wide range of questionable Congressional practices. Foremost among these are conflicts of interest that may prompt some legislators to cast votes favorable to powerful benefactors instead of their constituents. Some legislators regularly accept lecture fees from special-interest groups; others own shares of stock in corporations seeking Federal contracts or favorable legislation while others belong to law firms representing clients involved with the Federal government.

Congress has generally done a better job of insisting that others avoid conflicts—the Senate rejected Judge Clement Haynsworth's nomination to the Supreme Court partly because he had heard cases involving businesses in which he had a small equity—than it has in policing its own members. Unlike the Senate, the House does require that each representative file an annual public financial statement. But neither the House nor the Senate has moved with marked determination to set up a vigorous code of ethics—or punish members who violate the regulations that do exist. In the whole history of Congress only seven senators and eighteen representatives have been censured by their peers. Indeed, the current investigation of Florida Democrat Robert Sikes by the House ethics committee is the first time a House member has actually come under investigation by that panel since it was formed nine years ago in the aftermath of the Adam Powell case. Sikes is charged with voting for the 1974 Defense Appropriations bill that included a $73 million contract for Fairchild Industries—although he then owned 1,000 shares of Fairchild and supposedly should have abstained because of his direct pecuniary interest. Sikes has argued that the regulation in question—part of a Code of Ethics passed in 1958—applied only to the 86th Congress.

Most younger members—especially those elected on the basis of post-Watergate, clean-government campaigns—have relied wholly on their Congressional salaries ($44,625) to pay the family bills. But some of the Hill's most powerful veterans have long earned part of their income from outside business interests—and may be tempted to vote with their own bank accounts in mind when legislation affecting those interests has come before Congress.

House whip Thomas P. (Tip) O'Neill is active in real estate and insurance in Massachusetts, Minority Leader John Rhodes of Arizona is a director and vice president of a life-insurance company and scores of other senior members are involved with the banking industry, oil and gas companies and farming operations. Do these connections destroy their judgment? Not necessarily, argues Russell Long of Louisiana, chairman of the powerful Senate Finance Committee and a reliable defender of oil interests—who nevertheless refuses to disclose the size of his personal oil and gas holdings, most of them inherited from his father, former Gov. Huey Long. "A long time ago I became convinced that if you have financial interests completely parallel to your state, then you have no problem," says Long. "If I didn't represent the oil and gas industry, I wouldn't represent the state of Louisiana."

Even more difficult to trace is the influence of representatives who keep their law practices—and their clients, many of whom do business with the Federal government—when they become members of Congress. House rules require members to disclose the names of their firms, but not their clients, and the Senate does not even require practicing lawyers to identify themselves. In the case of Senate Minority Leader Hugh Scott, however, sworn testimony alleged that he asked the Gulf Oil Co. to continue paying his firm a retainer for his services. Gulf refused, according to the testimony, but agreed to pay Scott $10,000 a year in cash instead, a matter still under scrutiny by the Watergate special prosecutor.

Until recently, one of the most common grounds for what, at the very least, may be the appearance of a conflict of interest was the widespread Congressional sideline of collecting fees for speech-making and authorship. In 1974, according to the Congressional Quarterly, celebrity senators like Hubert Humphrey, Howard Baker, William Proxmire and Mark Hatfield each added between $40,000 and $50,000 to their government salaries through honorariums given for speaking engagements. Large chunks of the money that year came from special-interest groups, such as the Jewish National Fund ($15,050 to eight senators) and the American Bankers Association ($12,000 to eight). "Usually there is no conflict because the speaker is already somebody who has sided with the interest group," says one prominent lobbyist. Still, a reform-minded Congress in 1974 put a $15,000 ceiling on the amount a senator or congressman could earn from outside speeches and writing (often prepared free by Hill staffers) or from media appearances. Apparently feeling the pinch, however, Congress this year voted to raise that limit to $25,000—plus expenses.

As many congressmen and their aides explain it, the real problem is that Americans simply don't pay their legislators well enough to begin with. "These guys have to get the hell out of town practically every weekend to make a speaking date in Chillicothe or Bowling Green so they can make ends meet," notes the executive assistant of one Senate Democrat. "They're expected to entertain [constituents], but where do they get the money?" One longtime political advisor and former Senate aide argues that Congress "ought to raise the salaries to a realistic level and cut out having to beat it out of town every weekend to make a speech. But they're the only ones who can raise the salaries—and if they do, they're criticized for that."

Perks and Junkets

For all that kind of poor-mouthing, most Americans find it hard to think of the Capitol as a welfare ward. More often it seems a white-domed Xanadu where a congressman's every whim is catered to—usually at the taxpayer's expense. It wasn't always that way. Back in 1789, the first U.S. Congress voted to pay members $6 a day, and in the same measure approved the first Congressional perquisite in the form of a travel allowance of 30 cents a mile. Not until 1885 did the Senate vote pay for an aide to each senator (again, $6 a day), and the House waited until 1893 to provide $100 a month for a clerk to each representative. Since then, however, the perks have peaked to the point where the reform-minded Americans for Democratic Action now calculates their value at about half a million dollars for every member— including everything from staff salaries to free parking spaces, expense-paid travel (at home and abroad) and even the loan of two paintings (reproductions, actually) every year from the National Gallery.

There is, of course, nothing intrinsically wrong with some of the perks and privileges congressmen enjoy, be it a $2 haircut (Senators can have them in their own offices), a $1.90 chef salad in the House or Senate dining room (hardly *haute cuisine*), free mailing for newsletters and press releases or a $3,000 tax deduction for living expenses. But at the very least they may constitute a considerable advantage to incumbents in any political race, and they often lead to abuses that the Congressional system seems designed *not* to police.

The architect of the current system, ironically, is none other than Rep. Wayne Hayes. In 1971, Hays engineered a House vote that gave his House Administration Committee exclusive authority over the amount of allowances granted members for almost every conceivable expense—and thus for the way such allowances are actually used. "I do not know whether deviousness was intended, but it certainly will result and we shall rue the day," said New York Republican Barber Conable at the time.

A prime example is the stationery allowance: $7,500 a year for each House member—in addition to free envelopes (480,000 of them) and about $7,000 for reproduction of newsletters and air-mail and special-delivery stamps. Withdrawals from stationery accounts do not have to be specified on vouchers and the allowance actually constitutes a bonus to the member's salary (taxes must be paid on the allowance if it is not spent on official business). "Some guys never spend it," says one committee member. "One congressman let it build up for years, and when he left he took it with him."

House members (though not senators) are also permitted to set up private office funds to cover nonreimbursable expenses without identifying the interest groups that contribute to them. The potential for improper influence in such slush funds is obvious. "You'd be surprised at the people who call and say, 'We know how hard it is to get along,' and offer you money," says Florida Democrat Charles Bennett. "It makes you suspicious when they don't even come from your district."

Congressional travel provides even more temptation for abuse—and not only the headline-snatching junkets. For example, each House member is allowed 26 free trips to and from his home district every year, while senators have from 40 to 44 depending on the population of their home states. But according to a six-month investigation by the Wall Street Journal, some congressmen routinely put in for twice their actual expenses by claiming the trips were made by auto instead of air. Among those named: Louisiana's Otto Passman, Margaret Heckler of Massachusetts and Missouri's Clay. Chairman Hays simply suggested that members who filed their vouchers "incorrectly" might make restitution. So far, few have, but last week a Buffalo, N.Y., law student prompted the Justice Department to sue Clay for the return of almost $20,000 for payments he collected for trips home that he apparently never made at all. Clay blamed clerical errors.

Still, it is the international junket that generates the most flak for congressmen—about half of whom now take their wives along, according to one Hill source. And while many of these expeditions have at least some rationale—the annual NATO conference, the Paris air show, surveys of foreign political developments—others seem bizarre. Sen. Vance Hartke of Indiana, chairman of the Senate Veterans Affairs Committee, recently spent more than $14,000 in government money to visit several African nations, Hong Kong and elsewhere, presumably studying the way they deal with veterans' problems. Moreover, vouchers showing the expenses of individual junketeers are not available for public inspection; only the totals are reflected in semiannual reports.

Staffing and Nepotism

Perhaps the most potent perk of all today is the sizable staff each congressman can command. Nepotism, though somewhat reduced since a major scandal in 1959, continues to plague both chambers, but a larger problem seems to be the improper use of certain staffers for a member's own personal or political affairs. There are also reports that a few congressmen give raises to staffers, then demand that part of the money be kicked back in political donations or other contributions. "It's awfully hard to prove," says a former congressman. "The victims are just plain afraid to blow the whistle. And in many cases they are happy enough with the extra money to turn some of it over to the boss."

The size of Congressional staffs has increased slowly but steadily in recent years—although many Hill veterans argue it is still inadequate to handle the tenfold increase in constituent traffic faced by congressmen and a burgeoning of the Federal bureaucracy with which the committee system must cope. Each representative is now allowed to spend up to $204,720 per year for a maximum of eighteen staffers in his Washington and district offices (only a third of the members actually have that many), while the average senator is permitted to spend about $500,000 on staff salaries. Where many of the legislators really build their private empires, however, is in the network of committees and subcommittees under their control. Democratic Sen. Birch Bayh of Indiana, for example, heads a Judiciary subcommittee on constitutional amendments and one on juvenile delinquency. Together with his personal staff, they give the senator over 70 employees and a $1.4 million budget.

Despite their job titles, Hill staffers may be asked to perform almost any kind of task for the legislators they serve. A former aide says New York's Rep. Bella Abzug once called her at 1 a.m. and demanded that she come to Abzug's apartment to fix a stuffed toilet. (The staffer has since resigned.) Another congresswoman not only has her male aide serve as a chauffeur and escort at parties, but also sends him shopping for pantyhose and other personal items.

But congressmen may move from simple indignities to downright impropriety when they have committee staffers—hired to work on legislation—engage in election-year campaigning. Larry Conrad, for example, the chief counsel for Senator Bayh's constitutional amendments subcommittee back in 1968, was also a key aide in Bayh's re-election campaign. (Conrad is currently secretary of state in Indiana and the Democratic nominee for governor.) Some longtime observers of Congress believe that top staffers themselves are distorting the system by taking a far more influential role in the shaping of legislation than was ever envisioned by the Founding Fathers. Some key staff people actually call most of the shots on legislative proposals that the congressmen for whom they work have too little time or interest to consider for themselves.

Nepotism, strictly speaking, has been prohibited by various rules in the Senate and—to a lesser degree—in the House. But in both chambers members get past the restrictions by hiring each other's relatives or those of important contributors and other VIP's, particularly for summer jobs. And with payroll vouchers almost as well-kept a secret as travel vouchers, it is difficult to figure out whose back is being scratched by whom. "It's just a cute game they're playing," says one lobbyist. "There's still a lot of nepotism. It's just harder, sometimes impossible, to track down."

Drinking and Senility

Sins of weakness—as opposed to personal or political aggrandizement—are apparently on the wane in today's Congress. Senility has not constituted a serious problem since 1969 and the final days of Sen. Carl Hayden of Arizona, then 91, who—legend has it—once walked off the Senate floor into a telephone booth and said, "Up!" Still, some current Hill veterans "are not the men they used to be," associates say. Often mentioned are Senate Commerce Committee chairman Warren Magnuson, 71, Senate Appropriations chairman John McClellan, 80, and Senate Foreign Relations chairman John Sparkman, 77, who says he no longer dozes off in committee meetings. "You just go to a doctor and he gives you some tablets," adds Sparkman, who claims he no longer uses the pills, and hints that he may be retiring.

The big drinkers are also gone—or considerably constrained in their indulgence. Just before Christmas three years ago, for example, "there were so many cases of liquor in the halls that a half dozen men were moving it around on hand trucks," recalls one Senate aide. Last year, by contrast, the corridors were almost totally dry. According to a Senate staff director, "The really notorious drunks have gone, although chronic dependence on alcohol is widespread. A lot of them start nipping at mid-afternoon, but you don't see anybody stumbling and mumbling any more." Rep. Mendel Rivers of South Carolina is dead, Sen. Harrison Williams of New Jersey has been on the wagon for years—now joined by Arkansas's Wilbur Mills since his famous fling with Fanne Foxe—and Senator Long, who once had a serious problem, hardly ever takes a drink.

Along with alcoholism, absenteeism is also down. Senate Whip Robert Byrd of West Virginia and some other leaders are notably intolerant of truancy—and coverage by the newspapers back home has grown so sharp-eyed that members find it increasingly tough to cheat on attendance and still win re-election. As a result, the average daily attendance for floor sessions is 90 per cent. Among those with the worst records in this area for the first session of the 94th Congress were Congressman Hinshaw—who was on trial most of the time and made only 60 per cent of the votes—and Arizona Sen. Barry Goldwater, who was present for 67 percent.

Attendance at committee and subcommittee hearings is not nearly as high. "I have been up there recently and it is surprising how few members of the Senate actually sit in on regular hearings and meetings of their committees," says a former White House troubleshooter on the Hill. With most members holding an assortment of committee assignments, the average congressman shows up only for those sessions designed to generate a maximum of news.

Efforts at Reform

In the wake of the Hays affair, Congressional reformers hoped that pressure would build for changes more far-reaching than simply toppling Hays from several key chairmanships. Some serious reform may indeed be in the offing. Besides announcing his own retirement, Speaker Albert last week set up a special task force to "rationalize" the system of backdoor financing that Hays had perfected for congressmen's expenditures. And some thought that the 1971 decision to give the Administration Committee sole power over the perks might be reversed. "The heat is on and nobody can turn it off," said one member of the House leadership. The creation of task forces has often been just a way of buying time, of course, but a Common Cause spokesman said the citizens' group would keep the pressure on. The national press was also continuing to dig into the case, and the glare of an election year might well reinforce Congress's inclination to clean its House.

Beyond that, the scandal could only further discredit and weaken the Hill's Old Guard. With 100 first-termers already warming to the battle—and about 100 more expected next session—there was also new hope for pending or planned legislation to require sweeping financial disclosures by congressmen and Washington lobbyists, and perhaps to authorize Federal financing of Congressional elections. Even a Federal Elections Commission's ruling against the controversial House slush funds—thrown out by the House this year—might win support if the FEC issues it again. The reaction to the Hays-Ray scandal thus added up to a slow but steady cleansing process brought about by press scrutiny, public pressure—and the changing complexion of Congress itself.

6

Wincanton: the politics of corruption

*John A. Gardiner, with
the Assistance of David J. Olson*

In general, Wincanton represents a city that has toyed with the problem of corruption for many years. No mayor in the history of the city of Wincanton has ever succeeded himself in office. Some mayors have been corrupt and have allowed the city to become a wide-open center for gambling and prostitution; Wincanton voters have regularly rejected those corrupt mayors who dared to seek reelection. Some mayors have been scrupulously honest and have closed down all vice operations in the city; these men have been generally disliked for being too straitlaced. Other mayors, fearing one form of resentment or the other, have chosen quietly to retire from public life. The questions of official corruption and policy toward vice and gambling, it seems, have been paramount issues in Wincanton elections since the days of Prohi-

From the President's Commission on Law Enforcement and Administration of Justice: Task Force Reports: Organized Crime, Appendix B, John A. Gardiner, with the assistance of David J. Olson, Wincanton: The Politics of Corruption, pp. 61-70, 78-79. Footnotes omitted.

bition. Any mayor who is known to be controlled by the gambling syndicates will lose office, but so will any mayor who tries completely to clean up the city. The people of Wincanton apparently want both easily accessible gambling and freedom from racket domination.

Probably more than most cities in the United States, Wincanton has known a high degree of gambling, vice (sexual immorality, including prostitution), and corruption (official malfeasance, misfeasance and nonfeasance of duties). With the exception of two reform administrations, one in the early 1950's and the one elected in the early 1960's, Wincanton has been wide open since the 1920's. Bookies taking bets on horses took in several millions of dollars each year. With writers at most news-stands, cigar counters, and corner grocery stores, a numbers bank did an annual business in excess of $1,300,000 during some years. Over 200 pinball machines, equipped to pay off like slot machines, bore $250 Federal gambling stamps. A high stakes dice game attracted professional gamblers from more than 100 miles away; $25,000 was found on the table during one Federal raid. For a short period of time in the 1950's (until raided by U.S. Treasury Department agents), a still, capable of manufacturing $1 million in illegal alcohol each year, operated on the banks of the Wincanton River. Finally, prostitution flourished openly in the city, with at least 5 large houses (about 10 girls apiece) and countless smaller houses catering to men from a large portion of the state.

As in all cities in which gambling and vice had flourished openly, these illegal activities were protected by local officials. Mayors, police chiefs, and many lesser officials were on the payroll of the gambling syndicate, while others received periodic "gifts" or aid during political campaigns. A number of Wincanton officials added to the revenue from the syndicate by extorting kickbacks on the sale or purchase of city equipment or by selling licenses, permits, zoning variances, etc. As the city officials made possible the operations of the racketeers, so frequently the racketeers facilitated the corrupt endeavors of officials by providing liaison men to arrange the deals or "enforcers" to ensure that the deals were carried out.

The visitor to Wincanton is struck by the beauty of the surrounding countryside and the drabness of the tired, old central city. Looking down on the city from Mount Prospect, the city seems packed in upon itself, with long streets and red brick row houses pushing up against old railroad yards and factories; 93 percent of the housing units were built before 1940.

Wincanton had its largest population in 1930 and has been losing residents slowly ever since. The people who remained—those who didn't move to the suburbs or to the other parts of the United States—are the lower middle class, and less well educated; they seem old and often have an Old World feeling about them. The median age in Wincanton is 37 years (compared with a national median of 29 years). While unemployment is low (2.5 percent of the labor force in April 1965), there are few professional or white-collar workers; only 11 percent of the families had incomes over $10,000, and the median family income was $5,543. As is common in many cities with an older, largely working class population, the level of education is low—only 27 percent of the adults have completed high school, and the median number of school years completed is 8.9.

While most migration into Wincanton took place before 1930, the various nationality groups in Wincanton seem to have retained their separate identities. The Germans, the Poles, the Italians, and the Negroes each have their own neighborhoods, stores, restaurants, clubs and politicians. Having immigrated earlier, the Germans are more assimilated into the middle and upper middle classes; the other groups still frequently live in the neighborhoods in which they first settled; and Italian and Polish politicians openly appeal to Old World loyalties. Club life adds to the ethnic groupings by giving a definite neighborhood quality to various parts of the city and their politics; every politician is expected to visit the ethnic association, ward clubs, and voluntary firemen's associations during campaign time—buying a round of drinks for all present and leaving money with the club stewards to hire poll watchers to advertise the candidates and guard the voting booths.

In part, the flight from Wincanton of the young and the more educated can be explained by the character of the local economy. While there have been no serious depressions in Wincanton during the last 30 years, there has been little growth either, and more of the factories in the city were built 30 to 50 years ago and rely primarily upon semiskilled workers. A few textile mills have moved out of the region, to be balanced by the construction in the last 5 years of several electronics assembly plants. No one employer dominates the economy, although seven employed more than 1,000 persons. Major industries today include steel fabrication and heavy machinery, textiles and food products.

With the exception of 2 years (one in the early 1950's, the other 12 years later) in which investigations of corruption led to the election of Republican reformers, Wincanton politics have been heavily Democratic in recent years. Registered Democrats in the city outnumber Republicans by a margin of 2 to 1; in Alsace County as a whole, including the heavily Republican middle class suburbs, the Democratic margin is reduced to 3 to 2. Despite this margin of control, or possibly because of it, Democratic politics in Wincanton have always been somewhat chaotic; candidates appeal to the ethnic groups, clubs, and neighborhoods, and no machine or organization has been able to dominate the party for very long (although a few men have been able to build a personal following lasting for 10 years or so). Incumbent mayors have been defeated in the primaries by other Democrats, and voting in city council sessions has crossed party lines more often than it has respected them.

To a great extent, party voting in Wincanton follows a business-labor cleavage. Two newspapers (both owned by a group of local businessmen) and the Chamber of Commerce support Republican candidates; the unions usually endorse Democrats. It would be unwise, however, to overestimate either the solidarity or the interest in local politics of Wincanton business and labor groups. Frequently two or more union leaders may be opposing each other in a Democratic primary (the steelworkers frequently endorse liberal or reform candidates, while the retail clerks have been more tied to "organization" men); or ethnic allegiance and hostilities may cause union members to vote for Republicans, or simply sit on their hands. Furthermore, both business and labor leaders express greater interest in State and National issues—taxation, wage and hour laws, collective bargaining policies, etc.—then in local issues. (The attitude of both business and labor toward Wincanton gambling and corruption will be examined in detail later.)

Many people feel that, apart from the perennial issue of corruption, there really are not any issues in Wincanton politics and that personalities are the only things that matter in city elections. Officials assume that the voters are generally opposed to a high level of public services. Houses are tidy, but the city has no public trash collection, or fire protection either, for that matter. While the city buys firetrucks and pays their drivers, firefighting is done solely by volunteers—in a city with more than 75,000 residents. (Fortunately, most of the houses are built of brick or stone.) Urban renewal has been slow, master planning nonexistent, and a major railroad line still crosses the heart of the shopping district, bringing traffic to a halt as trains grind past. Some people complain, but no mayor has ever been able to do anything about it. For years, people have been talking about rebuilding City Hall (constructed as a high school 75 years ago), modernizing mass transportation, and ending pollution of the Wincanton River, but nothing much has been done about any of these issues, or even seriously considered. Some people explain this by saying that Wincantonites are interested in everything—up to and including, but not extending beyond, their front porch.

If the voters of Wincanton were to prefer an active rather than passive city government, they would find the municipal structure well equipped to frustrate their desires. Many governmental functions are handled by independent boards and commissions, each able to veto proposals of the mayor and councilmen. Until about 10 years ago, State law required all middle-sized cities to operate under a modification of the commission form of government. (In the early 1960's, Wincanton voters narrowly by a margin of 16 votes out of 30,000 rejected a proposal to set up a council-manager plan.) The city council is composed of five men—a mayor and four councilmen. Every odd-numbered year, two councilmen are elected to 4-year terms. The mayor also has a 4-year term of office, but has a few powers not held by the councilmen; he presides at council sessions but has no veto power over council legislation. State law requires that city affairs be divided among five named departments, each to be headed by a member of the council, but the council members are free to decide among themselves what functions will be handled by which departments (with the proviso that the mayor must control the police department). Thus the city's work can be split equally among five men, or a three-man majority can control all important posts. In a not atypical recent occurrence, one councilman, disliked by his colleagues, found himself supervising only garbage collection and the Main Street comfort station! Each department head (mayor and councilmen) has almost complete control over his own department. Until 1960, when a $2,500 raise became effective, the mayor received an annual salary of $7,000, and each councilman received $6,000. The mayor and city councilmen have traditionally been permitted to hold other jobs while in office.

To understand law enforcement in Wincanton, it is necessary to look at the activities of local, county, State, and Federal agencies. State law requires that each mayor select his police chief and officers "from the force" and "exercise a constant supervision and control over their conduct." Applicants for the police force are chosen on the basis of a civil service examination and have tenure "during good behavior," but promotions and demotions are entirely at the discretion of the mayor and council. Each new administration in Wincanton has made wholesale changes in police ranks—patrolmen have been named chief, and former chiefs have been reduced to walking a beat. (When one period of reform came to an end in the mid-1950's, the incoming mayor summoned the old chief into his office, "You can stay on as officer," the mayor said, "but you'll have to go along with my policies regarding gambling." "Mr. Mayor," the chief said, "I'm going to keep on arresting gamblers no matter where you put me." The mayor assigned the former chief to the position of "Keeper of the Lockup," permanently stationed in the basement of police headquarters.) Promotions must be made from within the department. This policy has continued even though the present reform mayor created the post of police commissioner and brought in an outsider to take command. For cities of this size, Wincanton police salaries have been quite low—the top pay for patrolmen was $4,856—in the lowest quartile of middle-sized cities in the Nation. Since 1964 the commissioner has received $10,200 and patrolmen $5,400 each year.

While the police department is the prime law enforcement agency within Wincanton, it receives help (and occasional embarrassment) from other groups. Three county detectives work under the district attorney, primarily in rural parts of Alsace County, but they are occasionally called upon to assist in city investigations. The State Police, working out of a barracks in suburban Wincanton Hills, have generally taken a "hands off" or "local option" attitude toward city crime, working only in rural areas unless invited into a city by the mayor, district attorney, or county judge. Reform mayors have welcomed the superior manpower and investigative powers of the State officers; corrupt mayors have usually been able to thumb their noses at State policemen trying to uncover Wincanton gambling. Agents of the State's Alcoholic Beverages Commission suffer from no such limitations and enter Wincanton at will in search of liquor violations. They have seldom been a serious threat to Wincanton corruption, however, since their numbers are quite limited (and thus the agents are dependent upon the local police for information and assistance in making arrests). Their mandate extends to gambling and prostitution only when encountered in the course of a liquor investigation.

Under most circumstances, the operative level of law enforcement in Wincanton has been set by local political decisions, and the local police (acting under instructions from the mayor) have been able to determine whether or not Wincanton should have open gambling and prostitution. The State Police, with their "hands off" policy, have simply reenforced the local decision. From time to time, however, Federal agencies have become interested in conditions in Wincanton and, as will be seen throughout this study, have played as important a role as the local police in cleaning up the city. Internal Revenue Service agents have succeeded in prosecuting Wincanton gamblers for failure to hold gambling occupation stamps, pay the special excise taxes on gambling receipts, or report income. Federal Bureau of Investigation agents have acted against violations of the Federal laws against extortion and interstate gambling. Finally, special attorneys from the Organized Crime and Racketeering Section of the Justic Department were able to convict leading members of the syndicate controlling Wincanton gambling. While Federal prosecutions in Wincanton have often been spectacular, it should also be noted that they have been somewhat sporadic and limited in scope. The Internal Revenue Service, for example, was quite successful in seizing gambling devices and gamblers lacking the Federal gambling occupation stamps, but it was helpless after Wincantonites began to purchase the stamps, since local officials refused to prosecute them for violations of the State anti-gambling laws.

The court system in Wincanton, as in all cities in the State, still has many of the 18th-century features which have been rejected in other States. At the lowest level, elected magistrates (without legal training) hear petty civil and criminal cases in each ward of the city. The magistrates also issue warrants and decide whether persons arrested by the police shall be held for trial. Migistrates are paid only by fees, usually at the expense of convicted defendants. All serious criminal cases, and all contested petty cases, are tried in the county court. The three judges of the Alsace County court are elected (on a partisan ballot) for 10-year terms, and receive an annual salary of $25,000.

Gambling and Corruptions: The Insiders

The Stern Empire

The history of Wincanton gambling and corruption since World War II centers around the career of Irving Stern. Stern is an immigrant who came to the United States and settled in Wincanton at the turn of the century. He started as a fruit peddler, but when Prohibition came along, Stern became a bootlegger for Heinz Glickman, then the beer baron of the State. When

Glickman was murdered in the waning days of Prohibition, Stern took over Glickman's business and continued to sell untaxed liquor after repeal of Prohibition in 1933. Several times during the 1930's, Stern was convicted in Federal court on liquor charges and spent over a year in Federal prison.

Around 1940, Stern announced to the world that he had reformed and went into his family's wholesale produce business. While Stern was in fact leaving the bootlegging trade, he was also moving into the field of gambling, for even at that time Wincanton had a "wide-open" reputation, and the police were ignoring gamblers. With the technical assistance of his bootlegging friends, Stern started with a numbers bank and soon added horse betting, a dice game, and slot machines to his organization. During World War II, officers from a nearby Army training base insisted that all brothels be closed, but this did not affect Stern. He had already concluded that public hostility and violence, caused by the horses, were, as a side effect, threatening his more profitable gambling operations. Although Irv Stern controlled the lion's share of Wincanton gambling throughout the 1940's, he had to share the slot machine trade with Klaus Braun. Braun, unlike Stern, was a Wincanton native and a Gentile, and thus had easier access to the frequently anti-Semitic club stewards, restaurant owners, and bartenders who decided which machines would be placed in their buildings. Legislative investigations in the early 1950's estimated that Wincanton gambling was an industry with gross receipts of $5 million each year; at that time Stern was receiving $40,000 per week from bookmaking, and Braun took in $75,000 to $100,000 per year from slot machines alone.

Irv Stern's empire in Wincanton collapsed abruptly when legislative investigations brought about the election of a reform Republican administration. Mayor Hal Craig decided to seek what he termed "pearl gray purity" to tolerate isolated prostitutes, bookies, and numbers writers but to drive out all forms of organized crime, all activities lucrative enough to make it worth someone's while to try bribing Craig's police officials. Within 6 weeks after taking office, Craig and District Attorney Henry Weiss had raided enough of Stern's gambling parlors and seized enough of Braun's slot machines to convince both men that business was over for 4 years at least. The Internal Revenue Service was able to convict Braun and Stern's nephew, Dave Feinman, on tax evasion charges; both were sent to jail. From 1952 to 1955 it was still possible to place a bet or find a girl. But you had to know someone to do it, and no one was getting very rich in the process.

By 1955 it was apparent to everyone that reform sentiment was dead and that the Democrats would soon be back in office. In the summer of that year, Stern met with representatives of the east coast syndicates and arranged for the rebuilding of his empire. He decided to change his method of operations in several ways; one way was by centralizing all Wincanton vice and gambling under his control. But he also decided to turn the actual operation of most enterprises over to others. From the mid-1950's until the next wave of reform hit Wincanton after elections in the early 1960's, Irv Stern generally succeeded in reaching these goals.

The financial keystone of Stern's gambling empire was numbers betting. Records seized by the Internal Revenue Service in the late 1950's and early 1960's indicated that gross receipts from numbers amounted to more than $100,000 each month, or $1.3 million annually. Since the numbers are a poor man's form of gambling (bets range from a penny to a dime or quarter), a large number of men and a high degree of organization are required. The organizational goals are three: have the maximum possible number of men on the streets seeking bettors, be sure that they are reporting honestly, and yet strive so to decentralize the organization that no one, if arrested, will be able to identify many of the others. During the "pearl gray purity" of Hal Craig, numbers writing was completely unorganized, many isolated writers took bets from their friends and frequently had to renege if an unusually popular number came up; no one writer was big enough to guard against such possibilities. When a new mayor took office in the mid-1950's, however, Stern's lieutenants notified each of the small writers that they were now working for Stern or else. Those who objected were "persuaded" by Stern's men, or else arrested by the police, as were any of the others who were suspected of holding out on their receipts. Few objected for very long. After Stern completed the reorganization of the numbers business, its structure was roughly something like this: 11 subbanks reported to Stern's central accounting office. Each subbank employed from 5 to 30 numbers writers. Thirty-five percent of the gross receipts went to the writers. After deducting for winnings and expenses (mostly protection payoffs), Stern divided the net profits equally with the operators of the subbanks. In return for his cut, Stern provided protection from the police and "laid off" the subbanks, covering winnings whenever a popular number "broke" one of the smaller operators.

Stern also shared with out-of-State syndicates in the profits and operation of two enterprises, a large dice game and the largest still found by the Treasury Department since Prohibition. The dice game employed over 50 men drivers to "lug" players into town from as far as 100 miles away, doormen to check players' identities, loan sharks who "faded" the losers, croupiers, food servers, guards, etc. The 1960 payroll for these employees was over $350,000. While no estimate of the gross receipts from the game is available, some indication of its size can be obtained from the fact that $50,000 was found on the tables and in the safe when the FBI raided the game in 1962. Over 100 players were arrested during the raid; one businessman had lost over $75,000 at the tables. Stern received a share of the game's profits plus a $1,000 weekly fee to provide protection from the police.

Stern also provided protection (for a fee) and shared in the profits of a still, erected in an old warehouse on the banks of the Wincanton River and tied into the city's water and sewer systems. Stern arranged for clearance by the city council and provided protection from the local police after the

$200,000 worth of equipment was set up. The still was capable of producing $4 million worth of alcohol each year, and served a five-State area, until Treasury agents raided it after it had been in operation for less than 1 year.

The dice game and the still raise questions regarding the relationship of Irv Stern to out-of-State syndicates. Republican politicians in Wincanton frequently claimed that Stern was simply the local agent of the Cosa Nostra. While Stern was regularly sending money to the syndicates, the evidence suggests that Stern was much more than an agent for outsiders. It would be more accurate to regard these payments as profit sharing with coinvestors and as charges for services rendered. The east coasters provided technical services in the operation of the dice game and still and "enforcement" service for the Wincanton gambling operation. When deviants had to be persuaded to accept Stern's domination, Stern called upon outsiders for "muscle" strong-arm men who could not be traced by local police if the victim chose to protest. In the early 1940's, for example, Stern asked for help in destroying a competing dice game; six gunmen came in and held it up, robbing and terrifying the players. While a few murders took place in the struggle for supremacy in the 1930's and 1940's, only a few people were roughed up in the 1950's and no one was killed.

After the mid-1950's, Irv Stern controlled prostitution and several forms of gambling on a "franchise" basis. Stern took no part in the conduct of these businesses and received no share of the profits, but exacted a fee for protection from the police. Several horse books, for example, operated regularly; the largest of these paid Stern $600 per week. While slot machines had permanently disappeared from the Wincanton scene after the legislative investigations of the early 1950's, a number of men began to distribute pinball machines, which paid off players for games won. As was the case with numbers writers, these pinball distributors had been unorganized during the Craig administration. When Democratic Mayor Gene Donnelly succeeded Craig, he immediately announced that all pinball machines were illegal and would be confiscated by the police. A Stern agent then contacted the pinball distributors and notified them that if they employed Dave Feinman (Irv Stern's nephew) as a "public relations consultant," there would be no interference from the police. Several rebellious distributors formed an Alsace County Amusement Operators Association, only to see Feinman appear with two thugs from New York. After the association president was roughed up, all resistance collapsed, and Feinman collected $2,000 each week to promote the "public relations" of the distributors. (Stern, of course, was able to offer no protection against Federal action. After the Internal Revenue Service began seizing the pinball machines in 1956, the owners were forced to purchase the $250 Federal gambling stamps as well as paying Feinman. Over 200 Wincanton machines bore these stamps in the early 1960's, and thus were secure from Federal as well as local action.) In the 1950's, Irv Stern was able to establish a centralized empire in which he alone determined which rackets would operate and who would operate them (he never, it might be noted, permitted narcotics traffic in the city while he controlled it). What were the bases of his control within the criminal world? Basically, they were three: First, as a business matter, Stern controlled access to several very lucrative operations, and could quickly deprive an uncooperative gambler or numbers writer of his source of income. Second, since he controlled the police department he could arrest any gamblers or bookies who were not paying tribute. (Some of the local gambling and prostitution arrests which took place during the Stern era served another purpose—to placate newspaper demands for a crackdown. As one police chief from this era phrased it, "Hollywood should have given us an Oscar for some of our performances when we had to pull a phony raid to keep the papers happy.") Finally, if the mechanisms of fear of financial loss and fear of police arrest failed to command obedience, Stern was always able to keep alive a fear of physical violence. As we have seen, numbers writers, pinball distributors, and competing gamblers were brought into line after outside enforcers put in an appearance. Stern's regular collection agent, a local tough who had been convicted of murder in the 1940's, was a constant reminder of the virtues of cooperation. Several witnesses who told grand juries or Federal agents of extortion attempts by Stern, received visits from Stern enforcers and tended to "forget" when called to testify against the boss.

Protection

An essential ingredient in Irv Stern's Wincanton operations was protection against law enforcement agencies. While he was never able to arrange freedom from Federal intervention (although, as in the case of purchasing excise stamps for the pinball machines, he was occasionally able to satisfy Federal requirements without disrupting his activities), Stern was able in the 1940's and again from the mid-1950's through the early 1960's to secure freedom from State and local action. The precise extent of Stern's network of protection payments is unknown, but the method of operations can be reconstructed.

Two basic principles were involved in the Wincanton protection system— pay top personnel as much as necessary to keep them happy (and quiet), and pay something to as many others as possible to implicate them in the system and to keep them from talking. The range of payoffs thus went from a weekly salary for some public officials to a Christmas turkey for the patrolman on the beat. Records from the numbers bank listed payments totaling $2,400 each week to some local elected officials, State legislators, the police chief, a captain in charge of detectives, and persons mysteriously labeled "county" and "State." While the list of persons to be paid remained fairly constant, the amounts paid varied according to the gambling activities in operation at the time; payoff figures dropped sharply when the FBI put the dice game out of business. When the dice game was running, one official was receiving $750 per week, the chief $100, and a few captains, lieutenants, and detectives lesser amounts.

While the number of officials receiving regular "salary" payoffs was quite restricted (only 15 names were on the payroll found at the numbers bank), many other officials were paid off in different ways. (Some men were also silenced without charge—low-ranking policemen, for example, kept quiet after they learned that men who reported gambling or prostitution were ignored or transferred to the midnight shift; they didn't have to be paid.) Stern was a major (if undisclosed) contributor during political campaigns— sometimes giving money to all candidates, not caring who won, sometimes supporting a "regular" to defeat a possible reformer, sometimes paying a candidate not to oppose a preferred man. Since there were few legitimate sources of large contributions for Democratic candidates, Stern's money was frequently regarded as essential for victory, for the costs of buying radio and television time and paying pollwatchers were high. When popular sentiment was running strongly in favor of reform, however, even Stern's contributions could not guarantee victory. Bob Walasek, later to be as corrupt as any Wincanton mayor, ran as a reform candidate in the Democratic primary and defeated Stern-financed incumbent Gene Donnelly. Never a man to bear grudges, Stern financed Walasek in the general election that year and put him on the "payroll" when he took office.

Even when local officials were not on the regular payroll, Stern was careful to remind them of his friendship (and their debts). A legislative investigating committee found that Stern had given mortgage loans to a police lieutenant and the police chief's son. County Court Judge Ralph Vaughan recalled that shortly after being elected (with Stern support), he received a call from Dave Feinman, Stern's nephew, "Congratulations, judge. When do you think you and your wife would like a vacation in Florida?"

"Florida? Why on earth would I want to go there?"

"But all the other judges and the guys in City Hall—Irv takes them all to Florida whenever they want to get away."

"Thanks anyway, but I'm not interested."

"Well, how about a mink coat instead. What size coat does your wife wear?"

In another instance an assistant district attorney told of Feinman's arriving at his front door with a large basket from Stern's supermarket just before Christmas. "My minister suggested a needy family that could use the food," the assistant district attorney recalled, "but I returned the liquor to Feinman. How could I ask a minister if he knew someone that could use three bottles of scotch?"

Campaign contributions, regular payments to higher officials, holiday and birthday gifts—these were the bases of the system by which Irv Stern bought protection from the law. The campaign contributions usually ensured that complacent mayors, councilmen, district attorneys, and judges were elected;

payoffs in some instances usually kept their loyalty. In a number of ways, Stern was also able to reward the corrupt officials at no financial cost to himself. Just as the officials, being in control of the instruments of law enforcement, were able to facilitate Stern's gambling enterprises, so Stern, in control of a network of men operating outside the law, was able to facilitate the officials' corrupt enterprises. As will be seen later, many local officials were not satisfied with their legal salaries from the city and their illegal salaries from Stern and decided to demand payments from prostitutes, kickbacks from salesmen, etc. Stern, while seldom receiving any money from these transactions, became a broker; bringing politicans into contact with salesmen, merchants, and lawyers willing to offer bribes to get city business; setting up middlemen who could handle the money without jeopardizing the officials' reputations; and providing enforcers who could bring delinquents into line.

From the corrupt activities of Wincanton officials, Irv Stern received little in contrast to his receipts from his gambling operations. Why then did he get involved in them? The major virtue, from Stern's point of view, of the system of extortion that flourished in Wincanton was that it kept down the officials' demands for payoffs directly from Stern. If a councilman was able to pick up $1,000 on the purchase of city equipment, he would demand a lower payment for the protection of gambling. Furthermore, since Stern knew the facts of extortion in each instance, the officials would be further implicated in the system and less able to back out on the arrangements regarding gambling. Finally, as Stern discovered to his chagrin, it became necessary to supervise official extortion to protect the officials against their own stupidity. Mayor Gene Donnelly was cooperative and remained satisfied with his regular "salary." Bob Walasek, however, was a greedy man, and seized every opportunity to profit from a city contract. Soon Stern found himself supervising many of Walasek's deals to keep the mayor from blowing the whole arrangement wide open. When Walasek tried to double the "take" on a purchase of parking meters, Stern had to step in and set the contract price, provide an untraceable middleman, and see the deal through to completion. "I told Irv," Police Chief Phillips later testified, "that Walasek wanted $12 on each meter instead of the $6 we got on the last meter deal. He became furious. He said, "Walasek is going to fool around and wind up in jail. You come and see me. I'll tell Walasek what he's going to buy."

Protection, it was stated earlier, was an essential ingredient in Irv Stern's gambling empire. In the end, Stern's downfall came not from a flaw in the organization of the gambling enterprises but from public exposure of the corruption of Mayor Walasek and other officials. In the early 1960's Stern was sent to jail for 4 years on tax evasion charges, but the gambling empire continued to operate smoothly in his absence. A year later, however, Chief Phillips was caught perjuring himself in grand jury testimony concerning kickbacks on city towing contracts. Phillips "blew the whistle" on Stern, Walasek, and members of the city council, and a reform administration was swept into office. Irv Stern's gambling empire had been worth several million dollars each year; kickbacks on the towing contracts brought Bob Walasek a paltry $50 to $75 each week.

Official Corruption

Textbooks on municipal corporation law speak of at least three varieties of official corruption. The major categories are nonfeasance (failing to perform a required duty at all), malfeasance (the commission of some act which is positively unlawful), and misfeasance (the improper performance of some act which a man may properly do). During the years in which Irv Stern was running his gambling operations, Wincanton officials were guilty of all of these. Some residents say that Bob Walasek came to regard the mayor's office as a brokerage, levying a tariff on every item that came across his desk. Sometimes a request for simple municipal services turned into a game of cat and mouse, with Walasek sitting on the request, waiting to see how much would be offered, and the petitioner waiting to see if he could obtain his rights without having to pay for them. Corruption was not as lucrative an enterprise as gambling, but it offered a tempting supplement to low official salaries.

Nonfeasance

As was detailed earlier, Irv Stern saw to it that Wincanton officials would ignore at least one of their statutory duties, enforcement of the State's gambling laws. Bob Walasek and his cohorts also agreed to overlook other illegal activities. Stern, we noted earlier, preferred not to get directly involved in prostitution; Walasek and Police Chief Dave Phillips tolerated all prostitutes who kept up their protection payments. One madam, controlling more than 20 girls, gave Phillips et al. $500 each week; one woman employing only one girl paid $75 each week that she was in business. Operators of a carnival in rural Alsace County paid a public official $5,000 for the privilege of operating gambling tents for 5 nights each summer. A burlesque theater manager, under attack by high school teachers, was ordered to pay $25 each week for the privilege of keeping his strip show open.

Many other city and county officials must be termed guilty of nonfeasance, although there is no evidence that they received payoffs, and although they could present reasonable excuses for their inaction. Most policemen, as we have noted earlier, began to ignore prostitution and gambling completely after their reports of offenses were ignored or superior officers told them to mind their own business. State policemen, well informed about city vice and gambling conditions, did nothing unless called upon to act by local officials. Finally, the judges of the Alsace County Court failed to exercise their power to call for State Police investigations. In 1957, following Federal raids on horse bookies, the judges did request an investigation by the State Attorney General, but refused to approve his suggestion that a grand jury be convened to continue the investigation. For each of these instances of inaction, a tenable excuse might be offered—the beat patrolman should not be expected to endure harassment from his superior officers, State police gambling raids in a hostile city might jeopardize State-local cooperation on more serious crimes, and a grand jury probe might easily be turned into a "whitewash" in the hands of a corrupt district attorney. In any event, powers available to these law enforcement agencies for the prevention of gambling and corruption were not utilized.

Malfeasance

In fixing parking and speeding tickets, Wincanton politicians and policemen committed malfeasance, or committed an act they were forbidden to do, by illegally compromising valid civil and criminal actions. Similarly, while State law provides no particular standards by which the mayor is to make promotions within his police department, it was obviously improper for Mayor Walasek to demand a "political contribution" of $10,000 from Dave Phillips before he was appointed chief in 1960.

The term "political contribution" raises a serious legal and analytical problem in classifying the malfeasance of Wincanton officials, and indeed of politicians in many cities. Political campaigns cost money; citizens have a right to support the candidates of their choice; and officials have a right to appoint their backers to noncivil service positions. At some point, however, threats or oppression convert legitimate requests for political contributions into extortion. Shortly after taking office in the mid-1950's, Mayor Gene Donnelly notified city hall employees that they would be expected "voluntarily" to contribute 2 percent of their salary to the Democratic Party. (It might be noted that Donnelly never forwarded any of these "political contributions" to the party treasurer.) A number of salesmen doing business with the city were notified that companies which had supported the party would receive favored treatment; Donnelly notified one salesman that in light of a proposed $31,000 contract for the purchase of fire engines, a "political contribution" of $2,000 might not be inappropriate. While neither the city hall employees nor the salesmen had rights to their positions or their contracts, the "voluntary" quality of their contributions seems questionable.

One final, in the end almost ludicrous, example of malfeasance came with Mayor Donnelly's abortive "War on the Press." Following a series of gambling raids by the Internal Revenue Service, the newspapers began asking why the local police had not participated in the raids. The mayor lost his temper and threw a reporter in jail. Policemen were instructed to harass newspaper delivery trucks, and 73 tickets were written over a 48-hour period for supposed parking and traffic violations. Donnelly soon backed down after national news services picked up the story, since press coverage made him look ridiculous. Charges against the reporter were dropped, and the newspapers continued to expose gambling and corruption.

Misfeasance

Misfeasance in office, says the common law, is the improper performance of some act which a man may properly do. City officials must buy and sell equipment, contract for services, and allocate licenses, privileges, etc. These actions can be improperly performed if either the results are improper (e.g., if a building inspector were to approve a home with defective wiring or a zoning board to authorize a variance which had no justification in terms of land usage) or a result is achieved by improper procedures (e.g., if the city purchased an acceptable automobile in consideration of a bribe paid to the purchasing agent). In the latter case, we can usually assume an improper result as well—while the automobile will be satisfactory, the bribe giver will probably have inflated the sale price to cover the costs of the bribe.

In Wincanton, it was rather easy for city officials to demand kickbacks, for State law frequently does not demand competitive bidding or permits the city to ignore the lowest bid. The city council is not required to advertise or take bids on purchases under $1,000, contracts for maintenance of streets and other public works, personal or professional services, or patented or copyrighted products. Even when bids must be sought, the council is only required to award the contract to the lowest responsible bidder. Given these permissive provisions, it was relatively easy for council members to justify or disguise contracts in fact based upon bribes. The exemption for patented products facilitated bribe taking on the purchase of two emergency trucks for the police department (with a $500 campaign contribution on a $7,500 deal), three fire engines ($2,000 was allegedly paid on an $81,000 contract), and 1,500 parking meters (involving payments of $10,500 plus an $880 clock for Mayor Walasek's home). Similar fees were allegedly exacted in connection with the purchase of a city fire alarm system and police uniforms and firearms. A former mayor and other officials also profited on the sale of city property, allegedly dividing $500 on the sale of a crane and $20,000 for approving the sale, for $22,000, of a piece of land immediately resold for $75,000.

When contracts involved services to the city, the provisions in the State law regarding the lowest responsible bidder and excluding "professional services" from competitive bidding provided convenient loopholes. One internationally known engineering firm refused to agree to kickback in order to secure a contract to design a $15 million sewage disposal plant for the city; a local firm was then appointed, which paid $10,700 of its $225,000 fee to an associate of Irv Stern and Mayor Donnelly as a "finder's fee." Since the State law also excludes public works maintenance contracts from the competitive bidding requirements, many city paving and street repair contracts during the Donnelly-Walasek era were given to a contributor to the Democratic Party.

Finally, the franchise for towing illegally parked cars and cars involved in accidents was awarded to two garages which were then required to kickback $1 for each car towed.

The handling of graft on the towing contracts illustrates the way in which minor violence and the "lowest responsible bidder" clause could be used to keep the bribe payers in line. After Federal investigators began to look into Wincanton corruption, the owner of one of the garages with a towing franchise testified before the grand jury. Mayor Walasek immediately withdrew his franchise, citing "health violations" at the garage. The garageman was also "encouraged" not to testify by a series of "accidents"—wheels would fall off towtrucks on the highway, steering cables were cut, and so forth. Newspaper satirization of the "health violations" forced the restoration of the towing franchise, and the "accidents" ceased.

Lest the reader infer that the "lowest responsible bidder" clause was used as an escape valve only for corrupt purposes, one incident might be noted which took place under the present reform administration. In 1964, the Wincanton School Board sought bids for the renovation of an athletic field. The lowest bid came from a construction company owned by Dave Phillips, the corrupt police chief who had served formerly under Mayor Walasek. While the company was presumably competent to carry out the assignment, the board rejected Phillips' bid "because of a question as to his moral responsibility." The board did not specify whether this referred to his poor corruption as chief or his present status as an informer in testifying against Walasek and Stern.

One final area of city power, which was abused by Walasek et al., covered discretionary acts, such as granting permits and allowing zoning variances. On taking office, Walasek took the unusual step of asking that the bureaus of building and plumbing inspection be put under the mayor's control. With this power to approve or deny building permits, Walasek "sat on" applications, waiting until the petitioner contributed $50 or $75, or threatened to sue to get his permit. Some building designs were not approved until a favored architect was retained as a "consultant." (It is not known whether this involved kickbacks to Walasek or simply patronage for a friend.) At least three instances are known in which developers were forced to pay for zoning variances before apartment buildings or supermarkets could be erected. Businessmen who wanted to encourage rapid turnover of the curb space in front of their stores were told to pay a police sergeant to erect "10-minute parking" signs. To repeat a caveat stated earlier, it is impossible to tell whether these kickbacks were demanded to expedite legitimate requests or to approve improper demands, such as a variance that would hurt a neighborhood or a certificate approving improper electrical work.

All of the activities detailed thus far involve fairly clear violations of the law. To complete the picture of the abuse of office by Wincanton officials, we might briefly mention "honest graft." This term was best defined by one

of its earlier practitioners, State Senator George Washington Plunkitt who
loyally served Tammany Hall at the turn of the century.

There's all the difference in the world between [honest and dishonest graft]. Yes, many of our men have grown rich in politics. I
have myself.

I've made a big fortune out of the game, and I'm gettin' richer
every day, but I've not gone in for dishonest graft—blackmailin'
gamblers, saloonkeepers, disorderly people, etc.—and neither has
any of the men who have made big fortunes in politics.

There's an honest graft, and I'm an example of how it works.
I might sum up the whole thing by saying: "I seen my opportunities and I took 'em."

Let me explain by examples. My party's in power in the city,
and it's goin' to undertake a lot of public improvements. Well,
I'm tipped off, say, that they're going to lay out a new park at a
certain place.

I see my opportunity and I take it. I go to that place, and I
buy up all the land I can in the neighborhood. Then the board of
this or that makes its plan public, and there is a rush to get my
land, which nobody cared particular for before.

Ain't it perfectly honest to charge a good price and make a
profit on my investment and foresight? Of course, it is. Well,
that's honest graft.

While there was little in the way of land purchasing—either honest or
dishonest—going on in Wincanton during this period, several officials who
carried on their own businesses while in office were able to pick up some
"honest graft." One city councilman with an accounting office served as
bookkeeper for Irv Stern and the major bookies and prostitutes in the city.

Police Chief Phillips' construction firm received a contract to remodel the
exterior of the largest brothel in town. Finally one councilman serving in the
present reform administration received a contract to construct all gasoline
stations built in the city by a major petroleum company; skeptics say that the
contract was the quid pro quo for the councilman's vote to give the company
the contract to sell gasoline to the city.

How Far Did It Go?

This cataloging of acts of nonfeasance, malfeasance, and misfeasance by
Wincanton officials raises a danger of confusing variety with universality, of
assuming that every employee of the city was either engaged in corrupt
activities or was being paid to ignore the corruption of others. On the contrary, both official investigations and private research lead to the conclusion
that there is no reason whatsoever to question the honesty of the vast majority of the employees of the city of Wincanton. Certainly no more than 10 of
the 155 members of the Wincanton police force were on Irv Stern's payroll

(although as many as half of them may have accepted petty Christmas presents—turkeys or liquor). In each department, there were a few employees who objected actively to the misdeeds of their superiors, and the only charge that can justly be leveled against the mass of employees is that they were unwilling to jeopardize their employment by publicly exposing what was going on. When Federal investigators showed that an honest (and possibly successful) attempt was being made to expose Stern-Walasek corruption, a number of city employees cooperated with the grand jury in aggregating evidence which could be used to convict the corrupt officials.

Before these Federal investigations began, however, it could reasonably appear to an individual employee that the entire machinery of law enforcement in the city was controlled by Stern, Walasek, et al., and that an individual protest would be silenced quickly. This can be illustrated by the momentary crusade conducted by First Assistant District Attorney Phil Roper in the summer of 1962. When the district attorney left for a short vacation, Roper decided to act against the gamblers and madams in the city. With the help of the State Police, Roper raided several large brothels. Apprehending on the street the city's largest distributor of punchboards and lotteries, Roper effected a citizen's arrest and drove him to police headquarters for proper detention and questioning. "I'm sorry, Mr. Roper," said the desk sergeant, "we're under orders not to arrest persons brought in by you." Roper was forced to call upon the State Police for aid in confining the gambler. When the district attorney returned from his vacation, he quickly fired Roper "for introducing politics into the district attorney's office."

If it is incorrect to say that Wincanton corruption extended very far vertically into the rank and file of the various departments of the city—how far did it extend horizontally? How many branches and levels of government were affected? With the exception of the local Congressman and the city treasurer, it seems that a few personnel at each level (city, county, and State) and in most offices in city hall can be identified either with Stern or with some form of free-lance corruption. A number of local judges received campaign finances from Stern, although there is no evidence that they were on his payroll after they were elected. Several State legislators were on Stern's payroll, and one Republican councilman charged that a high-ranking State Democratic official promised Stern first choice of all Alsace County patronage. The county chairman, he claimed, was only to receive the jobs that Stern did not want. While they were later to play an active role in disrupting Wincanton gambling, the district attorney in Hal Craig's reform administration feared that the State Police were on Stern's payroll, and thus refused to use them in city gambling raids.

Within the city administration, the evidence is fairly clear that some mayors and councilmen received regular payments from Stern and divided kickbacks on city purchases and sales. Some key subcouncil personnel frequently shared in payoffs affecting their particular departments—the police chief shared in the gambling and prostitution payoffs and received $300 of the $10,500 kickback on parking meter purchases. A councilman controlling one department, for example, might get a higher percentage of kickbacks than the other councilmen in contracts involving that department.

The Future of Reform in Wincanton

When Wincantonites are asked what kind of law enforcement they want, they are likely to say that it is all right to tolerate petty gambling and prostitution, but that "you've got to keep out racketeers and corrupt politicians." Whenever they come to feel that the city is being controlled by these racketeers, they "throw the rascals out." This policy of "throwing the rascals out," however, illustrates the dilemma facing reformers in Wincanton. Irv Stern, recently released from Federal prison, has probably, in fact, retired from the rackets; he is ill and plans to move to Arizona. Bob Walasek, having been twice convicted on extortion charges, is finished politically. Therefore? Therefore, the people of Wincanton firmly believe that "the problem" has been solved—"the rascals" have been thrown out. When asked, recently, what issues would be important in the next local elections, only 9 of 183 respondents felt that clean government or keeping out vice and gambling might be an issue. (Fifty-five percent had no opinion, 15 percent felt that the ban on bingo might be an issue, and 12 percent cited urban renewal, a subject frequently mentioned in the papers preceding the survey.) Since, under Ed Whitton, the city is being honestly run and is free from gambling and prostitution, there is no problem to worry about.

On balance, it seems far more likely to conclude that gambling and corruption will soon return to Wincanton (although possibly in less blatant forms) for two reasons—first, a significant number of people want to be able to gamble or make improper deals with the city government. (This assumes, of course, that racketeers will be available to provide gambling if a complacent city administration permits it.) Second, and numerically far more important, most voters think that the problem has been permanently solved, and thus they will not be choosing candidates based on these issues, in future elections.

Throughout this report, a number of specific recommendations have been made to minimize opportunities for wide-open gambling and corruption—active State Police intervention in city affairs, modification of the city's contract bidding policies, extending civil service protection to police officers, etc. On balance, we could probably also state that the commission form of government has been a hindrance to progressive government; a "strong mayor" form of government would probably handle the city's affairs more efficiently. Fundamentally, however, all of these suggestions are irrelevant. When the voters have called for clean government, they have gotten it, in spite of loose bidding laws, limited civil service, etc. The critical factor has been voter preference. Until the voters of Wincanton come to believe that illegal gambling produces the corruption they have known, the type of government we have documented will continue. Four-year periods of reform do little to change the habits instilled over 40 years of gambling and corruption.

7

Daley's machine in Chicago

Mike Royko

Kunstler: Mayor Daley, do you hold a position in the Cook County Democratic Committee?

Witness: I surely do, and I am very proud of it. I am the leader of my party.

Kunstler: What was that?

Witness: I surely do, and I am very proud of it. I am the leader of the Democratic party in Cook County.

Kunstler: Your honor, I would like to strike from that answer anything about being very proud of it. I only asked whether he had a position in the Cook County Democratic party.

Hoffman: I will let the words "I surely do" stand. The words after those may go out and the jury may disregard the expression of the witness that he is very proud of his position.

From the book *Boss: Richard J. Daley of Chicago* by Mike Royko pp. 59–69. Copyright © 1971 by Mike Royko. Published by E.P. Dutton & Co., Inc. and used with their permission.

The Hawk got his nickname because in his younger days he was the outside lookout man at a bookie joint. Then his eyes got weak, and he had to wear thick glasses, so he entered politics as a precinct worker.

He was a hustling precinct worker and brought out the vote, so he was rewarded with a patronage job. The Hawk, who had always loved uniforms but had never worn one, asked his ward committeeman if he could become a member of the county sheriff's police department. They gave him a uniform, badge, and gun, and declared him to be a policeman.

But the Hawk was afraid of firearms, so he asked if he could have a job that didn't require carrying a loaded gun. They put him inside the County Building, supervising the man who operated the freight elevator. He liked the job and did such a good job supervising the man who operated the freight elevator that the Hawk was promoted to sergeant.

When a Republican won the Sheriff's office, the Hawk was out of work for one day before he turned up in the office of the county treasurer, wearing the uniform of a treasurer's guard. His new job was to sit at a table near the main entrance, beneath the big sign that said "County Treasurer," and when people came in and asked if they were in the county treasurer's office, the Hawk said that indeed they were. It was a good job, and he did it well, but it wasn't what he wanted because he really wasn't a policeman. Finally his committeeman arranged for him to become a member of the secretary of state's special force of highway inspectors, and he got to wear a uniform that had three colors and gold braid.

The Hawk is a tiny piece of the Machine. He is not necessarily a typical patronage worker, but he is not unusual. With about twenty-five thousand people owing their government jobs to political activity or influence, nothing is typical or unusual.

The Hawk keeps his job by getting out the Democratic vote in his precinct, paying monthly dues to the ward's coffers, buying and pushing tickets to his ward boss's golf outing and $25-a-plate dinners. His reward is a job that isn't difficult, hours that aren't demanding, and as long as he brings out the vote and the party keeps winning elections, he will remain employed. If he doesn't stay in the job he has, they will find something else for him.

Some precinct captains have had more jobs than they can remember. Take Sam, who worked his first precinct forty-five years ago on the West Side.

"My first job was as a clerk over at the election board. In those days to succeed in politics you sometimes had to bash in a few heads. The Republicans in another ward heard about me and they brought me into one of their precincts where they were having trouble. I was brought in as a heavy, and I took care of the problem, so they got me a job in the state Department of Labor. The job was . . . uh . . . to tell the truth, I didn't do anything. I was a payroller. Then later I went to another ward as a Democratic precinct captain, where they were having a tough election. I did my job and I moved over to a job as a state policeman. Then later I was a city gas meter inspector, and a pipe fitter where they had to get me a union card, and an investigator for the attorney general, and when I retired I was an inspector in the Department of Weights and Measures."

The Hawk and Sam, as precinct captains, are basic parts of the machine. There are some thirty-five hundred precincts in Chicago, and every one of them has a Democratic captain and most captains have assistant captains. They all have, or can have, jobs in government. The better the captain, the better the job. Many make upwards of fifteen thousand dollars a year as supervisors, inspectors, or minor department heads.

They aren't the lowest ranking members of the Machine. Below them are the people who swing mops in the public buildings, dump bedpans in the County Hospital, dig ditches, and perform other menial work. They don't work precincts regularly, although they help out at election time, but they do have to vote themselves and make sure their families vote, buy the usual tickets to political dinners, and in many wards, contribute about two percent of their salaries to the ward organization.

Above the precinct captain is that lordly figure the ward committeeman, known in local parlance as "the clout," "the Chinaman," "the guy," and "our beloved leader."

Vito Marzullo is a ward committeeman and an alderman. He was born in Italy and has an elementary school education but for years when he arrived at political functions, a judge walked a few steps behind him, moving ahead when there was a door to be opened. Marzullo had put him on the bench. His ward, on the near Southwest Side, is a pleasant stew of working-class Italians, Poles, Mexicans, and blacks, A short, erect, tough, and likable man, he has had a Republican opponent only once in four elections to the City Council. Marzullo has about four hundred patronage jobs given to him by the Democratic Central Committee to fill. He has more jobs than some ward bosses because he has a stronger ward, with an average turnout of something like 14,500 Democrats to 1,200 Republicans. But he has fewer jobs than some other wards that are even stronger. Marzullo can tick off the jobs he fills:

"I got an assistant state's attorney, and I got an assistant attorney general, I got an electrical inspector at twelve thousand dollars a year, and I got street inspectors and surveyors, and a county highway inspector. I got an administrative assistant to the zoning board and some people in the secretary of state's office. I got fifty-nine precinct captains and they all got assistants, and they all got good jobs. The lawyers I got in jobs don't have to work precincts, but they have to come to my ward office and give free legal advice to the people in the ward."

Service and favors, the staples of the precinct captain and his ward boss. The service may be nothing more than the ordinary municipal functions the citizen is paying taxes for. But there is always the feeling that they could slip if the precinct captain wants them to, that the garbage pickup might not be as good, that the dead tree might not be cut down.

Service and favors. In earlier days, the captain could do much more. The immigrant family looked to him as more than a link with a new and strange government: he was the government. He could tell them how to fill out their papers, how to pay their taxes, how to get a license. He was the welfare agency, with a basket of food and some coal when things got tough, an entree to the crowded charity hospital. He could take care of it when one of the kids got in trouble with the police. Social welfare agencies and better times took away many of his functions, but later there were still the traffic tickets to fix, the real estate tax assessments he might lower. When a downtown office didn't provide service, he was a direct link to government, somebody to cut through the bureaucracy.

In poor parts of the city, he has the added role of a threat. Don't vote, and you might lose your public housing apartment. Don't vote, and you might be cut off welfare. Don't vote, and you might have building inspectors poking around the house.

In the affluent areas, he is, sometimes, merely an errand boy, dropping off a tax bill on the way downtown, buying a vehicle sticker at City Hall, making sure that the streets are cleaned regularly, sounding out public opinion.

The payoff is on election day, when the votes are counted. If he produced, he is safe until the next election. If he didn't that's it. "He has to go," Marzullo says. "If a company has a man who can't deliver, who can't sell the product, wouldn't he put somebody else in who can?"

Nobody except Chairman Daley knows precisely how many jobs the Machine controls. Some patronage jobs require special skills, so the jobholder doesn't have to do political work. Some are under civil service. And when the Republicans occasionally win a county office, the jobs change hands. There were more patronage jobs under the old Kelly-Nash Machine of the thirties and forties, but civil service reform efforts hurt the Machine. Some of the damage has been undone by Daley, however, who let civil service jobs slip back into patronage by giving tests infrequently or making them so difficult that few can pass, thus making it necessary to hire "temporary" employees, who stay "temporary" for the rest of their lives. Even civil service employees are subject to political pressures in the form of unwanted transfers, withheld promotions.

On certain special occasions, it is possible to see much of the Machine's patronage army assembled and marching. The annual St. Patrick's Day parade down State Street, with Daley leading the way, is a display of might that knots the stomachs of Republicans. An even more remarkably display of patronage power is seen at the State Fair, when on "Democrat Day" thousands of city workers are loaded into buses, trains, and cars which converge on the fairgounds outside Springfield. The highlight of the fair is when Daley proudly hoofs down the middle of the grounds' dusty racetrack in ninety-degree heat with thousands of his sweating but devoted workers tramping behind him, wearing old-fashioned straw hats and derbies. The Illinois attorney general's staff of lawyers once thrilled the rustics with a crack manual of arms performance, using Daley placards instead of rifles.

Another reason the size of the patronage army is impossible to measure is that it extends beyond the twenty to twenty-five thousand government jobs. The Machine has jobs at racetracks, public utilities, private industry, and the Chicago Transit Authority, which is the bus and subway system, and will help arrange easy union cards.

Out of the ranks of the patronage workers rise the Marzullos, fifty ward committeemen who, with thirty suburban township committeemen, sit as the Central Committee. For them the reward is more than a comfortable payroll job. If they don't prosper, it is because they are ignoring the advice of their Tammany cousin George Washington Plunkitt, who said, "I seen my opportunities and I took 'em." Chicago's ward bosses take 'em, too.

Most of them hold an elective office. Many of the Daley aldermen are ward bosses. Several are county commissioners. Others hold office as county clerk, assessor, or recorder of deeds and a few are congressmen and state legislators. Those who don't hold office are given top jobs running city departments, whether they know anything about the work or not. A ward boss who was given a $28,000-a-year job as head of the city's huge sewer system was asked what his experience was. "About twenty years ago I was a house drain inspector." "Did you ever work in the sewers?" "No, but many a time I lifted a lid to see if they were flowing." "Do you have an engineering background?" "Sort of. I took some independent courses at a school I forget the name of, and in 1932 I was a plumber's helper." His background was adequate: his ward usually carries by fifteen thousand to three thousand votes.

The elective offices and jobs provide the status, identity, and retinue of coat holders and door openers, but financially only the household money. About a third of them are lawyers, and the clients leap at them. Most of the judges came up through the Machine; many are former ward bosses themselves. This doesn't mean cases are always rigged, but one cannot underestimate the power of sentimentality. The political lawyers are greatly in demand for zoning disputes, big real estate ventures, and anything else that brings a company into contact with city agencies. When a New York corporation decided to bid for a lucrative Chicago cable TV franchise, they promptly tried to retain the former head of the city's legal department to represent them.

Those who don't have the advantage of a law degree turn to the old reliable, insurance. To be a success in the insurance field, a ward boss needs only two things: an office with his name on it and somebody in the office who knows how to write policies. All stores and businesses need insurance. Why not force the premium on the friendly ward boss? As Marzullo says, everybody needs favors.

One of the most successful political insurance firms is operated by party ancient Joe Gill. Gill gets a big slice of the city's insurance on public properties, like the Civic Center and O'Hare Airport. There are no negotiations or competitive bidding. The policies are given to him because he is Joe Gill. How many votes does Prudential Life deliver? The city's premiums are about $500,000 a year, giving Gill's firm a yearly profit of as much as $100,000.

Another firm, founded by the late Al Horan, and later operated by his heirs and County Assessor P. J. Cullerton gets $100,000 a year in premiums from the city's park district. Since Cullerton is the man who sets the taxable value of all property in Cook County, it is likely that some big property owners would feel more secure being protected by his insurance.

When the city's sprawling lake front convention hall was built, the insurance business was tossed at the insurance firm founded by George Dunne, a ward boss and County Board president.

Another old-line firm is operated by John D'Arco, the crime syndicate's man in the Central Committee. He represents the First Ward, which includes the Loop, a goldmine of insurable property. D'Arco has never bothered to deny that he is a political appendage of the Mafia, probably because he knows that nobody would believe him. A denial would sound strained in light of his bad habit of being seen with Mafia bosses in public. Besides, the First Ward was controlled by the Mafia long before D'Arco became alderman and ward committeeman.

D'Arco's presence in the Central Committee has sometimes been an embarrassment to Chairman Daley. Despite D'Arco's understandable efforts to be discreet, he can't avoid personal publicity because the FBI is always following the people with whom he associates. When D'Arco announced that he was leaving the City Council because of poor health, while remaining ward committeeman, the FBI leaked the fact that Mafia chief Sam Giancana had ordered him out of the council in a pique over something or other. Giancana could do that, because it is his ward; D'Arco only watches it for him. One of Giancana's relatives has turned up as an aide to the state Senate. At Daley's urging, the First Ward organization made an effort to improve its image by running a young banker for alderman. But the banker finally resigned from the council, saying that being the First Ward's alderman was ruining his reputation.

When he is asked about the First Ward, Daley retreats to the democratic position that the people elect D'Arco and their other representatives, and who is he to argue with the people? He has the authority, as party chairman, to strip the First Ward, or any ward, of its patronage, and there are times when he surely must want to do so. Raids on Syndicate gambling houses sometimes turn up city workers, usually sponsored by the First Ward organization. While he has the authority to take away the jobs, it would cause delight in the press and put him in the position of confirming the Mafia's participation in the Machine. He prefers to suffer quietly through the periodic flaps.

The question is often raised whether he actually has the power, in addition to the authority, to politically disable the Mafia. It has been in city government longer than he has, and has graduated its political lackeys to judgeships, the various legislative bodies, and positions throughout government. While it no longer is the controlling force it was in Thompson's administration, or as arrogantly obvious as it was under Kelley-Nash, it remains a part of the Machine, and so long as it doesn't challenge him but is satisfied with its limited share, Daley can live with it, just as he lives with the rascals in Springfield.

Ward bosses are men of ambition, so when they aren't busy with politics or their outside professions, they are on the alert for "deals." At any given moment, a group of them, and their followers, are either planning a deal, hatching a deal, or looking for a deal.

Assessor Cullerton and a circle of his friends have gone in for buying up stretches of exurban land for golf courses, resorts, and the like. Others hold interests in racetracks, which depend on political goodwill for additional racing dates.

The city's dramatic physical redevelopment has been a boon to the political world as well as the private investors. There are so many deals involving ranking members of the Machine that it has been suggested that the city slogan be changed from *Urbs In Horto,* which means "City in a Garden," to *Ubi Est Mea,* which means "Where's mine?"

From where Daley sits, alone atop the machine, he sees all the parts, and his job is to keep them functioning properly. One part that has been brought into perfect synchronization is organized labor—perhaps the single biggest factor in the unique survival of the big city organization in Chicago. Labor provides Daley with his strongest personal support and contributes great sums to his campaigns. Daley's roots are deep in organized labor. His father was an organizer of his sheet-metal workers' local, and Bridgeport was always a union neighborhood. With politics and the priesthood, union activity was one of the more heavily traveled roads to success. Daley grew up with Steve Bailey, who became head of the Plumbers' Union, and as Daley developed politically, Bailey brought him into contact with other labor leaders.

Thousands of trade union men are employed by local government. Unlike the federal government and many other cities, Chicago always pays the top construction rate, rather than the lower maintenance scale, although most of the work is maintenance. Daley's massive public works projects, gilded with overtime pay in his rush to cut ribbons before elections, are another major source of union jobs.

His policy is that a labor leader be appointed to every policy-making city board or committee. In recent years, it has worked out this way: the head of the Janitors' union was on the police board, the park board, the Public Buildings Commission, and several others. The head of the Plumbers' Union was on the Board of Health and ran the St. Patrick's Day parade. The head of the Electricians' Union was vice-president of the Board of Education. The Clothing Workers' Union has a man on the library board. The Municipal Employees' Union boss was on the Chicago Housing Authority, which runs the city's public housing projects. The head of the Chicago Federation of Labor and somebody from the Teamsters' Union were helping run the poverty program. And the sons of union officials find the door to City Hall open if they decide on a career in politics.

The third major part of the Machine is money. Once again, only Daley knows how much it has and how it is spent. As party chairman, he controls its treasury. The spending is lavish. Even when running against a listless nobody, Daley may spend a million dollars. The amount used for "precinct money," which is handed out to the precinct captains and used in any way that helps bring out the Democratic vote, can exceed the entire Republican campaign outlay. This can mean paying out a couple of dollars or a couple of chickens to voters in poor neighborhoods, or bottles of cheap wine in the Skid Row areas. Republicans claim that the Democrats will spend as much as $300,000 in precinct money alone for a city election. To retain a crucial office, such as that of county assessor, hundreds of thousands have been spent on billboard advertising alone. Add to that the TV and radio saturation, and the spending for local campaigning exceeds by far the cost-per-vote level of national campaigning.

The money comes from countless resources. From the patronage army, it goes into the ward offices as dues, and part of it is turned over to party headquarters. Every ward leader throws his annual $25-a-head golf days, corned beef dinners, and picnics. The ticket books are thrust at the patronage workers and they either sell them or, as they say, "eat them," bearing the cost themselves.

There are "ward books," with page after page of advertising, sold by precinct workers to local businesses and other favor-seekers. Alderman Marzullo puts out a 350-page ad book every year, at one hundred dollars a page. There are no blank pages in his book. The ward organizations keep what they need to function, and the rest is funneled to party headquarters.

Contractors may be the biggest of all contributors. Daley's public works program has poured billions into their pockets, and they in turn have given millions back to the party in contributions. Much of it comes from contractors who are favored, despite the seemingly fair system of competitive bidding. In some fields, only a handful of contractors ever bid, and they manage to arrange things so that at the end of the year each has received about the same amount of work and the same profit. A contractor who is not part of this "brotherhood" refrains from bidding on governmental work. If he tries to push his way in by submitting a reasonable bid, which would assure him of being the successful low bidder, he may suddenly find that the unions are unable to supply him with the workers he needs.

Even Republican businessmen contribute money to the Machine, more than they give to Republican candidates. Republicans can't do anything for them, but Daley can.

The Machine's vast resources have made it nearly impossible for Republicans to offer more than a fluttering fight in city elections. Daley, to flaunt his strength and to keep his organization in trim, will crank out four hundred thousand primary votes for himself running unopposed. His opponent will be lucky to get seventy thousand Republicans interested enough to cast a primary vote.

8

Mayor John Lindsay and the revenge of Boss Tweed

Jack D. Douglas

Almost all analysts of the politics of America's old industrial cities of the Northeast and Midwest (as well as of San Francisco and Los Angeles) would agree that pluralistic conflict is the dominant factor in local and state politics.

Almost all these cities are made up of mosaics of racial, ethnic, religious, economic, and cultural interest groups which are partially independent of, and even isolated from, each other, but which overlap and interact in complex and unpredictable ways in specific situations involving concrete issues. No single group, or small coalition of the largest groups, ever achieves dominace for long. These complex and changing conflicts produce what some an-

This article was prepared especially for this volume. It represents an abridgement of my longer essay which brings out the implications of this analysis. See Jack D. Douglas, "Urban Politics and Public Employee Unions" in *Public Employee Unions*. San Francisco: Institute for Contemporary Studies 1976. A much shorter article by the same name was published in *The Wall Street Journal*, June 30, 1976. References deleted.

alysts have called "immense centrifugal forces" what others more recently have called "fragmentation" and "polarization;" and what still others have despairingly described as a "Byzantine mosaic." Almost all major problems in these cities resolve around *the core problem of social order*, that is, how can anyone construct sufficient order among these groups to coordinate their efforts for successfully dealing with the problem? In all the cities, various coalition strategies and structural reforms (such as "strong mayor" systems and city managers) have been used in attempts to deal with this core problem. They are sometimes successful, but in every case, the success is only temporary. The best-constructed coalition eventually shatters under the strain of the conflicts, and all structural solutions are found to be largely, though not entirely, symbolic illusions which can only temporarily mask the realities of pervasive conflict. The result is a clearly discernible political cycle which generally falls roughly into three periods (with no common time or period observable).

The first stage in this political cycle is an amalgam (not yet a coalition) of the subcultures which comes to feel that the city faces major and urgent social problems. Less commonly, the first stage involves the leaders' coming to see a set of tempting opportunities for them in pursuing certain urban policies. (This is the less common reason of the two, because fear of civic problems seems a stronger prod to common action than the hope of gains.)

The second stage is the formation of a political coalition to deal with the problems. Unless the perceived problems are overwhelmingly frightening, which is rare, the coalition can succeed only in dealing with them by welding itself together through some form of public payoffs, or spoils. The more successful the coalition is in solving the problems (or, more likely, in simply surviving until the social perception of a problem wanes), the more the coalition must resort to payoffs in order to keep the subcultures working together. The association of payoffs with coalitions leads to their being seen as corrupt political machines. (The whole concept of a "machine" is mistaken because these coalitions never achieve the degree of rationalized coordination and functional interdependency summoned up by the image of a machine. All the elements of the machine envy and distrust the others. For example, a crucial link in the famous Tweed machine was the coalition of the Germans with the Irish. When the Germans, who resented the greater power and share of spoils of the Irish, supported Tilden's reformers, Tweed's fate was sealed. The more successful the machine, the more visible the success of the dominant elements in it, hence, the greater the envy and distrust of the lesser partners. Machines thus build up their own internal dissension, to match the external pressures on them. Only historical precedent justifies our use of the term "machine.")

The third stage of this political cycle is the period of reaction against the coalition, especially against the payoffs it uses to cement together the parts of the now-disintegrating machine. This is the reform stage, when other groups in the city attack the payoff system and form their own coalition, dedicated to ending corrupt politics. This begins with cutting back on taxes and on the payoff system. The reform coalition then discovers that once the old political machine is destroyed, it has growing difficulty in holding together its own coalition. This, combined with drastic cuts in taxes, makes it hard to deal with any new social problems that arise. The reform coalition is then easy prey for a new machine, unless it starts using rapidly increasing payoffs to create its own machine. Some reformers, like John Lindsay, seem to suffer from true political idealism. (The moral didacticism, or lecturing, is an outcome of the absolutist idealism of such men as Lindsay.) Not understanding that all the subcultures have their own absolutist rules within the pluralistic society, they alienate everyone by asserting their own morality. Lindsay's idealism created still more conflict and decreased his mayoral power. Idealistic politicians not only come into office opposed to the old machine, but immediately move to destroy part of their own political power base (through the "politics of disintegration," as Lowi calls it). This makes them easy targets for any coalition of other groups. (Lindsay did try to create his own patronage machine by using federal funds to build community action groups, but this failed.) They are then faced with almost certain defeat or with joining the coalition of opposing forces and using massive payoffs to hold them together. (This three-stage model is a modified, more complex version of what Lowi and others have called the "reform cycle" in New York politics. It is vital to understand, however, that it is common to most other major cities.

It is remarkable that all of the basic aspects of this complex cycle, including some of the same devices, were already operating in the machine politics of Boss Tweed in New York one hundred years ago. It is even more remarkable that, though Tweed himself understood the basic political forces at work, it took social scientists almost a century to understand them, probably because of the encrustations of moralism which for so long obscured the political forces at work.

William Marcy Tweed has come down in standard American history texts as a grotesque figure of political corruption, a man of vile ambitions who created an all-powerful political ring to rob the treasury of New York City. This is the picture that most of us got from the caricatures of Tweed by Thomas Nast, originally published in *Harper's Weekly,* as part of the reform campaign against Tweed. Those caricatures and many popular books, such as Denis Tilden Lynch's *"Boss" Tweed*, convinced most educated Americans that Tweed was simply a bad apple who used the democratic system of the city to enrich himself and others in his gang. It was not until the 1960s that a few historians, especially John Pratt and Seymour Mandelbaum, began to show the underlying social and political forces that led Tweed to launch his program and which eventually destroyed both him and his program. This analysis, together with Tweed's own statement after his fall, gives us a new

picture of Tweed as a masterful politician who understood the city's problems as few others have and who tried to solve them in the only way he
thought possible.

The New York City Tweed knew was roughly the same in its social
composition and political structure as the city is today. In 1860 the population was 813,669. Of this total, 203,740 had been born in Ireland;
119,984 in Germany; 27,082 in England, and so on. Fewer than
half—383,345—were native-born whites. While the city lacked large blocs of
blacks, Puerto Ricans, Italians, and Jews, the far greater proportions of the
foreign-born gave it at least as much heterogeneity as it has today. The
municipal government was even more decentralized and feudal than now; the
tug of war between state power and home rule was just as intense; and the
quasi-class conflicts between business taxpayers and those who demanded
public services were almost exactly the same. The large public employees'
organizations, especially the police and fire departments, were very powerful
politically; were paid off with special pension benefits; and were probably
more corrupt than they are today. Consequently, politics was every bit as
Byzantine then as now.

The only major difference between the politics of Tweed's day and today
is that, by our public standards, politics then was very corrupt. It is this
difference that led people to accept the caricatures of Tweed so willingly, and
to fail to see the lessons for our age in his downfall. Tweed lived within, and
wholeheartedly accepted, what we now stigmatize as "the spoils system"
and "The Glided Age."

The spoils system was the way of getting things done politically. It consisted primarily of the granting of political positions in exchange for personal favors and favors to the party, but it also included the increasingly
controversial practices of "tax farming," or the use of the powers of public
office to generate payment for an office holder. These age-old practices gave
the officeholder a cut in the proceeds of the office and, presumably, gave him
an incentive to increase those proceeds by applying more public pressure.
Such practices may have worked well in the small town, where there were
plenty of informal controls on abuse, but in the big city they caused tremendous controversy. They were combined with buying votes, stuffing
ballot boxes, and making no clear legal distinctions between campaign
contributions, personal gifts, and political bribes. All this produced a
situation we see today as extremely corrupt. In Tweed's day, those who were
out of power came to take the same view, but also used the same practices to
gain power. Most people, and certainly Tweed, accepted them as the reality
of the day. Tweed was a moral relativist who pragmatically negotiated and
used the moral standards of the different groups to build his own political
machine. As Tweed said of idealism in politics, "I don't think men are
governed in these [political] matters by ideas of what should be between man
and men."

Although Tweed used all these practices in order to gain personal power and wealth, he also did so to further a basic social program, without which he would not have had his large and devoted following. Boss Tweed, like John Lindsay and most New York politicians, presented himself as a reform candidate. He was able to put together a powerful coalition of offices and interests, and in 1869, overthrew the corrupt machine of Fernando Wood. Tweed made Democratic Tammany Hall his primary political base in order to succeed in this overthrow, but he then moved forcefully to create a power bloc of both Democrats and Republicans. The basic program of what was to become known as the Tweed Ring (or Tweed Gang) was the usual amalgam of conflicting goals. To his closest friends, the Irish workers of Tammany Hall, he offered a broad program of social welfare and justice, which included the right to form unions and to strike. Since the Irish at that time were in the position of the blacks in the 1960s, this right was very important to them and, by granting it, Tweed earned a devoted following. The police and fire departments were of crucial importance to his coalition and at times they used outright violence to support him. Tweed appealed to some business and presidential, as well as labor, interests by pushing through a public parks program, city construction, dock improvement, and other such municipal works which later became so widespread. At the same time—and vitally important to the businessmen in his coalition—he actually decreased the tax rate without raising tax assessments. As Seymour Mandelbaum summed it up, "His implicit motto was 'something for everyone.' His tactical plan was 'do it now.'"

As anyone could anticipate, this great increase in expenditures, combined with a decrease in taxes, produced a fiscal deficit. How was the deficit covered? As any one familiar with fiscal practices under John Lindsay might have guessed by now, Tweed sold short-term, revenue-anticipation bonds. (Revenue-anticipation bonds are bonds sold in anticipation that they will be repaid from tax revenues that fall due in a short time.) When Tweed's coalition took control of the city in 1869, the debt was approximately $40 million. In three years, his administration doubled that by selling short-term bonds to individuals and groups. Part of the bond issue was later converted into long-term (30-year) bonds for $15 million at 6% interest (an exorbitant rate in those halcyon days, and without tax subsidies). Many of these were sold to the Rothschilds.

These bonds were sold secretly and their totals were carefully hidden in secret records. By 1871, there were rumors about the secret bonds, and bankers began to speculate darkly about credit problems and of the danger that the city would not be able to meet its obligations if the credit markets were closed to it. Before anything much could come of this, *The New York Times*—which at that time was a Republican newspaper trying doggedly to expose the fiscal irresponsibility of Tweed's administration—got hold of a purloined copy of the city's books and began publishing excerpts to show that the Tweed Ring had committed fraud by paying phony bills and taking kickbacks on the vast profits. Bankers immediately refused to make further loans or to buy bonds, and the city faced default on its obligations unless it could pay the $2,700,000 interest due on its bonds by November first. By now, Tweed's colleagues were deserting him and denouncing him. A prominent member of the Ring, Judge Barnard, issued an injunction preventing the city from paying out any more money or buying any more bonds after September seventh. The crisis caused some small riots by workmen who were not paid for their services, and the municipal government, predictably, became panicky. But a new comptroller was appointed, the injunction was lifted, and the city narrowly avoided default—without federal guarantees.

Tweed, of course, was made the scapegoat. Everyone who was able to copped a plea by blaming Tweed for it all. Those who had been most deeply implicated in the kickback and book-manipulating schemes were the ones who testified against Tweed. He was the only one to go to prison. After a flamboyant escape to Spain, he was returned to prison, died there, and became a symbol of corruption for succeeding generations of Americans.

But why did he do it? Was it all personal greed, as Nast and the other anti-Catholic, anti-Irish forces insisted? If so, he must not have been terribly good at it, since he got so little out of it. Tweed explained his reasons very clearly to an Aldermanic Committee appointed to investigate the scandal: "The fact is New York politics were always dishonest—long before my time. There never was a time when you couldn't buy the Board of Aldermen. A politician in coming forward takes things as they are. This population is too hopelessly split up into races and factions to govern it under universal suffrage, except by the bribery of patronage and corruption." Tweed had brilliantly analyzed the conflict-ridden electorate and the weak government structure of New York City and had used what President Grover Cleveland later called "the cohesive ties of public plunder" to put together a complex coalition in order to achieve both personal power and a public program. Either he did not realize that such a massive payoff of voters, especially when financed by technically illegal means, would eventually produce fiscal disaster, or else he counted on getting up and out before the "fiscal chickens" came home to roost. He miscalculated, but the history of the city and of the state (and now perhaps the nation) shows that he had a masterful grasp of how to attack the complex problems of pluralistic and democratic society. He seems to have been striving to establish a highly centralized city government, and a less democratic one. His approach was to use massive payoffs in the short run in order to get the power to curtail these payoffs in the long run. But his attempts to increase his power gravely threatened some parts of the coalition, especially the one led by his archrival among the Democrats, Samuel J. Tilden. Tilden secretly schemed with Tweed's declared enemies, such as *The New York Times*, to overthrow him.

John Lindsay was to follow the Tweed scenario in almost all its details. He presented himself, sincerely enough, in the classic role of the reform politician who opposed Tammany Hall machine politics. He concentrated specifically on denouncing Mayor Wagner's budget deficit of $255 million which had been financed by selling short-term, revenue-anticipation bonds. (City Comptroller Abraham Beame, himself a Democrat, also denounced Wagner's plan as fiscally unsound and mounted an attack on the city's fiscal integrity. Lindsay denounced in particular the payoffs Wagner had given to his allies, the public employees' unions. But there was a crucial difference between Lindsay and Tweed. Not having come up through the ranks of city politics, Lindsay did not have a gut-level understanding of those politics. His understanding was based on abstract theories prevalent among academicians of the day, and on traditional Anglo-Saxon ideas of public morality. Even some academicians who knew the political problems involved supported his systemic approach to solving the city's problems. He took a structural and even rationalistic (computerized) view of the city's political problems. As late as 1969 Lindsay's own statements show very clearly that he continued to look at the feudal conflicts of the city's many agencies as a problem that could be solved by rational systematization. (See his book, *The City*, 1969:81–87.) He and his advisers were quite convinced that the feudal structure of the city administration, with all its rigorously independent and conflicting authorities, could be rationalized and that this would go a long way toward solving its problems. They failed to see that the feudal structure was very much a direct outcome of the complex compromises necessitated by the feudal realities of the city's heterogeneous subcultures and special interest groups. By expending so much effort on this rationalization drive, Lindsay and his men failed to deal with the real problems, aggravated the conflicting demands on the city, intensified the struggle for power, and actually undermined political support that could have been vital in dealing with their biggest political problems—the public employees' unions and the growing fiscal crisis.

The contrast between Robert Wagner's cautious, cunning, old-politics approach to governing New York and John Lindsay's impatient, optimistic, swashbuckling, idealistic approach was startling. Wagner knew the labyrinthine realities from the inside. He also knew the jealous cunning with which every minor feudal lord fought to protect the autonomy of his domain. Wagner saw that the only realistic role open to a mayor who lacked a powerful political coalition to support him was of settling disputes among the feudal lords, especially by slight readjustments of costs and benefits. With the major exception of his move to consolidate negotiations with the labor unions (which was not so catastrophic, as long as subsequent negotiations were carried out with his highly personal, feudal approach), Wagner more or less accepted the popular view of the city as "ungovernable." He adopted a minimax, or foxhole, strategy in his adjustment to working as mayor. That is, he tried to stir things up with inflammatory rhetoric and idealistic promises of sweeping reforms to solve every problem. Perhaps he understood, as Arthur Schlesinger, Jr. later said John Kennedy did, that any public social order in a society so full of conflict as ours is a thin membrane of civilization stretched over abysmal conflicts, and that *any* attempts at quick and sweeping changes will exacerbate the underlying conflicts in all the groups. When the conflicts are ignited by sweeping promises and real changes, various groups begin to fight over the proceeds of the body politic. For, in spite of what the absolutist morality of the idealist tells him, there are few or no shared values that permit agreement among groups about the just distributions of the proceeds. They all want more—and more—and every gain made by other groups creates greater demands. Even if each group gets the same amount, *each group feels it deserved what it got, but the other groups did not.* The end of moral crusades *within* a highly pluralistic society (as opposed to a popular crusade directed outside) is internal warfare which can be put down only by great force, which no city authority has, or by massive payoffs to a coalition of "the big brigades" (as the British call their massive special interest groups, the unions, which fatten themselves off the body politic).

Whether or not Wagner understood the abstract principles of the conservative (or Burkean) strategy for avoiding internal warfare, he acted in accordance with them. His motto appears to have been, "When in doubt, don't." Lindsay's approach was the opposite: "Don't doubt. Do something rational to produce sweeping changes." Barry Gatteher has captured the contrast beautifully:

Mayor Wagner was like a baseball batter who likes to wait out every pitch. Looking for a walk, swinging only when necessary, dependable but not colorful, and consistent but too cautious to break up a ball game. Lindsay, on the other hand, was a free swinger, going for anything close to the plate, looking for the big hit, colorful and able to break up a ball game, and inconsistent but dramatic even when he struck out.

"It is better to make 100 bold and imaginative decisions and chance being wrong five times, than to play it safe and make no decisions at all," Lindsay said. "If New York City is to be governed properly, its government should be intolerant of waste, impatient with delay and capable of fast, decisive action in carrying out its policies and programs."

The overall effect of Lindsay's idealistic rationalism was to exacerbate the conflicts, and so to create tremendous demands for ever-greater "services" (which have the same effect as political payoffs, because they alone can quiet the conflicts). He united the biggest of the big brigades, the public employees' unions, by placing them in direct negotiation with a single agency. In so doing, he deprived himself of any effective counterweight in political maneuvering.

Lindsay had long recognized that "the plight of the cities is on the bargaining table." What he did not understand when he took office was that this plight was a direct result of the complex political forces of the public employees' unions and of the traditional feudal politics of the cities. (We shall see in Chapter 9 that there were also many other payoffs of interest groups; but the payoffs to the middle-class public employees' unions were the biggest.) Most important of all, Lindsay did not realize that these unions had become extremely powerful in the city by the strong coalition they had formed during the Wagner years to present a united front to the city's negotiators. The reverse side of Lindsay's failure to understand union power was his failure to realize how limited his own powers were as mayor of New York, despite the relatively "strong mayor" system on the lawbooks. These misconceptions caused him to do things that actually reduced his power, at the same time he was taking on the unions in direct confrontation. His attacks on Wagner's payoffs to the unions and his "Yalie" manner angered the unions, making them eager to put him in his place. Only hours after he took office, he faced the stark power of the unions in the form of a crippling strike. His crushing defeat apparently taught him that something had to be done about the power of public employees' unions—whom he moralistically denounced as power brokers.

Anyone who understood what we now know about the complex politics of public employee unions and cities would have only two possible courses of action. First, he could try to bribe the union leaders with personal payoffs, thereby neutralizing their power and creating "sweetheart unions." Since the rank-and-file members would probably not have been deceived for long, this seems the less realistic of the two options. (Mayor Daley of Chicago, however, did this successfully. Second, he could try to build his own political power with the other major blocs in the city, as he moved to outwit the unions by political shrewdness. By doing this, he would be following Wagner's path of trying (not always successfully) to use every structure and device possible to diminish union power and increase his own. Given the intense conflict of the situation he faced, and the general political situation, this seems, in retrospect, to have been Lindsay's best strategy. Instead, he rationalized the gamut of city and union relations by introducing wholly new structures and professionalized negotiation procedures. He created the Office of Collective Bargaining, established tripartite negotiation procedures, and hired a corps of professional negotiators. Once again, he failed to see that no structure or procedure could possibly eliminate the pervasive feudal politics of the situation. He merely shifted politics to the negotiating table and wound up by giving the unions an even greater voice in the outcome. Perhaps most ironic of all, Lindsay's rationalistic systemization of the city's administrative procedures for dealing with the unions deprived him of one of the most potent weapons a weak political administrator can have in dealing with powerful employees—the weapon of stall and confusion. If a political administrator is weak, his only effective strategy in preventing massive payoffs may be to stall and confuse the demander by bogging him down in labyrinthine and conflicting bureaucracies, making it very hard for the leaders of the big brigades to even know who has the authority to pay them off. At the extreme, with such overlapping and confusing authority, it is even possible to cancel a prior settlement, if it can be proved that the employer who made it had no authority to do so. Instead, Lindsay swept away all of the hedgerows behind which he could have taken refuge from the ever-growing demands. As he later said,

In the field of labor relations there was no policy; labor relations were handled by the Budget Bureau on an ad hoc basis and there was no overall record of the more than two hundred separate contracts between the city and its public employees. Only with the establishment of our Office of Collective Bargaining did a systematic program begin to emerge (Lindsay, 1969:84).

What Lindsay accomplished was to make the process of making demands on the city much more efficient, speedy, and effective. As his own budget director pointed out, this rationalized procedure speeded up the payouts to the demanders, but it did so on the basis of pseudo-rationalistic premises and data:

Actuarial pension plans have typically [in the past] been set up and modified only after a careful and detailed examination of costs, benefits, actuarial and investment assumptions. On the other hand, pension provisions in the collective bargaining process have sometimes been resolved within a week or even a day. It is necessary to work with rough cost figures. The meaning of various provisions is often not totally clear to all parties. It was my experience as director of the budget that most such provisions have ultimately cost New York City more than the estimates at the time of bargaining.

Lindsay simply did not realize that most of the official information being used was itself often *necessarily* problematic, and even corruptible, so that the new, efficient administration wound up rapidly making bad decisions. It is really more rational to take three years to make a mistake than to do it in a few days, especially when the mistake leads immediately to increased expenditures in a city that is already going bankrupt.

Even when Lindsay did recognize that politics was involved, the unions moved to outflank and defeat him. The unions' strategy was symbolized by the struggle over the continued use of Theodore Kheel as a negotiator. Lindsay apparently suspected Kheel's negotiations to be too favorable to the unions for the city's fiscal health, so he tried to prevent his being used again. The unions, sagely recognizing an "impartial" negotiator when they saw one, adamantly insisted on his presence before they would negotiate. They won the battle and the war. The major pension benefits, which alone have left the city with accrued deficits of over $6 billion in its pension funds and threatens its entire future, were professionally and speedily negotiated through this rationalized process.

Almost all of America's old Northeastern and Midwestern cities face roughly the same situation, for the same reasons. Most of them have been rapidly increasing their tax rates, decreasing their employee productivity, eroding their tax bases, losing their middle-income population, losing their jobs, and increasing their welfare load. They often face growing deficits during recessions, steadily increasing their bond-indebtedness-to-revenue ratios, and accumulating deficits in pension funds that will have to be paid out of their shrinking tax bases in the decades ahead. Sometimes they resort to hiding the books and to making fraudulent revenue estimates. They incessantly do political frontwork (such as blaming their financial problems on welfare recipients or on federal tax shifts to the "sun belt") in their desperate efforts to get the federal government to bail them out. The major cities of the South (except for New Orleans) and the Southwest (excluding California, where Los Angeles and San Francisco are like the North and San Diego like the South) are facing the opposite problems of growth. The South and Southwest do not have powerful public employee unions for numerous political and legal reasons, in particular the general public opposition to unions. Though he himself was probably the greatest victim of these complex social forces, it is clear now that Boss Tweed was the first person to analyze them correctly. History has given him his revenge.

9

New York's fiscal crisis and the new welfare-state political machine

Jack D. Douglas

The fiscal crisis of New York City in the 1970s has become one of America's most tense news-dramas. It is political theater at its best and its worst. We are presented daily with front-page warnings and denunciations. We are presented with the fears of annihilation and the hope of salvation. We teeter, with the city, on the brink of total disaster and are pulled back at the last minute by the heroic acts of angry and lonely heroes who denounce their own fate as heroes. All the political shibboleths of the day are brandished wildly in what seems an exquisite morality play for our century.

Unfortunately, as in all the noisy productions of political theater today, the drama has little to do with the stark economic realities of the city's fiscal crisis or with their significance for us all. Indeed, many of the political proclamations and anguished cries of impending doom have been carefully orchestrated to hide the facts and the real issues from the public. The political orches-

This article is originally published in this volume.

trators obviously hope to continue substituting the rhetoric of political theater for the harsh economic realities. This, more than anything else, makes New York City a metaphor for what is going on in our society today.

Mayor Abraham Beame has even gone so far as to express his desire to banish "grim economic realities" from his attempts to deal with the problems. As he said on October 15, 1975, after presenting his plan for a $200 million reduction in the municipal budget, "We can take no pride in the plan, because it places a higher priority at this time on the grim economic realities confronting the city rather than upon the needs of our citizens." Put more simply, this statement means that he and his supporters could be proud of a plan only if it placed their self-defined "needs" *before* "grim economic realities." We are told that they *should* give priority to their self-proclaimed needs over whatever grim economic realities might face them, and that the nation should back them financially so they can continue to do so. That is just like telling someone that his desire to fly by jumping off a cliff and flapping his arms should take precedence over the grim realities of gravity. It denies that our desires should and must be formed by continual consideration of the practical constraints placed on us by the grim realities we face. Yet everyone knows that to insist on our desires in the face of reality is madness and the road to certain catastrophe. We have, then, a dramatic picture of the mayor of America's largest city proclaiming that he cannot be proud of a plan because it is *not* an example of economic madness. It is a truly revolutionary proclamation, and one that might startle a devotee of a psychedelic counter-culture. Yet it did not seem to shock many Americans. In fact, not a single voice has been raised against this example of the new politics of economic madness. I suggest this is simply because people are already used to it, and because so many people now share it. This is the point to which I shall return after considering the details of the grim economic realities which the mayor insists on fleeing.

The Grim Economic Realities of New York City

The most immediate grim reality facing the city was, of course, default on its approximately $3.3 billion in outstanding municipal bonds which came due June 1976. That grim reality was precipitated by the fact that prospective buyers no longer trusted the city to pay them when their bonds come due. Contrary to what the mayor would have us believe, investor distrust was firmly grounded in the grim realities of the city's recent past and of its projected future.

The grimmest reality of all, which has been slowly and tortuously brought to light, has been the way city officials have concealed and muddied the economic facts. Even after months of painstaking searching and auditing by the new independent state agency, the Municipal Assistance Corporation

("Big Mac"), set up to oversee the city's finances, no one seems sure exactly what the city's financial condition is. Because of the "fiscal magic" of the city's official "fiscal wizards," it was not until early 1976 that auditors realized that New York's accumulated operating deficits were approaching $3.3 billion. Before that, potential investors had no clear idea of the city's operating deficits. Even as late as summer 1975, the city comptroller reported to Big Mac that the accumulated deficit was probably more than $2.5 billion. It was, in fact, far more, and no one can be sure there will be no further discoveries of financial wizardry. A report by the state comptroller even raised serious questions about the legality of some of the city's deficit financing methods, by showing that the methods used to estimate potential assets (accounts receivable) grossly overestimated them by a factor of five. For whatever reasons, no indictments have been sought, but suspicions of fiscal malfeasance have been rampant. Senator James Buckley of New York has even called for an investigation by the Justice Department to determine whether federal laws against fraud were violated by city officials. And there is little doubt that fiscal misfeasance has been developed into a fine political art.

The general public, and probably most of the smaller investors who were left holding the city's unsalable bonds, had no idea that New York was financing its current operations through the sale of short-run municipal bonds. Furthermore, they had no idea that the total of these outstanding bonds was growing ominously larger as the city consistently expended about 6% more than it took in. This practice had begun quietly at the end of the Wagner administration in 1965 and was sternly denounced by the new mayor, John Lindsay. Lindsay apparently stopped selling short-term bonds during his first administration. But beginning in 1970, he and his city comptroller, Abraham Beame, began to "solve" the problems of the grim economic realities facing them by rapidly expanding short-run deficit financing through the sale of municipal bonds.

In 1970, the downturn in the city's revenues seemed to be the result of the nationwide recession. The fiscal wizards probably thought they were dealing with a short-run problem that would go away, perhaps with the help of federal aid to cities, legislation for which Mayor Lindsay became the most impassioned pleader.

But the problems have not gone away. The city lost 53,000 jobs in 1970. The city has been losing jobs ever since, and now has 400,000 fewer jobs than it had in 1969, despite a period of great economic boom in the nation as a whole up to 1974.

The reasons for this downturn are fairly obvious. As everyone knows, New York is no longer a nice place for most people to live. There probably have been people who left just because they were unhappy living there. But people usually make such decisions on the basis of the economic realities facing them. They live where the jobs are, and businessmen locate where they can operate their businesses successfully. The crucial problem in New York is not so much the quality of life, but the quantity of taxes.

Lindsay increased the city's expenditures by about 100% (for reasons we shall see below). The city now spends about $1,300 per person per year, more than any other major city, except for Washington, D.C., which is heavily subsidized by the federal government. Businesses have fled New York City for the same tax reasons they have fled most of the big Northern cities. They have moved to cities like Houston, where the tax rate is about one-sixth that of New York. Houston increases its population by almost 60,000 each year; has one of the lowest unemployment rates in the country (about 5%), had a budgetary surplus of $14 million in 1975, and, even with such a low tax rate, increased its total tax revenues from property taxes by 20% in one year. New York has eroded its tax base at a tremendous rate because it did not pay attention to the grim economic realities facing it. But why did it choose this path of increasing taxation, ever-growing deficits, and fiscal and political trickery to hide the ominous realities behind the bright facade?

The Welfare Liberal Herring

One of the common beliefs abroad in the land today is that New York has gone bust only because it is the most compassionate of cities and that, if only the cruel conservatives in the federal government assumed their rightful duties to poorer citizens, New York would not have to stoop to questionable fiscal practices. This is the belief that Mayor Beame was trying to keep alive when he cited the needs of his electorate as justification for his fiscal problems. Many liberal politicians have already bought this story. As Representative Gladys Spellman (Democrat, Maryland) told Mayor Beame during his appearance before the House Subcommittee on Economic Stabilization, "A lot of [people] aren't paying welfare because you are." But a careful examination of the facts reveals this picture of the "City with a Welfare Heart of Pure Compassion" to be just another bit of political illusion, a liberal herring used to hoodwink liberals and conservatives alike into guaranteeing the same bonds that previously hoodwinked investors are no longer willing to buy.

As *The Wall Street Journal* pointed out in an editorial, "New York Myths" (October 20, 1975), the city expends $2.4 billion a year on social services, exclusive of its share of Medicaid costs. But most of this sum is actually paid by the state and by federal subsidies to the city. The city government itself has estimated that the total direct cost of social services to the city, including administrative costs, is approximately $600 million a year. With a total budget of $12 billion a year, that comes to only 5% for social services. (In spite of that small percentage, the city is able to provide such social welfare luxuries as child day-care centers for *nonworking* mothers.) The city pays nearly three times that much annually to service its more than $12 billion in municipal bonds. Moreover, the proportion of New York residents who are below the federal poverty line has decreased in the past 15 years, from 15.2% in 1960 to 11.5% in 1970. Both figures are below the national average. The city is better off in terms of its welfare costs than many other major cities, none of which has yet come close to bankruptcy. Only 10.9% of New York's population is receiving Aid to Families with Dependent Children. In Newark, the percentage is 12.6%; in Philadelphia, 13.9%; in Baltimore, 14.5%; and in St. Louis, 15.8%.

An even more telling bit of wizardry by city politicians has been their success in convincing the nation that New York deserves federal assistance because it has chosen to shelter a vast horde of poor black immigrants from the South. New York's black population increased from 10% in 1950 to 21% in 1970. In Washington, D.C., the blacks now comprise 71.1% of the total population. Even Chicago, which has never had deficit financing, is 32.7% black. And Houston, which, as we have seen, is running up big tax surpluses while lowering tax rates, has a 25.7% black population. But, those under the spell of the wizards insist that New York's black are much poorer. In fact, in 1970 the median income for black families in New York was $8,107, compared to a national median of $6,279. Most of New York's new black citizens are hard-working, middle-class citizens who pay taxes to the city. It is a great disservice to these people for the fiscal wizards to portray them as non-working welfare recipients who are forcing the city into bankruptcy.

New York City does have to pay a higher share of welfare costs than most cities, and it has provided some luxuries to welfare recipients. But it is not these costs that have brought the city to the brink of bankruptcy, and those welfare luxuries (such as free college tuitions, rent subsidies, etc.) are probably more beneficial to the middle classes than to the poor blacks. Where, then, do these vast per capita expenditures go? In fact, rather than being spent on compassionate payments to the poor, most of this money has been spent in payments to the New Welfare-State Political Machine.

Going Broke to Pay Off the New Welfare-State Political Machine

People who know anything about New York City may scoff at the idea of a political machine in the city today. Everyone who reads the popular press knows that Chicago is the only city in America with a functioning political machine and that Mayor Richard Daley was the only boss left (until his death in 1976). They also know that men such as John Lindsay and Abraham Beame were ardent reform politicians who loudly opposed the remnants of the old political machines. Unfortunately, their reform rhetoric has been no more than old political rhetoric in a new guise. But it has prevented the public from seeing the rapid spread of worse machine abuses than the old machines were ever able to get away with.

Most people mistakenly assume that a political machine can have only one form, that of the traditional boss system, found in Chicago today, and in

New York during the reign of Tammany Hall. Yet this is the same mistake as thinking that a nation-state must be a monarchy, as political thinkers commonly thought during the early period of the rise of democratic nation-states. Power is certainly one of the necessary elements of a political machine, but it is by no means the only one, and it may take different forms. As almost anyone realizes, once he thinks about it, the most important part of a political machine is the so-called spoils system, or the use of government money to pay off the members of the machine so that they will continue their support of the would-be leaders. People often make the mistake of thinking a spoils system has to take the traditional form—a system of political favoritism, in which the leaders dispense jobs or financial benefits in *direct* payment for political support. But this is nonsense. Just as the power of the nation-state can be conferred by birth or by election, so the monetary spoils of the political machines can be dispensed by personal fiat, or they can be dispensed by means of civil service rules, in exchange for more indirect support at election time. The mainspring of the political machine is the *use of public monies to buy or encourage political support,* regardless of the means used. Once this is understood, it is perfectly obvious that New York's liberal politicians, whether they are Democrats, Republicans, or independents (as Lindsay was in his second administration), have been using the vast increases in public expenditures to pay off a New Welfare-State Political Machine, in exchange for votes. Even more striking, we find that the demands for payoffs have escalated, just as they did under the Tammany Hall machine in the nineteenth century. These demands have been met in exactly the way they were under Boss Tweed—by the sale of short-run municipal bonds. This corrupt practice has produced the same result of near-default on these bonds as it did when Boss Tweed vastly increased the city's debt while refusing to raise the tax rates.

If New York City is governed by a New Welfare-State Political Machine, who are the members of this machine? Even those who are convinced that New York politicians have been buying votes by promising and delivering more and more of the city's wealth to those who vote for them are apt to assume that those whose votes are bought are the poor, especially the poor blacks. But this is ridiculous. It is certainly true that the poor get their share of the tax-and-bond-revenue pie in exchange for their votes for the liberal (i.e., *spending*) politicians, but we have already seen that only about 12% of the city's population is poor, by federal definition. Even if we liberalize that percentage by doubling it, or radicalize it by tripling it, we still end up with a distinct minority of the population, and even fewer of the voters (since the poor always have low voting rates). No one can win many elections by paying off the poor with the tax monies of the middle classes. The middle classes make up the great majority of the population in New York, just as they do in the industrialized nations. If a candidate is to win an election in New York, he must have at least the support of large middle-class blocs to combine with the lower-class bloc. We shall see how the New York reform liberals courted the middle classes with political and fiscal magic.

New York has not suddenly discovered the political magic of exchanging tax money for middle-class votes. Large chunks of the city's budget have gone to the middle classes for many years. Such benefits as free tuition at the City University's 19 institutions and low-cost medical care at city hospitals are long traditions. The only things not traditional about them are the steeply rising costs, resulting from the great increases in college enrollment in the 1960s (220,000 students are enrolled in 1975), and the spiraling inflation of medical costs. New York has also given vast *indirect tax benefits* to many thousands of its middle-class citizens by maintaining strict rent controls on housing that would otherwise be yielding many millions in taxes. Rent controls have had an especially devastating effect ever since the great increases in fuel costs. The city, to appease the bloc of middle-class voters, has refused to allow landlords to raise rents to meet upwardly spiraling fuel prices. The average apartment owner now seems to be losing money, in spite of drastic cutbacks in maintenance and repairs. As a result, about 25% of apartment taxes are in arrears; approximately 40,000 apartment units are abandoned every year, sometimes leaving almost entire blocks of gutted apartments; and about 90 of the city's 125 subsidized apartment projects for middle-income residents nearly defaulted on mortgages in 1975–1976. In the same spirit many politicians supported a rent strike at New York's massive Co-op City housing development in 1976, which nearly bankrupted the state housing agency.

Most of these middle-class payoffs were demanded and given by the city before the Lindsay administration. Rent controls go back to the Second World War. But such payoffs became a much greater burden under the New Welfare-State Political Machine, and most politicians would not dare to curtail them, because that would cost them too many middle-class votes. In fact, taking away a benefit once bestowed produces more feelings of outraged deprivation than failing to give new benefits ever can. Even in the current fiscal maelstrom, which the wizards warn us may produce international catastrophes, no one has mentioned ending the sacred middle-class payoff of rent control, though small tuition fees were imposed in the city universities in 1976.

The distinctive, creative form of middle-class payoffs under the New Welfare-State Political Machine has, remarkably enough, proven to be exactly the same kind as that used by Tammany Hall in the nineteenth century—jobs and lucrative pension programs for city employees. City employees, who number more than 200,000 (no one knows exactly how many more), and their families, constitute the backbone of the new political machine. It is they whose votes can be counted before the elections; they whose presence can be counted on to get out the vote on Election Day; and, above all, it is they whose wrath must be feared, because a single transit workers' union can shut down much of the complex and interdependent metropolis.

The politicians' *fear* of the city employees' unions is the overriding reality of the new machine—the thing that makes it truly different from the old machines and, fiscally, far more dangerous. At times, the traditional machine used the power of its members against the rest of the city in order to wrest spoils from reluctant taxpayers. And certainly the bosses were, like all political leaders, partly dependent for their power on the will of the governed. But, even so, men like Richard Daley were *real* bosses. They had real power from the machine which they used to keep the members in line for the benefit of everyone in the machine. Moreover, the greater power within the machine made it possible to control the rest of the city, with a much smaller percentage of people living off the machine. The disciplined cadres were not only more effective against enemies, but that discipline made businessmen and others of substance willing to play ball with the machine. They knew the boss would deliver stability, or whatever he promised, precisely because he had discipline. In fact, it was most often a collusion of older elite groups, especially business groups, with new leaders of large voting blocs, that produced traditional machine politics. This is the conclusion of James C. Scott in his study of corruption and machine politics around the world, *Comparative Political Corruption:* "The growth of machine-style politics often represents a large-scale effort by elite groups to manage the problem of rapidly expanding political participation while at the same time retaining their control over state policy" (p. 145).

As long as the machine maintains discipline within its ranks, generally through a boss system, it can maintain a stable state of financial corruption, although it may go too far and precipitate crises, as the Tammany Hall machine did in the nineteenth century. The discipline of the party machine in Chicago allowed Mayor Daley to keep the city running smoothly and economically, with few or no strikes by city employees' unions, a relatively small municipal work force, and no deficit spending. He was able to offer the unions salaries and benefits not too far below those of New York, but at a far lower overall cost, and with far fewer of the union disruptions that drive businesses out as surely as tax increases do. The internal discipline made it unnecessary to pay off hundreds of thousands of other middle-class people through rent controls, free tuition, low-cost hospital care, and similar appeasements.

The reform liberals in New York did not have the advantages of machine discipline. Indeed, they were explicitly and vociferously against "dirty machine politics." They seemed to have been sincere in their opposition to machine politics, but equally dedicated to gaining and keeping power. (We must be cautious in assessing their motives. We must remember that Boss Tweed came to power under a cloak of respectability by demanding the overthrow of the corrupt machine of Fernando Wood.) Rather than being the machine wolves who ate the sheep, Lindsay's people seem to have been the sheep who were forced to become wolves in sheepskins or else be eaten by the powerful middle-class coalition of voters they had successfully courted.

Most important, while they were elected by a large coalition of middle- and lower-class voters, the reform liberals quickly found that the city employees' unions were real wolves who had to be paid off in massive amounts to prevent continual disruptions of all city services.

A few major transit and sanitation union strikes taught them their lesson. John Chamberlain put it graphically, in *The Wall Street Journal* (October 22, 1975), when he said, "In New York City, John Lindsay began his career in City Hall bravely by announcing his positive refusal to capitulate to Iron Mike Quill's transport workers. Alas, it was Lindsay's last act of noble defiance. Pressed by Governor Nelson Rockefeller, who could exert sufficient leverage from Albany to take over New York City's Sanitation Department at one point, Mr. Lindsay quickly made his peace with the municipal labor leaders. They rewarded him by reelecting him on an Independent ticket, but Mayor Beame is now paying for what Mr. de Toledano calls 'elephantiasis of the municipal budget.'"

Rather than a political machine with a strong boss system, the New Welfare-State Political Machine is thoroughly democratic at the top, and authoritarian at the middle level with the unions. The level at which any real authority rests always varies. In Great Britain, it is very low, so that the shop unions are powerful and the higher political levels weak. In America, the trade or craft union level is generally the strongest, especially in government employees' unions, while the locals and the federations are weak. The result is that any hopeful political leader in an American city is faced with really powerful trade union officials who have authority over the lower parts of their own unions, but are not subject to any significant authority from above. The municipal unions constitute America's new Urban Union Oligarchy. Political leaders are in a totally new situation, one of true democracy and little authority. Not only must the mayors and councilmen face elections every few years, but, unlike the union officials, they are continually undercut by their political competition. Then-Governor Rockefeller was already working to undercut Mayor Lindsay by making him look bad in handling the unions. And he did. Lindsay was left out on the front lines of the urban battlefield, facing a powerful oligarchy of union leaders who supported each others' pay demands, and who had no political pressures except for demands from their members for more and more money. The same situation has faced almost all mayors across the country. As John Chamberlain said of Mayor Alioto of San Francisco, "he begins by . . . [warning] his brother mayors that there must be no truckling to striking police. But then he folds completely, endorsing pay raises for strikers in order to get them back to work. Nobody in supposedly powerful office thunders anything, for none of our rulers has any conviction of sovereignty in a time when representative government no longer dares to represent the full body of taxpayers." Like Rockefeller before him, Jerry Brown, the governor of California, undercut the mayor of San Francisco in this police strike by refusing to take any

position on the strike while it was on; then by attacking the mayor's solution
once it was clear the taxpayers were angry about it. At the same time, he was
careful to continue his own support for collective bargaining rights for public
employees. All the mayors who survive learn quickly that they must play ball
with the Urban Union Oligarchy. In fact, the pattern of oligarchical bargaining
in our cities is now so well established that Professor Kurt Hanslowe has been
given the dubious honor of having it named after him, as the "Hanslowe
Effect." Chamberlain defines this as "the mutual back-scratching potential
inherent in compulsory public-sector bargaining laws whereby public employees and politicians 'reinforce the other's interest and domain.'" In short,
we now have a classic case of oligarchical price-fixing in our cities.

Mayor Lindsay learned very quickly and thoroughly how to play ball with
New York's stern union oligarchy. As Wyndham Robertson has shown in
Fortune (August 1975), between 1965 and 1969, Lindsay's first term, New
York experienced real prosperity. The population was stable, yet jobs increased by 220,000. But hidden in this overall picture was the ominous fact
that, with no increase in population, almost 80,000 of those new jobs were
city government jobs—unionized jobs. The nationwide recession struck in
1970 and the city lost 53,000 jobs in one year. But city jobs grew in number.
Between 1969 and 1975, the city lost 11% of all its jobs, more than 400,000
jobs. But municipal jobs increased every year.

The creation of these new patronage jobs caused much of the city's recent
fiscal crisis, especially when the Nixon administration refused to bail out
cities with massive government subsidies. (Most people have forgotten the
stern face of Mayor Lindsay on the television screen, when he threatened that
unless the federal government increased its subsidies to New York City by
billions, and to all cities by perhaps a hundred billion, there would be eternal
rioting. We now know why he was so anguished. Remembering earlier cries of
moralistic anguish helps to put the later ones in perspective.)

The sheer number of municipal jobs, not the pay rates, which are only
slightly higher than those in Chicago, is the shocking problem. True to the
principle that greater anger results from taking away patronage once granted,
than pleasure at the prospect of future patronage, Mayor Beame finds himself
unwilling to face the grim economic realities that would mean cutting back
the municipal labor force to a level commensurate with the city's continually
shrinking population. He has promised to reduce it by about 20,000, but that
is still probably five times too few. To propose any measure commensurate
with the grim economic realities of the city would be a truly grim political
reality.

New York's Hidden Grim Economic Realities

But there is a still more frightening economic reality facing the city,
which has been almost totally unreported in the nation's news media, with
the exception of *The Wall Street Journal.* The union oligarchy was quietly

working its political will at both the city and state levels during Lindsay's second term, in order to pull off a truly staggering coup. This had to do with union pension payoffs. In the nineteenth century, the police and firemen were the hard core of the city employees in the old boss-run machines. They were, accordingly, paid very well. But, as politicians have always found, tax-payers scream in protest and vote against them if they discover they are openly being ripped-off. The public must, then, be secretly ripped-off through *hidden taxes,* and those who profit from the rip-offs must receive these profits secretly, through *hidden benefits.* If this is done discreetly, the public almost never realizes what has happened, because they, and most of the news media, cannot follow such complex and hidden maneuvers. (At the national and state levels, most massive general tax increases are hidden by placing them on corporations as corporate taxes and employer contributions, which are then passed on to consumers. Or, individuals pay higher taxes in the form of Social Security or property reassessments, or inflation of the money supply.) In the nineteenth century, New York helped to pioneer the hidden machine payoffs to police and firemen through lucrative pension plans. Now standard throughout the nation, these pensions normally pay a minimum of one-half of final-year salaries after only twenty years of active service. The bene-ficiaries of these plans then get as much as the average person, who must work at least twice as long. During the Lindsay administration, New York took a giant step forward in hidden payoffs by providing transit workers, teachers, sanita-tion workers, and then general city workers the same benefits (with some modifications, such as minimum age requirements).

But city benefits do not stop there. The average employer contribution to pension plans is under 10%. New York pays about 20%. But that is not all. As Wyndham Robertson argues, there are hidden ways in which the union retirees can greatly boost their pension pay beyond what is recorded in the city's union contracts. "Traditionally, the base [salary for pension payments] had been the average of the employee's salary in the five years prior to retirement. The new legislation led to changing the base to the final year's salary. Because of earlier laws passed in the fifties, the base salary also in-cludes overtime, so nowadays employees about to retire take a sudden interest in their work and pile up mounds of overtime in that last year."

To a politician seeking votes from demanding unions *and* angry taxpayers, the wonderful thing about pension benefits (and many other side payments) is not only that they are hidden, but that they do not come due until many years after the politician has moved on—to higher office, perhaps. They have thus become a favorite ploy in the politicians' basic strategy of *up and out before the fiscal chickens come home to roost.* Even the taxpayer who learns of their existence is likely to feel, "It's too far off to worry about." Perhaps this same indifference explains why the news media has paid so little atten-tion to New York's great pension rip-offs.

But to anyone concerned with the financial status of all governments in the year ahead, New York's pension obligations are of great significance. Unlike congressmen and average citizens, every serious potential investor now knows that these future pension obligations are *the* hidden grim economic reality facing the city. Jonathan Schwartz has stated in *The Money Manager* (September 29, 1975), that the city has a vast, and possibly undeterminable, accrued deficit in these pension funds which runs into billions—the figure is often set at $6 billion, but it is possibly much higher. He estimates that the city will have to increase its contributions to four of its five pension funds by about $300 million a year over the next 15 or 20 years, while the fifth, the firemen's pension fund, will require an increase of 80% in contributions, by *both* the city and the firemen to meet its obligation.

That seems serious enough in a city which is rapidly losing its population, and losing its jobs and its tax base even faster. But its portent is more serious still. As *The Wall Street Journal* (October 15, 1975) concluded, "Governments, whether in New York, Albany or Washington, operate on cash-flow (or yearly intake and outgo). They assume that taxes can be raised in the future to meet future liabilities. The lesson of New York City is that this assumption is erroneous. New York politicians and editorial writers left, right, and center acknowledge that taxes can't be raised to meet past commitments or future liabilities, that increased rates would *reduce* revenues by eroding the tax base. What they still do not see, or will not admit, is that the city's credit cannot be restored merely by drawing a plan to balance the city's cash-flow budget over the next two or three years. Only a decrease in future liabilities can persuade the credit markets that New York City will be able to meet its obligations without raising taxes."

The debate in Congress and in the news media has focused on the city's annual operating deficit of about $300 million. This has led them to assume that the city will be financially viable if it reduces that deficit to zero within three years, while being propped up by federal government guarantees of its bonds. The city's actual deficit (cash-flow and accrued) is at least twice that great and the politicians have not dared to face it. Presumably, they are continuing to use the up-and-out ploy at the same time they are using the *bait-and-hook ploy*. City officials assume that they will be out of office by the time the shaky structure collapses due to growing pension fund shortfalls. At the same time, they make it look so easy to bail them out (it *only* takes a guarantee of $9 billion in bonds), in the hope the taxpayers will bite and only later discover there is a hook to the whole thing—outright tax subsidies in the future to prevent default of federally guaranteed bonds.

The Grim Lesson for America in New York's Fiscal Crisis

There are many clear lessons for other cities in New York's current dilemma. Most of our old, large urban centers in the North are eroding their tax bases in the same way as New York, though generally less spectacularly so. Most of them are doing it for the same reasons, especially that of giving in to all major demands by government employees' unions. If the true dimensions of New York's economic crisis are broadcast and brought home dramatically by actual bond default, people might become more aware of the New Welfare-State Political Machine, and the many forms of fiscal corruption it is using to pay off its voter members. Many of them will look behind the yearly accounts to discover that their cities already have huge accrued deficits in pension funds that will begin to be crushing burdens in the not-too-distant future. Some people may even become astute enough in the new oligarchic politics—with its emphasis on quickie up-and-out policies and dramatic playing-to-the-mass-media pronouncements—to expose it as it is being perpetrated, rather than waiting until all the grim realities are revealed. There have already been some steps taken in this direction. The new president of the League of California Cities, Mayor Pete Wilson of San Diego, has warned that passage of binding arbitration legislation for public employees (which has received strong support from Governor Brown and has already been enacted for California teachers) could create fiscal chaos in other cities, similar to that in New York.

The grim realities in New York may even make the nation recognize and accept the simple fact that we are now undergoing another old-fashioned American social movement. Just as the past century has been one of massive urbanization, so will the next be one of massive decentralization. People are moving out of cities at increasing rates, both because of the push of rising taxes and urban problems and because of personal preference. We no longer need heavy concentrations of industry and population in a few centers in order to make production possible. Indeed, we are steadily decreasing the percentage of population that is involved in basic production. We are becoming a knowledge-centered, service economy that can be based almost anywhere—including far-flung multinational bases around the world.

But these are the brighter sides to the lessons New York's plight can teach us. As with all political problems, there is a less pleasant side. New York's lesson in going-bust is only a very small game in a much larger game of going-bust that is being played out in many parts of the world.

It is certainly being played out in New York state in many of the same ways. In fact, the city's fiscal wizardry and the dangers of bond default came to light in good part as a result of the brief default on bonds of the state's Urban Development Corporation in February 1974. This default led bankers and bond underwriters to begin looking closely at the financial statements made by the city in support of its bond issues. And in October 1975 state Comptroller Arthur Levitt revealed that several of the state's agencies faced default in the next year. Most immediately, the state's Housing Finance Agency, created to provide low- and middle-income housing support, faced default on almost $300 million in bonds by the end of 1975. This agency's problems were largely precipitated by the rent strike against New York's Co-op City, a strike supported by many city politicians for the usual political reasons. The state itself must refinance about $3 billion in bonds throughout 1976. Yet the state's taxes have had similar, though less severe, eroding effects on its tax base as on the city's. Businesses leaving New York, but wishing to relocate nearby, have found New Jersey far more hospitable than New York state.

But that too is just a small part of the going-bust game. Almost every major nation in the Western world is now firmly set on a similar course. All of them have a majority of Liberal or Social Democratic voters and political leaders, who are elected predominantly on the simple premise that they can and will overcome grim economic realities, in order to provide quick satisfaction for the self-stated needs of the largest bloc of consumers—the lower to middle classes. (Some observers might point to France as a possible exception, but Valéry Giscard d'Estaing won the presidency by a tiny 1% majority over Francois Mitterrand, the candidate of the Socialist and Communist coalition. His victory was probably a lingering effect of the Gaullist era.) The names of the parties differ, ranging from Socialist to Liberal. But everywhere the thrust is the same, and it is so powerful that even supposedly conservative parties tend to move in the same direction in order to save themselves from overwhelming defeat. In Great Britain, Edward Heath did precisely this during his prime ministership in the early 1970s, and most British observers feel that any serious move to fiscal conservatism by the Conservative party will lead to a prolonged decline.

All the major governments have, to varying degrees and in varying ways, committed themselves to paying off voters by greatly and steadily increasing short-run consumption. They can do this only by increasing transfer payments away from those with high investment rates (the well-off) to those with low and zero investment rates (the large bloc of voters), or by extensive deficit financing. The use of transfer payments is the least apt to produce quick economic decline because it merely slows investment, so that everyone just gets poorer slowly. But it is also tremendously disruptive politically, because the middle to upper classes resent losing even more than the middle to lower classes like gaining. Deficit financing has almost always proven the more politicially popular means of rapidly increasing consumption of the welfare state bloc of voters. But deficit financing can only work over the years to increase the relative consumption rates of some, if it is actually serving as a hidden tax on others, through inflation. And even when it does that, it has sharp effects on the prices paid by the middle-to-lower class electors of the liberal spenders. They develop a subjective feeling that they are losing more than they are gaining, even when this is clearly absurd to economists. This leads to the spiraling wage demands so obvious in Great Britain over the past years, and in lesser powers, like Italy and Argentina, for many years. Most important, as all the major nations embark on the same deficit-financed consumption binge at the same time, the inflationary pressures on consumer goods become intense, and the entire Western market faces the danger of such severe recession that everyone gets much poorer very fast.

But there is a more dangerous form of fiscal wizardry that nations may use in much the same way New York's politicians used the municipal bond route. Instead of relying only on internal debt to finance the deficit spending used to quickly spur consumption, they can try to pay off voters with external debt. That is, they may borrow from foreign investors to pay for the rapidly growing internal consumption rates. That, of course, is more or less what cities like New York are forced to do. And that is what some nations, notably Great Britain, have done. For many years, Great Britain relied overwhelmingly on internal debt to finance its ever-increasing deficits. But growing inflation, heavy taxation (now running as high as 58% in all its national and local forms), and resulting low investment rates which erode the tax base have forced the government to look abroad for money to maintain its consumption rates. Great Britain now has a national deficit estimated by the Chancellor of the Exchequer, Denis Healey, to be about $19 billion per year, but most economists believe it will become significantly higher. Since Great Britain's gross national product is about one-seventh or less that of the United States, that is equivalent to the United States having a national deficit of about $150 billion. And it will not be for one year, or two. Great Britain is now borrowing more than $5 billion a year abroad, to help maintain consumption rates and to keep down the price inflation that would be so greatly increased by raising all the debt at home.

Foreign investors are not ignorant of the long-run decline of Great Britain and of the inflationary pressures on the pound, caused by the continual use of deficit financing to maintain consumption rates. The British, therefore, have had to use collateral to secure these foreign bonds. New York had to do the same, so it used anticipated taxes, bonds, and other receivables. Great Britain has used its North Sea oil resources. New York officials were apparently hoping that they would be saved by some magical increase in federal revenue-sharing—billions of dollars for the City of Compassion. And they are still hoping there will be a last-minute salvation by a congressional underwriting of their current rates of consumption and deficit financing. The British are also using anticipation notes. They and their foreign investors are assuming that the oil, which so far is just a trickle, will come on time in great quantities by the end of the 1970s; that the costs will not be greater than projected; and that the oil prices engineered by OPEC will remain in effect, since the costs of drilling for North Sea oil are so high that it must bring a basic price not much below current prices in order to show a profit. New York did not get its revenue-sharing. It is still trying for its last-ditch federal salvation. The North Sea oil has proven more costly to get than had been projected; the delivery dates are slipping; and moreover, no international cartel has succeeded for long in maintaining vastly inflated prices. Rarely has a great city so tied its fiscal status to the slim anticipations of future outside help. Rarely has a great nation so tied its fiscal status to slim anticipations of future wealth from a single resource. In one generation, New York City went from wealth to vast deficits and to corrupt financial practices to cover up the deficits. In one generation, Great Britain went from an empire on which the sun never set, to the banana republic of Europe, basing much of its future financing on one roll of the international economic dice.

New York will not go under financially, whether or not it receives federal support. It might go bankrupt, but bankruptcy is usually short-lived. It is the politicians, those caught out when the fiscal chickens came home to roost, who will go bust, unless they are saved from the outside. The city can always drastically curtail its expenditures. It might even be able to slow its tax base erosion by ending rent controls and by taking other such measures. But any internally based corrective measures seem destined to produce a gradual decline of the city that will last for many years.

It seems less likely that Great Britain will go bankrupt. Even if their North Sea gamble does not pay off, the British can always pay off their foreign anticipation notes by vastly increasing domestic debt or, if the bond buyers are wary of gambling, by vasting increasing taxation. But that would produce a severe run on sterling, a further inflationary spiral, and a severe drop in internal consumption. It seems likely that, like Italy, Great Britain will turn in the end to the European Economic Community and the United States for bailouts, just as New York is now turning the the federal government.

The crucial question is not whether small segments of the Western world can overcome their problems by internal reform or by outside bailouts. The question is whether the whole Western world can continue to pursue fiscal policies that erode the investment necessary for the production base, while vastly increasing consumer demand, and still hope to forever put off the day of reckoning with grim economic realities. If a day of default comes, it will probably come in the form of a severely disruptive recession, produced by the accelerating inflationary spiral, and there will be no one outside to come to the rescue. One might hope that a reading of the lessons of New York, of Great Britain, of Italy, of Denmark, of Argentina, of Uruguay, of Sri Lanka (Ceylon), of Chile, and of other nations would serve as a warning to those who voted in fiscally irresponsible leaders. But anyone who has watched the developments of these fiscal crises would be foolish to bet on it.

part IV

Federal usurpations of power

Official deviance currently enjoys topical popularity, largely because of the events surrounding Watergate, which led to the resignation of President Richard Nixon, and to a lesser extent because
of the public revelations of CIA and FBI abuses of power which
followed the Watergate investigation. These topics have generated
great concern among Americans recently, but it is impossible to
say whether or not this concern will be transitory, or whether it
will lead to significant changes in our political institutions. The
six readings in Part IV document and analyze recent usurpations
and abuses of power by those in federal authority. These abuses
have been so widespread and so complex that we cannot present
many specific details about them. Such documentation fills
volumes of official commission reports, newspaper accounts, and
other writings. We have assumed that our readers will be to some
extent familiar with these activities, and so we have selected the
chapters for Part IV on the basis of how well they illuminate and
analyze our recent history.

We begin this selection with a brief excerpt from the testimony of John W. Dean, President Nixon's former White House counsel before the Senate Select Committee. It gives a brief glimpse into the atmosphere of distruct within the White House inner circle. An interpretation is presented in Reading 11, "Watergate: Harbinger of the American Prince," in which Jack Douglas argues that Watergate, rather than being the outcome of pyramiding of power by dominant elites, resulted from the *loss* of social power by once powerful elite groups in the United States. Douglas also tries to draw broader implications from his anlysis, and extrapolates about the future.

Reading 12, an excerpt from the Rockefeller Report to the President on CIA Activities, documents the activities of a Special Operations Group ("Operation CHAOS") which was authorized to collect various kinds of information on American dissenters, and which far exceeded its mandate in the process. The next two readings detail some of the illegal activities of FBI agents directed toward the same goals, including 238 illegal break-ins. Part IV concludes with Arthur Vidich's analysis of the Watergate events, "Political Legitimacy in Bureaucratic Society" (Reading 15), an excellent sociological analysis of the traditional sources of political legitimacy in our society; how these have changed over time; and how they are related to the massive usurpations and abuses of power by our federal authorities. According to Vidich, the evidence shows that modern bureaucratic states are not characterized by any universal criteria of assent and legitimacy, nor do they need these to survive, despite what many functionalist, Marxist, and critical sociologists would have us believe. Observations of the increasing fragmentation, politicization, and polarization of American society, such as those by Douglas and Vidich will be further analyzed in several of the chapters in Part VIII.

10

Senate testimony by John W. Dean 3d

June 25 Asserts Nixon took part in Watergate coverup for eight months and says he warned him that Watergate was "a cancer growing on the Presidency." / June 26 Says Nixon misled the nation with Watergate denials, insists charges against the President are factual. / June 27 Details lists of White House political enemies and outlines purpose of lists. / June 28 Tells of White House concern over demonstrations and recalls plan for using I.R.S. audits as a political weapon. / June 29 Recounts his accusations against the President, saying he is prepared to stand on his word.

June 25, 1973

MR. DEAN: To one who was in the White House and became somewhat familiar with its interworkings, the Watergate matter was an inevitable outgrowth of a climate of excessive concern over the political impact of demonstrators, excessive concern

109

over leaks, an insatiable appetite for political intelligence, all coupled with a do-it-yourself White House staff, regardless of the law. However, the fact that many of the elements of this climate culminated with the creation of a covert intelligence operation as part of the President's re-election committee was not by conscious design, rather an accident of fate.

It was not until I joined the White House staff in July of 1970 that I fully realized the strong feelings that the President and his staff had toward antiwar demonstrators—and demonstrators in general.

The White House was continually seeking intelligence information about demonstration leaders and their supporters that would either discredit them personally or indicate that the demonstration was in fact sponsored by some foreign enemy. There were also White House requests for information regarding ties between major political figures (specifically members of the U.S. Senate) who opposed the President's war policies and the demonstration leaders.

I also recall that the information regarding demonstrators—or rather lack of information showing connections between the demonstration leaders and foreign governments or major political figures—was often reported to a disbelieving and complaining White House staff that felt the entire system for gathering such intelligence was worthless. I was hearing complaints from the President personally as late as March 12 of this year.

Approximately one month after I arrived at the White House I was informed about the project to restructure the Government's intelligence gathering capacities vis-à-vis demonstrators and domestic radicals.

After I was told of the Presidentially approved plan that called for bugging, burglarizing, mail covers and the like, I was instructed by Haldeman to see what I could do to get the plan implemented. I thought the plan was totally uncalled for and unjustified.

I talked with Mitchell about the plan, and he said he knew there was a great desire at the White House to see the plan implemented, but he agreed fully with F.B.I. Director Hoover, who opposed the plan, with one exception: Mitchell thought that an interagency evaluation committee might be useful, because it was not good to have the F.B.I. standing alone without the information of other intelligence agencies. After my conversation with Mitchell, I wrote a memorandum requesting that the evaluation committee be established, and the restraints could be removed later.

The interagency [Intelligence] Evaluation Committee was created, as I recall, in early 1971. I requested that Jack Caulfield, who had been assigned to my office, serve as the White House liaison to the I.E.C., and when Mr. Caulfield left the White House, Dr. David Wilson of my staff served as liaison. I am unaware of the I.E.C. ever having engaged in any illegal assignments, and certainly no such assignment was ever requested by my office. The reports from the I.E.C., or summaries of the reports, were forwarded to Haldeman and sometimes Ehrlichman.

In addition to the intelligence reports from the I.E.C., my office also received regular intelligence reports regarding demonstrators and radical groups from the F.B.I. and, on some occasions, from the C.I.A.

I became directly and personally aware of the President's own interest in my reports regarding demonstrations when he called me during a demonstration of Vietnam Veterans Against the War on the Mall in front of the Capitol. This was the occasion in May 1971, I believe that is the date, when the Government first sought to enjoin the demonstration and later backed down. The President called me for a first-hand report during the demonstration and expressed his concern that I keep him abreast of what was occurring. Accordingly, we prepared hourly status reports and sent them to the President.

I was made aware of the President's strong feelings about even the smallest of demonstrations during the late winter of 1971, when the President happened to look out the windows of the residence of the White House and saw a lone man with a large 10-foot sign stretched out in front of Lafayette Park.

I ran in to Mr. Dwight Chapin who said that he was going to get some "thugs" to remove that man from Lafayette Park. He said it would take him a few hours to get them, but they could do the job. I told him I didn't believe that was necessary. I then called the Secret Service and within 30 minutes the man had been convinced that he should move to the back side of Lafayette Park. There the sign was out of sight from the White House. I told Mr. Chapin he could call off the troops.

I also recall that the first time I ever traveled with the President was on his trip in 1971 to the Football Hall of Fame.

When the President arrived at the motel where he was spending the night in Akron, across the street were chanting, Vietcong-flag-waving demonstrators. The President told the Secret Service agent beside him, in some rather blunt synonyms, to get the demonstrators out of there. The word was passed, but the demonstrators couldn't be moved.

In early February of 1972, I learned that any means—legal or illegal—were authorized by Mr. Haldeman to deal with demonstrators when the President was traveling or appearing someplace. I would like to add that when I learned of the illegal means that were being employed, I advised that such tactics not be employed in the future and if demonstrations occurred—they occurred.

We never found a scintilla of viable evidence indicating that these demonstrators were part of a master plan; nor that they were funded by the Democratic political funds; nor that they had any connection with the McGovern campaign. This was explained to Mr. Haldeman, but the President believed that the opposite was, in fact, true.

11

Watergate: harbinger of the American prince

Jack D. Douglas

A basic test of scientific theories is their ability to predict specific events. It seems quite relevant today to assess the value of our sociological theories of deviance by asking whether they could have predicted the many forms of official deviance revealed by Watergate.

Let me begin by pointing out the obvious. No one *did* predict these concrete events—and that emphatically, and most significantly, includes the participants in Watergate. Had the participants themselves been able to predict, whether by sociology or scapulomancy, the concrete events as they have unfolded, they would certainly not have done the things that helped to produce the events—their very predictability would have prevented them, thereby destroying their predictability, as Popper and many other social thinkers have long pointed out. No sociologist or student

This is a revision of an essay originally published in *Theory and Society*, 1 (1974) 89–97 © Elsevier Scientific Publishing Company, Amsterdam– Printed in The Netherlands.

who has gone beyond the myths of introductory sociology would expect sociology to predict such concrete events. Human beings are necessarily partially free to construct the concrete events that occur in this world and no theory, notwithstanding the "law" of large numbers, can predict just what these concrete constructions will be. But human beings are also partially constrained in making their choices by the "realistic alternatives" they believe exist in the physical and social world in which they live, so there are partial, though changing, uncertain and conflicting patterns in our social lives. (These basic issues of freedom and constraints, certain and uncertain, order and disorder, predictability and unpredictability, have been dealt with in such nauseating detail in earlier works, such as my own works on *American Social Order* and *Existential Sociology,* that I need hardly elaborate upon them here.) The only serious issue of predictability for sociologists concerns whether we can predict the vague and conflicting trends or patterns of events in our society, how concrete these predictions can be, and whether such predictions actually flow from our theoretical understandings or merely from our common-sense understanding of the trends in society.

Rather than tantalizing the reader's imagination by holding the answer for the end, let me say that I think any number of us have long "predicted" such events, that these predictions have been both general and low level, and that our sociological understanding was combined with our "cultural wisdom" in making such predictions. Let me point out also that our sociological understandings lead us to predict more such events.

There are at least two levels of generality of events of this sort which were expected. The most general level of events worthy of consideration here is that of the extralegal use of power by individuals with some form of official sanction to achieve their personal and political goals. The more specific level of events that concerns us is that of the use of such extralegal means by individuals working in some way with or for those officially entrusted with power at the highest levels of our society.

Predicting the use by officials of means which a vast majority of people define as extralegal takes no special sociological knowledge. Any man of practical affairs in American society knows that there are always extralegal means of doing things, that the ways in which laws are administered depend very much on personal and political factors, and that those involved in administering the laws and exercising official power are generally aware that this is so and are quite aware that their rhetorical flurries about the supremacy of the law, etc., are largely just that—rhetoric. Sociologists have long known this at the local levels and about specific official organizations. Westie's studies of the deliberate use of beatings by police to "enforce the laws" when they did not think they could do so legally is only one instance of many such findings. Anybody who knows anything about the "criminal justice" system knows that it works not by ideas of justice, but primarily by very hard-nosed, practical compromises. Anyone busted for selling dope is not "given justice" as demanded by the code books, but a chance to "work it off kilo for kilo."

When Judge John Sirica used the cruel and unusual punishments of the inquisition, such as forty-year sentences held in abeyance until the individual pleaded guilty and implicated his friends, he was only returning tit for tat to the conspirators. They used illegal means, so he will use quasi-legal torture to force them to cop a plea, to serve the ends of "justice." The President's men used illegal means to "get Ellsberg;" so too, Woodward and Bernstein used the illegal means of publishing the jury proceedings to arouse the public against the conspirators and, as they admitted, Judge Sirica "admonished" them to stop—but did not demand prosecution.

What is legal and what is illegal? The claims and counterclaims raging on all sides of this controversy are beautiful examples of the problematic and conflicting nature of the meanings and uses of rules in our society today. We know of state legislators who have passed laws they themselves believed to be unconstitutional, but very useful in preventing some evil events, such as the election of progressives in an election to be held too soon for the courts to intervene. We know of the systematic violations of antitrust laws by corporations who do not believe in them; of the systematic violations of the rules of the National Labor Relations Board by companies; of the systematic use of violence and intimidation by unions to achieve their ends against the same businesses; of the student "protesters against the crimes in Vietnam" committing crimes of violence to stop "crimes of violence;" of the systematic use by police and national guardsmen of brutal force against almost anyone who looked like a student on such occasions; of the use by police of immense firepower against their enemies, all covered by a hail of public relations talk about the enemies attacking first; and the use of violence by demonstrators to stop the police, political parties, or anyone else who opposed their use of illegal means. We know from all accounts that bugging, spying, bribing, use of call girls, and so on, are endemic to many forms of business, most forms of national "intelligence" work, many forms of police work, and much of politics. We know also that almost all of these activities are commonly hidden from public view behind carefully guarded fronts of public respectablity that exclude all but the guilty from the inner secrets of the organizations. We know also that these activities in different forms go on in almost all groups, including universities.

I say we "know" these things, many as informed citizens and many others as sociologists. We do not all know it, or, rather, as sociologists we do all know these things, but we do not all accept them as important realities that must be understandable and generally predictable from our sociological theories. The traditional sociological theories, such as functional theory, look at such events as "deviant" from the normal, value-determined, systematically bounded events of the social world. But it is precisely the failure of such theories to explain and predict the pervasiveness of such events that led so many sociologists to reject them, or let them die of disuse. The major contenders for the so-called sociological theories of deviance (which many now recognize as a misnomer inherited from our antecedents) all now accept these as pervasive and important, even fundamental, aspects of our social world. In the usual manner of theories, they are both the result of such events and the predictors of further such events. They do differ in the degree to which they emphasize such things, and to which they see them as basic throughout society, but all of them to some degree see all social meanings, and certainly moral meanings, as problematic for the members and in some way as conflicting. They do not see the world as made up of good guys fighting bad guys, but as a struggle between individuals and groups with overlapping but different and often conflicting interests and meanings which have uncertain relations to many of the situations and events in their lives.

Some of us have insisted that these things are true of any society to some extent, but they are crucial to understanding American society, because its great pluralism, rapid change, and high degree of individual freedom make all these conflicts more intense. My own work, especially in *American Social Order* and *Existential Sociology*, has led me to see these problems of meanings and conflicts as so pervasive and intense that the basic stuff of all sociological theories, from the code-book values of functionalism to the linguistic accounts of ethnomethodologists, has missed the very nature of human social life by taking our fronts for our realities. Law as used in American society is largely a front, a myth to hide what is going on.

But those kinds of understandings and predictions are still some distance from "predicting" Watergate-type events in our society. Certainly they would lead us to expect that those who have succeeded in getting the most political power have been deeply involved in such practices. Certainly they would lead us to suspect that almost anyone who has been highly successful has become a master artificer at frontwork. The political frontwork of a Spiro Agnew forcing officials to allow him to cop a plea to minor charges by threatening to wreak political havoc on the nation, and then presenting himself as a national hero for copping that plea, may be *ne plus ultra* in frontwork, but is it also representative of routine political hackwork. These understandings lead us to expect also, without yet having penetrated the official organizations enough to get the evidence, that the FBI and all other official agencies, right up to the attorney general's office, have been involved in such general practices. It's not at all surprising that antitrust laws are enforced more under Democratic administrations than under Republican ones; or that Robert Kennedy turned the full force of the Justice Department against Jimmy Hoffa and put him in prison; or that Richard Nixon got him out when the Teamsters demonstrated their love for Republicans; or that Sam Ervin and the Democratic congress were outraged over Watergate but not over the Daley machine's throwing the election to Kennedy in 1960 by stuffing ballot boxes; or that Republican party workers are outraged that Ervin and company will not admit their demagoguery on national television, while not being outraged over their own lies, or a whole lot of other things.

Do these sociological theories allow us to understand and predict the kinds of extralegal, tyrannical uses of federal, especially presidential, power which we witness in the Watergate proceedings? Do they allow us to understand and predict that most of the top personal workers and friends of a president elected by a landslide majority would be involved in consciously subverting the very laws they swore to uphold? I think they do in one sense, though I would again emphasize that the specific nature of these events was very much a matter of individual construction to meet the unexpected demands of a terribly confused situation which none of them seemed to have grasped in its entirety, until it was all over, except for providing the frontwork of ex post facto public accounts.

A number of us, especially those taking an existential perspective on the social world, have long argued that in our society meanings are becoming so pluralistic, problematic, and conflicting that the members themselves have become increasingly aware of this and to believe that they cannot expect rational and morally correct solutions to their problems. The people recognize that they cannot expect others to share their feelings, ideas, values, and decisions on actions. In this situation, individuals retreat more into their private lives, shunning all the kooks and weirdos. When they must deal with others, they are more willing to use force, lies and any other means. Politicans come increasingly to believe that they cannot convince people to do anything because it is right or reasonable. They recognize that there is a growing chaos of values and ideas about government. They recognize also that there is a growing unwillingness to believe what the officials say.

There is a growing "unmasking" of the social world, aided by the development of sociology into a cornerstone of mass education. In this situation, political actors rely increasingly on power to construct social order, to get people to do what they want them to do. If you have legitimate power, use it. If not, use illegitimate power, if you believe you can avoid getting caught. Street demonstrators believed the same things: you can't trust the president or Congress because they lie and are trying to use you; attack them with physical force, make them do what you want. The politicians and their workers believed the same things about the street people and about the rest of society. Some of them attacked those people with the means they found at their disposal—some known to be legal, some known to be illegal, some not known one way or the other.

A popular form of structural sociology has led many people to believe— or, at least, to assert as political rhetoric—that there is an establishment, the power elite of the WASPs, that really determines what goes on in American society. This popular idea, like structural sociology before it, has led its proponents to believe that there is already a tyranny in the land and that Watergate is its outcome. This idea is really just a successor to the nineteenth-century ideological rhetoric of Marxism, which has already spawned most of the so called conflict theories of society. The Marxists, such as Herbert

Marcuse, believe that American society is already run by an efficient, but "comfortable," form of tyranny, a corporate power elite manning the techno-logical society. Most of them, of course, look at the "Watergate Follies" as merely another form of "fascist tyranny." All of these ideas of pop-and-ideologue sociology are mere stuff and nonsense. (I've never been able to understand why any so-called sociologist would prefer to take a "Marx hath said" stance toward American society when he could get an immensely more realistic, detailed analysis of what goes on in this society from any hack political reporter. The best I've been able to do in explaining this aberration is to view it as another instance of the Mystique-of-the-Written-Word which has misinspired so much of Western thought since the first scribes befuddled *hoi polloi* with their symbol-legerdemain. The Great-Man-with-the-Great-Book is a sure sign of an intent to mystify the masses into submission.)

These pop ideas are just the opposite of the truth. In fact, the growing forms of extralegal and quasi-legal power, such as Watergate, are the result of a *loss* of power by the once-dominant power group in American society. In the nineteenth century, the early American elite, the intellectual and upper-class WASPS, so cherished and well represented by the Henry Adamses of that day, was replaced by a new power elite, the corporate leaders and their middle-class minions, also largely WASPs. But in the twentieth century, this group's power was counterbalanced by the growth of new power groups, such as the political power of the lower classes and the ethnic blocs. As the century wore on, power became progressively fragmented as the values, other social meanings, and material interests of the nation became more pluralistic and uncertain, and as new groups, such as the academics and intellectuals, joined the fray, some of them introducing real leftist politics.

A highly pluralistic society was left without a power center. This condi-tion was long obscured by international conflicts, but with the waning of the cold war in the 1960s, it became all too clear to large segments of the people. Extremist politics broke out on many different sides—everything from youth rebellions to gay rebellions, from urban riots to campus riots. And there was no central power able to stop them. At the same time, the highly in-flammatory rhetoric of revolution of the new leftists fanned the deepest fears of social chaos, and even murder, among many of the power groups in the society. Even with this, they could not unite effectively around any program because their feelings, ideas, values, interests, and power were so uncertain and so conflicting. The only thing the great mass of people could agree on was rejecting any group with clear, unconflicting, uncompromising, extreme positions. They rejected what they saw as the extreme right (Goldwater) and the extreme left (McGovern).

Anybody who managed not to appear at the extremes split the society right down the middle. Kennedy and Nixon won by chance events, or corrup-tion, when not opposed by extremes. The Nixon people could not get the political support they needed to stop the Ellsberg leaks or do anything much else they felt necessary to stop what they believed to be the disintegration of society. Out of a lack of legitimate, legal power, they resorted to the use of extralegal and quasi-legal power. This was done largely to try to gain legitimate power, and, above all, to produce a great new coalition of power groups. Watergate was the outcome of a fragmentation of power in a time of crisis, of deep fears of chaos, rather than an instance of the exercise of extralegal power by a clearly dominant elite.

There is a seeming paradox in this picture of the helpless giant of "the imperial presidency," as Arthur Schlesinger, Jr. has called the modern American presidency. On the one hand, it is perfectly obvious that the federal government and most local governments have grown massively and become many times more powerful in our lives than they were a mere forty years ago. But, on the other hand, as Robert Nisbet, Alexander Bikel, Theodore Sorenson, and many others have argued so convincingly, Big Government has been less able to achieve its goals than any government before. The paradox is only apparent. Our Big Government has been less able to achieve its goals because it goals, those of meeting the ever-growing demands for services of our myriad Big Interest Groups, have increased faster than its ability to meet the demands. This, in turn, has undermined the legitimate authority of Big Government, causing still more fragmentation. At the same time, as government becomes bigger, and dispenses ever more payoffs to the conflicting Big Interest Groups, it creates more conflict among those interest groups and further undermines its own authority. The very process of trying to do more and more destroys Big Government's authority, so Big Government increasingly must resort to extralegal, quasi-legal, ad hoc, and even illegal means to achieve any of its goals—but especially those that crosscut the goals of the Big Interest Groups.

Fragmentation of power and Big Government are the clear realities of our society today, but I believe this is an unstable state of affairs that will be replaced by a new form of "democratic" tyranny. As long as this fragmentation continues, we shall have more forms of extralegal official actions. Under the new tyranny, they will not be necessary, except in the sense that, under tyranny, all government powers will be illegitimate. This, however, is irrelevant, since the new tyranny will not arise until the mass media are brought under sufficient control to prevent the people from knowing that the new government is a tyranny.

There is no one set of interests, values, or meanings dominant in our society today. That means that power must increasingly be used to maintain social order. But there is no dominant power group, so government has less authority. If anything, authority is becoming more fragmented at the same time as meanings become more fragmented. Power is not given; it is seized. Power becomes increasingly tyrannical, extralegal, and extra-moral. The twentieth century thus becomes the beginning of the Age of the American Prince. Watergate is the tip of the iceberg. It is a growing tip because its base is growing and pushing it upward. It will contine to grow, though it is unlikely that anyone will be so dumb as to repeat these exact follies. Human beings caught in the fearful chaos we face are vicious, but become more cunningly vicious, not stupidly so.

I have already emphasized that our theoretical perspective leads us to predict more such extralegal uses of power. This means not only more Watergates, but more lying in official statistics; more manipulation of fronts through political tricks; more secret taxation by using Newspeak to name taxes "insurance" (Social Security, unemployment, etc.), and by printing more money that causes inflation; and more secret leaks by newspapers and television aimed at destroying political enemies (especially the political enemies of newspapers and television). But let me go beyond simple extrapolation into the really dangerous waters of predicting social events, to predict what will be done to change the present situation.

Most important, I believe this fragmentation will not last. It will not last, primarily because too many of the interest groups are in the same boat in an increasingly difficult international situation, and because their desire to get more and more in government payoffs and the fears of chaos that grow with fragmentation will lead too many of them to accept almost any practical order. But there is no reason at all to believe we shall see a rebirth of democratic controls and authority. I do not believe there will be any leap into outright blatant forms of tyranny. A wise politician in a democracy or republic always uses traditional forms to mask his revolutionary moves. Augustus Caesar hid behind senatorial forms. Tyrannical power in America will be wrapped in democratic forms—indeed, in a *glorification* of those democratic forms. This will be all the more possible and likely because such a tyranny will have to be based in good part on the power of the mass media: Television will trumpet the revival of the Great American Democracy. Richard Nixon discovered the vast power potential of a coalition of the affluent blue-collar workers and the rural and Southern fundamentalists with the vast economic power of the corporate world. He made the mistake of not controlling the mass media and, worse, of making them his enemies. He was working to bring them under control and eventually to bring them into the coalition. But the unpredictable occurred—somebody got caught doing dumb things and the media, predictably, struck back at their mortal enemy.

Some happy Democratic warriors, such as Arthur Schlesinger, Jr. predict that this gloomy (to me) scenario will not unfold, because Watergate and related events have made it possible to restrict the power of the Presidency by having Congress reseize such power. Nonsense. The vast increases in the power of the Presidency have come about because of the almost universal demands of America's myriad Big Interest groups for more and more services (payoffs to voters), which can be provided only by an increasingly powerful, centralized bureaucratic government. Congress cannot meet those demands alone because it is the most fragmented, conflict-ridden, inept, and corrupt branch of the federal government. The drive toward centralized executive power will continue, and with it will come a new form of democratic tyranny. As John Adams, Thomas Jefferson, and almost all the founding fathers argued, Big Government will eventually produce usurpations of power, or tyranny. This new democratic tyranny will certainly be a comfortable tyranny in which masses are paid off with liberal reforms, such as guaranteed incomes and health "insurance." But it will still be a cradle-to-grave tyranny, in which the truth is kept from the people and they are manipulated through the mass media.

Having said that, let me reiterate the proviso about all social predictions with which I began this discussion. Men are partially free to construct their social world. My prediction of the continuing growth of a new form of tyrannical power in America is based on the presumption that Americans will not become aware of these dangers, or they will not choose to act in time to prevent them. I also expect that our massive interest groups, from Big Business and Big Labor to Big Agriculture and Big Welfare, will all continue to demand their government payoffs, while denouncing both the rip-offs of other groups *and* the Big Government their effective demands have created. But my expectation is not absolute. There are still those lingering doubts raised by the necessary, if partial, freedom of human beings, especially of Americans. If the Watergate conspirators could choose to do some of the dumb things they did, it's still just possible the American people might choose to do some wise things about their society that might prevent the rise of a new democratic tyranny. It is still possible that Big Interest groups will recognize that their short-run payoffs are producing Big Government which, in the long run, is dangerous to all of them. And it is just barely possible that they will choose to cut back on their short-run payoffs, restore little government, and thus restore and safeguard the individual rights of all.

But let me not end on an optimistic note. The times do not justify it. Every one of our Big Interest Groups is growing and demanding more and more from Big Government. Thus, Big Government grows bigger and bigger. Thomas Jefferson feared for the future of American democracy in an age when men would be corrupted by the greed and complex evils of urban living. His prognosis seems frighteningly convincing today when our greatest city has been bankrupted by greedy Big Interest Groups, and a so-called conservative president subverts the rule of law.

12

Special operations group– "operation chaos"

The Rockefeller Commission

Responding to Presidential requests to determine the extent of foreign influence on domestic dissidence, the CIA, upon the instruction of the Director of Central Intelligence, established within the Counterintelligence Staff a Special Operations Group in August 1967, to collect, coordinate, evaluate and report on foreign contacts with American dissidents.

The Group's activities, which later came to be known as Operation CHAOS, led the CIA to collect information on dissident Americans from its overseas stations and from the FBI.

Although the stated purpose of the Operation was to determine whether there were any foreign contacts with American dissident groups, it resulted in the accumulation of considerable material on domestic dissidents and their activities.

During six years, the Operation compiled some 13,000 different files, including files on 7,200 American citizens. The documents in these files and related materials included the names of

From *The Rockefeller Report to the President By The Commission on CIA Activities*, 1975.

more than 300,000 persons and organizations, which were entered into a computerized index.

This information was kept closely guarded within the CIA to prevent its use by anyone other than the personnel of the Special Operations Group. Utilizing this information, personnel of the Group prepared 3,500 memoranda for internal use; 3,000 memoranda for dissemination to the FBI; and 37 memoranda for distribution to high officials.

The Operation ultimately had a staff of 52, who were isolated from any substantial review even by the Counterintelligence Staff of which they were technically a part.

Beginning in late 1969, Operation CHAOS used a number of agents to collect intelligence abroad on any foreign connections with American dissident groups. In order to have sufficient "cover" for these agents, the Operation recruited persons from domestic dissident groups or recruited others and instructed them to associate with such groups in this country.

Most of these recruits were not directed to collect information domestically on American dissidents. On a number of occasions, however, such information was reported by the recruits while they were developing dissident credentials in the United States, and the information was retained in the files of the Operation. On three occasions, agents of the Operation were specifically used to collect domestic intelligence.

Part of the reason for these transgressions was inherent in the nature of the task assigned to the Group: to determine the extent of any foreign influence on domestic dissident activities. That task necessarily partook of both domestic and foreign aspects. The question could not be answered adequately without gathering information on the identities and relationships of the American citizens involved in the activities. Accordingly, any effort by the CIA in this area was bound, from the outset, to raise problems as to whether the Agency was looking into internal security matters and therefore exceeding its legislative authority.

The Presidential demands upon the CIA appear to have caused the Agency to forego, to some extent, the caution with which it might otherwise have approached the subject.

Two Presidents and their staffs made continuing and insistent requests of the CIA for detailed evaluation of possible foreign involvement in the domestic dissident scene. The Agency's repeated conclusion in its reports—that it could find no significant foreign connection with domestic disorder—led to further White House demands that the CIA account for any gaps in the Agency's investigation and that it remedy any lack of resources for gathering information.

The cumulative effect of these repeated demands was the addition of more and more resources, including agents, to Operation CHAOS—as the

Agency attempted to support and to confirm the validity of its conclusion. These White House demands also seem to have encouraged top CIA management to stretch and, on some occasions, to exceed the legislative restrictions.

The excessive secrecy surrounding Operation CHAOS, its isolation within the CIA, and its removal from the normal chain of command prevented any effective supervision and review of its activities by officers not directly involved in the project.

A. Origins of Operation CHAOS—August 1967

In the wake of racial violence and civil disturbances, President Johnson on July 2, 1967, formed the National Commission on Civil Disorders (the Kerner Commission) and directed it to investigate and make recommendations with respect to the origins of the disorders. At the same time, the President instructed all other departments and agencies of government to assist the Kerner Commission by supplying information to it.

On August 15, 1967, Thomas Karamessines, Deputy Director for Plans, issued a directive to the Chief of the Counterintelligence Staff instructing him to establish an operation for overseas coverage of subversive student activities and related matters. This memorandum relayed instructions from Director Richard Helms, who, according to Helms' testimony, acted in response to continuing, substantial pressure from the President to determine the extent of any foreign connections with domestic dissident events. Helms' testimony is corroborated by a contemporaneous FBI memorandum which states:

> The White House recently informed Richard Helms, Director, CIA, that the Agency should exert every possible effort to collect information concerning U.S. racial agitators who might travel abroad * * * because of the pressure placed upon Helms, a new desk has been created at the Agency for the explicit purpose of collecting information coming into the Agency and having any significant bearing on possible racial disturbances in the U.S.

The question of foreign involvement in domestic dissidence combined matters over which the FBI had jurisdiction (domestic disorder) and matters which were the concern of the CIA (possible foreign connection). The FBI, unlike the CIA, generally did not produce finished, evaluated intelligence. Apparently for these reasons, the President looked to the Director of Central Intelligence to produce a coordinated evaluation of intelligence bearing upon the question of dissidence.

When the Kerner Commission's Executive Director wrote to Helms on August 29, 1967, requesting CIA information on civil disorders, Helms offered to supply only information on foreign connections with domestic disorder. Ultimately, the CIA furnished 26 reports to the Kerner Commission, some of which related largely to domestic dissident activities.

B. Evolution of Operation CHAOS—The November 1967 Study

The officer selected to head what became the Special Operations Group was a person already involved in a counterintelligence effort in connection with an article in *Ramparts* magazine on CIA associations with American youth overseas. In connection with his research and analysis, the officer had organized the beginnings of a computer system for storage and retrieval of information on persons involved in the "New Left."

By October 1967, this officer had begun to establish his operation concerning foreign connections with the domestic dissident scene. In a memorandum for the record on October 31, 1967, he indicated that the CIA was to prepare a study on the "International Connections of the United States Peace Movement."

The CIA immediately set about collecting all the available government information on dissident groups. All field stations of the CIA clandestine service were polled for any information they had on the subject of the study. Every branch of the intelligence community was called upon to submit whatever information it had on the peace movement to the Special Operations Group for cataloging and storage. Most of the information was supplied by the FBI.

All information collected by the Special Operations Group was forwarded to the CIA Office of Current Intelligence, which completed the study by mid-November. Director Helms personally delivered the study to President Johnson on November 15, 1967, with a covering note stating that "this is the study on the United States Peace Movement you requested."

The study showed that there was little evidence of foreign involvement and no evidence of any significant foreign financial support of the peace activities within the United States. As a result of the information gathered for the study, however, the Special Operations Group gained an extensive amount of data for its later operations.

On November 20, 1967, a new study was launched by the CIA at the request of the Director of Central Intelligence. This study was titled "Demonstration Techniques." The scope of the study was world-wide, and it concentrated on antiwar demonstrations in the United States and abroad. The procedure used on the earlier study was also employed to gather information for this new project.

The CIA sent an updated version of the Peace Movement Study to the President on December 22, 1967, and on January 5, 1968, Director Helms delivered to the White House a paper entitled "Student Dissent and Its Techniques in the United States." Helms' covering letter to the President described the January 5 study as "part of our continuing examination of this general matter."

Again, the information bank of the Special Operations Group was increased by the intelligence gathered for these studies.

C. Evolution of Operation CHAOS—Domestic Unrest in 1968

Continuing antiwar demonstrations in 1968 led to growing White House demands for greater coverage of such groups' activities abroad. As disorders occurred in Europe in the summer of 1968, the CIA, with concurrence from the FBI, sought to engage European liaison services in monitoring United States citizens overseas in order to produce evidence of foreign guidance, control or financial support.

In mid-1968, the CIA moved to consolidate its efforts concerning foreign connections with domestic dissidence and to restrict further the dissemination of the information used by the Special Operations Group. The Group was given a cryptonym, "CHAOS." The CIA sent cables to all its field stations in July 1968, directing that all information concerning dissident groups be sent through a single restricted channel on an "Eyes Only" basis to the Chief of Operation CHAOS. No other dissemination of the information was to occur.

Some time in 1968, Director Helms, in response to the President's continued concern about student revolutionary movements around the world, commissioned the preparation of a new analytic paper which was eventually entitled "Restless Youth." Like its predecessor, "Restless Youth" concluded that the motivations underlying student radicalism arose from social and political alienation at home and not from conspiratorial activity masterminded from abroad.

"Restless Youth" was produced in two versions. The first version contained a section on domestic involvements, again raising a question as to the propriety of the CIA's having prepared it. This version was delivered initially only to President Johnson and to Walt W. Rostow, the President's Special Assistant for National Security Affairs. Helms' covering memorandum, dated September 4, 1968, stated, "You will, of course, be aware of the peculiar sensitivity which attaches to the fact that CIA has prepared a report on student activities both here and abroad."

Another copy of the first version of "Restless Youth" was delivered on February 18, 1969, after the change in Administrations, to Henry A. Kissinger, then Assistant to President Nixon for National Security Affairs. Director Helms' covering memorandum of February 18 specifically pointed out the impropriety of the CIA's involvement in the study. It stated:

In an effort to round-out our discussion of this subject, we have included a section on American students. This is an area not within the charter of this Agency, so I need not emphasize how extremely sensitive this makes the paper. Should anyone learn of its existence it would prove most embarrassing for all concerned.

A second version of "Restless Youth"·with the section on domestic activities deleted was later given a somewhat wider distribution in the intelligence community.

The CHAOS group did not participate in the initial drafting of the "Restless Youth" paper, although it did review the paper at some point before any of its versions were disseminated. Intelligence derived from the paper was, of course, available to the group.

E. The June 1969 White House Demands

On June 20, 1969, Tom Charles Huston, Staff Assistant to President Nixon, wrote to the CIA that the President had directed preparation of a report on foreign communist support of revolutionary protest movements in this country.

Huston suggested that previous reports indicated inadequacy of intelligence collection capabilities within the protest movement area. (Helms testified that this accurately reflected the President's attitude.) According to Huston's letter, the President wanted to know:

—What resources were presently targeted toward monitoring foreign communist support of revolutionary youth activities in this country;

—How effective the resources were;

—What gaps existed because of inadequate resources or low priority of attention; and,

—What steps could be taken to provide maximum possible coverage of the activities.

Huston said that he was particularly interested in the CIA's ability to collect information of this type. A ten-day deadline was set for the CIA's reply.

The Agency responded on June 30, 1969, with a report entitled, "Foreign Communist Support to Revolutionary Protest Movements in the United States." The report concluded that while the communists encouraged such movements through propaganda and exploitation of international conferences, there was very little evidence of communist funding and training of such movements and no evidence of communist direction and control.

The CIA's covering memorandum, which accompanied the June 30 report, pointed out that since the summer of 1967, the Agency had attempted to determine through its sources abroad what significant communist assistance or control was given to domestic revolutionary protests. It stated that close cooperation also existed with the FBI and that "new sources were being sought through independent means." The memorandum also said that the "Katzenbach guidelines" of 1967 had inhibited access to persons who might have information on efforts by communist intelligence services to exploit revolutionary groups in the United States.[1]

1. In 1967 President Johnson appointed a committee including Nicholas Katzenbach, John Gardner, and Richard Helms to investigate charges that the CIA was funding the

E. CHAOS in Full-Scale Operation—Mid-1969

By mid-1969, Operation CHAOS took on the organizational form which would continue for the following three years. Its staff had increased to 36. (Eventually it totaled 52.) In June 1969, a Deputy Chief was assigned to the Operation to assist in administrative matters and to assume some of the responsibilities of handling the tightly held communications. There was a further delegation of responsibility with the appointment of three branch chiefs in the operation.

The increase in size and activity of the Operation was accompanied by further isolation and protective measures. The group had already been physically located in a vaulted basement area, and tighter security measures were adopted in connection with communications of the Operation. These measures were extreme, even by normally strict CIA standards. An exclusive channel for communication with the FBI was also established which severely restricted dissemination both to and from the Bureau of CHAOS-related matters.

On September 6, 1969, Director Helms distributed an internal memorandum to the head of each of the directorates within CIA, instructing that support was to be given to the activities of Operation CHAOS. Both the distribution of the memorandum and the nature of the directives contained in it were most unusual. These served to underscore the importance of its substance.

Helms confirmed in the September 6 memorandum that the CHAOS group had the principal operational responsibilities for conducting the Agency's activities in the "radical milieu." Helms expected that each division of the Agency would cooperate "both in exploiting existing sources and in developing new ones, and that [the Special Operations Group] will have the necessary access to such sources and operational assets."

Helms further stated in the memorandum that he believed the CIA had "the proper approach in discharging this sensitive responsibility while strictly observing the statutory and *de facto* proscription on Agency domestic involvements."

The September 6 memorandum, prepared after discussions with the Chief of the Operation, among others, served at least three important functions: First, it confirmed, beyond question, the importance which Operation CHAOS had attained in terms of Agency objectives. Second, it replied to dissent which had been voiced within the CIA concerning the Operation. Third, it ensured that CHAOS would receive whatever support it needed, including personnel.

National Student Association. The charges were substantiated, and the Katzenbach Committee's recommendation that the government refrain from covert financial support of private educational organizations was adopted as government policy.

F. Agent Operations Relating to Operation CHAOS

Within a month after Helms' memorandum of September 6, an operations or "case" officer was assigned from another division to Operation CHAOS. The Operation thus gained the capacity to manage its own agents. A full understanding of the Operation's use of agents, however, requires some appreciation of similar proposals previously developed by other components of the CIA.

1. "Project 1"

In February 1968, the CIA's Office of Security and a division in its Plans Directorate jointed drafted a proposal for "Project 1," which was initially entitled "An Effort . . . in Acquiring Assets in the 'Peace' and 'Black Power' Movements in the United States." The project was to involve recruitment of agents who would penetrate some of the prominent dissident groups in the United States and report information on the communications, contacts, travel and plans of individuals or groups having a connection with a certain foreign area. The proposal was rejected by Director Helms in March 1968 on the ground that it " would appear to be" beyond the Agency's jurisdiction and would cause widespread criticism when it became public knowledge, as he believed it eventually would.

Shortly thereafter, the proposed Project was modified to include a prohibition against domestic penetration of dissident groups by agents recruited by the CIA. Any contact with domestic groups would be incidental to the overall objective of gaining access overseas to information on foreign contacts and control.

This modification was consistent with Helms' instruction that the Agency was not to engage in domestic operational activity directed against dissident groups. The modified plan was approved by the Deputy Director of Plans, subject to conditions to ensure his tight supervision and control over its activities, but no evidence could be found that the project ever became operational.

The history of Project 1 clearly reflected the CIA's awareness that statutory limitations applied to the use of agents on the domestic dissident scene. "Penetration" of dissident groups in the United States to gain information on their domestic activities was prohibited.

2. "Project 2"

A second program, "Project 2," was initiated in late 1969 by the same office in the CIA's Plans Directorate which had developed Project 1. Under Project 2, individuals without existing dissident affiliation would be recruited and, after recruitment, would acquire the theory and jargon and make acquaintances in the "New Left" while attending school in the United States. Following this "reddening" or "sheepdipping" process (as one CIA officer described it), the agent would be sent to a foreign country on a specific intelligence mission.

Project 2 was approved on April 14, 1970, by the Assistant Deputy Director for Plans, who stated that no Project 2 agent was to be directed to acquire information concerning domestic dissident activities. Only if such information was acquired incidentally by the agents during the domestic "coloration" process would it be passed to Operation CHAOS for forwarding to the FBI.[2]

Renewals of Project 2 were approved annually during 1971–1973 by the Deputy Director for Plans. The Project was also reviewed and approved in the fall of 1973 by William E. Colby, by then Director of Central Intelligence. In granting his approval on September 5, 1973, Director Colby, in language which paraphrased the original Project 1 guidelines, stated that:

Care will be taken that, during the training period of [Project 2] agents within the United States, they will not be operated by CIA against domestic targets.

During the period 1970–1974 a total of 23 agents were recruited for the project, of which 11 completed the prescribed development process in the United States. Each agent was met and debriefed on a regular schedule in this country by Project 2 case officers. The agents were told repeatedly of the limitations on their activities in the Unites States.

The Project 2 case officers used debriefing sessions as one method of assessing an agent's effectiveness in reporting facts precisely and accurately, obviously an essential skill to any intelligence agent. "Contact reports" were prepared after the sessions. Although the reports contained a substantial amount of information on agents' observations of domestic activities, no evidence was found that Project 2 itself opened any files based upon any of the information.

Copies of all contact reports with Project 2 agents, however, were provided to Operation CHAOS, and that Operation made a detailed review of the information contained in the reports. Information on both individuals and activities which was contained in the reports and which was deemed significant by CHAOS was incorporated into the raw data files of the operation and indexed into its computer system. Depending upon the nature of the information, it might eventually be furnished by Operation CHAOS to the FBI.

Thus, while Project 2 agents were not assigned collection missions in the United States, the tandem operation of CHAOS with Project 2 nevertheless did result in collection and dissemination by the CIA of a limited quantity of intelligence on domestic dissident activities. Director Helms testified that he was not aware of this collection and dissemination.

2. Prior to the April 14 approval of Project 2, Operation CHAOS personnel had requested that a proviso be added to the Project that Operation CHAOS would coordinate Project 2 recruits during the 'coloration" process in the United States. The proviso was rejected.

Furthermore, despite efforts by Project 2 case officers to have their agent trainees avoid taking an activist role in domestic dissident groups, that did occur upon occasion. One of the agents became an officer in such a group, and on at least one occasion the agent provided Project 2 with copies of minutes of the group's meetings.

A Project 2 agent also became involved as an adviser in a United States congressional campaign and, for a limited period, furnished reports to CHAOS of behind-the-scenes activities in the campaign.

3. CHAOS Agents

During the first two years of its existence, Operation CHAOS gathered the bulk of its information from reports issued by other governmental agencies or received from CIA field stations abroad.

By October 1969, this approach had changed almost completely. Operation CHAOS' new case officer was beginning to contact, recruit, and run agents directly for the operation. This reversal of approach appears to be attributable primarily to three factors:

—First, and most important, an increasing amount of White House pressure (for example, the June 20, 1969, letter from Tom Charles Huston, Staff Assistant to the President) was brought to bear on the CIA to provide more extensive and detailed reporting on the role of foreign connections with American dissident activities;

—Second, Operation CHAOS had been relatively unsuccessful in obtaining meaningful information through agents associated with other agencies;

—Third, the tempo of dissident activities had increased substantially in the United States.

The extent of CHAOS agent operations was limited to fewer than 30 agents. Although records of the Operation indicate that reporting was received from over 100 other agent sources, those sources appear to have been directed abroad either by other governmental agencies or by other components of the CIA. The information which these sources reported to Operation CHAOS was simply a by-product of other missions.

Operation CHAOS personnel contacted a total of approximately 40 potential agents from October 1969 to July 1972, after which no new agent recruitments were made. (The case officer left the Operation on July 12, 1972.) Approximately one-half of these individuals were referred to the Operation by the FBI, and the remainder were developed through various CIA components.

All contact, briefing and debriefing reports prepared by the case officer concerning all potential and actual agents, from whatever source, became part of the records of the Operation. These reports, often highly detailed, were carefully reviewed by CHAOS personnel; all names, organizations and significant events were then indexed in the Operation's computer. Upon occasion, the information would be passed to the FBI.

The individuals referred to Operation CHAOS by the FBI were past or present FBI informants who either were interested in a foreign assignment or had planned a trip abroad. Eighteen of the referrals were recruited. Only one was used on more than one assignment. In each instance the Operation's case officer briefed the individual on the CHAOS "requirements" before his trip and debriefed him upon his return. After debriefing, the agents once again became the responsibility of the FBI.

In one instance, the FBI turned an individual over to Operation CHAOS for its continued use abroad. Before going overseas, that agent was met by the Operation's case officer on a number of occasions in the United States and did report for several months upon certain domestic contacts.

Seventeen agents were referred to Operation CHAOS by other CIA components. Ten were dropped by the Operation for various reasons after an initial assessment. Four were used for brief trips abroad, with reporting procedures which essentially paralleled those used for the FBI referrals.

The remaining three individuals had an entree into anti-war, radical left, or black militant groups before they were recruited by the Operation. They were used over an extended period abroad, and they were met and debriefed on numerous occasions in the United States.

One of the three agents traveled a substantial distance in late 1969 to participate in and report on major demonstrations then occurring in one area of the country. The CHAOS case officer met and questioned the agent at length concerning individuals and organizations involved in the demonstrations. Detailed contact reports were prepared after each debriefing session. The contact reports, in turn, provided the basis for 47 separate disseminations to the FBI, the bulk of which related solely to domestic matters and were disseminated under titles such as: "Plans for Future Anti-War Activities on the West Coast."

The second of these agents regularly provided detailed information on the activities and views of high-level leadership in another of the dissident groups within the United States. Although a substantial amount of this agent's reporting concerned the relationship of the dissident group with individuals and organizations abroad, information was also obtained and disseminated on the organization's purely domestic activities.

The third agent was formally recruited in April 1971, having been initially contacted by Operation CHAOS in October 1970. During the intervening months the CIA had asked the agent questions posed by the FBI concerning domestic dissident matters and furnished the responses to the Bureau.

Two days after the official recruitment, the agent was asked to travel to Washington, D.C. to work on an interim basis; the mission was to "get as close as possible" and perhaps become an assistant to certain prominent radical leaders who were coordinators of the imminent "May Day" demonstrations. The agent was to infiltrate any secret groups operation behind the scenes and report on their plans. The agent was also asked to report any information on planned violence toward government officials or buildings or foreign embassies.

This third agent traveled to Washington as requested, and was met two or three times a week by the CHAOS case officer. After each of these meetings, the case officer, in accordance with the standard procedure, prepared contact reports including all information obtained from the agent. These reports, many of which were typed late at night or over weekends, were passed immediately to the Chief of Operation CHAOS. And when the information obtained from the agent was significant, it was immediately passed by the Chief to an FBI representative, generally orally.

The Operation's use of these three agents was contrary to guidelines established after Director Helms rejected the initial proposal for Project 1 in March 1968. Helms testified that he was not aware of the domestic use of these agents.

The Commission found no evidence that any of the agents or CIA officers involved with any of the dissident operations employed or directed the domestic use of any personal or electronic surveillance, wiretaps or unauthorized entries against any dissident group or individual. Any reporting by CHAOS agents in the United States was based upon information gained as a result of their personal observations and acquaintances.

G. Collection, Indexing, and Filing of Information by Operation CHAOS

The volume of information passing through the CHAOS group by mid-1969 was great. As Director Helms pointed out in his September 6, 1969, memorandum to the Directorates, the Operation's main problem was a backlog of undigested raw information which required analysis and indexing.

Not only was the Agency receiving FBI reports on antiwar activities, but with the rise of international conferences against the war, and student and radical travel abroad, information flowed in from the Agency's overseas stations as well.

The Operation had gathered all the information it could from the Agency's central registry. According to the Chief of the Operation, that information for the most part consisted of raw data gathered on individuals by the FBI which had not been analyzed by the Agency because the information contained nothing of foreign intelligence value.

CHAOS also availed itself of the information gained through the CIA's New York mail intercept. The Operation supplied a watch list of United States citizens to be monitored by the staff of the mail intercept. The number of mail items intercepted and sent to CHAOS during its operation were sufficient in number to have filled two drawers in a filing cabinet. All of these items were letters or similar material between the United States and the Soviet Union.

In addition, Operation CHAOS received materials from an international communications activity of another agency of the government. The Operation furnished a watch list of names to the other agency and received a total of approximately 1100 pages of materials overall. The program to furnish the Operation with these materials was not terminated until CHAOS went out of existence. All such materials were returned to the originating agency by the CIA in November 1974 because a review of the materials had apparently raised a question as to the legality of their being held by CIA. The materials concerned for the most part anti-war activities, travel to international peace conferences and movements of members of various dissident groups. The communications passed between the United States and foreign countries. None was purely domestic.

During one period, Operation CHAOS also appears to have received copies of booking slips for calls made between points in the United States and abroad. The slips did not record the substance of the calls, but rather showed the identities of the caller and the receiver, and the date and time of the call. The slips also indicated whether the call went through.

Most of the officers assigned to the Operation were analysts who read the materials received by it and extracted names and other information for indexing in the computer system used by the Operation and for inclusion in the Operation's many files. It appears that, because of the great volume of materials received by Operation CHAOS and the time pressures on the Operation, little judgment could be, or was, exercised in this process. The absence of such judgment led, in turn, to the inclusion of a substantial amount of data in the records of the Operation having little, if anything, bearing upon its foreign intelligence objective.

The names of all persons mentioned in intelligence source reports received by Operation CHAOS were computer-indexed. The computer printout on a person or organization or subject would contain references to all documents, files or communications traffic where the name appeared. Eventually, approximately 300,000 names of American citizens and organizations were thus stored in the CHAOS computer system.

The computerized information was streamed or categorized on a "need to know" basis, progressing from the least sensitive to the most sensitive. A special computer "password" was required in order to gain access to each stream. (This multistream characteristic of the computer index caused it to be dubbed the "Hydra" system.) The computer system was used much like a library card index to locate intelligence reports stored in the CHAOS library of files.

The files, like the computer index, were also divided into different levels of security. A "201," or personality, file would be opened on an individual when enough information had been collected to warrant a file or when the individual was of interest to another government agency that looked to the CIA for information. The regular 201 file generally contained information such as place of birth, family, occupation and organizational affiliation. In addition, a "sensitive" file might also be maintained on that same person. The sensitive file generally encompassed matters which were potentially embarrassing to the Agency or matters obtained from sources or by methods which the Agency sought to protect. Operation CHAOS also maintained nearly 1000 "subject" files on numerous organizations.[3]

Random samplings of the Operation's files show that in great part, the files consisted of undigested FBI reports or overt materials such as new clippings on the particular subject.

An extreme example of the extent to which collection could go once a file was opened is contained in the Grove Press, Inc., file. The file apparently was opened because the company had published a book by Kim Philby, the British intelligence officer who turned out to be a Soviet agent. The name Grove Press was thus listed as having intelligence interest, and the CHAOS analysts collected all available information on the company. Grove Press, in its business endeavors, had also produced the sex-oriented motion picture, "I Am Curious Yellow" and so the Operation's analysts dutifully clipped and filmed cinema critics' commentaries upon the film.

From among the 300,000 names in the CHAOS computer index, a total of approximately 7,200 separate personality files were developed on citizens of the United States.

In addition, information of ongoing intelligence value was digested in summary memoranda for the internal use of the Operation. Nearly 3,500 such memoranda were developed during the history of CHAOS.

Over 3,000 memoranda on digested information were disseminated, where appropriate, to the FBI. A total of 37 highly sensitive memoranda originated by Operation CHAOS were sent over the signature of the Director of Central Intelligence to the White House, to the Secretary of State, to the Director of the FBI or to the Secret Service.

H. Preparation of Reports for Interagency Groups

Commencing in mid-1970, Operation CHAOS produced reports for the interagency groups discussed in the previous chapter. One such report was prepared by the Operation in June 1970. Unlike the June 1969 study, which was limited to CIA sources, the 1970 study took into account all available

3. The organizations, to name a few, included: Students for a Democratic Society (SDS); Young Communist Workers Liberation League (YCWLL); National Mobilization Committee to End the War in Vietnam; Women's Strike for Peace; Freedomways Magazine and Freedomways Associated, Inc,; American Indian Movement (AIM); Student Non-Violent Coordinating Committee (SNCC); Draft Resistance Groups (U.S.); Cross World Books and Periodicals, Inc.; U.S. Committee to Aid the National Liberation Front of South Vietnam; Grove Press, Inc.; Nation of Islam; Youth International Party (YIP); Women's Liberation Movement; Black Panther Party (BPP); Venceremos Brigade; Clergy and Laymen Concerned About Vietnam.

intelligence sources. In the 1970 analysis, entitled "Definition of Existing Internal Security Threat—Foreign," the Agency concluded that there was no evidence, based on available information sources, that foreign governments and intelligence services controlled domestic dissident movements or were then capable of directing the groups. The June 1970 Report was expanded and republished in January 1971. It reached the same conclusions.

I. Relationship of Operation CHAOS to Other CIA Components

Substantial measures were taken from the inception of Operation CHAOS to ensure that it was highly compartmented. Knowledge of its activities was restricted to those individuals who had a definite "need to know" of it.

The two or three week formal training period for the Operation's agents was subject to heavy insulation. According to a memorandum in July 1971, such training was to be carried out with "extreme caution" and the number of people who knew of the training was to be kept to "an absolute minimum." The Office of Training was instructed to return all communications relating to training of CHAOS agents to the Operation.

The Operation was isolated or compartmented even within the Counterintelligence Staff which, itself, was already a highly compartmented component of the CIA. The Operation was physically removed from the Counterintelligence Staff. Knowledge within the Counterintelligence Staff of proposed CHAOS operations was restricted to the Chief of the Staff and his immediate assistants.

The Counterintelligence Chief was technically responsible in the chain of command for Operation CHAOS, and requests for budgeting and agent recruitment had to be approved through his office. But the available evidence indicates that the Chief of Counterintelligence had little connection with the actual operations of CHAOS. According to a CIA memorandum in May 1969, Director Helms specifically instructed the Chief of the Operation to refrain from disclosing part of his activities to the Counterintelligence Chief.

The Counterintelligence and the CHAOS Chiefs both agree that, because of the compartmentation and secrecy of CHAOS, the actual supervisory responsibility for the Operation was vested in the Director of Central Intelligence. This was particularly so beginning in mid-1969. In fact, the Chief of CHAOS, later in history of his Operation, sought unsuccessfully to have his office attached directly to that of the Director.

Director Helms testified that he could recall no specific directions he gave to the CHAOS Group Chief to report directly to him. To the contrary, Helms said, he expected the Chief to report to the Chief of Counterintelligence, who in turn would report to the Deputy Director for Plans and then to the Director.

The sensitivity of the Operation was deemed so great that, during one field survey in November 1972 even the staff of the CIA's Inspector General was precluded from reviewing CHAOS files or discussing its specific operations. (This incident, however, led to a review of the Operation by the CIA Executive Director—Comptroller in December 1972.)

On another occasion, an inspection team from the Office of Management and Budget was intentionally not informed of the Operation's activity during an OMB survey of CIA field operations.

There is no indication that the CIA's General Counsel was ever consulted about the propriety of Operation CHAOS activities.

It further appears that, unlike most programs within the CIA clandestine service, Operation CHAOS was not subjected to an annual review and approval procedure. Nor does there appear to have been any formal review of the Operation's annual budget. Such review as occurred seems to have been limited to requests for authority to assess or recruit an American citizen as an agent.

The result of the compartmentation, secrecy and isolation which did occur seems clear now. The Operation was not effectively supervised and reviewed by anyone in the CIA who was not operationally involved in it.

Witnesses testified consistently that the extreme secrecy and security measures of Operation CHAOS derived from two considerations: First, the Operation sought to protect the privacy of the American citizens whose names appeared in its files by restricting access to those names as severely as possible. Second, CHAOS personnel were concerned that the operation would be misunderstood by others within the CIA if they learned only bits of information concerning it without being briefed on the entire project.

It is safe to say that the CIA's top leadership wished to avoid even the appearance of participation in internal security matters and were cognizant that the Operation, at least in part, was close to being a proscribed activity and would generate adverse public reaction if revealed.

Despite the substantial efforts to maintain the secrecy of Operation CHAOS, over six hundred persons within the CIA were formally briefed on the Operation. A considerable number of CIA officers had to know of the Operation in order to handle its cable traffic abroad.

Enough information concerning CHAOS was known within the CIA so that a middle-level management group of 14 officers (organized to discuss and develop possible solutions to various CIA problems) was in a position to write two memoranda in 1971 raising questions as to the propriety of the project. Although only one of the authors had been briefed on CHAOS activities, several others in the group apparently had enough knowledge of it to concur in the preparation of the memoranda.

Opposition to, or at least skepticism about, the CHAOS activities was also expressed by senior officers in the field and at headquarters. Some area division chiefs were unwilling to share the authority for collection of intelligence from their areas with the Operation and were reluctant to turn over the information for exclusive handling and processing by the Operation. When CHAOS undertook the placement of agents in the field, some operations people resented this intrusion by a staff organization into their jurisdiction.

In addition, some of the negativism toward CHAOS was expressed on philosophic grounds. One witness, for example, described the attitude of his division toward the Operation as "total negativeness." A May 1971 memorandum confirms that this division wanted "nothing to do" with CHAOS. This was principally because the division personnel thought that the domestic activities of the Operation were more properly a function of the FBI. As a result, this division supplied the Operation with only a single lead to a potential agent, and its personnel has little to do with the on-going CHAOS activities.

Apparently the feelings against Operation CHAOS were strong enough that Director Helms' September 6, 1969 memorandum was required to support the Operation. That memorandum, sent to all deputy directors in the CIA, assured them that the Operation was within the statutory authority of the Agency, and directed their support.

Director Helms' attitude toward the views of some CIA officers toward Operation CHAOS was further summarized in a memorandum for the record on December 5, 1972, which stated:

CHAOS is a legitimate counterintelligence function of the Agency and cannot be stopped simply because some members of the organization do not like this activity.

J. Winding Down Operation CHAOS

By 1972, with the ending of the American involvement in the Vietnam War and the subsequent lower level of protest activities at home, the activities of Operation CHAOS began to lag. The communications traffic decreased, and official apprehension about foreign influence also abated. By mid-1972, the Special Operations Group began to shift its attention to other foreign intelligence matters.

At the end of August 1973, William E. Colby, the new CIA Director, in memoranda dealing with various "questionable" activities by the Agency, ordered all its directorates to take specific action to ensure that CIA activities remained within the Agency's legislative authority. In one such memorandum, the Director stated that Operation CHAOS was to be "restricted to the collection abroad of information on foreign activities related to domestic matters. Further, the CIA will focus clearly on the foreign organizations and individuals involved and only incidentally on their American contacts."

The Colby memorandum also specified that the CIA was not to be directly engaged in surveillance or other action against an American abroad and could act only as a communications channel between the FBI and foreign services, thus altering the policy in this regard set in 1968 and reaffirmed in 1969 by Director Helms.

By August 1973, when the foregoing Colby memorandum was written, the paper trail left by Operation CHAOS included somewhere in the area of 13,000 files on subjects and individuals (including approximately 7,200 personality or "201" files);[4] over 11,000 memoranda, reports and letters from the FBI; over 3,000 disseminations to the FBI; and almost 3,500 memoranda for internal use by the Operation. In addition, the CHAOS group had generated, or caused the generation of, over 12,000 cables of various types, as well as a handful of memoranda to high-level government officials.

On top of this veritable mountain of material was a computer system containing an index of over 300,000 names and organizations which, with few exceptions, were of United States citizens and organizations apparently unconnected with espionage.

K. Operation CHAOS Terminated

On March 15, 1974, the Agency terminated Operation CHAOS. Directions were issued to all CIA field stations that, as a matter of future policy, when information was uncovered as a byproduct of a foreign intelligence activity indicating that a United States citizen abroad was suspect for security or counterintelligence reasons, the information was to be reported to the FBI.

According to the CHAOS termination cable, no unilateral action against the suspect was to be taken by the CIA without the specific direction of the Deputy Director for Operations and only after receipt of a written request from the FBI and with the knowledge of the Director of Central Intelligence.

The files and computerized index are still intact and are being held by the Agency pending completion of the current investigations. According to the group chief who is custodian of the files, many of the files have little, if any, value to ongoing intelligence operations. The CIA has made an examination of each of the CHAOS personality files and has categorized those portions which should be eliminated. Final disposition of those files, as noted, awaits the completion of the current investigations.

Conclusions

Some domestic activities of Operation CHAOS unlawfully exceeded the CIA's statutory authority, even though the declared mission of gathering intelligence abroad as to foreign influence on domestic activities was proper.

Most significantly, the Operation became a repository for large quantities of information on the domestic activities of American citizens. This information was derived principally from FBI reports or from overt sources and not from clandestine collection by the CIA. Much of the information was not

---

4. A CIA statistical evaluation of the files indicates that nearly 65 percent of them were opened to handle FBI information or FBI requests.

directly related to the question of the existence of foreign connections with domestic dissidence.

It was probably necessary for the CIA to accumulate an information base on domestic dissident activities in order to assess fairly whether the activities had foreign connections. The FBI would collect information but would not evaluate it. But the accumulation of domestic data in the Operation exceeded what was reasonably required to make such an assessment and was thus improper.

The use of agents of the Operation on three occasions to gather information within the United States on strictly domestic matters was beyond the CIA's authority. In addition the intelligence disseminations and those portions of a major study prepared by the Agency which dealt with purely domestic matters were improper.

The isolation of Operation CHAOS within the CIA and its independence from supervision by the regular chain of command within the clandestine service made it possible for the activities of the Operation to stray over the bounds of the Agency's authority without the knowledge of senior officials. The absence of any regular review of these activities prevented timely correction of such missteps as did occur.

Recommendation (5)

a. Presidents should refrain from directing the CIA to perform what are essentially internal security tasks.

b. The CIA should resist any efforts, whatever their origin, to involve it again in such improper activities.

c. The Agency should guard against allowing any component (like the Special Operations Group) to become so self-contained and isolated from top leadership that regular supervision and review are lost.

d. The files of the CHAOS project which have no foreign intelligence value should be destroyed by the Agency at the conclusion of the current congressional investigations, or as soon thereafter as permitted by law.

13

FBI admits it opened mail in 8 cities in illegal program parallel to that of CIA

Robert L. Jackson

WASHINGTON—The FBI said Wednesday it had opened mail illegally in Los Angeles, San Francisco and six other cities in a program paralleling that of the CIA.

Providing the first details of its mail surveillance project, James B. Adams, deputy associate director, said that FBI agents opened mail for "national security" purposes between 1940 and 1966.

In New York City, an estimated 42 million pieces of mail were examined by agents from Oct. 1, 1959, to July 22, 1966, he said. Of these, 1,011 pieces were opened, Adams told members of a House postal facilities subcommittee.

Rep. Charles H. Wilson (D-Calif.), the subcommittee chairman, said that the figure sounded too low and instructed Adams to supply details on the other cities. Adams said he would try to do so, but insisted, "We do not have adequate records on this program."

In addition to New York, Los Angeles and San Francisco, letters were opened in Boston, Washington, Detroit, Seattle and Miami, Adams said.

After Adams gave additional testimony in closed session, a subcommittee source termed the program "very indiscriminate." The mail of antiwar groups and political extremists often was opened under the mandate of national security, the source said.

Adams did not explain why the FBI's mail program was terminated in 1966. This was the same year, however, that the late J. Edgar Hoover, then FBI director, also gave written orders ending break-ins in "domestic subversion cases."

As described by Adams, the FBI's mail program was similar to that of the CIA, which opened an estimated 13,000 letters a year to and from Communist countries between 1953 and 1973. Wilson's subcommittee has been investigating since the two agencies acknowledged the practice earlier this year.

The FBI sought to find foreign agents in the United States and U.S. citizens who might "sell out this country to hostile foreign powers," Adams said. The CIA's mail project was aimed principally at gathering foreign intelligence, but copies of thousands of letters a year also were passed to the FBI by the CIA.

Adams testified that there was "no statutory basis" for the FBI's actions. But after the program was abandoned in 1966 the bureau continued to accept mail intelligence from the CIA—ranging from 6,256 letters in 1967 to 1,353 in 1972, he said.

Wilson's subcommittee has found no indication so far that any President knew about or approved these projects.

According to previous testimony, the CIA's mail project was terminated under pressure from the Postal Service in February, 1973. CIA director William E. Colby has called the activity improper.

Declaring that the FBI mail program had been useful, Adams told the subcommittee that a U.S. citizen who had offered to sell antiballistic missile information to a foreign agent had been detected through a letter.

Asked later by reporters if the citizen had been prosecuted, Adams said no. He said government lawyers had decided that the evidence was tainted because the FBI lacked authority to open mail.

By law, the FBI may open mail only upon issuance of a warrant by a federal judge. No warrant is needed, however, for local, state, or federal agencies to institute a "mail cover," which means secretly examining the envelopes.

Adams said the FBI currently has 79 mail covers in progress.

14

Senate probers tell of 238 break-ins by FBI against subversive targets

Robert L. Jackson

WASHINGTON—FBI agents conducted at least 238 break-ins over a 26-year period against "domestic subversive targets" in the United States, mostly radical political groups, Senate investigators said Thursday.

Documents released by the Senate Select Committee on Intelligence Activities showed that the FBI regarded its break-ins as "clearly illegal" and took steps to hide and later destroy records of them.

According to available documents, J. Edgar Hoover, the late FBI director, emphasized in memos in 1966 and 1967 that these "black bag" jobs should be terminated. But the break-ins continued until at least April, 1968, committee officials said.

Sen. Frank Church (D-Ida.), the committee chairman, said the subject of domestic break-ins was still so sensitive that FBI Director Clarence M. Kelley had not yet declassified all of the details surrounding them. As a result, the committee cannot reveal specific break-ins at this time, Church said.

He said the FBI informed the committee that "at least 14 domestic subversive targets were the subject of 238 entries from 1942 to April, 1968." Three additional domestic targets were subjected to "numerous entries" during part of this period, but no total figure was available, Church said.

It was understood that these statistics referred mainly to such extremist groups as the Ku Klux Klan, the Black Panther Party, the Communist Party and Students for a Democratic Society.

Government sources have said the FBI has also broken into foreign embassies in the United States in connection with its counter-espionage duties, but no statistics on these activities were furnished Thursday.

In a memo entitled "Black Bag Jobs" that the committee released, William C. Sullivan, former head of the FBI's domestic intelligence division, reported on July 19, 1966:

"We do not obtain authorization for 'black bag' jobs from outside the bureau. Such a technique involves trespass and is clearly illegal; therefore, it would be impossible to obtain any legal sanction for it.

"Despite this, black bag jobs have been used because they represent an invaluable technique in combating subversive activities of a clandestine nature aimed directly at undermining and destroying our nation."

The memo added that a break-in had to be approved by the special agent in charge of an FBI field office and an assistant director at FBI headquarters. Approval hinged on the assumption that a break-in "can be safely used without any danger or embarrassment to the bureau," Sullivan's memo said.

Describing how records of break-ins must be hidden, the memo said reports were forwarded to Hoover or his longtime assistant, the late Clyde Tolson, "under a 'do not file' procedure."

Sullivan explained that the field agent then prepared "an informal memorandum" showing he had obtained approval for the illegal entry. This memo was kept in his safe for bureau inspectors to read, and was later destroyed, Sullivan wrote.

At the bottom of this memo Hoover had written in longhand: "No more such techniques must be used."

Hoover wrote a later memo, dated Jan. 6, 1967, reiterating that "surreptitious entrances upon premises of any kind . . . will not meet with my approval in the future."

Charles D. Brennan, a former FBI intelligence chief, told the committee Thursday that Hoover's later opposition to "black bag" jobs—after having approved of them for years—might have resulted partly from his turning 70 years old in 1965.

This meant that President Lyndon B. Johnson had to grant Hoover a year-by-year waiver of the mandatory retirement age, Brennan said. He testified that Hoover believed himself "somewhat vulnerable" under this arrangement and probably feared that disclosure of illegal burglaries could affect his reappointment.

Sen. Robert Morgan (D-N.C.) objected to Brennan's testimony on this point as "speculative." Fritz Schwarz, the committee's chief counsel, said later that other FBI officials thought Hoover's opposition to break-ins was based solely on moral principle.

In 1970, Hoover objected to illegal break-ins as part of the White House "Huston Plan" to control domestic disorders. His opposition has been credited with killing the plan shortly after former President Richard M. Nixon had authorized it.

However, Church said the committee had evidence that the FBI greatly expanded its surveillance of campuses in the fall of 1970, just three months after a Huston Plan proposal to do this had been voided.

Brennan said break-ins had been used mainly against extremist groups to obtain their membership lists and financial records. He agreed with Sen. Richard S. Schweiker (R-Pa.) that under the FBI's "do not file" system, bureau officials could certify in court that they had found no records of a break-in.

"It's really the perfect cover-up," Schweicker said.

Despite years of investigation—much of it under pressure from Presidents Johnson and Nixon—the FBI never found evidence of substantial foreign funding of U.S. radical and antiwar groups, Brennan said. There was ample evidence, however, that American antiwar leaders had attended conferences in Havana, Moscow and Hanoi, he said.

Sen. Howard H. Baker Jr. (R-Tenn.) asked Brennan: "Did the FBI ever get caught?"

"I don't think we did, senator," he replied. Calling the FBI "the finest group of individuals I have ever worked with," Brennan said the bureau could benefit from better supervision by Congress.

"What are the guidelines?" he asked. "What do you want us to do? What are the limits of our activities? We would be glad to comply."

15

Political legitimacy in bureaucratic society: an analysis of Watergate

Arthur J. Vidich

Jürgen Habermas, in his essay "What Does a Crisis Mean Today? Legitimation Problems in Late Capitalism,"[1] has argued that capitalist countries face increasingly difficult problems in gaining consent from significant constituencies. He states that groups such as youth, women, pacifists, Jesus people, apprentices, and others experience political alienation and that their withdrawal from the politicoeconomic system constitutes a growing threat to the late-capitalist system. The crisis of legitimation that one would expect from such political alienation is avoided, he maintains, only because the politicoeconomic system has been "uncoupled" from the cultural system. A legitimation crisis would occur "if the basic convictions of a communicative ethics and the experience complexes of countercultures . . . acquired a motive-forming

From *Social Research*, Vol. 42, No. 4, Winter, 1975. pp. 778–811. Reprinted by permission.

1. *Social Research.* XI (Winter 1973), 641–677. See also Jürgen Habermas, *Legitimation Crisis* (Boston: Beacon Press, 1973).

power determining typical socialization processes."[2] In other words, once the attitudes of alienation that now exist are built into the socialization process of capitalist culture, we can expect that capitalism will no longer be able to successfully claim legitimacy for itself. In Habermas's words, this projection is stated as follows:

Such a conjecture is supported by several behavior syndromes spreading more and more among young people—either retreat as a reaction to an exorbitant claim on the personality-resources; or protest as a result of an autonomous ego organization that cannot be stabilized without conflicts under given conditions. On the activist side we find: the student movement, revolts by high-school students and apprentices, pacifists, women's lib. The re-treatist side is represented by hippies, Jesus people, the drug subculture, phenomena of undermotivation in schools, etc. These are the primary areas for checking our hypothesis that the late-capitalist societies are endangered by a collapse of legitimation.[3]

I do not question the existence of discontent, dissatisfaction, or aliena-tion on the part of these groups. It may well be that not only these groups but many others as well lack an ideological commitment to the capitalist system, and that they withhold the granting of legitimacy to it. They may even regard their government, their leaders, and their political system as illegitimate.

However, by focusing his attention on finding the weaknesses in the systems of legitimation of "so-called" capitalism, late capitalism, and post-capitalism, Habermas has failed to notice the possibility that social systems may exist without a dominant system of legitimation. It may be that modern industrialized and bureaucratized societies can be governed without a domi-nant legitimating ideology designed to secure consent. In this paper I will consider the possibility that many legitimating ideologies can coexist and compete and that acceptance or rejection of such ideologies is not always necessary to processes of governance in bureaucratic society.

Of Laws and Men

Through July and August of 1974, during Watergate, major political con-stituencies in the United States withdrew support from a popularly elected president and his inner-governing circle. Voters who had voted for President Nixon considered their vote to have been fraudulently claimed and felt be-trayed by the candidate for whom they had voted. Other citizens and leaders who had not voted for Nixon no longer felt a commitment to respect the results of the election. The withdrawal of support and consent from the

2. *Ibid.*, p. 667.
3. *Ibid.*

ruling circle of political leaders resulted in a virtual paralysis of governmental operations.

During the last stages of the paralysis in August, the sources of the legitimacy of governmental actions were difficult to locate. Governmental departments such as Defense, State, Health, Education and Welfare, and bureaus such as the FBI and CIA were presumably acting on their own cognizance since the president was discredited and most of the inner circle of government under whose direction existing policies had been set were either in jail or on their way to criminal prosecutions that would put them in jail. At the last moments of the Nixon presidency, the secretary of the armed forces, James Schlesinger, took it upon himself to screen any communications that might have come from the White House to the military services. Presumably he was suspicious of a last-minute presidential attempt to save power by means of force. By so doing, however, Schlesinger arrogated to himself the direct powers of government and came perilously close to accomplishing what he was trying to avoid. The legitimacy of a duly elected president and his government was abandoned on the grounds that the president was possibly a criminal. The vacuum created by these events was filled by self-appointed guardians of authority whose claims to legitimacy rested on discrediting traditional forms of legitimation.

In democratic society the idea of the supremacy of the electoral mandate is basic to its legitimacy. Early in the development of capitalism, the bourgeoisie in its efforts to express its sense of self-worth made claims for participation in the political process. Except for such movements as Bonapartism, Nazism, and Fascism, the electoral affirmation and support of a government and its policies by the majority of its citizens has been thought necessary to the legitimacy of governance. Electoral legitimation has been distinguished from the mass support achieved by Fascism and Nazism because the latter used political processes that violated the institution of free elections. Popular elections involving competing parties have come to be thought of as the fundamental instrument for securing consent and for making claims to legitimacy.[4]

But in the history of capitalism and democracy, the electoral process has been constrained by a larger legitimating idea known as the "rule of law."[5] Legality, as represented in such documents as constitutions, bills of rights, and statutes supported by judicial procedures are in Weber's terms the basis on which legitimacy is claimed under a system of rational legal authority. Thus legitimacy granted by the electoral process is limited and restricted by the parameters of the law. When engaging in actions for which routine legal

4. For a cogent statement of this position, see Hans J. Morgenthau, "Decline of Democratic Government," *The New Republic,* CLXXI (Nov. 9, 1974), 13–18.

5. For a contemporary version of this statement, see John R. Silber, "The Thicket of Law and the Marsh of Conscience," *Harvard Magazine,* November, 1974, pp. 14–18.

acceptance cannot be expected, leaders have been careful to find in advance explicit legal justifications for such actions, or, if necessary, as for example in the Gulf of Tonkin resolution, to create laws in advance of the use of authority which might otherwise be regarded as of dubious legality. When legality has not been adhered to, recourse has been had to clandestine actions in agencies such as the CIA and FBI, or to the subcontracting of illegal work to private businesses such as the Mafia. Since these latter actions have been kept secret in the sense that it was difficult in pre-Watergate times to discuss them publicly, they could be thought to either not exist or to represent only an occasional lapse into illegality. Legitimacy is thus ultimately based on claims of legal rationality supported by rhetorical invocation of "government of laws, not of men."[6]

However, the rhetoric of the rule of law as indicated by secret governmental operations has been muddied by the growth of the administrative state and by the bureaucratization of the presidency. President Nixon and his inner circle seemed to act outside the framework of established law. Congressional investigators tried to act within the law in carrying out their investigations, but they engaged in unofficial "plea bargaining" with witnesses and the accused in order to facilitate their legal actions. Judges refused to accept the testimony of witnesses whom they knew had perjured themselves and made deals with other witnesses for reduced sentences in exchange for confessions. The president himself was pressured into resigning by some of his closest associates and friends. Finally, it appears that the resignation of the president may have involved informal agreements concerning the terms of the resignation and that the investigators may have been consulted about the acceptability of these terms. Illegal or extralegal actions were used to restore the rule of law. It would appear that the rule of law requires as a prop the rule of men.

Watergate revealed that the restoration of legitimacy could be granted only by men who as self-appointed guardians of authority choose to restore legitimate rule of law. Both the resignation under pressure and the restoration of legal authority revealed the previous absence of law. Seen in this light, we may return to the fundamental question raised by Habermas—the alleged withdrawal of consent by significant constituencies. Habermas's point is independent of Watergate, but if Habermas is right, Watergate should have exacerbated this process.

Legitimation Problems Revealed by Watergate

It is generally agreed that the Nixon administration had no legal justification for the bombing of Cambodia, the theft of Ellsberg's psychiatric files, the break-in of the Democratic party's national offices in the Watergate

6. "Our constitution works; our great Republic is a government of laws and not of men," stated Gerald Ford upon assuming the presidency.

building, the attempts to suppress the investigation of Watergate, and, finally, the efforts to conceal and destroy legal evidence related to the Watergate cover-up. Some of these illegal activities were ordered by the president himself. Others were ordered and executed by officials appointed by the president acting on the strength of his office. All of these acts were committed while Richard M. Nixon was president of the United States. None was challenged until after he was inaugurated for his second term of office, an election he won by one of the largest electoral majorities in modern times.[7] Most of these crimes were reported in the press but were played down and little noticed. Only after the Watergate break-in trial and the resignation of Elliot Richardson after the election did the public respond to facts that were already reported. In spite of or perhaps because of his alleged crimes, it is clear that Nixon convinced many citizens of his qualifications for the presidency. This fact alone calls for some explanation in the sources of legitimation of the American government in the actions of the leader himself.

Moreover, it was only because of the naive discovery of the Watergate break-in by a night watchman who took his job seriously and was helped in his work by the apparent overconfidence of the Watergate burglars that the train of events leading to the Watergate investigation was initiated. Similarly, Nixon's demise might never have occurred if he had not, because of the tapes, supplied the hard evidence to refute his own denials. Presumably, without the discovery of the break-in and the existence of the tapes, Richard Nixon would still be president of the United States, the crisis of legitimacy created by Watergate would not have occurred, and the concept of "government of laws, not of men" would still be intact, at least for those who accept this conception. The maintenance of secrecy supports legitimacy and becomes a part of it. It would appear that the processes by which Watergate was brought to the attention of the governed are also a part of the problem of legitimacy. Mass communications, counterintelligence, mutual covert surveillance, propaganda and public opinion, while having no place in received theories of legitimation and delegitimation, must be made part of the analysis.

In the administrative state, mass communications and image management (propaganda) are also branches of government which are not part of the traditional language of the "rule of law." Thus the rules and regulations (the ethics and morality) governing the competition for the attention of the public are neither specified nor codified. Competitive struggles to claim the right to the attention of constituencies and to define political issues are linked to free speech and free press, but can also include struggles to define and specify the grounds of legitimacy itself. The concepts of public opinion, intelligence, and political legitimacy are closely related.

7. The fact that the Democratic party failed to make an issue of the Watergate break-in during the election would suggest that its leaders were neither morally outraged nor regarded it as an issue. Presumably this form of interparty spying is regarded as the norm in Washington.

Historically, the ideas of knowledge and of intellectual enlightenment have been associated with the slogans "freedom of speech" and "freedom of the press." The right to freely transmit information and news was thought of as a powerful instrument not only for resisting the tyranny of government but also for the creation of an educated political community. The safety and well-being of democracy were thus linked to an intellectually enlightened public. With the advent of mass media and highly complex institutions of opinion formation, the slogan "freedom of speech and press" has been extended to cover these newer media. However, the media are highly complex bureaucracies which specialize in gathering and transmitting news and information. As corporate structures, which are similar to business corporations, they have claimed under the legal fiction of the corporate individual equal rights to freedom of speech and press. The success of this claim has given to the media a powerful voice in supporting or denying the legitimacy of slogans.

The conflict between government and media includes vast administrative and organizational struggles to appropriate the power of slogans. The marketplace in which these struggles occur bears no relationship to the marketplace of free speech as conceived by liberals in the nineteenth century. The administrative and organizational apparatus employed in these struggles is not part of any tradition of rule of law as related to constitutionalism.

The absence of formal rules for the regulation of competition between government and media has meant that the relationship between these two institutions is regulated by other means. At times, their representatives may negotiate formal contracts, but at other times the relationship may rest on informal understandings, threats, bribes, and blackmail. Thus, in both government and the institutions of the mass media, there is a backstage of administrative process which is managed by political and administrative bureaucrats who make laws and break them and at the same time manage the appearance of legality.[8] So long as frontstage and backstage are kept apart—in our terms, so long as the propaganda remains intact—crises of legitimacy are not likely to occur.[9]

8. Jonathan Schell's series of six essays in *The New Yorker*, June–July 1975, presents a thorough recapitulation of the illegal and extralegal underpinnings of Nixon's presidency. By his reassessment of almost all of Nixon's private presidential actions after the fact of the exposures, Schell presents in combination the secret and official sides of government. His simultaneous juxtaposition of rhetoric and reality within the Nixon administration reveals the two faces of the rule of law. A similar analysis of the mass-media industry has not yet appeared, although David Halberstam has laid out the contours for such an analysis in "Press and Prejudice: How Our Last Three Presidents Got the Newsmen They Deserved," *Esquire*, LXXXI (April 1974), 109–114.

9. At least some members of the journalism profession were chastened by the power of the press in penetrating government operations during the Watergate affair. See Katharine Graham, "The Press after Watergate: Getting Down to New Business," *New York*, Nov. 4, 1974, pp. 69–72, where the point is made that Congress allowed the press to do its investigative work and that the journalists overly enjoyed it because they felt

Backstage political processes may be conveniently referred to as the invisible government.[10] In the invisible government, relations among leaders are based on powerful forms of clique group loyalty. The inner clique or cliques, whose existence in the Nixon administration were so fully revealed during the Watergate investigations, play an autonomous—that is, not legitimated—role in the governing process. Because they can strengthen the appearances of frontstage politics, their role can include the maintenance of beliefs in legitimacy. A key question in the study of the problem of legitimacy is: What are the circumstances under which front- and backstage are broken down sufficiently to reveal to believers that their faith has not been justified?

An answer to this question involves several political processes whose examination may shed some light on the problems of legitimation in modern industrial, bureaucratic society:

• On what grounds do the groups, classes, and individuals who are the governed grant consent to be governed? We do not assume that all groups grant consent for the same reason—that is, there do not necessarily exist overarching legitimacy symbols and ideologies.

• Who among the totality of political actors will assume responsibility for exposing backstage politics to the point of threatening the faith of large numbers of citizens?

• Once political faith is destroyed, what processes are available for its re-creation, and who will elect those who administer the restoration?

Varieties of Consent

If the values governing consent are different for different groups, it follows that assessments of what is legitimate government and what is illegitimate will also vary among different constituencies. In this brief essay I cannot discuss the full array of groups in American society, so I will limit the discussion to the older middle classes, the industrial and factory working classes, and the new middle classes. The choice has the advantage of including Habermas's alienated constituencies while not excluding groups which have granted their acceptance to governing elites in the United States.[11]

---

that Nixon had deceived and tricked them. This author argues that the press damaged itself by overstepping its role, but offers no clear definition of what its role is or should be.

10. See Arthur J. Vidich and Joseph Bensman, *Small Town in Mass Society*, rev. ed. (Princeton: Princeton University Press, 1968), chap. 9, for a description and analysis of this form of government.

11. While it would be helpful to examine the political ideologies of the social and economic upper classes, they are less well known now than they were thirty or forty years ago because since then their economic and social commitments and identifications have become internationalized and therefore their conceptions of legitimacy may transcend the nation-state.

The Old Middle Classes

Throughout the course of Nixon's impeachment proceedings, the opinion polls reported a stable 25 percent of the electorate to be in support of the president and his government. For these citizens, legality or illegality was not at issue in their acceptance of Nixon. Neither the admission of outright lies nor attempts to cover up lies were sufficient to disabuse them. At the time, the summer of 1974, analysts believed that this constituency was made up of middle-American middle classes whose loyalty was to conservatism and to the Republican party.[12] My own studies, with Joseph Bensman, of American society confirm this interpretation.[13] We called this group the "old middle classes" to distinguish them from the new middle classes, who are bureaucrats, managers, administrators, and professionals employed in public and private bureaucracies.[14]

The political experience of the old middle classes is most likely to have been shaped in towns, smaller cities, and county governments. In our study of Springdale, we found that this group under the leadership of Jones routinely had recourse to the use of extralegal measures in local politics. In a later essay,[15] we described the position of the old middle class relative to newer cultural and political movements in American society and pointed out that they could be both defensive and at times desperate because of their fear of losing control. We would argue that Nixon represented the conservatism and Republicanism of this older-middle-class tradition and simply enacted on the national stage the political style Jones enacted in Springdale. Thus, for them, Nixon's "criminal" conduct did not depart from tradition but upheld basic American moral values. As a result, Nixon's conduct did not call for reactions of moral revulsion or withdrawal of credence but required support and loyalty in the face of adversity. Defense of party and patronage and of the American system were more important as issues than mere legality or illegality.

In this view, victory at the polls guarantees four years of rule and grants to the victors the choice of political means. Surely, many in the older generation of the Republican old middle class could remember their defeats at the hands of Franklin D. Roosevelt in the 1930s and 1940s. They remember having suffered the "regulation of business," the introduction of the welfare

12. These are the remnants of the old middle classes described in C. Wright Mills, *White Collar* (New York: Oxford University Press, 1951).

13. Vidich and Bensman, *Small Town in Mass Society*; and Joseph Bensman and Arthur J. Vidich, *The New American Society* (Chicago: Quadrangle Books, 1971).

14. For further clarification of the distinction between these two groups, see our debate with Ivan Light in "Recent Developments in American Society: Reply to Ivan Light," *Theory and Society*, II (1975), 125–133.

15. See Vidich and Bensman, *Small Town in Mass Society*, chap. 12, "A Theory of the American Community," pp. 317–347.

state, and the attempted packing of the Supreme Court. Many regarded Roosevelt to have exceeded the legal limits of the presidency and thought him to be a criminal. Yet they would say that they accepted the electoral process as the source of governmental legitimacy and did not run Roosevelt out of the White House. They would agree with Nixon, who throughout Watergate seemed to be saying, "I won the election, why can't I be president for four years?"

Legitimacy based on party victory rests upon mutual acceptance by opposing parties of the results of elections.[16] Victors, in this tradition, are free to choose political means, including those used to gain victory. Losers do not accept the legitimacy of the rule of the victors, but agree only to accept their own defeat on the grounds that they will have a chance to try for victory at a later time. Legitimacy for both winners and losers resides in the hope of future victories.[17] Crises of legitimacy are avoided or forestalled because all contenders for power can hope that power will be theirs in the future. The expectation of future victory results in political self-restraint, unwillingness to use violence to gain power, and acceptance of the authority of the victors. Thus Nixon did not use force to retain power because he could entertain the hope of a political comeback.

The Industrial and Factory Working Classes

In their daily work, industrial and factory workers (hard hats), as distinguished from service and white-collar employees, tend to confront inert objects rather than people or paper. Their routine work activities involve neither psychological sensitivity to clients nor bookish or literary kinds of intellectuality. For the most part these workers, except for some younger ones who have had college educations, are defensive with respect to their abilities to understand the complexities of the culture and politics of modern industrial society. They are likely to prefer clear-cut political choices that enable them to take a political stand without the need for knowledge in

16. There is some indication that Nixon felt cheated by his loss to John F. Kennedy in the 1960 election. In that election, the last votes to be counted were Mayor Daley's votes in Cook County, Illinois, and the absentee ballots in the state of California. The election hinged on how these votes would be counted because they would determine the electoral votes of both states. The California vote went to Nixon and the Illinois vote to Kennedy, so that the election was won for Kennedy by the Cook County results. Nixon apparently agreed not to challenge the legality of these results and accepted his defeat, though not without bitterness.

17. This system places heavy emphasis on the politics of means. Nixon and his inner group never thought of themselves as having committed crimes. They operated on the principle of a higher morality in the cause of saving the country from its enemies. Gordon Liddy, one of the Watergate conspirators, stated this position most fully in "Gordon Liddy: A Patriot Speaks," *Harper's*, CCIL (October 1974), 45–51, where he invokes the revolutionary spirit and the lawlessness of the founding fathers to justify his moral duty to protect American values.

depth. As hard hats, they are likely to be suspicious and perhaps resentful of the wordiness and intellectual sophistication of "eggheads." George Meany, president of the AFL-CIO, has embodied the attitude and style of political gruffness and bluntness that is representative of the communicative level preferred by these workers.

President Nixon, as part of his political strategy, addressed the hard hats on their terms. He also made direct advances to George Meany and gained his political support. His appeals to workers consisted in clear definitions of the meaning of loyalty and patriotism to the nation, and included an image of a tough president who opened the White House to hard hats at the expense of intellectuals. This working-class constituency, relatively new to the Republican party, was one of Nixon's creative innovations which, incidentally, confounded both the Democratic party and the socialist and Marxist political left. Later, when he recognized that he had been taken, it was also a source of embarrassment to George Meany.

I exclude the white-collar working and service classes from this analysis because they have a much greater familiarity with the inner workings of bureaucracies and because to them "paper and pencil work" comes easily. Bureaucratic procedures such as filing, pre- and postdating letters, rigging tax returns, destroying correspondence, fixing conferences, placing blame on scapegoats, sandbagging, stonewalling, protecting the boss and so forth are all part of everyday work experiences. In their case, the revelations about the inner workings of the White House were recognizable, comprehensible, and believable. For this group, a critical point in the erosion of the president's creditability occurred when Rose Mary Woods, in a photo reproduced in newspapers throughout the country, demonstrated how she accidentally destroyed a portion of a tape while transcribing it. Miss Woods was shown operating the transcribing device with one leg fully extended and operating a telephone with one arm fully extended in the opposite direction. The critical eighteen minutes of erased tape were attributed to this maneuver. Secretaries and office workers would know from their daily work that this pose was unbelievable. A difference in an ability to see (through) a rigged scenario suggests the difference in political skill between white-collar as opposed to industrial and factory workers. Such differences in political skills among the working groups in society suggests that even workers are not a unitary constituency whose grounds for granting or withdrawing consent are common.[18]

18. Even here, however, one could argue that knowledge of the inner operations of bureaucracy does not automatically account for the political disenchantment of white-collar, bureaucratically employed groups. It is possible that each individual regards his own work situation as unique and, as a result, fails to generalize his experience as the norm rather than the exception. Psychological processes of particularization prevent an awareness of the general phenomenon and enable the individual to preserve illusions about the nature of political bureaucracies. When such beliefs in exceptionalism are violated as was the case during Watergate, political disenchantment can be prevented only by a purge of those who by their actions have threatened the illusions. The purge restores credence and reconfirms the belief in exceptionalism.

For the industrial and factory working classes the will to believe in the image of Nixon as a leader was built on themes such as: (a) the tough, shrewd, political tactician who held close reins over irresponsible congressmen; (b) the bold leader who would restore order to American society after the civil rights, racial, and student disorders which the Democratic party had tolerated during the 1960s; (c) the rational administrator who as president was reasserting control over an overexpanded, frequently autonomous Federal bureaucracy; (d) the world statesman, tough on Communism, but unafraid to deal with the Communists in order to promote American interests. In short, major segments of the working class could place faith in Nixon and be assured that their political interests were protected.[19]

At the time the Watergate scandal began to unfold, the honeymoon between President Nixon and the workers was still in effect. However, as the investigations continued, seeds of doubt were sown and workers became less sure of their new-found political ally. The major feature of the Watergate investigations and the impeachment hearings was precisely that they lacked clarity, simplicity, and comprehensibility. They were highly technical and legalistic in form, and were frequently ambiguous and difficult to follow. To attempt to understand them required close and sustained attention, and even then it was difficult to follow the twists, turns, implications, and ramifications of the proceedings and the intentions of the antagonists. The working classes in particular were neither equipped to digest this material nor capable of easily judging truth and falsity. Nixon's outright denials and brazen efforts to conceal could appeal only to those who wished to avoid involvement in the political complexities of the situation. One must understand that what was later called his duplicity may have been a conscious effort on Nixon's part to retain a positive working-class public opinion by giving workers an opportunity to make a simple choice based on loyalty and patriotism. It was to this class more than to any other that Nixon offered a simple choice when he defended the presidency rather than himself. At this point Nixon's claim was to the sanctified legitimacy of the office, not to himself or the law.

The Watergate and cover-up investigations created confusion and uncertainty and perhaps even fear in the working classes. Since the basis of faith in Nixon rested on trust, the violation of trust resulted in feelings of betrayal and a moral crisis for believers, including political disenchantment and reversion to more customary forms of cynicism—"all politicians are crooks"— characteristic of America's working classes. However, though the disenchantment of the working classes came late, it represented a major source of delegitimation of the Nixon administration. The meaning of this delegitimation must be made clear.

The working classes accepted the legitimacy of Nixon and his government

19. The acceptance of President Nixon on these terms was characteristic of other groups as well. By November 1972, the belief in Nixon's political mastery was held by most Americans.

because Nixon recognized and accepted them and, equally importantly, relieved them of the responsibility for understanding the process of government. Thus a group's willingness to be co-opted cognitively and spiritually (for whatever reason) may be a basis for the consent necessary for political legitimacy. However, this type of legitimacy is effective only so long as the co-optation, the will to believe, is not violated by a shattering of the faith, by the feeling of having been double-crossed. When faith is shattered, withdrawal from co-optation occurs.

However, withdrawal from the co-optation left the working classes in the same position they had been in before—political powerlessness—until some other leader or agency offered to co-opt them. The critical factor, then, is not that government needs acceptance of its legitimacy from the working classes but rather the kinds of political roles that are assigned to them by the ruling elite. Thus there need not be a *common* belief in the rule of law or rational-legal legitimacy as a prerequisite for the operations of modern governments. Other, short-term bases for legitimacy may be created by political leaders when it is convenient for them to do so, or such belief may be simply regarded as unnecessary regardless of basic ideology or belief.

The New Middle Classes

The new middle classes are different from the bourgeoisie identified with the nineteenth-century development of democratic institutions as described by Marx. This bourgeoisie made its claim to political participation on the strength of its new industrial capital and on the economic power which accrued to it as a result of the success of capitalist business enterprise. The new middle classes neither base their social and political position on ownership of business capital, nor do they necessarily commit themselves to ideologies of capitalism. Their claim to status and income is based on education, skilled expertise in the tasks required of large-scale bureaucracies and professions, and their ability to participate through their occupational roles in decision-making that affects the society as a whole.[20] One of its problems has been to find a political role that would be consistent with a moderately successful, educated, and cultivated self-image.

As the educated elite of the society, they hold key technocratic positions in some of the older as well as newer public institutions. The university is one of the older institutions that have become major sources of their support. Through the university and university-related institutions such as institutes of higher learning and think tanks, they have had access to policy-makers in education, defense, planning, and public opinion. More importantly, however, modern institutions of public opinion have not only been a major source of economic support but also a crucial channel of access to information-consuming publics. Thus news commentators, foreign correspondents,

20. See Bensman and Vidich, *The New American Society,* chaps. 9–10, pp. 161–188.

journalists, editors of scholarly and unscholarly magazines, public-opinion pollsters, advertising men and public-relations counsels contribute to the formation of public opinion. In an epoch when the educated can believe in the social construction of reality, the importance and effectiveness of knowledge and propaganda cannot be underestimated. The new middle classes in part have made their claims to privileged political participation on the mystique of controlling knowledge and intelligence.

The idea of natural law, of God and divine justice, and of Adam Smith's free market as the basis of economic justice are not parts of their ideology. Bentham's slogan, "the greatest good for the greatest number," is likely to be invoked when it is recognized that a particular policy involves a clash of interests. The concept of the public interest is not regarded as transcendent but rather is a link to ideologies of democratic pluralism and to the possibility of a managed balance of social and economic justice by the operators of the bureaucratized corporate society. The public interest is also the slogan which justifies claims to the privileged role of technical intelligence in politics.

The rise in political importance of the educated new middle class has been associated with the growth in organizational and bureaucratic complexity of the opinion, propaganda, and communications industries. As an occupational group, it monopolizes technologies of production in symbol-making industries and is the source of supply for the consumers of opinion and communication.[21]

The educated elites of the new middle classes are still in the process of attempting to find ideologies to support and justify their ascendency and their claims to political participation. Robert Lilienfeld's essay in this issue of *Social Research* describes the ideology of systems theorists who make their claim to authority on the grounds of scientific rationality applied to societal administration. For systems theorists, the public interest is represented by the rational objectivity inherent in the logics of the system. Peter Ludz's essay in this issue[22] describes the application of this ideology to Eastern European nations where the ruling administrative classes are attempting to replace outmoded revolutionary ideologies with ideologies of systems functions. If the system can be said to be functionally interrelated at all managerial levels, then all participants ought to share in the operation of society. Thus the unantici-

---

21. To the extent that there are social and occupational relations between members of this class, their influence may be extended through the informal socializing they carry out with each other. Thus we have the phenomena of literary establishments, writers' cliques, *samizdat* journalism, "fixed" reviews, orchestrated literary attacks, and so forth. For a time, the CIA organized and rationalized all these methods for coordinating the viewpoints of the media and communications industries. Because the CIA's activities were unsuspected, it was able to coordinate opinion more effectively than Russia's Agitprop, which lacks a credible front.

22. See also Peter C. Ludz, *The Changing Party Elite in East Germany* (Cambridge: The MIT Press, 1972), especially Part IV, for a comprehensive discussion of East European managerial ideologies.

pated growth of the state bureaucracy in socialist countries is solved as a problem because the rewards of state power ought to be distributed to participants at all levels in the social system. The result would be a withering away of the state and fulfillment of a revolutionary promise.[23] Another example is the work of John Kenneth Galbraith, who, writing from the perspective of liberalism, came close to supplying an ideology for state economic planners when he described the functions of the technostructure in *The New Industrial State*. Other similar claims have been made by those who have proclaimed the end of ideology in postindustrial society. As a substitute for the end of ideology, they have proposed rational planning based on social-scientific analysis of social indicators by social scientists. Their claim to predict the future through futurology is a claim for authority based on a mystique of foreknowledge. The efforts of all these theorists are attempts to supply an ideological underpinning to the ascendency of what Djilas called for Eastern Europe the new class[24] and what I have referred to as the new middle class. A key dimension of Watergate was the relationship between this class and the Nixon administration.

In contrast to the 1968 election, when Richard Nixon did not have the support of this class, a substantial portion of it, including university professors and journalists and writers, voted for him in 1972. By 1972, President Nixon had recast his image from one based upon his defeat of Helen Gahagan Douglas and his prosecution of Alger Hiss to an image of the masterful professional politician who could be trusted with the administration of domestic and international affairs in contrast to his opponent, George McGovern, who appeared naive, disorganized, uncertain, and overly responsive to hippies and student radicals. Thus, this class could identify with Nixon the astute political bureaucrat even though this claim to rule violated some elements in such ideologies as pluralism, futurology, and technical planning rationality. It was not until the Watergate exposures, however, that this class, much like the working classes, began to feel the sense of betrayal and the loss of trust which became the basis for a reassertion of its sense of political morality independently from its occupational ideologies.

The Political Bureaucrat and the Management of Ideology

In his actions as president of the United States, Richard M. Nixon not only rejected the claims of these newer middle-class ideologies but also their claimants. He represented the ideology of the rational political bureaucrat whose *modus operandi* depends upon the blind loyalty of clique associates and not upon the acceptance of alternative ideologies. He used his own corps

23. But of course bureaucracy would replace the state.
24. Milovan Djilas, *The New Class* (New York: Praeger, 1957).

of managerial technocrats as a vehicle for his illegalities and his programs, but he did not ideologize them. In fact he did this while attacking governmental bureaucracy and the civil service. Thus the vast majority of the new middle class were psychologically, occupationally, and politically excluded from both participation and a sense of participation. The administration's techniques of media and opinion management were employed at the expense of the new middle classes.

The role of the new middle class in the legitimation process was revealed during the Watergate scandal and the resignation of President Nixon. I will argue that it opposed Nixon because he excluded it from levels of political participation deemed consonant with its self-image.

President Nixon centralized the power of the presidency to a greater extent than previous presidents. He consolidated his power in five major areas of government and party operations:

● Foreign affairs were placed in the White House by the simple method of abandoning cold-war policies to which other Federal bureaucracies, especially the State Department and the Department of Defense, were still committed. By inaugurating détente as a policy and keeping its contours secret until dramatic public announcements could be made, Nixon immobilized other agencies; lacking information, they could not publicly debate the issue, let alone oppose the policy. Thus Nixon and Kissinger could dominate a major reversal of foreign policy largely without reference to the Federal bureauracy of Congress.

● The Office of Management and Budget was set up within the executive branch as a watchdog agency designed to scrutinize government operations in all spheres. Administratively, it stood between the president and his own cabinet members and was the device by which the president undercut their authority. The key administrative technique included in this by-passing of the traditional authority of the cabinet was to assign a representative of OMB (in effect a presidential agent) to policy-making positions in each department of government. The penetration of departments by a presidential agent who had direct access to the White House was a formalization of interorganizational clique control[25] over all branches of government, thus rendering impotent alternative sources of authority and policy.

● The systematic presidential practice of impounding congressionally approved expenditures deprived congressmen of one of their main sources of rewards to their constituents, that of bringing money into their districts and states. Impounding of funds weakened the position of congressmen in relation to their constituencies, weakened their bargaining position with lobbyists

---

25. See Bensman and Vidich, *The New American Society,* pp. 91–103, for a description of the characteristics of interinstitutional power cliques and the coordination of bureaucracies by cliques.

who had already paid for their share of funds that were blocked by impounding, and made them more dependent on the president for campaign funds and
other patronage.

• Revenue-sharing or the direct grants of Federal funds to state, town,
and country governments on a prorated scale again deprived congressmen of
the right to claim credit for Federal expenditures in their voting districts. In
effect, traditional patronage rights to which congressmen had become accustomed were being claimed by the White House itself. This was a hardship for
urban liberal congressmen who had grown accustomed to taking credit from
blacks and other minority and disadvantaged constituencies for funds channeled through OEO, welfare programs, educational spending, federal support
of urban renewal, housing, and so forth.

• The traditional campaign and electioneering apparatus of the Republican party was circumvented and rendered impotent by the creation of the
Committee to Re-elect the President (Creep). Again, Creep was controlled by
the White House, and campaign contributions were controlled by the White
House, and campaign contributions were channeled through Creep rather
than through the party, which as a result had almost no role in the 1972
campaign.

Nixon's successful domination of the Federal bureaucracy, Congress, and
the Republican party enabled him to centralize societal administration in a
manner that can be compared to the situation in Russia when the secretary-
ship of the Communist party and governmental administration are combined
in one person. Such centralization makes possible the orchestration of administrative actions related to widely disparate sectors of society. Not only
does the society appear to be managed with some measure of rationality, but
it becomes apparent to some of those who are so managed that they have
been excluded from participation by the process of management. It is quite
obvious that this process was not complete by the time of Watergate or there
would not have been a Watergate crisis. But it is also obvious that the process
was well underway.

However, since not all groups claim their right to participate, Nixon's
policies of exclusion did not affect all groups equally. For purposes of this
analysis I will mention only those groups on which Nixon's policies had a
negative effect. The excluded groups included the following:

• Congress, because legislative and patronage initiatives were monopo-
lized by the White House. Congressmen were offered the alternative of accepting White House policy or being penalized for rejecting it.

• Bureaucrats in almost all branches of government, because they discovered they were surrounded by Nixon men in their own bureaus. Bureaucrats could either accept their impotence or could fight back by counter-
spying on the White House (e.g., the Department of Defense and the CIA), or
by sabotaging White House policy by legalism, delay, news leaks, and planned
inefficiencies.

• The press, because it was denied access to the policy-making secrets of the White House and, when it attempted to pierce the managed veil, was denounced as the tool of an un-American, eastern radical establishment and subjected to threats of loss of licenses and of prosecutions for tax evasion. So tight was White House control over news releases and news leaks that the press corps was almost reduced to an agitprop branch of government.

• Universities and university-based consultants had their funds sharply curtailed and their services were not utilized. This was a particularly stunning blow to many university professors and administrators who had been sup- porters of government policies throughout the cold-war period. President Nixon's failure to defend them even after they defended government- supported operations in the universities against radical students left them free and resentful.

• New middle classes, which had grown accustomed to being recipients of educational, cultural, transportation, and welfare benefits, because the White House redirected these funds to another class of recipients under its program of revenue-sharing.

President Nixon's politics of exclusion were carried out largely within the framework of the law. The use of organized power cliques, employment of persons wholly dependent on the president, use of budgetary methods to destroy competition, reversals of policy to by-pass existing centers of authority, and administrative reorganizations to redistribute power were legal methods of administration. Where the success of these policies depended on bureaucratic technique, no laws existed which could be invoked against the administrative methods used. At the level of governmental operations Presi- dent Nixon's extraordinary success as a political bureaucrat reduced his opposition to impotence. If President Nixon had continued to manage the society under his terms, there would have been no necessity for a government of law or of rational legitimacy. All that would have been required was an effective control of public opinion.[26]

The Failure of Nixon's Claim to Legitimacy

The evidence from the Watergate example shows that industrial, bureau- cratic society functions without a dominant ideology of legitimation based on rational-legal authority. However, while arguing against the Weberian concept

26. In Russia, the knowledge and communications industries have been under central government control since shortly after the revolution. In the Russian political system, control of these industries at the level of influencing the political "line" has indicated both who is in power and whose power is likely to be legitimated. In the United States, as shown by Watergate, these industries may play an independent role and are not wholly controlled by the central government.

Klaus Mueller, in *The Politics of Communication: A Study in the Political Sociology of Language, Socialization, and Legitimation* (New York: Oxford University Press, 1973), argues that all communication in "late capitalist" society is both managed and distorted

of rational-legal legitimacy as the basis of modern society, I have also noted the existence of a multiplicity of other ideologies and bases of legitimacy that can coexist and occasionally merge with each other. Class, occupational, and educational interests are alternative bases for ideologies which can coexist with the "rule of law" as legitimating ideologies. Even the idea of "administrative necessity" which replaces ideological justification can be the basis for an alternative ideology.

The basis of legitimacy in modern society need not be only the rule of law—rational-legal authority, so defined—but can be defined separately to meet the aspirations of new classes, elites, and occupations. Thus modern legitimacy can be based on managerial or scientific necessity, a special technique or function, special kinds of knowledge (scientific systems, futurology, dialectics), judgment and political intelligence, and morality, to mention only a few.

President Nixon attempted to base his ideology of legitimacy on practical political intelligence while subverting the rule of law even while he preserved its public forms. He also exalted the charisma of his office, the presidency, over and above the rule of law. Ultimately, President Nixon, the masterful politician, demanded the *trust* of others on the basis of his political know-how supported in part by some redneck, Protestant, practical morality (if it works, it's good). He supported this claim by simultaneously attempting to withdraw legitimacy from other claimants who based their claims on science, systems analysis, and universal morals. His claim was sustained by the appearance of success, carefully managed by stage managers and image makers.

Part of President Nixon's success was based on his ability to make his enemies and opponents appear to be incompetent, bumbling, or foolish—above all, incapable of operating the American political system because they were too idealistic, unable to create efficient organizations, not politically hard-headed, too ideological or too flabby in their liberalism. By his formula for legitimation, success could only breed success, and it appeared that in 1972 the majority of Americans were prepared to accept both the appearances of success and the legitimacy claims.

In terms of this argument, President Nixon's *failure* can be attributed to the appearance of incompetence, ambivalence, and hesitancy in his political mismanagement of the Watergate cover-up. By revealing incompetence and an inability to cope with his opponents and enemies, he violated his own claim to legitimacy based on mastery of politics. This failure made it necessary for President Nixon to introduce into his political style complexity, evasion,

---

by the political system. If this were the case, a phenomenon like Watergate could not have happened because the "political system" would have been successful in its ability to distort and control. The Watergate exposures provide sociologists with a vast amount of empirical data for the analysis of the operations of the political processes of American society. Such analysis would require the revision of Mueller's thesis in its application to capitalist societies. Very probably, however, this thesis might hold if applied to Russia.

defensiveness, and trickiness, thus violating his promise of simplicity and confidence. Loss of his claim to trust was experienced as a betrayal by many who had accepted the claims, especially his new working- and middle-class constituencies. This gave a new chance to all those with competing legitimacy claims to press their claims to the newly created audiences of the betrayed who apparently were prepared to shift from a legitimacy ideology based on practical political success to a legitimacy ideology based on morality.

But the idea of the rule of law and even perhaps the notion of basic inalienable rights had some deeper resonances during the late stages of Watergate. It may take enormous amounts of immorality and criminality to evoke these resonances, but when evoked they resulted in an extremely intense reaction against Nixon by a majority of the citizens. In this extreme instance, the individual citizen perhaps feels or sees that his own political fate may indeed be connected to an ideology of the rule of law.

The Process of Relegitimation

The forces at work in the resignation of President Nixon involved more than legal and judicial processes. They included not only a clash of class and political-party interests but also a significant role for the opinion and media industries. Moreover, class and party interests intersected within these industries when there was a mutuality of interests between them. These interests included claims to power, protection of jobs, and the preservation of a sense of self-worth and self-mastery in the face of emasculation by higher bureaucrats.[27] The question is, how were threats to these interests transformed into a withdrawal of consent?

Those who claim a right to grant legitimacy are limited to those who have access to the attention of publics. In this perspective, the concept of legitimate authority has a much narrower meaning than is usually attributed to it in conventional theory. Democratic, pluralist, and radical-left theories of legitimation represent no more than the ideologies of specific interest groups who make their claim to participation on the strength of these ideologies. Thus the new middle classes connected to the knowledge and opinion industries make their claims with ideologies that claim privileged participation for

27. In this respect, see David Halberstam's comparative analysis (in "Press and Prejudice") of John F. Kennedy, Lyndon B. Johnson, and Richard M. Nixon in their relations with the press. Halberstam argues that Kennedy succeeded in controlling the press by appealing to the vanity of the members of the press corps, and that the press protected Kennedy from exposure because Kennedy supported the journalists' image of their own importance. Nixon, apparently, was incapable of performing this kind of psychological bribery. As a result, Kennedy was a popular president, but we know much less about the operations of his government than we do of the Nixon administration. President Ford is following the unique policy of attempting to bribe the press by giving it an oversupply of information about past secret governmental operations, thereby directing its attention away from the actions of his own government. The press appears to have accepted this bribe because it offers unlimited opportunities for headlines and by-lines.

themselves. This phenomenon has been commonplace in the history of class ideologies, but it is unique in modern society because its claimants are the professors, academicians, journalists, writers, opinion specialists, social scientists, and others who play special roles in the historically unique institutions of opinion, communication, and knowledge dissemination—that is, the institutions through which claims and counterclaims to legitimacy are made. The concept of legitimation is thus restricted to those groups capable of either making a claim or refusing to accept the claims of others. Ordinarily these claims have been made at the time of elections, and elections have been thought to validate the claims. Watergate represents a rejection of the legitimacy of the electoral claim without a testing of the legality of the rejection in an impeachment process.

The work of the media industries in their reporting of the congressional investigations destroyed Nixon's legitimacy not by attacking policy but by attacking the moral tone and illegalities of his administration. The revelation of backstage bureaucratic acts such as spying, lying, sabotage, intimidation, bribery, payoffs, co-optation, stonewalling, blackmail, and so forth were exposed to public view. Exposure of these bureaucratic ethics and morality by the press created new constituencies of nonbelievers in the legitimacy of political institutions. Nixon, too, became aware that the grounds for his claim to legitimacy had shifted from electoral victory and political mastery to the ethics and morality of his bureaucratic conduct when he felt obliged to declare to the nation, "I am not a crook." In making this statement, he indicated his acceptance of his opponents' rules of legitimation. His acceptance gave courage and conviction to the press that their standards of legitimacy were morally correct and justified.

Equally important was acceptance by Nixon and his circle of opinion pollsters' reports throughout the summer of 1974 that only 25 percent of the public supported the government. Nixon attempted to redress this low percentage rating by engaging in dramatic foreign-policy activities designed to make a claim to Americans that protection of national interests by the master diplomat was sufficient grounds for legitimacy, but because of détente no clear international enemy existed and sentiments of nationalism based on national security appeared not to carry weight in support of this claim. In the late stages of Watergate, no claims other than morality and legality were effective. Upon resigning, President Nixon justified his resignation on the grounds that he had lost his support in Congress. In his terms, he had lost his political base. In our terms, he had lost his legitimacy because he had accepted the claims to legitimacy of others.

In Latin American countries, Nixon's resignation would be regarded as a *golpe*—a coup d'état—and another political party would take power. As an American-style *golpe*, Watergate did not have this result. Legality was maintained by the ascension of a previously appointed vice-president.

Apart from this thin but important observation of the rules of legality, we may ask where it was that legality resided before and during the *golpe*. The answer to this question seems to be that it inhered in those people, such as Alexander Haig,[28] who prepared President Nixon to accept his own resignation, and the circle of Gerald Ford's friends, who appointed themselves to plan and manage governmental operations in anticipation of President Nixon's resignation.[29] When Vice-President Ford became involved in his friends' plans to inaugurate him and chart the course of his administration, he acted on the basis of a claim to future legitimacy: the legitimacy of his actions rested upon the expectation of Nixon's resignation. All of these actions were the actions of our then existing invisible self-legitimating government.

During the congressional investigations, the impeachment hearings, and the resignation, no challenge to the legitimacy claims of others was made by either left revolutionary groups, militarists, or conservative businessmen. No attempt was made to seize the reins of government and rule on the basis of another set of claims. In point of fact, all of these groups were united by anti-Nixon ideology that had as its central tenet the desirability of removing him from office. Yet throughout the period of investigations and the paralysis of executive leadership, the government continued to function at the level of its bureaucratic mechanics. No class or group was prepared to press a counter-claim even though there was a vast disenchantment with the members of the ruling elite. While the symbols of governmental legitimacy had been destroyed, and Nixon's specific claims were rejected, no new ones replaced them. The delegitimation of past symbols appears to be the only basis upon which the citizenry is prepared to consent to be governed. It is in this negative sense, perhaps, that the new middle class can achieve an ultimate sense of its self-worth and its sense of importance in the governing of modern society.

President Ford has made his appeals for support on the basis of candor, honesty, and political accessibility, replacing the appeals of intelligence and political practicality used by Nixon prior to Watergate. He has stressed the morality and legality of his presidential actions, and he has followed a policy of allowing full disclosure of past immoralities and illegalities in such agencies as the CIA, FBI, and Department of Justice. The American public seems to have accepted President Ford's claim, and journalists have been content to focus their attention on past indiscretions and illegalities. Thus President Ford, up to October, 1975, has been able to govern with a relatively high

28. See Theodore H. White, *Breach of Faith: The Fall of Richard Nixon* (New York: Atheneum, 1975) for documentation of the role of Alexander Haig. White claims that Haig managed the country during the weeks preceding Nixon's resignation.

29. See *The New York Times,* Aug. 26, 1974, p. 1, for James M. Naughton's story "The Change in Presidents: Plans Began Months Ago," where the activities of the group headed by Philip W. Buchen are described in detail.

public-opinion rating and with relatively little backstage scrutiny by the press. The legitimacy of government has been temporarily restored simply because President Ford's claims have not been rejected, for whatever reasons.

Radicalism, Morality, and Legitimacy

Ideologists of the left, even when they claim descent from Marx, have abandoned the idea of economic class and class-based ideologies. For them, class has been replaced by the values of science and technology as central categories of analysis. Ideologies of acceptance or rejection of these values define for them the scope of legitimacy problems of late capitalism. Since science and technology are spheres of activity managed by academicians, administrators, bureaucrats, and technocrats, the left criticism is an attack on the political role of the right and middle sectors of the new middle classes. Thus left ideologists support those within the middle classes like youth, women, and communitarians who reject the results of modern science and technology. Their overall attacks on the social structures of late capitalistic societies have stressed the irrationalities of the productive and distributive systems. Because of these irrationalities they have called for a delegitimation of prevailing capitalistic institutions and governing methods. All of these political approaches are premised on the assumption that institutional and societal rationality are achievable by other means (a higher rationality than even that of science—perhaps the dialectic) and that these alternative approaches would product results that would better serve society (the public interest).

Commitment to the ideology of a higher rationality has influenced their attitude toward violence and revolution. The disorder, confusion, and uncertainty of revolutionary violence run counter to order and rationality. It is perhaps for this reason that critical sociologists have not followed the politically activist dimensions of Marxism, but have confined their energies to a criticism of the irrationalities of late capitalism. However, even the revolutionary left in its own way is committed to a rational reconstruction of society for the purpose of fulfillment of fundamental human needs not now being met by late capitalism. Thus their rationality includes an attempt at an even more comprehensive rational organization of society than the rationality of those who only criticize. However, in the case of the revolutionary left, the rational organization of society is deferred until after the revolution.

The differences in ideological claims for privileged political participation made by the various sectors of the middle classes conceal the ideological similarities among them. As the educated, intellectual sector of society, the middle classes have stressed the functional necessity of rationality in governance. The rationality of science and technology has been absorbed into a legitimacy claim for the class itself. When science and technology are regarded as antirational in their consequences—that is, producing socially undesirable effects—resort is had to the moral condemnation of the bearers of science and technology. When use of legal rationality by government results in political defeats that retard class ascendency or class interests, legal rationality is either repressive or is regarded as immoral in its consequences. Terms such as rationality, irrationality, legality, and repressiveness stand as code indices for a belief by these classes that they are the moral arbiters of society. They are the definers of rationality and the designers of the future ideal society. Claims to moral righteousness thus relativize and make arbitrary the traditional rhetorics for legitimacy based on "rule of law," legality, and electoral results.[30]

The combining of rationality and morality as conditions for acceptance of governmental legitimacy has posed problems for the bureaucratic state because the moral codes that are invoked cannot be adhered to by the political bureaucrat who holds the power of government in his hands. At one extreme the Weatherman Underground Organization claims moral justification for its armed attacks on the institutions of government,[31] and on the other hand the CIA has justified to itself the moral necessity of spying on other branches of government. The arrogation of the moral authority to claim legitimacy for all varieties of political action places the politician in a defensive position because it constrains him to appear to be moral under circumstances where political choice involves moral compromises. Under these rules of politics the legitimacy of rulers can be challenged easily.

The radical left and critical sociologists have pointed to the decline in the legitimacy foundations of political authority in so-called late capitalistic societies. In focusing specifically on the weaknesses in the legitimating structures of governments in capitalist countries they have failed to notice similar or even more pronounced problems of legitimation in many of the Communist

30. John R. Silber, in "The Thicket of Law and the Marsh of Conscience," takes this position when he argues that President Ford's unilateral pardon of former president Richard M. Nixon could have been used as an occasion for the restoration of the rule of law if Nixon had pleaded guilty prior to the pardon. He writes (p. 17): "Mr. Ford has told us that only he could write 'The End' on what he called the American tragedy of Watergate. Mr. Ford is wrong, for only the law can put an end to Watergate. But that end would be swiftly accomplished even now, were Mr. Nixon to sit down with the Prosecutor, agree on charges, plead guilty and thus complete the legal process. . . . As soon as Mr. Nixon admits his guilt to properly drawn charges, President Ford's pardon restores are expectation of equal justice under law and mercifully closes the book of Watergate for Mr. Nixon." Professor Silber seems to be unaware that he has granted to Nixon the power to restore the rule of law. In his terms, because Nixon has not confessed to his crimes we do not have a rule of law. This explanation is excessively simple. It also has the disadvantage that it places Professor Silber in the position of being the moral arbiter of President Nixon's actions.

31. "The Weather underground organization is responsible for over 25 armed actions against the enemy. . . . This includes the attack on the Pentagon in 1972 and on the State Department in 1975. Ten actions were directed against the repressive apparatus: courts, prisons, and in support of Black Liberation. This includes attacks on New York City Police Headquarters. . . . Together they have resulted in approximately $10 million damage to the imperialists and a significant blow to their arrogance. . . ." (Osawatomie, No. 2 [Summer 1975], p. 2).

countries of the world. In many of those countries the original claims for legitimacy which were based on successful revolution have not been replaced by an alternative basis of legitimacy claims even though the revolutionary elites over time have been replaced by bureaucratic elites. Russia under Stalin is an extreme example of a case where the legitimacy of the entire regime rested solely on one person, but in principle the same holds for Khrushchev and Brezhnev. Tito of Yugoslavia provides a similar example. However, Tito recognized the political need for consent to his rule, and attempted to solve his legitimacy problem by setting up workers' councils and self-management mechanisms that would at least give the appearance that authority resided in the workers themselves. Legitimation as a problem under this practice was "resolved" by denying that a centralized authority existed and pretending that authority existed in the actions of the worker participators themselves. It is not entirely clear whether this solution will succeed, since its success depends upon concealing the role of the party apparatus and other agencies of control.

In countries such as Russia and Yugoslavia where the prerevolutionary bourgeoisie had been weak, nonexistent, or was eliminated during the revolution, the pressure to create legally based legitimations for the rising bureaucratic classes did not exist. Peasants were the largest part of the postrevolutionary populations. They accepted state power in its own right with little need for ideologies or rhetorics to justify its use. For the Communist or socialist countries the need for legitimate authority may become a problem as the educated middle classes increase in size and begin to demand forms of participation in governance that is consistent with their enhanced self-image. Perhaps the radical left and critical sociologists have not been concerned with legitimacy problems in Communist and socialist countries because until recently such problems have not existed as they had in capitalist industrial democracies, where the self-esteem of the middle classes was already high. The lesson of Communist and socialist countries, where the need for legitimacy in the bourgeoisie sense as some form of "natural law" and the inalienable rights of man does not exist, may be that the centralized bureaucratic state can indeed be self-legitimating.

But, while there are a multitude of ways in which legitimacy can be challenged in modern society, consent and belief in legitimacy or illegitimacy are not required from all groups. The claims for legitimacy made by dissident groups—whether based on moral, radical, or reactionary ideologies—do not necessarily destroy a system of legitimacy or societal structure. Thus the attribution of absolute requirements for assent and universal legitimacy assumed to be necessary by some critical sociologists is more a product of their own need to believe and their own need for self-legitimation than it is an attribute of the social system.

The amount of withdrawal of consent necessary to overturn a system is substantial and would depend not only on the strategic position, numbers, and strength of dissidents, but also on the capacity of the system to maintain a minimal level of routine operations if only based on habit and inertia. It is in this sense that one can speak of legitimacy as mechanical or routinized in contemporary industrial-bureaucratic societies.

part V

Official violence

Several chapters in the preceding section documented usurpations and abuses of power by the CIA, the FBI, and other federal agencies. There are many complicated and interwoven factors in these conditions and what led to them, among which are the competing claims to political authority and legitimacy, as noted by Arthur Vidich in Chapter 15. We should not, however, be tempted to think that these were only symbolic political struggles, devoid of any real consequences for the citizens involved. The lives of many individuals were affected by these usurpations and abuses, and for some, their lives were destroyed. Part V includes four readings which tell us about the circumstances in which 43 private citizens were killed by acts of official violence. Chapters 16 and 17 discuss the deaths of four Kent State University students who were killed by gunfire from National Guardsmen in May 1970. And Chapter 18 discusses the circumstances of the killing of 39 inmates by New York State Police at the Attica prison in September 1971—the bloodiest one-day encounter between Americans since the Civil War. While the implied threat of force or of extralegal violence is much more common (and much more effective) than the actual use of such force most of the time, the use of violence is the most significant kind of official seizure of power. Extralegal violence is a basic ingredient of all political tyrannies, and it is destructive of all constitutional guarantees of individual freedom.

Social science concepts of civil disorder and organized protests have been greatly influenced by liberal political sentiments which assume that official actions are a functional response to such situations and which tend to control them. The problem for liberal social scientists, then, is to seek out factors of the predisorder situation (such as the protesters' psychological or social backgrounds) in an attempt to understand what led to the provocation of violence in the first place. But, as sociologist Gary T. Marx argues in Reading 19, "Civil Disorder and the Agents of Social Control," this approach fails to see that many cases of official violence stem from the complex interaction that occurs when civil protesters confront official authorities. Marx argues that many situations involving collective behavior have an emergent quality to them, which means that much of what happens emerges from the interactional context itself, rather than from whatever preceded it. In this respect, the mental attitudes and expectations that armed officials bring to these encounters are highly critical to their outcome. Marx sees official violence as being closely related to the officials' state-of-seige anticipations and their "get-tough" attitudes. Marx concludes by discussing one of the classic questions of political science and philosophy: "Who controls the agents of social control?" This crucial issue is one to which we shall return in Part VIII.

16

A boy who was just 'there watching it and making up his mind'

John Pekkanen

On the morning of the day Bill Schroeder died the alarm went off at 7 a.m. He slept through it and his roommate had to turn it off. At 8:15 he finally got up, dressed in the blue denim jacket his grandfather gave him and the orange bellbottoms he called his "Brian Jones pants" after the late member of the Rolling Stones. ("He owned every record the Stones ever made," a friend remembers.) Leaving his house at 603 Franklin Street, only a few blocks from the Kent State University campus, he drove to class. "I went with him," one of his five housemates said. "He was wearing a purple flower and a yellow flower in each lapel of his jacket. He joked that the purple flower was his Purple Heart." Crossing the campus, Bill found a spent tear gas canister. He picked it up and turned it over to a nearby National Guardsman.

His first class was ROTC, compulsory for Bill because he had transferred to Kent State as a sophomore last fall on an ROTC scholarship. He ranked second among his ROTC classmates academically. "We used to kid him about it," his roommate said, "because ROTC isn't something very popular on campuses these days." But if the kidding bothered him it didn't show. "It wasn't like he had to choose. He was in ROTC and he didn't like Vietnam and Cambodia but if he had to go to Vietnam he would have gone." He once confided to Gene Pekarick, a close friend and fellow psychology major, that he strongly disagreed with another ROTC student who, in discussing a hypothetical military operation, suggested the way to succeed was to "go in there and wipe them out." "Bill was just disgusted by that. He said, 'What kind of mentality is that?' He hated the thought of this kind of senseless killing this guy talked about."

The burning of the Kent State ROTC building the preceding Saturday night had bothered him a lot. He mentioned it on Sunday when he called home to his parents in Lorain, Ohio, a steel town about 60 miles from Kent. He assured his parents that he was all right and planned to take advantage of the disturbances by staying inside and studying.

The rally had been scheduled for noon on Monday on the commons, a gently rolling area now fresh with the burst of spring. Bill and Gene met after class and instead of going to lunch began walking to the rally. "He went because he was curious to see it. He wasn't a participant and he wasn't just a bystander. He was open-minded. He went there to observe."

As they moved toward the commons there was an edge of confrontation in the air, but no expectation of violence. Bill had earlier told his roommate that he didn't like the prospect of going to class under martial law. But as he and Gene walked past some Guardsmen, Gene said, "I hope none of those guys have itchy fingers," and it was Bill who reassured him. "Don't worry about it. They don't even have clips in their rifles."

They mingled in the rally, along with some 1,000 other students, most of whom shared their frame of mind—curious and a bit angry, but not outraged. "Nobody seems to understand," a student said later, "we just wanted the Guard off our campus. They were making everything worse." The metallic voice of the Guard bullhorn ordered the rally to disperse. Rights of assembly were suspended, it declared, authoritatively, anonymously. "A jeep came up toward us. They kept telling us to disperse. We just scattered and in the confusion I momentarily lost sight of Bill," Gene recalls. "The kids were strung out all over the area."

A cluster of students soon collected, shouting "Pigs off campus" at the Guard. Some of them, perhaps no more than 20, lobbed stones and the Guard responded with tear gas. Students hurled canisters back. The Guard ran out of tear gas and, confronted by a skirmish line of several hundred students, drew together to regroup. Bill was standing about 100 feet from the Guardsmen, between them and the main body of students, when the Guardsmen opened fire. According to Gene, Bill wasn't shouting at the Guard or throwing rocks at them.

Gene, like the others around him, hit the ground. "Some girls had fainted. I looked over and saw a girl lying on the ground. She wasn't moving. It looked like Allison [Allison Krause, one of the four students who died]. I didn't really know her but she went out with a guy down the hall from me. A beautiful, happy girl. Then my roommate came running down the hill shouting at me, 'Do you know who they shot?' I said I think they shot Allison. 'No. They shot your buddy.' I ran up the hill and three people were around Bill. A crowd had gathered and then people moved away to give him room. He was alive and was able to speak. He just said, 'Where's an ambulance?' His voice was weak, like a whisper. An ambulance was nearby but it took another injured student away. About 10 minutes later one came for Bill. As they put him on the stretcher, he moved his leg up to help them. When they drove away I didn't even think he was hurt that bad." Ten hours later the university news service issued a statement: "Schroeder, Wm. K., 19, sophomore, DEAD. Five minutes after arrival."

Tuesday morning, after the National Guard had ordered everyone off campus until further notice, Bill Schroeder's housemates on Franklin Street prepared to leave for home. A group of them came out on the front porch and refused to allow anyone to enter the house. "Don't use our names," one said. "Just say we were a family and one of us was killed."

One of them, who identified himself as Bill's roommate, had known him since junior high school in Lorain and lived a block from his home. Monday night he had gone to the county morgue to make a positive identification of Bill. "We did everything together. Took walks, played basketball. Bill was good at everything he tried. He had a mind, I mean a real mind." Their high school principal said the same. Bill had an A-minus average at Lorain Senior High School and had the highest rating in every attitude category from citizenship to attendance. At Kent State his average was B-plus. "He wanted to get into psychology," his roommate said. "He liked it here. We would spend a lot of nights together just talking, sometimes to 4 or 5 in the morning. He told us once that he really wanted to be a writer. He's been writing poetry for the last few years but he'd always hide it."

The boy spoke haltingly, unable at times to control his trembling. "Make sure you say one thing if nothing else. Say that Bill was not throwing rocks or shouting at the Guardsmen. It would have never crossed his mind to do that. He was there watching it and making up his own mind about it and they shot him." Then Bill Schroeder's friends went back into the house and began packing his clothes.

17

Kent state: how it happened

*The President's Commission
on Campus Unrest*

Blanket Hill is a grassy knoll in the center of the campus of Kent
State University, named by students who use it as a place to sun
themselves in the day and to romance at night. From here, shortly after noon on a sunny spring day, a detachment of Ohio
National Guardsmen, armed with World War II-vintage army
rifles, fired a volley of at least 61 shots killing four college students and wounding nine.

Kent State University is a state-supported school with some
20,000 students, more than four-fifths of them graduates of Ohio
high schools. Its main gate is only four blocks from the center of
the business district of Kent, a city of some 30,000.

Compared with other American universities of its size, Kent
State had enjoyed relative tranquility prior to May 1970, and its

From *The Report of the President's Commission on Campus Unrest*
(Washington: Government Printing Office, 1970).

student population had generally been conservative or apolitical. Under state law, the university must accept any graduate of an accredited Ohio high school, and five out of six Kent State students are from Ohio, mostly from Cleveland and Akron, from the steel towns of Lorain and Youngstown, and from small rural towns. They are predominantly the children of middle-class families, both white collar and blue collar, and in the main go on to careers as teachers and as middle-level management in industry.

On the night of Thursday, April 30, President Richard M. Nixon announced that United States troops were being ordered into Cambodia.

Kent State President White did not hear President Nixon's speech. When his wife told him about it later, he had a "sinking feeling," he said. Downtown, in the North Water Street bar area, slogans denouncing the Cambodian action were being painted on walls. Many students viewed the move as a shocking reversal of President Nixon's announced policy of withdrawal from Vietnam and as an aggressive action which flouted widespread antiwar sentiment in the United States.

The first disturbance began Friday evening on North Water Street, a downtown area where six bars, popular with young people, are located. Some of these bars feature rock bands. The sale of 3.2 beer to persons 18 or older, and of liquor to 21 year olds, is legal in Kent. Because several surrounding counties prohibit the sale of beer or liquor, the Kent bars draw young people from as far as 50 miles away in addition to Kent State students.

May 1 was one of the first warm Friday nights of the spring. A sizable crowd of young people, some of whom were discussing Cambodia, gathered in and around the bars. About 11:00 p.m., they began to jeer passing police cars.

Kent's small police force had fewer than 10 men on duty when the disturbance began. Four of these men in two patrol cars were specifically assigned to North Water Street.

The crowd grew increasingly boisterous. They began to chant slogans, and a motorcycle gang called the "Chosen Few" performed some tricks with their bikes. Shortly before 11:30 p.m., someone threw a bottle at a passing police car. The Kent city police ceased efforts to patrol the street and waited for reinforcements from the day shift and from other law enforcement agencies.

Some of the crowd, which had grown to about 500, started a bonfire in the street. Soon the crowd blocked the street and began to stop motorists to ask their opinion about Cambodia.

One motorist accelerated when approached, narrowly missing people standing in the street. This incident, according to witnesses, angered bystanders. Shortly thereafter a false rumor that black students were "trashing" on campus circulated among the crowd.

Some demonstrators began to break store windows with rocks. A few items were stolen from the display windows of a shoe store and a jewelry store. A fertilizer spreader was taken from a hardware store and thrown through the window of a bank. In all, 47 windows in 15 establishments were broken, and two police officers were cut by thrown missiles.

At 12:30 a.m., after the trashing had begun, Kent Mayor LeRoy M. Satrom declared a state of emergency and ordered the bars closed. The assembled force of city police and sheriff's deputies then moved to clear the street, which became even more crowded as evicted patrons poured out of the bars.

Between 1:00 and 2:00 a.m., a force composed of 15 Kent city police and 15 Portage County deputies used tear gas to force the student crowd out of the downtown area, up East Main Street for several blocks, and back onto the campus through the main gate at Lincoln and East Main streets.

City police, who would not enter the campus, and students faced each other over the border of the campus, and a virtual stand-off developed. A freak automobile accident on Main Street is generally credited with dispersing the crowd.

An electrical repairman was standing on his truck repairing a traffic light in front of Prentice Gate. A car hit the truck, knocking the scaffold from beneath the repairman and leaving him hanging onto the traffic light above the pavement. His odd predicament completely captured the attention of the crowd. They drifted away quietly after he was rescued.

Fifteen persons, all with Ohio addresses, were arrested that night, most of them on charges of disorderly conduct.

The disturbance on North Water Street angered and frightened many merchants and left the city administration fearful that it did not have enough manpower available to keep order. On the next day, these circumstances were to lead to the calling of the Ohio National Guard.

Many of the students who were in the crowd on North Water Street were there only because the bars were closed. Some were disgruntled because they had paid cover charges to hear rock bands and then had to leave before they felt they had had their money's worth.

The pattern established on Friday night was to recur throughout the weekend: There were disorderly incidents; authorities could not or did not respond in time to apprehend those responsible or to stop the incidents in their early stages; the disorder grew; the police action, when it came, involved bystanders as well as participants; and, finally, the students drew together in the conviction that they were being arbitrarily harassed.

The ROTC building was an obvious target. It was a two-story wooden structure—an old World War II-type Army barracks—and it looked easy to ignite. Many students saw it as evidence that the university supported the Vietnam war effort by maintaining a military training program on campus.

About 8:10 p.m. [Saturday evening], a few students began to throw rocks at the ROTC building. In a short while, flying rocks had broken some of the building's windows. A few in the crowd appeared to have brought bags of rocks to the scene. A group used an ash can as a battering ram to break in a window: some started throwing lighted railroad flares into and onto the building. A curtain caught fire. In the crowd, someone burned a miniature American flag. A student taking pictures was attacked and wrestled to the ground, and his film was taken and exposed. Professor Frank said that when he intervened in the student's behalf, he was grabbed from behind. Frank was saved from further attack only when recognized by one of his students. Finally, a young man dipped a cloth into the gasoline tank of a parked motorcycle. Another young man ignited it and set the building afire. The building began to burn about 8:45 p.m.

The mood of the part of the crowd nearest the ROTC building was one of anger. "I have never in my 17 years of teaching," said Frank, "seen a group of students as threatening or as arrogant or as bent on destruction as I saw and talked to that night." Faculty marshals did not intervene.

Many spectators behaved around the ROTC fire as though they were at a carnival. Only a dozen or so persons appeared to have made active efforts to set the building afire, and another two or three dozen threw stones, but many others cheered and shouted with glee as the building was destroyed and sat on the hills surrounding the Commons to watch the conflagration.

One student protested the burning of the ROTC building, telling his fellows, "You can't do this." He was shouted down. A faculty marshal who feared that the student was in danger of physical injury led him from the area.

About 9:00 p.m., a truck from the Kent fire department arrived. No police protection was provided. Members of the mob grabbed the hose from the firemen. They slashed and stabbed the hose with pocket knives, an ice pick, and a machete. They threw rocks at the firemen, who then withdrew.

When the building was burning furiously and live ammunition was exploding inside, the campus police appeared. The police fired tear gas at the crowd, which then left the ROTC building area and moved across the Commons to the tennis courts. Some students bent down the strong metal fence around the courts.

About 9:30 p.m., near the tennis courts, a small shed which was used to store archery equipment was set afire. Flames shot up from the shed and threatened nearby trees. Students hurried into buildings, filled wastebaskets with water, and put out the fire.

Aware of the turmoil on campus, Mayor Satrom had called General Del Corso's office at 8:35 p.m. to renew his request for troops.

At 9:30 p.m. Generals Del Corso and Canterbury arrived in Kent. As their troops were pulling into town, the flames from the burning ROTC building lit up the horizon.

The generals went to city hall and were briefed by Mayor Satrom. Del Corso then dispatched one detachment of guardsmen to prevent students from entering downtown Kent and sent another detachment to protect firemen who were returning to the burning building. As a Guard unit rode down East Main Street, it was stoned by persons hiding among trees.

The National Guard cleared the campus with dispatch, using tear gas freely. Some students had to spend the night in dormitories other than their own because the cleanup was so quick and emphatic.

When a group of faculty marshals wearing blue armbands attempted to identify themselves as guardsmen approached, the guardsmen knelt in a skirmish line and pointed rifles at them. Abandoning explanations, the marshals fled.

The university had made no effort beforehand to prepare the students for the possibility that the Guard might come to the campus. Administration officials had met with student leaders several times during the day, but the discussions were confined to the subject of dances and other diversionary social events. There was no discussion of what might happen if another disorder occurred—a subject administrators discussed only among themselves or with city officials.

President White and his wife were at the home of his sister-in-law in Mason City, Iowa, all day Saturday. After repeated telephone conversations Saturday morning with his aides in Kent, he called for the Kent State airplane to be sent to bring him back to his troubled campus. He took off for Ohio early Sunday morning.

As the ROTC building burned, the pattern of the previous night was repeated—authorities arrived at the scene of an incident too late to apprehend the participants, then swept up the bystanders and the participants together in their response. Students who had nothing to do with burning the building—who were not even in the area at the time of the fire—resented being gassed and ordered about by armed men. Many students returning to campus on Sunday after a weekend at home were first surprised at the Guard's presence, then irritated when its orders interfered with their activities. Student resentment of the Guard continued to grow during the next two days.

At 10:00 a.m. Sunday, while Kent State President White was on his way home from Iowa by plane, Governor Rhodes arrived in Kent and held a news conference.

After referring to recent disturbances at two other Ohio universities, Governor Rhodes said:

We have the same groups going from one campus to the other and they use the universities state-supported by the state of Ohio as a sanctuary. And in this, they make definite plans of burning, destroying, and throwing rocks at police and at the National Guard and at the Highway Patrol.

"We are going to eradicate the problem," Governor Rhodes said. "We are not going to treat the symptoms."

Rhodes described the troublemakers as

worse than the brown shirts and the communist element, and also the night-riders and the vigilantes. They are the worst type of people that we harbor in America. And I want to say this—they are not going to take over the campus and the campus now is going to be part of the county and the state of Ohio. It is no sanctuary for these people to burn buildings down of private citizens, of businesses in the community, then run into a sanctuary. It is over with in the state of Ohio.

Many persons felt that the governor had spoken firmly and forthrightly. Others felt that his remarks were inflammatory and worsened an already tense situation. Some, including many Kent students, believed the governor was hoping that his words and actions at Kent would win him additional votes in the primary election, to be held two days later, for nomination to the United States Senate.

After the governor departed, widespread uncertainty regarding rules, prohibitions, and proclamations remained. Many people were unsure about what was to be legal and what not, particularly with respect to rallies and demonstrations.

On Sunday afternoon, the campus was generally quiet, and many students felt the worst was over. Sightseers visited the ruins of the ROTC building, and some students conversed with guardsmen.

Students began gathering on the Commons about 8:00 p.m. The crowd was peaceful and included a group of coeds kicking a soccer ball around. But by 8:45 p.m., it had grown so large that campus police and the Highway Patrol suggested to Colonel Finley that the 1:00 a.m. campus curfew be cancelled and an immediate curfew imposed. As a result, shortly before 9:00 p.m., Major Jones read the Ohio Riot Act to the crowd on the Commons and gave them five minutes to disperse. When they did not, police proceeded to disperse them with tear gas. One group headed toward President White's house, another toward Prentice Gate. .

The students were driven away from White's home by tear gas. At Prentice Gate, there was a more serious confrontation. A sizable crowd sat down in the intersection of Lincoln and Main, next to the gate, and asked to speak with Satrom and White about six demands: abolition of ROTC; removal of the Guard from campus by Monday night; lifting of the curfew; full amnesty for all persons arrested Saturday night; lower student tuition; and granting of any demand made by the BUS [Black United Students].

An unidentified young man who was permitted to use the police public address system told the crowd that Mayor Satrom was coming to discuss their demands and that efforts were being made to contact President White. (John Huffman, Matson's executive assistant, later said he had just told the young man specifically that White was not coming.) The young man said that if the students would move out of the street, the guardsmen at the scene would reciprocate by moving off campus. Both the Guard and the students did in fact withdraw slightly.

At 11:00 p.m., police were told that the two officials would not talk to the demonstrators. The Riot Act was read to the crowd, and Colonel Finley told them the curfew was in effect as of 11:00 p.m.

The students, previously nonviolent, became hostile. They felt that they had been double-crossed. They cursed the guardsmen and police and threw rocks at them. Tear gas was fired and the crowd ran back from the gate across the campus lawn.

During the confusion of the dispersal, two students were bayoneted and sustained minor cuts. Three guardsmen received cuts and bruises from thrown stones and a wrench.

With tear gas, guardsmen drove one group of about 300 young persons across the campus to the Tri-Towers dormitory area. A helicopter had been hovering over the Prentice Gate sit-in. Its spotlight illuminated the scene, following the students as they ran. Its wash increased the effective of the gas along the ground. Among the fleeing Kent State students was Allison Krause.

Another group of students ran to the Rockwell Memorial Library, the building closest to the gate, and climbed through windows to get inside. A coed was reportedly bayoneted as she attempted to climb through a window. Some of the library windows were broken by rocks. The night guard locked the doors, sealing the students inside. They were later given a 45-minute grace period to leave the building and return to their dormitories.

Fifty-one persons were arrested Sunday night, most of them for curfew violations. They brought the total of arrests to more than 100 since the disturbances had begun.

Despite the day's promising start, the situation at Kent State had appreciably worsened by Sunday night. Students were more resentful of the Guard as a result of what they considered to be broken promises at Prentice Gate. The university was anxious to restore normal conditions, and law enforcement officers and guardsmen seemed to be growing more impatient with student curses, stones, and refusals to obey.

[On Monday,] as they lined up opposite students on the Commons shortly before noon, the three National Guard units involved in the Kent State shooting had had an average of three hours of sleep the night before.

Throughout the morning, guardsmen patrolled the campus without notable incident. About 11:00 a.m., students began gathering on the Commons, apparently for a variety of reasons. Some had heard vaguely that a rally would be held. Some came to protest the presence of the Guard. Some were simply curious, or had free time because their classes had been cancelled. Some students stopped by on their way to or from lunch or class. The Commons is a crossroads between several major university buildings.

Many students who described themselves as "straight," or conservative, later attributed their presence at the rally to a desire to protest against the

National Guard. This attitude was reflected in the testimony of one Kent State coed before the Commission:

I just couldn't believe that my campus had been taken over by Guards. You know, they said I couldn't cross the campus, they said we can't assemble on the campus. I stood on the Commons. I was watching the Guards and thinking, they are telling us to leave, but this is our campus, we belong here and they don't. That is why I stayed mostly.

This coed was gassed on the Commons, moved back over Blanket Hill to the Prentice Hall parking lot, and was within three feet of Allison Krause when Miss Krause was killed.

A Kent State policeman, Harold E. Rice, stood near the ROTC ruins and, using a bullhorn, ordered the students to disperse. It is doubtful that Rice was heard over the noise of the crowd. A jeep was brought up. Rice, a driver, and two Guard riflemen drove out across the Commons toward the crowd. Rice gave the dispersal order again.

The students responded with curses and stones. Some chanted "Pigs off campus" and "One, two, three, four, we don't want your fucking war." Rocks bounced off the jeep, and Rice said the occupants were hit several times.

At 11:58 a.m., as the jeep returned, Canterbury ordered the 96 men and seven officers to form a skirmish line, shoulder to shoulder, and to move out across the Commons toward the students. Each man's weapon was locked and loaded. Canterbury estimated the size of the crowd on the Commons at about 800; another 1,000 or more persons were sitting or milling about on the hills surrounding the Commons. His goal as he moved out was to disperse the crowd.

The guardsmen generally felt that the students, who had disobeyed numerous orders to disperse, were clearly in the wrong. The razing of the ROTC building had shown them that these noisy youths were capable of considerable destruction.

Many students felt that the campus was their "turf." Unclear about the authority vested in the Guard by the governor, or indifferent to it, some also felt that their constitutional right to free assembly was being infringed upon. As they saw it, they had been ordered to disperse at a time when no rocks had been thrown and no other violence had been committed. Many told interviewers later, "We weren't doing anyting."

The guardsmen marched down the east slope of Blanket Hill, across an access road, and onto the football practice field, which is fenced in on three sides. The crowd parted to let them down the hill to the field and then reformed in two loose groups—one on Blanket Hill, above the football field, and the other in the Prentice Hall parking lot at the north end of the field. The crowd on the parking lot was unruly and threw many missiles at guardsmen on the football field. It was at this point that the shower of stones apparently became heaviest. Nearby construction projects provided an ample supply of rocks.

Tear gas canisters were still flying back and forth; after the Guard would shoot a canister, students sometimes would pick it up and lob it back at the guardsmen. In some cases, guardsmen would pick up the same canister and throw it at the students. Some among the crowd came to regard the situation as a game—"a tennis match" one called it—and cheered each exchange of tear gas canisters. Only a few students participated in this game, however. One of them was Jeffrey Glenn Miller. A few minutes later, Miller was fatally shot.

As the confrontation worsened, some students left the scene. Among those who departed was a student who had gone to the rally with a classmate, William Schroeder. Subsequently, Schroeder was killed.

While on the football field, about a dozen guardsmen knelt and pointed their weapons at the students in the Prentice Hall parking lot, apparently as a warning or a threatening gesture. Whether any shot was fired on the field is in dispute.

After the guardsmen had been on the football field for about 10 minutes, Canterbury concluded that his dispersal mission had been sufficiently accomplished. He ordered his troops to retrace their steps back up Blanket Hill. He also thought—wrongly—that his men had exhausted their supply of tear gas.

The Guard's march from Blanket Hill to the football field and back did not disperse the crowd and seems to have done little else than increase tension, subject guardsmen to needless abuse, and encourage the most violent and irresponsible elements in the crowd to harass the Guard further.

As the guardsmen withdrew from the field, many students thought either that they had run out of tear gas or that there was nothing more they could do in their strategically weak position. Many felt a sense of relief, believing all danger was over. Most expected the Guard to march back over Blanket Hill to the ROTC building.

Some students grew more aggressive. A small group of two to four dozen followed the Guard closely. Some came as close as 20 yards, shouting and jeering and darting back and forth.

Many witnesses said that during the Guard's return march the intensity of rock-throwing appeared to diminish. The witnesses also said that most rock-throwers remained so far away from the guardsmen that most of their stones fell short, but several guardsmen were hit and some rocks bounced off their helmets. Other student witnesses said the rock-throwing never slackened, and some say it grew heavier as the Guard mounted the hill.

Near the crest of Blanket Hill stands the Pagoda, a square bench made of 4-by-4 wooden beams and shaded by a concrete umbrella. The events which occurred as the Guard reached the Pagoda, turned, and fired on the students, are in bitter dispute.

Canterbury, Fassinger, and Jones—the three ranking officers on the hill—all said no order to fire was given.

Twenty-eight guardsmen have acknowledged firing from Blanket Hill.

Four persons were killed and nine were wounded.

As the shooting began, students scattered and ran. In the parking lot behind Prentice Hall, where two were killed and two were wounded, students dove behind parked cars and attempted to flatten themselves on the pavement. On the slope east of Taylor Hall, where four were wounded, students scrambled behind a metal sculpture, rolled down the incline, or sought cover behind trees. The scene was one of pell-mell disorder and fright.

Many thought the guardsmen were firing blanks. When the shooting stopped and they rose and saw students bleeding, the first reaction of most was shock. Jeffrey Miller lay on the pavement of an access road, blood streaming from his mouth.

Then the crowd grew angry. They screamed and some called the guardsmen "murderers." Some tried to give first aid. One vainly attempted mouth-to-mouth resuscitation on Sandra Lee Scheuer, one of the fatalities. Knots of students gathered around those who had fallen.

[Dead or dying were:]

Sandra Lee Scheuer, 20, a junior, is believed to have been on her way to a 1:10 p.m. class in the Music and Speech Building when she was struck. She has not been identified in any available photographs as having attended the prohibited noon rally on the Commons.

Allison B. Krause, 19, a freshman, was among the group of students gathered on the Commons by the Victory Bell shortly before noon. After her death, small fragments of concrete and cinder block were found in the pockets of her jacket.

Jeffrey Glenn Miller, 20, a junior, was present in the crowd on the Commons when the dispersal order was given and made obscene gestures with his middle fingers at guardsmen. He also threw back a tear gas canister at the Guard while it was on the football practice field.

William K. Schroeder, 19, a sophomore, was an ROTC cadet. A photograph shows him retreating up Blanket Hill from the rally on the Commons, but he is not shown taking part in any of the harassment of the Guard.

At the moment of the firing, most of the nine wounded students were far beyond a range at which they could have presented any immediate physical threat to the Guard.

18

Bloody Attica

*New York State Special
Commission on Attica*

Forty-three citizens of New York State died at Attica Correctional Facility between September 9 and 13, 1971. Thirty-nine of that number were killed and more than 80 others were wounded by gunfire during the 15 minutes it took the State Police to retake the prison on September 13. With the exception of Indian massacres in the late 19th century, the State Police assault which ended the four-day prison uprising was the bloodiest one-day encounter between Americans since the Civil War.

In attempting to answer the first major question presented by its mandate—why did Attica explode—the Commission was presented with no lack of explanations.

Correction personnel and some older inmates tended to take a conspiratorial view of the uprising, calling it the work of left-wing

From New York State Special Commission on Attica, *Attica: The Official Report* (New York: Bantam 1972), excerpted from pp. 104–330. Some material has been transposed in order to amplify selected parts of the report's summary.

radicals and "troublemakers" among the inmate population and insisting that it was planned in advance.

No less pat are explanations found in the blossoming literature of the "prisoners' liberation" movement. Those partisans would be the last to dispute the conclusion that the uprising was spawned "for political reasons." But they would glorify the prison rebels as heroes and place the blame squarely on the political and economic system against which the uprising was, in their view, directed. "The realization is growing, especially in the black community," wrote one such advocate, "that prisoners are the real victims of this society. One must look outside the prisons for the criminals." According to that thesis, revolts such as Attica "will recur so long as men and women are put behind bars for disobeying the inhuman laws of the society and struggling against its inequities—that is, as long as capitalism remains intact."

Contrary to these popular views, the Attica uprising was neither a long-planned revolutionary plot nor a proletarian revolution against the capitalist system.

Attica happened at the end of a summer marked by mounting tensions between inmates and correction officers, but also by rising expectations and improving conditions. Attica was no longer the jim crow institution it was even in the early sixties. Prison discipline had become more relaxed. The courts had responded to inmates' complaints and begun to order limited reforms. And the new Commissioner had liberalized rules and was promising new programs, new facilities, and a a new attitude, toward inmate problems.

But the new Attica was increasingly populated by a new kind of inmate. Attica, like most of our prisons, had become largely a black and Spanish-speaking ghetto, and the new inmate was shaped by the same experiences, expectations, and frustrations that culminated in eruptions in Watts, Detroit, Newark, and other American cities. The young inmate was conscious of the changes in attitudes in the black and Puerto Rican communities, on the campuses, in the churches, and in the antiwar movement. The increasing militancy of the black liberation movement had touched him. Names like Malcolm X, George Jackson, Eldridge Cleaver, Angela Davis had special meaning to him.

The new inmate came to Attica bitter and angry as a result of his experiences in the ghetto streets and in the morass of the criminal justice system. Very likely, he already did, or would soon, see himself as a "political prisoner"—a victim, not a criminal. For all its changes, Attica was still a prison, the very symbol of authoritarianism, and in the summer of 1971, it was caught up in an era of decline and rejection of authority.

Many inmates came to believe that they were "political prisoners," even though they had been convicted of crimes having no political motive or significance. They claimed that responsibility for their actions belonged not to them—but to a society which had failed to provide adequate housing, equal educational opportunities, and an equal opportunity to compete in American life. Believing themselves to be the victims, not the aggressors, they claimed that the public should concentrate its efforts on rehabilitation of society and not of them. To them, such prison programming and job training as existed did no more than prepare them for a submissive role in a racist and unfair society.

There were many men in Attica in 1971 who held the view that they were victims of society. They must be distinguished, however, from the small group who, like Samuel Melville, were totally committed to a firm political ideology of revolution. Melville had been convicted of bombing public buildings for political purposes. The bond between these two brands of self-proclaimed political prisoners was their common rejection of established authority and their denunciation as barbaric of the wages, programs, hygiene, medical care, censorship, and other conditions at Attica.

In contrast to this new breed of inmate were the older inmates—black, white, and Spanish-speaking—who had come to accept prison conditions: they made few demands upon the officials, proclaimed at most their innocence, but not society's guilt, kept their frustration and anger to themselves, and accepted the word of the guards as law. Many who were interviewed by the Commission expressed deep antagonism toward younger inmates who were not prepared to "do their own time," and insisted on defying authority.

The older inmate may have remembered when prison conditions were worse, but the improvements made no impression on the younger one. It did not matter to the younger inmate that he was not required to move in a lockstep shuffle; that he was not required to work 12 to 14 hours a day; that he had a makeshift handball court and a basketball hoop and television in his exercise yard; that there was a prison library and commissary for his use. To the young inmate, it was enough that he was still a faceless number in a silent formation of marching men; that he was assigned to meaningless, unpleasant work details for reasons of administrative efficiency having nothing to do with rehabilitation; that for many months of the year his exercise yard was buried in four feet of snow; that he was entitled to only one shower a week in all seasons of the year; that he was paid, on the average, 25¢ a day for his labor, half of which officials saved for his release, and was expected to buy his own cigarettes and toiletries from his wages; and that he saw a correction staff that did not include one black or Puerto Rican officer and that exhibited the same "remember your place and do as you're told" attitude that his people had been rebelling against for the last decade. The new inmate was not about to submit to these conditions simply because he had been convicted of a crime.

Attica's all-white correctional staff from rural western New York State was comfortable with inmates who "knew their place," but unprepared and untrained to deal with the new inmate, much less to understand him. Unused to seeing their authority challenged, officers felt threatened by the new inmate. Viewing the recent relaxations of rules and discipline, the intervention of the courts, and the new programs for inmates, they felt that their authority was being undermined by Albany and that their superiors were not backing them up. The officers became increasingly resentful and insecure. The result was, inevitably, daily confrontations between the new inmate and the old-style officer.

The Commission discussed the problem of the new inmate and the "political prisoner" with more than 200 of Attica's correction officers. Their responses varied from understanding to racist interpretations of inmates' complaints. But one theme stood out above all others and made any meaningful meeting of minds between inmates and correction officers almost impossible: "These men are not in here for missing Sunday School," said one officer. Another exclaimed, "No one comes here for just playing jacks on the sidewalk." An inmate's very presence at Attica was regarded as sufficient evidence that he had voluntarily forfeited, by his own actions, many of the rights the new inmate insists upon retaining. In speaking of the rights of prisoners, correction officers often turn the question to the rights of their victims. "They cry about their rights," correction officers say, "but what about the rights of their victims? Did they worry about the rights of the man they killed or the woman they raped?" The inmate who refused to regard himself only as a criminal simply could not relate in any meaningful, constructive manner with a prison staff that could not regard him as anything else.

Thus, correction officers frequently found themselves demanding adherence to rules which inmates would not accept. As the number of confrontations increased during this period, so did the intensity. An officer's orders to stop talking, for example, were first questioned, later ignored, and finally ridiculed.

Moreover, inmates challenged one of the oldest codes of the maximum security prison: "Do your *own* time." Inmates demanded the right to gather and form associations for religious and political purposes. Finding strength in numbers, many new inmates joined organizations which stressed ethnic identity, such as the Muslims, the Black Panthers, the Young Lords, and the Five Percenters.

"Now, one inmate's trouble was everybody's trouble," explained one officer. Although not overtly threatened, officers who singled out an inmate for discipline began to find themselves acutely and uncomfortably aware of the hostile glares of many inmates. Instead of retreating from a confrontation, inmates realized they could intimidate many officers simply by standing fast. They soon learned that they could communicate their hostility and their resentment and their unacceptance merely by their silent, ominous presence together. The politics of confrontation had come to prison.

The confrontations were accompanied by increasing societal awareness among inmates and the growth of organizations inside the institution determined to spread the consciousness and try to make changes. Groups such as the Muslins, Black Panthers, and Young Lords gained adherents and held meetings, but quarrels and rivalries among them and their leaders prevented them from coming together in concerted action.

Largely as the result of these groups' efforts, discussion groups began in the exercise yards. By the summer of 1971, an inmate-instructed sociology class in the school had become an informal forum for ideas about effecting change. There was, finally, a series of organized protest efforts at Attica in the months prior to September 1971. Some had moderate success, but others ended only in the discipline of participants. The reaction of the authorities became increasingly one of isolating and transferring suspected "ringleaders" and "troublemakers."

An inmate manifesto setting forth a series of moderate demands, and including a commitment to peaceful change, was sent to the Commissioner and the Governor in July 1971. The Commissioner responded with an acknowledgment and with a [promise to visit] Attica early in September. In the intervening eight weeks, tensions at Attica had continued to mount, culminating in a day of protest over the killing of George Jackson at San Quentin, during which few inmates ate at lunch and dinner and many wore black armbands. The inmates had demonstrated their ability and their willingness to act en masse, and there was now some talk about organizing a prisonwide sit-down strike. When Commissioner Oswald's visit produced nothing more than a taped speech promising future changes and asking for patience, the stage was set. No one really expected a violent take-over of the prison, but few at Attica thought the summer would pass without a major incident.

How It Happened

The initial explosion on Thursday, September 9, came in reaction to an incident the previous day which provoked anger and resentment among inmates in two companies in A block. A misunderstanding in the exercise yard on Wednesday afternoon led to an unusually intense confrontation between officers and inmates, during which a lieutenant was struck by an inmate. The officers were forced to back down, but that evening, two inmates were removed from their cells to HBZ, precipitating angry name-calling, hurling of objects from cells, and vows of revenge along the two galleries.

The following morning, uneasiness lingered on in one of the two companies, comprised largely of inmates considered "difficult" by the administration. An inmate who had been locked in his cell for throwing a soup can at an officer the previous evening was released from his cell by fellow inmates. After breakfast, a lieutenant who had been involved in the incident on Wednesday approached the company as it was lined up in A tunnel on its way back from breakfast. He intended to try to persuade the inmates to return to their cells, but as he reached them, he was attacked, and the uprising was underway.

After an initial outburst of chaotic violence, rebellious A block inmates regrouped and set upon the locked gate at Times Square, which separated A block from the rest of the institution. A defective weld, unknown to officers and inmates alike, broke and the gate gave way, giving the rioters access to the center square and the keys which unlocked the gates in three directions. From Times Square, inmates from A block spread throughout the institution with little resistance, attacking officers, taking hostages, destroying property. As the rebellion reached other areas, some inmates joined in actively, but the majority tried to escape to secure areas, or were simply caught up in the tide.

The authorities were slow in responding, due largely to the absence of a riot control plan, the lack of available manpower, and an antiquated communications system. Connected with other parts of the prison only by single-line telephones, those in the administration building could not appreciate the full extent of the trouble, or summon help, until it was too late. By 10:30 A.M. the inmates had obtained control of four cellblocks and all of the yards and tunnels, and 1,281 inmates had gathered in D yard with over 40 hostages. Only then did the rudiments of organization begin to appear, with leaders of preexisting groups, inmates well versed in law, and other natural leaders among the inmates emerging as spokesmen. Most of those who took an active role in organizing the yard, drafting demands, and, later, negotiating with the state, had not been involved in the initial outbreak of violence and did not join in it when the rioters reached their area of the prison.

Was It Planned?

The Commission has found no evidence that the Attica uprising was planned, either by avowed revolutionaries or anyone else. All of the objective evidence, especially the course the uprising actually took, points in the other direction.

To begin with, if a take-over was planned, it would not have been planned to commence in an enclosed area, such as A tunnel, where access to the rest of the prison was presumably sealed off by iron gates. The mess halls or exercise yards, where there were concentrations of inmates, were more logical choices. The company which started the violence had just come from the mess hall, where hundreds of other inmates were present, had passed through Times Square, where the keys to four corridor gates were kept, and had seen the Times Square gates locked behind them, all without incident. A planned rebellion, even if the planning were limited to that company, would surely have been touched off before the moment the inmates were confined to A tunnel, with no immediately apparent avenue of escape and no guarantee of access to the rest of the institution.

No one could have anticipated that the Times Square gate would give way. Had it held, as everyone expected it would, the uprising would have been limited to A block and A yard—where at that hour fewer than 300 inmates and 10 correction officers were located. Before the gate broke, the A block rebels called to inmates trapped in other corridors to join in the uprising, but their entreaties fell on deaf ears.

Only after the totally fortuitous failure of the Times Square gate were the rebels able to get the keys to other gates and gain access to the metal shops, where they obtained tools, acetylene torches, and an electric truck for use in breaking through still more gates. Had an uprising been planned, inmates in other areas of the prison would surely have been alerted to begin hostile action before the rioters from A block reached their areas. In fact, however, no violence erupted, no damage was done, and no hostages were taken anywhere in the institution until inmates who had broken into Times Square arrived. Even then, most inmates just did their best to stay out of the way. Significantly, most of the inmates who were later to emerge as leaders and negotiators in D yard were not part of the first wave of violence and destruction.

The rioters did not take over the prison according to any rational plan. After the initial flare-up, before times Square fell, there was a 10-minute lull during which A block inmates hurriedly gathered sports equipment and broom handles, broke up benches in A yard, and fashioned makeshift masks from bed sheets. During this lull, some inmates retrieved crude weapons from old hiding places. But the quick emergence of homemade weapons is no indication of advance planning, since inmates in prisons everywhere keep such weapons hidden for self-protection or "just in case."

After the violence had subsided and the hostages were taken, the inmates continued for at least an hour to act in a manner inconsistent with the idea that there were any preexisting plans. They raided the commissary and officers' mess in helter-skelter fashion, not at first stockpiling supplies or preserving them for future use. Before the commissary could be completely stripped of food, it was set on fire and destroyed. Once the metal shops were entered and over 20 hostages taken, fires were set and the inmates deserted the shops, leaving behind large quantities of volatile materials, tools, metal scraps, and machines that could be used for making weapons.

When the uprising broke out, only one correction officer and two civilians were on duty in the powerhouse, control of which would include the capacity of cutting off the electricity in the entire institution. Yet, inmates never made a concerted effort to take over the powerhouse. Even when they all reached D yard, there was a long period of chaos and internal bickering among inmates before organization emerged.

The lieutenant who had first been struck in A tunnel told the Commission that while he was hiding in an A block cell, he heard an inmate somewhere in A block shout, "Squad 1, go to your area, Squad 2, go to your area." To him, and others at Attica, this was a strong indication of preexisting inmate organization and planning. No similar reports were received from other sources and, in months of investigation, the Commission was never informed of the existence of inmate "squads."

It is unclear exactly when the remark was heard, but it may well have been a considerable time after the initial flare-up, when the beginnings of inmate organization were emerging. Then, too, it is clear that tightly disciplined organizations, such as the Muslims, did exist at Attica and that they attempted soon after the uprising began to make some order out of the chaos. A group of Muslims, operating in A block, were responsible for protecting and releasing several injured officers that morning. Throughout the four-day uprising, the Muslims were always well disciplined and continued to protect the hostages from harm. The commands overheard by the lieutenant may well have been a part of that discipline. Standing alone, his report does not constitute persuasive evidence that the uprising was planned.

The Commissioner's Decision

[Commissioner of Correctional Services] Oswald had warned [Governor Nelson Rockefeller] in May 1971 that prison unrest was increasing, "fomented and exacerbated by internal and external revolutionary political activities which were increasingly zeroing in on the criminal element in our society."

The Governor viewed the Attica rebellion as another step in an ominous world trend. As he told the Commission:

... one of the most recent and widely used techniques of modern-day revolutionaries has been the taking of political hostages and using the threat to kill them as blackmail to achieve unconditional demands and to gain wide public attention to further their revolutionary ends. I have followed these developments with great interest and considered that, if tolerated, they pose a serious threat to the ability of free government to preserve order and to protect the security of the individual citizen.

Therefore, I firmly believe that a duly elected official sworn to defend the constitution and the laws of the state and the nation would be betraying his trust to the people he serves if he were to sanction or condone such criminal act by negotiating under such circumstances.

In the handling of the Attica uprising, the Governor found that these views conflicted with his belief in delegation of responsibilities to the department heads he had selected. Despite his own convictions against negotiating with the holders of the hostages, the Governor chose not to overrule the man whom he had named and he supported Oswald's decision to attempt a negotiated settlement.

When Oswald informed the Governor that he was prepared to accept the 28 Points, the Governor backed him up with the assurance that he would recommend the legislation contemplated by the Points.

The Governor stood firm, however, on one matter—he told Commissioner Oswald that even if he had the power to grant amnesty, which he and his counsel agreed he did not have—he would not grant it as a matter of principle. The Governor drew a sharp distinction between amnesty, which he considered a "political" objective not negotiable with the holders of hostages, and penal reform promised in the 28 Points, which he testified Oswald "had in mind anyway."

Moreover, the Governor, with his concern that "revolutionaries" were playing a major role in the Attica uprising, concluded that [a personal visit to the scene by him] would be exploited by those "who were not interested in seeing the settlement or seeing a reform, but who wanted to drag this out, preserve the theater for worldwide coverage relating to revolutionary forces."

From the outset, the Governor perceived the Attica uprising as more than a prison riot. The uprising constituted an insurrection against the very authority of the state, and to tolerate it was to concede a loss of sovereignty over the rebels.

Sooner or later, the state's paramount interest in restoring order would have to be asserted. That point was really reached on Saturday night, when a settlement based on the 28 Points was rejected by the inmates. Despite the frantic efforts of Sunday, Oswald's attempt to avoid the use of force to end an uprising had, as the Governor testified, "proven to be a failure."

The decision to retake the prison was not a quixotic effort to rescue hostages in the midst of 1,200 inmates; it was a decisive reassertion of the state of its sovereignty and power. While all state officials were concerned about the safety of the hostages, they had finally reached the conclusion that, after four days of negotiations, the need to reassert the authority of the state over the rebels outweighed the risks of an assault.

Many inmates still believed, when the helicopters first appeared over D yard on Monday morning, that the balance of power was controlled by hostages, not guns. They failed to realize that once the state decided that the rebellion was no longer tolerable, the lives of the hostages were expendable.

Officially, the decision to commence the assault was made by Oswald as the official in charge of all correctional facilities, and authorized and approved by the Governor. In fact, the decision was inevitable once the negotiations seemed hopeless.

19

Civil disorder and the agents of social control

Gary T. Marx

The number of popular and scholarly perspectives that can be brought to bear on the interpretation of civil disorder in the United States seems limited only by the breadth of one's imagination and reading. Some of the more prominent would undoubtedly include those that emphasize the increased radicalism of social movements as they evolve; the relevance of world revolutionary struggle; the importance of external warfare; limited political access of certain groups; various types of social and political frustration; conspiracy and agitation; the mass media; relative deprivation and heightened aspirations; our frontier tradition and history of racial and labor violence; lower class and criminal subcultures; and youthful, Hobbesian, biological or territorial man.

From Gary T. Marx, ed., *Muckraking Sociology,* New Brunswick, N.J.: Transaction Books, 1972, pp. 75–97. Reprinted by permission.

All of these perspectives focus on factors in the predisorder situation conducive to violence. Each also tends to correspond either to a particular left- or right-wing ideology. Thus conservatives tend to see disturbances as meaningless, irrational events caused by agitators who prey upon the degenerate character of the lower classes, while liberals are more likely to see them as spontaneous patterned protests caused by the deprivation of these same classes. One perspective, however, finds support among both the extreme left and right, and seeks the cause in the disturbance situation itself. This is the view which suggests that the police cause riots (though, to be sure, the Right blames the police for being too soft, while the Left blames them for being too harsh).

Unintended Consequences of Social Action

One justification for social research is that it goes beyond our common-sense views of the world. Robert Merton has suggested that an important task of social research is to point out the latent or unintended consequences of human action. For example, however corrupt early twentieth-century political machines were, they also helped the Irish and other immigrants to assimilate. Prostitution, whatever its moral implications, sometimes makes an important contribution to family stability. There are other cases with unintended consequences: propaganda designed to reduce prejudice may actually reenforce it; youth institutions may create juvenile delinquents who are later made into knowledgeable and embittered criminals by the prison system; mental hospitals may reinforce mental illness; welfare institutions may create dependency; and doctors sometimes injure or even kill patients.

In the same fashion a review of police behavior in civil disorders through the summer of 1967 suggests a number of instances in which the behavior of some agents of social control seemed to create as much disorder as it curbed. Some of the ways in which the behavior of various agents of control has had these unintended consequences are examined in this chapter.

As Park and Blumer and other researchers have noted, collective behavior has an emergent character. It involves elements that can't very well be predicted by a static consideration of conditions preceding the disturbance. Civil disorder involves a social process of action and counteraction. It is here that a consideration of police behavior is relevant.

I have found it useful to organize police behavior that was ineffective or seemed to create rather than control the disorders into the following three categories: inappropriate control strategies, lack of co-ordination among and within various control units, and the breakdown of police organization. I will be concerned primarily with police behavior up to the end of the summer of 1967.

Inappropriate Control Strategies

Crowd Dispersal.

In the spirit of Gustav Le Bon, it is sometimes assumed that crowds are uniformly like-minded, anarchic, irrational and hell-bent on destruction. From this it may follow that all people on the street are actual or potential rioters, that crowds must always be broken up, that a riot will not terminate unless it is put down, and that only a technical approach involving the use of massive force is adequate.

In all too many cases police are still following nineteenth-century methods; a riot manual of the period stated that "crushing power, exercised relentlessly and without hesitation is really the merciful, as it is necessary, course to be pursued." Police are often responsible for the initial crowd, which gathers when they respond to fairly routine incidents with a large number of squad cars with loud sirens and flashing lights. In some cities I studied the traditional strategy of dispersing the crowd had unanticipated consequences and served to escalate and spread disorder. The problem then shifted from controlling a crowd to coping with guerrilla-like hit-and-run activities.

While the initial formation of a crowd seemed to be an important factor in most disturbances I studied, it does not follow that crowds should always be dispersed, nor that when they are dispersed, force is the only means that should be used. While a crowd may encourage its members to lose some of their inhibitions, their anger may be heightened and released by precipitous police action.

In New Haven in 1967, for example, the crowd's mood was still tentative in spite of some initial minor violence. A small crowd walked down the street toward police lines. As the perimeter of the lines was reached, police fired three canisters of tear gas. The crowd then ran back, breaking windows and began seriously rioting.

According to a report on the 1964 Harlem riot, New York City's Tactical Police Force attempted to clear an intersection by swinging their clubs and yelling "Charge!" As they plowed into the crowd and broke it into smaller segments, "Hell broke loose in Harlem." The angry but until then peaceful crowd began pulling fire alarms, starting fires and beating up whites.

In Englewood, New Jersey, police efforts to force black bystanders into houses, whether or not they belonged to them, angered and sparked violence on the part of young men. In Rockford, Illinois, instances of rock and bottle throwing were inspired by police efforts to move a late-night bar crowd off the streets.

A peaceful rally protesting school practices in Philadelphia was violently broken up by the Civil Disobedience Squad using "riot plan number three." This elicited a violent response from the black youth. The Superintendent

and President of the School Board subsequently blamed the police for starting the riot.

Contrary to official riot control manuals (and usually the wishes of higher
authorities) as police encounter a crowd they may break ranks, raise their
night sticks above their shoulders and hit people on the head rather than the
body.

Beyond the issue of police provoking a hostile but as yet nondestructive
crowd to retaliatory violence or committing a symbolic act that serves as a
catalyst for the expression of the crowd's anger, the members of the crowd,
once dispersed, may do more damage than the crowd itself. Here an analogy
might be what happens when one beats a burning log to put out a fire, only
to see the sparks and embers scatter widely. Both the Milwaukee and New
Haven disorders were spread in this fashion. Scattered bands of rioters may
have presented police with a more difficult control situation than the original
crowd.

Failure to Negotiate

The treatment of disorder as a technical problem of law and order to be
solved only by force has meant that negotiations and the use of counterrioters were often ruled out. Such ironclad rules popular in many police
circles has completely obscured the variation in types of disorder. When the
disturbance seems apolitical, unfocused and primarily expressive, and is not
related to current issues or demands, and when there is no minimal organization among rioters and no one willing to take counterriot roles, authorities
may have no alternative—from their viewpoint—but the graduated use of
force. However, when the disturbance develops out of specific issues (the
demand for receiving promised jobs, a particular instance of police brutality,
discrimination by a business firm, disagreement over school policies and so
forth), when grievances and demands are clearly articulated, when there
seems to be some organization among rioters and actual or would-be spokesmen and potential counterrioters come forth, the disturbance may be stopped
or dampened by entering into a dialogue, considering the grievances, and
using counterrioters. To resort to force is more likely to inflame the situation
and increase the likelihood of future disorders.

The refusal to negotiate and use strategies other than a show of white
force may have had disastrous consequences in Watts. The director of the Los
Angeles Human Relations Commission had worked out a plan to send in
black plainclothes officers and antipoverty workers to make inconspicuous
arrests and spread positive rumors ("the riot is over") and to withdraw white
officers to the perimeter. Young gang leaders promised to use their influence
to stop the riot and were led to believe that the above conditions would be
met.

The Deputy Chief of Police rejected this proposal stating among other
things that he was not going to be told how to deploy his troops and that,

"Negro police officers are not as competent as Caucasian officers and the only reason for sending them in would be because they have black skins and are invisible at night." To the Director of the Human Relations Commission he said, "I don't want to hear anything you have got to say, you're part of the problem. *We know how to run a riot* and we are going to handle it our way." In response to the promises of gang leaders to stop the riot, he stated, "We are not going to have hoodlums telling us how to run the police department." And, "We are in the business of trying to quell a riot and we haven't got time to engage in any sociological experiments." Following his refusal a full-scale riot ensued.

All Blacks are Rioters

Just as it is sometimes erroneously assumed that all men at a gay bar are gay or all women standing on certain street corners at a particular time are prostitutes, so to the police any black person out on the street during a period of civil disorder may be suspect. In some cities, orders to clear an area and the panicky use of force (along with beliefs about the efficacy of getting tough) have resulted in indiscriminate abuse of anyone with a black face, including innocent bystanders, government officials, policemen in civilian clothes, ministers and Negro youth trying to stop the disorder.

Previous role relationships have an important effect on behavior in disaster situations. While collective behavior is essentially defined by the emergence of new, spontaneous norms, it nevertheless occurs within a context of ongoing familial, religious, economic, political and social relationships. In many cities the resources of the black community were effectively used in counterriot activities—quelling rumors, urging people to go home, and trying to channel indignation into less destructive protest.

During the summer of 1967, in some cities such as Tampa, Florida, and Elizabeth, New Brunswick and Plainfield, New Jersey, police were even ordered out of the disturbance area and local residents successfully patrolled the streets. The issue of whether or not police should be withdrawn is a complex one that far transcends the simplistic rhetoric of its opponents and supporters. While it was successful in the above cities, in several other cities it had the opposite effect. Counterriot sentiment was generally not counter-protest and in many cases represented considerations of strategy rather than principle. However, the *existence* of a sizeable reservoir of counterriot sentiment that can be activated in the place of, or alongside, other control activities is not really at issue. And motivation aside, failure to effectively use counterrioters may have prolonged a number of disturbances.

In Cincinnati, despite an agreement between the Mayor and black leaders that the latter would be given badges and allowed to go into the riot area to help calm things, police refused to recognize the badges and arrested some of their wearers on charges of loitering. A somewhat similar situation resulted in Milwaukee. In Newark the Mayor and Governor gave permission to Negro volunteers to go among the people to calm the situation. Their activities were inhibited by enforcement personnel. According to the Governor, they ". . . were chased around so much by people who suspected them as participating in the riot that they had to abandon their efforts."

Beyond the general confusion in the disorders and a racially inspired (if not racist) inability to differentiate among Negroes, police harassment was related to their view of the disorders as a technical problem to be met only by a show of force and their feeling that police competence and jurisdiction were being infringed upon. Because counterrioters were often black activists, and in some cases youthful gangs, their feelings may have been accentuated.

Official Anticipation

Thus far, I have considered disturbances that had a pattern of riotous or at least disorderly Negro behavior followed and sometimes encouraged by the official response. However, in other instances the dynamics of the disturbance worked in the opposite direction. Here authorities (with poor intelligence reports) precipitated confrontation by anticipating violence where none was imminent and by overreacting to minor incidents that happened to occur when a major riot was going on elsewhere.

While adequate planning and preparation are vital to effective control, they may help create a state-of-siege mentality, increase susceptibility to rumors, and exert a self-fulling pressure. This is particularly true when they are accompanied by a get-tough, act-quickly philosophy. Following the Newark riot, disorders broke out in 14 cities in the surrounding area, and after Detroit, eight additional Michigan cities reported disorders. An important factor in the spread of violence from major urban centers to outlying communities was the expectation of a riot and subsequent overreaction on the part of white authorities.

In New Jersey, a month and a half before Newark erupted, there were reports of planned violence, and counterplans were designed. On June 5, 1967, the police chiefs of more than 75 New Jersey communities met in Jersey City to discuss the supposed plans of militant blacks to foment violence. Jersey City, Newark and Elizabeth were reportedly given "triple A" ratings for violence over the summer. The authorities drew up plans to coordinate control efforts and rehearsed procedures for calling in the National Guard and state police. Riot control training was held in a number of communities.

When Newark finally erupted many officials found their expectations confirmed and they acted on their fears of anticipated local violence. In one New Jersey city officials reacted to the rumor that Stokely Carmichael was bringing carloads of black militants into the community, although Carmichael was in London at the time. In Jersey City 400 armed police occupied the black area several days before any disorders occurred. In Englewood, where police outnumbered participants three to one, black residents had earlier been angered by riot control exercises in which the wind blew tear gas into surrounding Negro homes. In Elizabeth, police greatly increased patrols in the black area and residents expressed opinions such as, "The community felt it was in a concentration camp." The appearance of armed police patrols increased the likelihood of confrontation and greatly strained relations with local Negroes. Whatever an individual's feelings about civil rights, having its neighborhood saturated with armed men in uniform in the face of minimal, sporadic or sometimes no disorders often created indignation. A frequent demand was for police withdrawal or a less visible show of arms. In six of seven New Jersey cities that had disorders at the time of Newark, removal of police from the ghetto signalled an end to violence.

Sniping

While much sniping was attributed to police and other control agents firing at each other, firecrackers and the snapping of broken power lines, response to the sniping that actually did occur was inadequate. Mass firing at buildings by men on the ground, who often used their private weapons, occurred, and an inadequate system of accounting for ammunition and lack of supervision by a superior officer all created havoc. Many innocent people were killed and wounded which helped to escalate the violence. Such firing in some cases created the very sniper fire it was supposedly trying to stop, as angry Negroes retaliated. In Detroit the fact that a policy of not shooting rioters was reversed without public announcement may have increased the death toll.

Lack of Coordination Among Control Units

In the face of major, unanticipated disorders involving a wide area and large numbers of people engaged in hit-and-run guerrilla-like tactics, decentralized, autonomous local police, organized primarily to fight crime, control traffic and keep the peace, were usually ineffective. The control of such disturbances requires training and actions that are almost opposite to those used in normal police operation. As a result, other control units differing in training, organizational structure, ethos and familiarity with the local area were often called in. Not surprisingly difficulties resulted.

The inability to admit failure, bureaucratic entanglements, petty rivalries and political considerations usually delayed the calling out of higher levels of force, and lack of prior planning and an unclear chain of command all meant further delays once other control agents finally did arrive on the scene.

Local, state and National Guard units did not merge easily. Guard units, accustomed to acting in patrols, were fragmented and guardsmen were isolated from commanding officers, while police used to working as one or two-man autonomous patrol units had to become disciplined members of military units relying on commands from superiors instead of their own discretion. While officers from different units were together, they often responded to separate orders. In Newark the three enforcement agencies were issued separate orders on weapons use.

Technical as well as social communication problems contributed to ineffective coordination of control activities and clearly furthered the disorders. Regular radio frequencies were heavily overtaxed, and local police, state police and the National Guard operated on different frequencies. Though this had been a problem two years earlier in Watts, little had changed by the time of Detroit and Newark. In the beginning stages of the latter riot, state police were unable to get a clear definition of riot perimeters or where activity was heaviest. They could not obtain information about the movement of local police patrols and were obliged to follow local police and fire trucks responding to citizens' calls. Inability to communicate was a factor in police and guardsmen firing at each other and in the belief in widespread sniping.

Poor communication within departments also had serious consequences. One reason the Los Angeles Police Department failed to employ sufficient manpower was the reluctance of subordinate commanders to expose themselves to ridicule and downgrading by possible overreaction. While the Los Angeles police possess some of the most skilled investigators in the world, trained to deal with master criminals, they could not get a true picture of what was happening in the early stages of Watts. Early on the third day of the riot, field forces knew the situation was out of control but the downtown command post was still optimistic. This is the classic problem of information flow in a bureaucracy. A highly professional department was unable to admit that a handful of what it considered hoodlums could create a major disturbance that it couldn't control.

In Plainfield, contrary actions by county and city police greatly inflamed the disorders. Plainfield was primarily a political disturbance, with meetings and negotiations between blacks and city authorities alternating with violence. At one such meeting, held under the auspices of community-relations personnel and with the understanding of city police, several hundred young men gathered in a county park to discuss their grievances and to choose leaders to represent them. During the meeting the violence greatly subsided. Peace was short-lived, however, as the assembly was abruptly broken up by county police who said they could not meet in the park without a permit. This incensed the young men. Within an hour violence flared and that night a patrolman was killed and the destruction reached its highest point.

Further conflict among different levels of authority emerged in Plainfield between the police and local and state officials. Police felt "left out," "tired" and "poorly treated" and threatened to resign *en masse* (and to some observers almost mutinied) after they were excluded from negotiations that led to the release of arrested rioters, the institution of a policy of containment following the killing of a fellow officer, and the termination (by a State official) of a house-to-house search for stolen carbines. The New Jersey riot inquiry felt that the circumscription of local police activities was such "as virtually to destroy the department's morale . . . (and) to limit seriously the effectiveness of the force."

In still other cases, as in Los Angeles, Boston and New York, agreements reached by the mayor's special representatives, human relations officials and police-community relations officers who had rapport with rioters were not honored by other policemen, creating great indignation and a sense of betrayal.

In Los Angeles, the police community relations inspector was reportedly not called into the inner circle of police advisors. The Chief of Police was unaware that his department had been represented at an important community meeting held during the riot.

A potentially ugly incident might have emerged in Detroit (May 21, 1968) when mounted police outside a building tried to drive supporters of the Poor People's March back into a building, while police on the inside were trying to drive them out.

In Rockford, Illinois, in 1967, as people poured out of bars that were closing, police tried to drive them off the street that other police had already barricaded.

In Birmingham in 1963 police circled several thousand blacks, on one side swinging their clubs and from the other side turning water hoses on them catching bystanders as well as protesters. This was no doubt all too well coordinated.

Breakdown of Police Organization: One Riot or Two?

An additional source of police ineffectiveness and abuse stems from the breakdown of organization within enforcement agencies.

In most discussions of riots undue emphasis has been given to the behavior of rioters. The normal concepts used to analyze collective behavior have been applied to them—emotional contagion, the spread of rumors, panic and the expression of frustration, the lessening of inhibitions, innovative behavior. Yet in several major disturbances, these concepts might equally be applied to the police. Police, lacking training and experience and often uncertain of what they were to do, sometimes became fatigued (frequently working 12-hour or more shifts with insufficient rest and little food). They were likely to be thrown off balance by the size of the disturbance and by being drawn frantically from one area to another, in some cases because of false alarms seemingly coordinated with attacks and looting. As large numbers of people taunt, defy, insult and attack them and they see their fellows injured and in some cases killed, patience thins and anger rises. Rumors about atrocities committed against them may spread.

Police may take violent black rhetoric and threats (which are partly related to expressive oral traditions, ritual posturing and political infighting) too literally; for few police are killed by snipers and there are reports that some snipers misfire on purpose. The lack of attacks on known racists certainly indicates this.

The belief may spread that they are in a war and all black people are their enemy. Traditional misconceptions about riotous crowds may contribute to an exaggeration of the dangers confronting them. And as police control of the "turf" is effectively challenged and rioters gain control of the streets by default, the word may spread (as in Watts, Newark, and Detroit) that rioters have "beat the police." Losing face, humiliated by their temporary defeat and with their professional pride undermined, police may have a strong desire for revenge and to recoup their "honor."

In a context such as the above, superior officers may lose the power to control their men. The chain of command and communication between and within enforcement agencies, often unclear to begin with, may completely break down. The most dangerous part of the disturbance is now at hand as the environment changes from riot to a war. Some police behavior seems as much, or more, inspired by the desire for vengeance, retaliation and "to teach the bastards a lesson" as by the desire to restore law and order.

The words of Lee and Humphrey, written shortly after the 1943 Detroit riot, are clearly relevant 26 years later. "War is to the army much what civilian outbreaks are to the police. Both offer socially acceptable outlets for the residuum of aggressiveness characteristic of each."

On the third day of the Detroit riot, an officer was overheard telling a young black on a newly stolen bicycle, "The worm is turning." And turn it did as the police took off their badges, taped over squad car numbers (this, of course, greatly reduced the number of complaints filed), and began indiscriminantly and excessively using force against rioters, bystanders and in some cases each other. The death and injury toll climbed rapidly. Some of the firing stopped only when control officials ran out of ammunition. At this time the Algiers Motel killings or "game" (from the perspective of involved police) occurred. According to an account by John Hersey, one of the police officers involved in this incident stated ". . . there was a lot of roughhousing, you know, everything just went loose, [following the killing of a police officer on the third day of the riot]. The police officers weren't taking anything from anyone." This would seem to be something of an understatement.

According to one high police official in secret testimony, by the fourth day of the riot "the police were out of control." There are some reports of police keeping looted goods taken from prisoners and robbing them, and of doing damage to "soul brother" stores spared by the rioters. Claims of brutality filed included charges of the mistreatment of women and the carving of initials on prisoners.

The chairman of the Newark Human Rights Commission reported that ". . . men were being brought in, many of them handcuffed behind their backs, being carried like a sack of meal, and the fifth policeman would be hammering their face and body with a billy stick. This went on time after time. Many times you would see a man being brought into the police station without a mark on his face and when he was taken out he was brutally beaten." It has been said in jest, although there is an element of truth in it, that Newark was a classical race riot except the Italians wore blue uniforms.

Police behavior often seems to become progressively worse as the disorders wear on. In Watts, Newark and Detroit this was partly related to the entrance of higher level control units into the disturbance. The assignment of Guardsmen to accompany policemen may be seen by the latter as offering a chance to reverse earlier humiliation and gain revenge for injury and death suffered by the police. At the same time, inexperienced Guardsmen, isolated from the authority of their commanding officers, may become subject to the same collective behavior phenomena as police and blacks, further adding to the disorder. Police may come to see rioters and suspected rioters, like those convicted of crimes, as having forfeited their civil rights.

The head of the Detroit police, a former reporter, was hesitant to call out the Guard. According to a report by Garry Wills, he said "I've been on too many stories where the guard was called up. They're always shooting their own people. . . . These poor kids were scared pissless; and they scared me."

What is especially tragic is that the symbols of police legitimacy become the cloak under which indiscriminate force is exercised upon the Negro community. It is a mistake to attribute such behavior only to the desire for revenge or a hatred of Negroes. Part of it would seem to be equivalent to the behavior of front-line soldiers who kill many of their own men in their first combat experience. That the breakdown of police organization transcends racism may also be seen in their response to student protests such as at Columbia Unversity and various antiwar demonstrations.

It is important to recognize that not only was police behavior in the latter stages of several major riots excessively brutal and probably ineffective, but that such acts were not idiosyncratic or random but were woven into a social fabric of rumor, panic, frustration, fatigue, fear, racism, lack of training and inexperience and the breakdown of police organization. While such a situation creates widespread fear in the Negro community and may inhibit some rioters, it can lead to (and partly results from) escalation in the level of black violence as the same social processes go on.

There is an interaction process and gradual reciprocal increases in the severity of action taken on both sides. The fact that police abuses were most pronounced in Newark and Detroit, where disturbances were the most serious, does not necessarily lend itself to a one-sided causal interpretation. Here we see the emergent character of the disorders. Just as the belief that blacks want to kill them spreads among police so it may spread among black people.

An additional element in the misuse of official force is the view held by some policemen that they can (and indeed must) "hold court in the street," given the presumed leniency and complexity of the legal system. Gathering evidence that will hold in court during mass disorders and demonstrations is difficult; those arrested can often be charged with nothing more than a misdemeanor; sentencing for riot offenses tends to be lighter than for similar offenses committed in nonriot situations. The use of violence in such situations may also be related to the policemen's effort to save face and their belief that respect for their authority must be reestablished.

Yet police in Japan and Britain have learned to cope with similar provocations. Even in the United States police overreaction is the exception rather than the rule. We simply don't hear about the large number of instances when police show professional behavior and restraint because they are not newsworthy. Unlike the more enduring problems of reducing the crime rate and eliminating corruption, this is one area where real change is possible if the police are given appropriate leadership, training and strategy.

The breakdown of police organization and the misuse of force has not happened to anywhere near the same extent in all cities that have had demonstrations and riots. An important question for analysis is why did this breakdown occur in the ghetto riots of Watts, Newark and Detroit—but not in Cincinnati or Boston? Why at the Chicago Democratic Convention but not at the counter-inaugural in Washington, D.C. where many of the same groups were involved? Why at Columbia and Harvard but not at M.I.T. or Dartmouth? Why at the People's Park in Berkeley but not at Woodstock? Given the immense number of factors involved and the variability of confrontations, the conditions under which such police behavior appears can never be exactly predicted. Yet it would seem to be related to some things which cannot readily be changed, such as the extent to which police disagree with, or are threatened by, the issues raised by protestors, whether police expect disturbance participants to be sufficiently punished by the legal system, the extent of injuries and provocation faced by police and the size and length of the disorders. Yet factors that *are* amenable to change may be even more important. Among them are training, the extent to which a flexible approach to crowds is used, that doesn't rely only on force and stresses communication between authorities and protestors and the right of peaceful assembly, the extent to which police share social characteristics with protestors, the clarity of orders stressing restraint, the general climate created by officials and the tightness of the police command structure. Other factors are whether civilian monitors and high-level government and police officials are on the scene, and whether it is made clear to police that they will be punished for misbehavior. Filming the scene and having names or numbers on helmets and sewn on uniforms might also increase accountability.

Quia Custodiet Ipsos Custodes?

A crucial question raised by some of this material is "Who controls the agents of social control?" One of the central intellectual problems for social analysts is the basis of social order. If one resolves the question of social order by relying on shared values and the internalization of standards then there may not be much of an issue. Yet even those who answer the question of social order by stressing the importance of external force usually ignore the problem of controlling the agents of control. In several major disturbances the tragic answer to the question of "who guards the guards" seemed to be "no one."

One of the manifestly unfair aspects of social organization is that those with official power are usually those (or are intimately tied to those) who possess the power to legitimately sanction the misuse of this power.

One means by which the police have traditionally been controlled is by the exclusionary rule of the courts, whereby illegal means used in acquiring evidence or making arrests are grounds for the dismissal of a case. However, this rule only has an effect when convictions are sought (a factor often beyond the control of the police). In addition many police abuses do not involve the gathering of evidence. The closeness of the police to the courts and their interdependence may inhibit the regulatory role of the latter, particularly at lower levels.

Individuals can also bring costly and time-consuming civil damage suits against the police, although those most likely to need redress may be least likely to have the resources necessary for a long court struggle—and establishing proof is difficult. The anonymity and confusion of a crowd situation and the tendency to remove badges makes identification of offending officials unlikely. In the rare cases where police are criminally prosecuted for riot offenses, juries tend to find in their favor. In most states National Guardsmen are granted immunity from criminal and/or civil liability.

Police have also been controlled through direct political means. The rise of "good government"-inspired civil service reforms and the decline of the urban political machine makes this less likely today. Most of the now-defunct Civilian Review Boards met with great police resistance, had no formal enforcement power and could not initiate inquiries.

The means of control favored by the police is self-regulation, in a fashion analogous to specialized professions such as medicine or law. It is argued that police work is highly technical and only those who practice it are competent to judge it. Internal review mechanisms have been inadequate to say the least; there is evidence to suggest that, like the rest of us, the police can resist anything but temptation. Knowledge that they are unlikely to be subjected to post-riot sanctioning may have lessened restraints on their use of violence. In many departments there is a strong norm of secrecy surrounding police misbehavior; even when known, infractions often go unpunished.

The consequences, costs and benefits of various means of regulating the police have not been carefully studied. It is clear from some of the data considered in this chapter and from more recent events such as the Chicago Democratic Convention, the People's Park episode in Berkeley and attacks on groups such as the Black Panthers that the control of the police is sometimes not much affected by the courts, various other checks and balances, internalized norms of fair play, nor internal police organization. The question of control and responsiveness of the police is certainly among the most pressing of domestic issues.

It has been often suggested that the most hideous crimes have been committed in the name of obedience rather than rebellion. In the Gordon Riots of 1780, demonstrators destroyed property and freed prisoners but evidently did not kill anyone, while authorities killed several hundred rioters and hanged an additional 25. In the Reveillon Riots of the French Revolution, several hundred rioters were killed, but rioters killed no one. Up to the end of the summer of 1967, this pattern was being repeated; police, not rioters, are responsible for most of the more than 100 riot deaths that have occurred. To an important extent this pattern stems not from differences in will, but from the greater destructive resources of those in power, from their holding power to begin with, and from their ability to sanction. In a related context, the more than 100 civil rights murders of recent years have been matched by almost no murders of racist whites. (Since 1968, this pattern may be changing.)

As long as racism and poverty exist American society needs relentless protest. It also needs police. It is increasingly clear that police are unduly scapegoated, stereotyped and maligned; they are, as well, often underpaid, undertrained, given contradictory tasks, and made to face directly the ugly consequences of the larger society's failure to change. It is equally clear that solutions to America's racial problems lie much more in the direction of redistributing power and income, eliminating discrimination and exploitation than in changing the police. Nevertheless, one important change called for in the Kerner Commission's plea to "end the destruction and violence, not only in the streets of the ghetto but in the lives of the people" is surely more enlightened police behavior.

part **VI**

Official deviance in regulatory and planning agencies

Several of our earlier readings have noted that current public concern with acts of official deviance and corruption has increased proportionately to the mass media coverage of the more dramatic events, such as the Kent State and Attica killings, the Watergate hearings, and the congressional hearings on CIA and FBI abuses of power. Although all of these are of great importance to those of us interested in usurpations and abuses of political power, even when they are taken together, their consequences probably do not exceed those of the less dramatic, but more pervasive, forms of official deviance. Abuses of power occur routinely within the administrative, regulatory, and planning agencies charged with carrying out official policies. The appearance of new kinds of official deviance also cannot be overemphasized. We have had to be very selective in our choice of readings and have presented only four chapters which deal with these concerns. The magnitude and significance of official deviance within regulatory and planning agencies, however, is very great indeed, and, in all likelihood, it will become even greater in the future.

Political scientists have been the only ones to study the activities of regulatory agencies in any depth, and there is a large body of literature on this subject. Sociologists have conspicuously ignored these agencies. But, just as one of the most consistent findings of sociological studies has been that bureaucratic agencies tend toward autonomy over time, political scientists have found that regulatory agencies become "captured" over time by the interests of those they are supposed to regulate. These findings are analyzed in the chapters that follow. In Chapter 20, Justice William O. Douglas provides us with an excellent account of how the Army Corps of Engineers has evolved to the point where it serves primarily its own ends. Chapter 21 presents an excerpt from the Knapp Commission Report which studies the connections between construction industry leaders in New York City and the political officials charged with controlling them. According to the Knapp Commission findings, "Corruption is a fact of life in the construction industry." In other words, we, as citizens and consumers, must subsidize corruption in the form of higher costs of government, higher construction costs, and the amplification effect these have in inflationary prices and wages. In Chapter 22, "HUD's Bonanza for Suburbia," Al Hirshen and Richard Le Gates provide us with a similar account of one of our federal agencies. Finally, in "Lethal Smokescreen" (Chapter 23), Associated Press reporter Dan Berger gives us an excellent description of the political shenanigans of the Federal Aviation Administration (FAA) and the aviation industry. Berger's chapter is especially noteworthy because he shows how federal regulations, originally issued to serve the FAA's definition of the public interest—in this case, the saving of air passengers' lives—not only resulted in higher consumer prices (which all of us would favor to achieve that goal) but actually *endanger* passengers' lives.

20

The public be dammed

Justice William O. Douglas

"The Army Corps of Engineers is public enemy number one." I spoke those words at the annual meeting of the Great Lakes Chapter of the Sierra Club, early in 1968; and that summary supplied an exclamation point to a long discussion of the manner in which various Federal agencies despoil the public domain.

It is not easy to pick out public enemy number one from among our Federal agencies, for many of them are notorious despoilers and the competition is great for that position. The Tennessee Valley Authority, for example, like the Corps of Engineers, has an obsession for building dams, whether needed or not. Its present plan to wipe out the Little T River and its fertile valley is rampant vandalism. TVA is also probably the biggest strip miner in the country, using much coal for its stand-by steam plants. The sulphuric acid that pours out of strip mines, running downstream waters, is TVA acid.

The Bureau of Mines sits on its hands in Washington, D.C., pretty much a captive agency of the coalmine owners, and does precious little about strip mining.

The Public Roads Administration has few conservation standards; it goes mostly by engineering estimates of what is feasible and of cost. In the Pacific Northwest, it has ruined 50 trout streams through highway design. Everywhere—East and West—the Administration aims at the heart of parklands, because they need not be condemned, and plays fast and loose with parts of the public domain that were reserved for wildlife and outdoor recreation.

The list is long; and when the names of Federal agencies are all in, the balloting for public enemy number one will not be unanimous. But my choice of the Army Engineers has a powerful case to support it.

The Corps is one of our oldest Federal agencies. It is small and elite, highly political and very effective. It is honest and, with exceptions I will note, quite efficient. It is also largely autonomous and inconsiderate of the requirements of conservation and ecology.

There has been a recurring effort to get rid of it. The Hoover Commission Task Force on Water Resources and Power recommended in 1949 that the functions of the Corps and the Bureau of Reclamation be transferred to the Secretary of a proposed Department of Natural Resources and consolidated there in an agency to be known as the Water Development Service. The training provided "in peacetime for the 215 Army engineers at present utilized on this civilian program can surely be secured in some far less costly fashion."

In 1966, Senators Joseph S. Clark, Lee Metcalf and Frank E. Moss sponsored a bill that would have turned the Department of the Interior into a Department of Natural Resources and transferred the Corps to that new department. But the power of the Corps is so strong that that bill died in committee. Indeed, Senators and Congressmen who are so bold as to urge that the Army Engineers be abolished find themselves wholly out of favor when it comes to projects for their states.

At the time of the Hoover Report, the budget of the Corps was about $440,000,000 a year. It is now 1.3 million dollars and is expected to reach three billion dollars in the 1980s. So the Corps shows no sign of diminishing political influence.

Its specialty is in pork-barrel legislation on the Hill. It commonly outmaneuvers the President and has its way, irrespective of his wishes. The Corps gave F.D.R. one of his soundest political thrashings. The Corps also has few public critics; it has become one of the sacred cows of Washington.

The Corps farms out many of its research and development projects. There is hardly a Federal agency in Washington that is not offered a piece of it in amounts from $200,000 to $400,000 or more a year. Federal bureaucrats love that kind of money, for they do not have to depend on Congress for it. There is a rule of thumb in Washington that 15 percent of an amount obtained in an appropriation is used for permanent overhead. That means that if agency A receives $500,000 for research on siltation, water purification, or what not, it uses $75,000 to add to its permanent personnel and the rest for the current annual project. But agency A, like the other agency donees who receive funds from the Corps, is anxious to have a similar amount, year after year. Therefore, never do they raise their voices against ill-conceived projects; never, when the Corps is throwing its weight around and the public is protesting, do these Federal agencies align themselves with the people.

In the late Fifties, I was a member of a group of conservationists fighting the Corps on the high River Bend Dam on the Potomac River. The dam was virtually useless as a power project and of no value for flood control. Its justification was the creation of a head of water that could be used to flush the polluted Potomac of sewage. Some of the huge Federal agencies were silently opposed; but none would speak up, for fear of losing the Corps' good will and its research and development funds. We ended by getting an independent engineering study that actually riddled the project. That dam—which would have flooded 80 miles of river and shown a drawdown of 35 vertical feet—would have been known in time as the nation's greatest folly. It would have despoiled a historic river; and the 35-foot vertical drawdown would have resulted in several hundred yards of stinking mud flats exposed to public view. Yet the Corps had the nerve to get a public relations outfit to make an estimate as to the millions of tourists who would be drawn to this ugly mudhole from all over the East.

The Engineers gave up on River Bend and offered an alternative of an upstream dam at Seneca for water power. Public hearings exposed its destructive qualities. It, too, would ruin a beautiful free-flowing river. Moreover, there was a growing awareness that dams for municipal water are unnecessary along the Potomac; for the estuary in front of Washington, which is 20 miles long and moved by the tides, contains billions of gallons of potable water, which is all the water the metropolitan area will ever need.

At the peak of its promotional activities along the Potomac, the Corps has plans for 16 big dams and 418 small ones. How many were actually discarded? I do not know. But their active promotion of Potomac river dams has shrunk from 434 to 6. Those six are for water for metropolitan use—a needless expenditure, because of the ample supply of estuary water.

The estuary water is polluted, but so is the entire Potomac. Why not expend our energies and fortunes in building sewage disposal plants, not dams that put fertile bottom lands under muddy waters from now to eternity and drive thousands from their homes?

As I said, the Corps sometimes turns out to be mightier than the Commander-in-Chief, the President of the United States.

Franklin D. Roosevelt tried to draw the lines of authority governing the Corps quite sharply: If a project was primarily concerned with navigation or flood control, then the Army Corps of Engineers had jurisdiction; if, however irrigation and power were the dominant features of the project, then the Bureau of Reclamation would be in charge. The matter came to a head in 1944, when the Kings River project and the Kern River project—both part of a development program for California's Great Central Valley—were before Congress. Roosevelt was firmly on record as having said, "I want the Kings and Kern River projects to be built by the Bureau of Reclamation and not by the Army Engineers."

But the Corps had its way before both the House and the Senate. Roosevelt countered by directing the Secretary of War to make no allocation of funds nor submit any estimate of appropriations without clearing the matter with the Bureau of the Budget. F.D.R. provided funds in his new budget only for the Bureau of Reclamation respecting these projects. But before the budget cleared the House, the Army Engineers got included in the budget funds for initial work on the projects.

F.D.R. signed the bill reluctantly, saying he would ask Congress to transfer jurisdiction over all these Central Valley projects to the Department of the Interior. Then he died and Truman took over the problem. The maneuvering against Truman was long and involved. In time, the Corps had pretty much its own way (A) by taking the stump against the White House in California to elicit the support of greedy landowners who wanted the benefit of irrigation without paying the costs as provided by law, and (B) by lobbying in Congress.

Every President has known something of the freewheeling nature of the Corps and its tendency to undercut the White House and curry favor with its friends on the Hill. Early in 1968, it was busy dodging the Bureau of the Budget on six Potomac dams and making its own recommendations to Congress. L. B. J., probably the dearest friend the Corps has had, tried to keep the Engineers in line. But the Corps is incorrigible, violating the fundamental principle that while an administrative agency is the creation of Congress, it must report through the Chief Executive, in order for a centralized, coordinated plan of administration to be successful. Even though the President advises that a Corps project is not in accord with White House policy, the Corps transmits its report to Congress anyway, sometimes, though not invariably, including in the transmittal a statement of the President's position. In this sense, the Corps is *imperium in imperio*, enjoying a status no other administrative agency has.

The Corps goes way back in our history, the present one dating from March 16, 1802. It is a small, elite group of officers, not many over 200 in number. But it supervises over 40,000 full-time civilian employees.

The permanent staff of civilian employees obtains its pay *only* when there is some public-works program to which the salary can be charged. That is why every civilian member is eager to suggest, initiate or create a role for the Corps that will keep everyone employed. In time of war, the Corps has military assignments, but its essential work over the years is concerned with civil functions. The Chief of Engineers is responsible to the Secretary of Defense regarding his civil duties and does not report to the Chief of Staff nor to any general. Actually, the Corps in operation is largely independent of the Secretary.

The committees of the House and Senate through which it operates are the Public Works committees. The inception of a Corps project starts with the Congressman or Senator representing the district where the project will be located. What member of Congress does not want $10,000,000 or, preferably, $100,000,000 coming into his district? He therefore tries to get the item included in an omnibus bill authorizing a preliminary examination. Once that is done, the preliminary examination may or may not be made. The appropriation is in a lump sum and there is usually not enough to make all the investigation authorized. So the Corps, at its own discretion, decides which has priority.

The Corps finally obtained by an act of Congress special permission to spend up to $10,000,000 on any project without approval by Congress, provided the project has been approved by resolutions adopted by the Senate and House committees. This is an advantage shared by no other Federal agency; and it is a measure of the rapport between Congress and the Army Engineers. Moreover, it gives the Corps a tremendous momentum. Once $5,000,000 or $10,000,000 is spent on a project, the pressure to get on with it and finish it is tremendous.

A member of Congress who is in good with the Corps will receive favors; those who may have been critical of it will be kept waiting. The game is boondoggling played for high stakes by clever, cunning men.

There are few members of Congress who do not early learn the lesson that an obsequious attitude pays off when it comes to pumping millions of dollars into a district that may save an election for a deserving Democrat or Republican but destroy a lovely free-flowing river.

The Corps operates in part through NRHC, the National Rivers and Harbors Congress. Five of the 21 directors are members of Congress. Ten are national vice-presidents. The all-important operative committees are, with one exception, chaired by members of Congress. At its annual meeting, the National Rivers and Harbors Congress decides which rivers and harbors projects it should present to Congress and then the Congressional members change hats and go to work lobbying one another.

One who is in a campaign opposed to the Corps has very few important allies. I remember the Buffalo River in Arkansas and the Saline River in the same state—both destined by the Army Engineers to be destroyed as free-flowing rivers. The Buffalo I knew well, as I had run it in canoes and fished for bass in shaded pools under its limestone cliffs. Much of the land bordering the Buffalo is marginal wood-lot acreage. Those who own that land were anxious to sell it for a song to Uncle Sam. Chambers of commerce blew their horns for "development" of the Buffalo. Bright pictures were drawn of motels built on the new reservoirs where fishing would abound and water-skiing would attract tourists.

The Corps has introduced Arkansas to at least 14 such river projects that buried free-flowing streams forever under muddy waters. The fishing is good for a few years. Then the silt covers the gravel bars where bass spawn and the gizzard shad—a notorious trash fish—takes over.

The people are left with the dead, muddy reservoirs. There is electric power, to be sure; but Arkansas already has many times the power that it can use. So why destroy the Buffalo? Why destroy the Saline?

What rivers are there left where one can go, camp on a sandpit, and rid himself of the tensions of this age? These are questions people are beginning to ask. And these questions eventually won over enough of the Arkansas delegation to save the Buffalo—at least temporarily—but the Saline is still in jeopardy.

Down in Kentucky last year, my wife and I led a protest hike against the plans of the Corps to build a dam that would flood the Red River Gorge. This gorge, which is on the north fork of Red River, is a unique form of wilderness that took wind and water some 60,000,000 years to carve out.

This is Daniel Boone country possessed by bear, deer and wild turkey. It has enough water for canoeing a few months out of the year. It is a wild, narrow, tortuous gorge that youngsters 100 years from now should have a chance to explore.

The gorge is only about 600 feet deep; but the drop in altitude in the narrow gulch produces a unique botanical garden. From March to November, a different wild flower blooms every day along the trails and across the cliffs.

This is wonderland to preserve, not to destroy.

Why should it be destroyed?

Flood control has been brought into the story; but it is a makeshift, for flood control could be achieved with a dam farther downstream that would preserve the gorge. The same can be said for water supply. The real reason: recreation. The Corps and promoters of the dam say that the reservoir will attract tourists who will spend their money in motels, lodges and boat docks. That's the way the dam was sold to the local people, who naïvely expect to get rich by the influx of tourists.

And so Red River Gorge was preserved when Senator John Sherman Cooper of Kentucky and Governor Lottie B. Nunn proposed an alternative plan to save the gorge by putting the dam farther downstream. The Corps, minding its politics, accepted the proposal; and the names Cooper and Nunn have become revered by the Sierra Club and all other conservationists for that move.

(Army Engineers now have plans for the big south fork of the Cumberland in Kentucky. It is one of the very best white-water canoe rivers we have left. It is a wild, unspoiled waterway running through uninhabited lands; and those who know and love it are now mustering their forces for another great contest.)

The Corps is an effective publicist. After my wife and I led the protest march against the Red River Gorge project, we flew back to Washington, D. C. that night. The next day was Sunday; and that morning, every paper I saw had a wire-service story saying that we had been driven out of Kentucky by 200 armed men who did not want "a senile judge" telling them how to run their affairs. It was not until two days later that the conservationists had their statement ready for the press.

The most alarming thing is the very number of dams proposed by the Corps. One of our wild, wild rivers is the Middle Fork of the Salmon in Idaho—a 100-mile sanctuary that should be preserved inviolate like the Liberty Bell. White sandpits make excellent campsites. The waters so abound with trout that barbless hooks should be used. Mountain sheep look down on the river from high embankments. Deer and elk frequent the open slopes. When I ran that scenic river and returned to Washington, I discovered that there were dams planned for the Middle Fork.

The most recently outraged citizens are the Yuki Indians of Round Valley, California. The Corps dam on the Eel River will flood the historic "Valley of the Tall Grass." But what difference do 300 Indians make? "Progress" must go on until we are all flooded out.

The problem with dams is that they silt in: Mud, carried to the dam by its source waters, settles in the reservoir and accumulates steadily. In time, the silt completely replaces the water. The Corps faces this prospect everywhere. Some dams in Texas lose eight percent of their capacity annually due to silting. Numerous ones lose two percent a year and at least six lose three percent or more. Most of those I examined were not Corps dams; but its Texas dams suffer the same fate. Once a dam is silted in, there is no known way to remove the silt and make the dam useful again.

The Waco Dam in Texas is a classic failure of the Engineers. Inadequate testing of the foundation shales below the embankment was the cause of the disaster. Parts of the embankment slid 700 feet from the dam axis. Correcting the failure amounted to about four percent of the original estimated cost of the dam.

The Corps has been embarrassed by hush-hush dams that are so leaky that the waters run under—not over—the dams. This failure is due to gypsum beds that underlie the reservoirs, a mineral that seems to baffle the dam builders and causes them to fall into all kinds of traps.

One conservationist, in speaking of a dam that carried water under, not over it, said rather whimsically, "This may be the perfect solution. The Corps and the Congressmen get the dam constructed, the money pours into the district, yet the river valley is saved. We should encourage gypsum bases for all Corps dams."

But the two dams where the water ran under—rather than over—have now been fixed. So the hope to make them monuments to the folly of the Engineers has vanished.

The trend is ominous. The Corps expects by 1980 to flood new areas about the size of Maryland (6,769,280 acres).

I mentioned how the Engineers planned to build a dam on the Potomac to flush the river of sewage. That is by no means the sole example. The Oakley Reservoir on the Sangamon River in Illinois has been proposed to create a huge reservoir that will wash the river of sewage from Decatur on downstream. The trouble is that a reservoir large enough will inundate Allerton Park, a unique bottom land owned by the University of Illinois where valued research in biology and ecology goes forward.

The Corps has curiously become one of our greatest polluters. It is dedicated to the task of dredging channels in rivers and in the mouth of harbors so that vessels can get in and out. These days, the bottoms of channels are not mud but sludge formed from sewage and industrial wastes. The Corps takes these dredgings and dumps them into Lake Michigan. In fact, the lake is used as a dumping ground for 64 separate dredging operations. There was a public uproar in 1967 and 1968 and hearings were held. Lake Michigan is going the way of Lake Erie, which has become a big bathtub full of stinking waste material. Lake Erie is dead; and it is feared that Lake Michigan is on its way.

The dredging of estuaries has had a similarly shocking effect. A third of San Francisco Bay—or 257 square miles—has been filled in or diked off and is now occupied by homes, shopping centers and the like. Oyster production is ended; so is clam production; only a minimal amount of shrimp production remains. There are 32 garbage-disposal sites around the shores of the Bay. Eighty sewage outfalls service the Bay. Daily, over 60 tons of oil and grease enter the estuary, the cradle of the sea. The Army Engineers are not responsible for the pollution; but they are responsible for the dredging. The National Sand and Gravel Association has the estuaries marked for billions of tons of sand and gravel for the next 30 years. The Corps issues dredging permits; and ten years of dredging, according to the experts, makes an estuary a biological desert.

But the Corps has no conservation, no ecological standards. It operates as an engineer—digging, filling, damming the waterways. And when it finishes, America the beautiful is doomed.

The ecologists say that estuaries are 20 times as productive of food as the open sea. An estuary has been called a "nutrient trap." Being shallow, it is exposed to the energy of sunlight. Rooted plants of the land and drifting plants of the sea commingle. Thick beds of grasses, sea lavender, bulrushes and cattails provide hiding areas, as well as food, for minute forms such as diatoms and for young fish, clams, mussels and oysters as well. Indeed, it is estimated that two-thirds of our ocean catch has been estuary dependent for part of its life. The reality is that by the year 2000, California will not have a single running river to the ocean. What will be left, for example, of San Francisco Bay will be dead salt-water sewage.

The Corps seems destined to destroy our esturies. The estuarine areas of our coast line have distinctive features. South of Boston are salt marshes where flounders spawn and grow to a size that permits their exit to the ocean. Down in Florida, the estuaries attract many species of commercial and sport fish and the valuable pink shrimp as well. The shrimp breed there and the young stay in the estuary until they are large enough to risk the Gulf. And so it goes from estuary to estuary. The estuaries have one thing in common—a balance between fresh water and salt water. Once the fresh water dries up and salinity increases, the estuary is avoided entirely by some species and used by the remaining species for a lesser time.

The results are revolutionary. The birds that are dependent on these sloughs for their feed must leave. The wood ibis, for example, which nests in the mangroves of Florida and feeds on the teeming estuarine life, flourishes when the annual flow of fresh water is 315,000 acre feet or more and does not nest successfully when the flow is less than that amount. Some dominant water-fowl foods—notably chara and naiad—tolerate only mild salinity. They have all but disappeared in Coot Bay in the Everglades, as a result of a Corps canal. With the elimination of those foods, the number of waterfowl in Coot Bay has declined more than nine tenths.

The Cape Fear River development is now booming along in North Carolina. In 1934, the Corps reported that flood control was not justified in the lower Cape Fear basin. In 1947, after a disastrous flood, it again reported that no dam was justified. In the 1960s, the Engineers have been saying that Cape Fear flood control is essential. They add that if flood control is not needed, a dam or a series of dams will make great recreational areas. The principal rivers feeding the main reservoir are the Haw and the New Hope, both heavily polluted. The estimated cost will be $72,000,000 plus. Residents of the valleys where 35,000 acres of choice lands will be taken are much opposed. Those are farm units handed down from generation to generation and greatly loved. It is tragic to hear them talk about the conversion of those gorgeous acres into a gigantic cesspool for raw sewage on which enthusiastic tourists are destined, it is said, to shout with joy.

Since 1936, Federal investment in flood protection, largely through Corps activities, has amounted to more than seven billion dollars. Despite this massive investment, flood damages (according to the President's Task Force that reported in 1966) have been as much as ten times what they were in 1936. The Corps approach is purely an engineering approach. What is needed are conservation standards that regulate land use and reduce the risk that land will be so used as to accentuate run-offs and actually imperil property and lives because of man's grotesque ways of despoiling the earth. But these are no concern of the Corps. It exists to turn rivers into sluiceways and to raise the height of levees, so that man's misuse of the land may be borne by all the taxpayers. The report of the President's Task Force is a severe indictment of the Corps' mentality and techniques in dealing with water.

The disease of pouring money into sluiceways and levees is a pernicious one. The Army Engineers dredge channels, build levees and erect dams. Getting a man off heroin is easy compared with getting Congress off the kind of pork barrel the Corps administers. On July 30, 1968, Congress approved a one-and-a-quarter-billion-dollar appropriation for the civil activities of the Army Engineers. Forty-seven states were included. Texas, as might be expected, was granted 24 projects for construction during fiscal year 1969 that amounted to almost $40,000,000. Everybody is taken care of: under the cloak of flood benefits, recreation benefits and the like, great vandalism is committed. Beautiful river basins are wiped out forever and one of our most pressing problems—water pollution and sewage—goes begging.

The Everglades National Park in Florida is a unique national treasure. It lies in a shallow limestome bowl not higher than 12 feet above sea level. Its life-blood is the gentle, persistent flow of fresh water from the northern part of Florida, mostly the overflow from Lake Okeechobee. The biological and botanical life of the Everglades is intricate and amazing. The lowly gambusia fish and the alligators are the key, the gambusia feeding on mosquito larvae and starting the food chain for 150 species of fish that, in turn, nourish the alligator. The alligator wallows and forms the mudholes where this chain of aquatic life is maintained. Moreover, within the Everglades are 95 percent of all of our remaining crocodiles.

The birds come to nest and to feed on fish—white-crowned pigeons, white ibis, herons, roseate spoonbills, wood ibis, swallow-tailed kites, great white pelicans, millets, black-necked stilts, boat-tailed grackle, the anhinga. The most vulnerable of all fish is the bass that is dependent on the oxygen in the water. So when there is a drought, bass die by the hundreds. Since the garfish and the bowfin surface to get oxygen, they survive droughts somewhat better. But severe droughts kill everything; and the Corps, with no conservation standards, is the greatest killer of them all.

The park has 47 species of amphibians, all dependent on standing water for reproduction. The reptiles are dependent almost entirely on aquatic food. Of the 200 species of birds in the park, 89 are almost totally dependent on aquatic food. Five thousand pairs of wood storks, for example, require more than 1,000,000 pounds of small live fish to raise 10,000 young. Of the 12 different mammals in the park, most are amphibious or partly so. The 150 species of fish in the park are mostly dependent on estuaries for their existence. The invertebrates are also estaurine. The vegetation of the park is dominantly aquatic.

The Corps decided with the connivance of real-estate developers and prospective tomato farmers to divert all the overflow of Lake Okeechobee to the Atlantic or the Gulf. It sponsored and promoted various canals, which directly or indirectly served that end. Over the years, the Corps juggled costs and benefits—it lowered construction costs though they had risen some 36 percent; it found "land enhancement" values theretofore overlooked; but, naturally, it failed to deduct the destruction of the Everglades, a unique bit of Americana, and beautiful free-flowing streams such as the Oklawaha River, which it would destroy.

Over the past ten years, the toll dropped drastically between 1961 and 1966. Thousands of birds and tens of thousands of fish died. Watery expanses of saw grass became stinking mud flats where nothing could live. There were no fish even to feed the young in the rookeries. The rains in 1966 saved the Everglades; but over the years, it cannot survive on rain alone. It needs the oozing fresh water from the north.

The Corps, greatly criticized for bringing the Everglades close to complete destruction, has come up with a plan to provide the park with fresh water—a plan that has just been presented to Congress. The plan is to raise the levees around Lake Okeechobee to provide for additional water storage; it would improve the canal system leading south toward the park to provide additional capacity for conveying water into the park.

But the plan, though noble on its face, utterly lacks schedules showing the guaranteed deliveries of acre feet, come the dry season or drought weather. A contest is on between fresh water for real-estate developers and farmers and the park; and the Army Engineers are strangely allied with economic interests. The concept of the public welfare that those special interests have is how well lined their pockets are with public money.

One of the worst things the Corps is doing is the methodical destruction of our riverways. Some of its plans call for a conversion of river beds into sluiceways that eliminate gravel beds for spawning of fish and islands where birds nest. In the state of Washington, the Corps is bent on destroying the last piece of the native Columbia River.

From Bonneville Dam to Grand Coulee, there are now 11 dams on the Columbia, the only natural part of the river left being a 50-mile stretch from Richland to Priest Rapids. The plans of the Corps to install Benjamin Franklin Dam will destroy that peice of the river, making all of it a big lake or reservoir.

The reason advanced is commercial. It is pointed out that with the locks of Benjamin Franklin, the apple growers of Wenatchee will be able to float their apples to the Portland market. The difficulty is that an apple traveling that distance through that hot, bleak area of eastern Washington would not be edible by the time it reached Portland.

Be that as it may, the Corps would never be building Benjamin Franklin Dam if it had any conservation standards.

This section of the river is the last natural piece of the river left. The spring and summer run of salmon enter *the tributaries* of the Columbia for spawning. But the fall run of the Chinook salmon spawn *in the main bed;* and upstream from Richland are the last spawning grounds left in the main river. Due to the disappearance of other spawning areas, this stretch of the river has become increasingly important. The 20-year average of spawning beds is 902; in 1965, there were 1770 spawning beds; in 1966, 3100; in 1967, 3267. This area now accounts for about 30 percent of all the fall Chinook production. Where they will go if the river becomes a lake, no one knows.

This stretch of the river is also an important breeding ground for small-mouthed and largemouthed bass, white sturgeon and whitefish. It is also a natural spawning ground for steelhead trout, an operation greatly aided by a state hatchery. At least 30,000 steelmouthed trout a year are produced here; and the summer run is so excellent that sportsmen now catch 11,000 there.

The Benjamin Franklin Dam would wipe out 20 natural islands that are breeding grounds for the Canada goose and for several species of gulls, including the California and the ring-billed. The nesting geese number about 300 adult pairs and they produce about 1000 goslings a year. The dams with their resultant impoundments have greatly reduced, in all of the upper Columbia, the goose population from 13,000 to less than half. With all the dams being completed, the upper Columbia will have fewer than 3500 geese.

The river above Richland accommodates as many as 200,000 wintering waterfowl on a single day. Most of the facilities for these wintering inhabitants will be destroyed by the Benjamin Franklin Dam.

The destruction of these spawning grounds and breeding areas is a form of official vandalism. No Federal agency with any concern for the values of conservation would be implicated in such a senseless plot.

Much of the river to be destroyed is now a part of a reservation of the Atomic Energy Commission, which uses the river to run its plutonium reactors. The AEC knows enough to realize how destructive the plans will be to the Columbia's natural wonders. But the AEC will not promote the dam nor oppose it. It is on the Corps' payroll and, like other similar Federal agencies, it is beholden.

The conservation cause is therefore handicapped. A stalwart group is fighting the dam. But public opinion is difficult to muster, as only a few people can enter the sacred precincts of the AEC reservation. So the river has few knowledgeable friends.

The Corps is now starting a vast internal canal-building project to build waterways into the dry, desert-blown parts of America. What chamber of commerce does not long to make its forgotten city a great port?

Will Rogers used to joke that the best thing to do with the Trinity River at Fort Worth, Texas, was to pave it, the stream being a bare trickle at times. That wild idea is now a reality. Construction of a 370-mile canal from Fort Worth to Houston is under way, with 20 new dams (multipurpose) and 20 locks.

Rogers used to twit the Corps about getting him "a harbor on the Verdigris at Oologah" in Oklahoma. That 1.2-billion-dollar project is now under way—a 539-mile canal reaching into the heart of Oklahoma. The plan includes 18 locks and dams that will lift river traffic 530 feet from the Mississippi to the level of Catoosa, the head of navigation.

In 1967, the Corps approved a $316,000,000 Tennessee-Tomlingbee waterway as justified by a benefit-cost ratio of 1.24 to 1. The Secretary of the Army, Stanley Resor, sent the report to Congress with his own contrary conclusion that the project did not have the requisite "margin of economic safety." But the interested Congressmen ignored Resor's conclusion, did not take the issue to Congress, but in committee ordered the Engineers to start the controversial canal that is to run 253 miles.

The most brazen project of all is known as Mike Kirwan's Big Ditch, linking Lake Erie with the Ohio River. Kirwan is chairman of the subcommittee of the House Appropriations Committee on Public Works. Eighty-year-old Kirwan has long been a stern opponent of national-park development. "The U.S. owns too much land" is his position. A member of his subcommittee who opposes him is in a perpetual doghouse, never getting any favors of his own. So they all—mostly all—meekly fall into line.

Kirwan's Big Ditch would be 120 miles long, with a 35-mile reservoir to supply the canal with Erie's sewage water. Nearly 90,000 acres of the nation's finest dairy farms would be inundated and more than 6000 people would lose their homes.

The idea is an old one, going back to George Washington; but today the experts think it is utterly worthless.

The Corps benefit-cost ratio was juggled to suit its needs; obvious costs to the tune of at least $170,000,00 were left out. Benefits were rigged. Thus, "recreation" was valued at $17,000,000 a year—a sum that could be reached only if 500,000 sportsmen descended on this stinking sewage water on a normal Sunday.

The Corps approved the project, estimating the cost at over a billion dollars. It let Kirwan make the announcement. Kirwan managed it through the House; and the Senate—without a roll call—approved.

Two million of the needed one billion dollars plus for Mike Kirwan's Big Ditch was in L. B. J.'s budget, a budget in which, L. B. J. said, "Waste and nonessentials have been cut out. Reductions or postponements have been made wherever possible."

And so the skids were greased. But the voice of Pennsylvania spoke up in opposition; and the Big Ditch has been delayed. Yet the momentum is so great in Washington, that if Texas and Oklahoma can have their worthless canals, so can Ohio.

The truth is that our waterways present staggering problems demanding money, engineering skills and ecological insights. These critical problems are not being managed by the Army Engineers.

Instead, the Corps is destroying free-flowing streams to make unnecessary dams. It is trying to turn natural rivers into sluiceways; it is destroying our estuaries. Having no conservation standards, the Corps can easily destroy the Everglades in favor of get-rich real-estate promoters.

The Corps, presently headed by the efficient General William F. Cassidy, has a long and illustrious record, completely free of fraud, mismanagement or other types of scandal. By 1942, it had built two and a half billion dollars' worth of facilities in a year and a half; and during World War II, ten billion dollars' worth in four years. In terms of coverage, it has included navigation, flood control, hydro-power, beach erosion, water supply, fish and wildlife preservation, hurricane protection and related subjects. Since 1824, it has built most of the nation's harbors and navigable waterways. From the beginning, it was active in flood control; and when the first national Flood Control Act was passed by Congress in 1917, it became very active, especially in the Mississippi Valley. One who tours America will see many great and useful structures built by the Corps. Certainly, the Corps is unlike the Mafia; it has no conspiratorial function. It is honest and aboveboard.

The difficulty is, however, that we are running out of free-flowing rivers and healthy estuaries. The traditional engineering functions no longer fit our needs. Our need is to preserve the few remaining natural wonders so that we can make them clean and sparkling and fit for use by humans and by the vast world of birds, fish, reptiles and crustaceans that possess our waters.

We need the Corps. But we need also to redefine its functions and change its focus.

We pay farmers not to plant Crops. Let's pay the Corps not to build dams, dredge estuaries, convert rivers into sluiceways or build inland canals.

We can accomplish that goal by a few simple amendments to the Corps' basic statutory authority.

First, its projects for river improvement should now be conditioned by conservation standards. Will the project protect the marshlands? Will it provide the needed fresh water for sanctuaries such as the Everglades? Will it preserve the bottom lands sorely needed for ecological studies?

Second, the Corps' statutory authority should be enlarged to authorize it to construct sewage-disposal plants. It has no such authority. It can be busier at that than at dam building. Its large civilian staff, dependent on Federal largess for salaries, can fatten on sewage as well as on flood control and navigation.

The Corps needs statutory redesigning to meet modern urban and technological needs.

One billion dollars is needed in the Lake Erie complex to restore that dead lake, so that swimming, boating and fishing are once more possible. Mike Kirwan would not get a Big Ditch under this new regime. But he might get a big sewage-disposal plant named for him.

These are rewards enough, even at the level of pork barrel, if the Corps concentrates on socially useful projects that are desperately needed. Now is the chance to save the rest of our rivers by proclaiming our love of the land and our determination to preserve its natural wonders, even against despoilers as professionally competent as the Army Corps of Engineers.

21

Official corruption and the construction industry

Knapp Commission

"It is virtually impossible for a builder to erect a building within the City of New York and comply with every statute and ordinance in connection with the work. In short, many of the statutes and rules and regulations are not only unrealistic but lead to the temptation for corruption."

So said H. Earl Fullilove, Chairman of the Board of Governors of the Building Trades Employers Association of the City of New York, in testimony before the Commission on October 29, 1971, summing up a situation which has led to extensive graft in the construction industry. The Commission found that payments to the police by contractors and subcontractors were the rule rather than exceptions and constituted a major source of graft to the uniformed police. It must be noted that policemen were not

From Commission to Investigate Allegations of Police Corruption and the City's Anti-Corruption Procedures (Knapp Commission), *Commission Report*, pp. 123–132.

alone in receiving payoffs from contractors. Much larger payoffs were made to inspectors and permit-granting personnel from other agencies.

The Investigation

In its initial investigation into corruption in the construction industry, the Commission came up against a stone wall. Sixteen veteran job superintendents and two project managers interviewed at construction sites solemnly denied that they had ever paid off the police or known anyone who had. Similar denials were made under oath by other construction people and by three patrolmen and their precinct commander, who were subpoenaed by the Commission. Later, in private talks with members of the construction industry, quite a different story began to emerge. From information obtained in these lengthy, off-the-record interviews, the Commission was able to piece together a detailed picture of corruption in the construction industry.

Although several of these sources were unusually helpful to the Commission in private talks, only one agreed to testify extensively in executive session (and then only under the cloak of anonymity) and none would testify at the public hearings. Their testimony could at no time be compelled, because the Commission lacked the power to obviate claims of Fifth Amendment privileges by conferring immunity. However, it was arranged that the construction industry would be represented at the public hearings by Mr. Fullilove, whose association is made up of 800 contractors and subcontractors, including industry giants as well as smaller companies.

Speaking for his membership, Mr. Fullilove said, "Many—if not most—people in the industry are reluctant to appear at an open hearing and to testify on these matters. Our members feel that unless the entire situation can be remedied in one fell swoop, it's a tremendous burden on a member to become a hero for a day and then suffer the consequential individual harassment." He then went on to detail the laws and ordinances leading to police harassment and consequent graft. This information was corroborated and buttressed by the testimony of Patrolmen William Phillips and Waverly Logan.

Reasons for Police Corruption in Relation to Construction

Corruption is a fact of life in the construction industry. In addition to extensive payoffs contractors make to police and others in regulatory agencies, there is evidence of considerable corruption within the industry itself. Contractors have been known to pay owners' agents to get an inside track on upcoming jobs; subcontractors pay contractors' purchasing agents to receive projects or to get information helpful in competitive bidding; sub-subcontractors pay subcontractors; dump-truck drivers exact a per-load payment for taking out extra loads they don't report to their bosses; and hoist engineers get money from various subcontractors to insure that materials are lifted to high floors without loss or damage. In this climate, it is only natural that contractors also pay the police.

The heart of the problem of police corruption in the construction industry is the dizzying array of laws, ordinances, and regulations governing construction in the City. To put up a building in New York, a builder is required to get a minimum of forty to fifty different permits and licenses from various City departments. For a very large project, the total number of permits needed may soar to 120, 130 or more. These permits range in importance from the initial building permit down through permits required for erecting fences, wooden walkways and construction shanties, to seemingly petty ones like that required whenever a track vehicle is moved across a sidewalk. "This [latter] regulation is often violated," Mr. Fullilove told the Commission, "because it is [a] tremendous inconvenience to obtain a one-shot permit to move a bulldozer over a five-foot stretch of sidewalk." In practice, most builders don't bother to get all the permits required by law. Instead, they apply for a handful of the more important ones (often making a payoff to personnel at the appropriate agency to insure prompt issuance of the permit). Payments to the police and inspectors from other departments insure that builders won't be hounded for not having other permits.

Of the City ordinances enforced by the police which affect construction, most relate to use of the streets and sidewalks and to excessive dust and noise. Ordinances most troublesome to contractors are those which prohibit double-parking, flying dust, obstructing the sidewalk, or leaving it strewn with piles of sand and rubble, and beginning work before 7:00 a.m. or continuing after 6:00 p.m. (This last is for the protection of neighborhood residents already subject to eleven legal hours a day of construction noise.)

Most large contractors seem to regard all of the ordinances mentioned above and many of the permit requirements simply as nuisances which interfere with efficient construction work. Thus, they are willing parties to a system which frees them from strict adherence to the regulations.

Police Enforcement of Laws Regulating Construction

Although building inspectors are responsible for enforcement of regulations concerning construction techniques, the responsibility for inspecting certain permits and enforcing the ordinances outlined above lies with the police. The police officers charged with this responsibility have always been faced with a particularly tempting opportunity for corruption. The Department has attempted, since the Commission hearings, to lessen the opportunities by cutting back on enforcement. It has ordered its men to stop enforcing all laws pertaining to construction, unless pedestrians are endangered or traffic is impeded. If a patrolman observes a condition which affects pedestrians or traffic, he is to call his superior to come to the site and take whatever action is needed. Nevertheless, pending a revision of the laws to make them more realistic, they cannot go entirely unenforced and whoever is given the job will meet the same pressures found by the Commission.

Traditionally, construction enforcement was the function of one foot patrolman in each precinct called the "conditions man" who concentrated on construction enforcement. At the time of the investigation, a growing number of precincts had abolished the post, leaving the responsibility for construction enforcement to other officers, such as "summons men" who had broader responsibilities for issuing summonses in other areas. Foot patrolmen and those in patrol cars were also empowered to go onto any site in their sectors to check for violations. In any case, the patrolman whose duty it was to enforce construction laws was, at the time of the investigation, required to make periodic checks of all construction sites in the precinct to make sure that they 1) had the proper permits, 2) conformed to the limitations of those permits, and 3) adhered to all City ordinances not covered by the permits. If he found any violations, he was supposed to issue a summons. Department regulations provided that he make a notation in his memo book whenever he visited a construction site and maintain a file at the precinct with a folder for each construction job in his jurisdiction, containing copies of all permit numbers for the site and a record of all civil summonses it had received.

In practice, the Commission found, officers responsible for enforcing ordinances relating to construction simply kept pro forma files and pretty much let the job go at that. Examination of conditions men's memo books in the Twentieth Precinct, where there were between twenty and fifty construction projects underway at one time, indicated that a grand total of thirty-nine visits were reported to have been made to construction sites over the two-year period from March, 1969, to March, 1971, with over half those visits recorded as having been for the purpose of copying down permit numbers. The patrolmen whose notebooks were examined admitted under oath that they did not follow Department regulations in getting permit numbers from new sites or in making entries in their memo books every time they entered a site. In short, the Commission found that these patrolmen had not been doing their jobs properly, were aware that they weren't, and knew that their work would not be reviewed by senior officers.

These rules were designed to facilitate control of corruption. Where the rules were ignored by supervisors, the spread of corruption was almost inevitable.

Patterns of Police Corruption in Construction

The most common pattern of police payoffs in the construction industry, as described to the Commission by police officers and by contractors and their employees, involved payment to the sector car of a fixed monthly or weekly fee, which varied according to the size of the construction job. Occasionally, the sergeants would also have a pad, and in larger jobs, the precinct captain sometimes had one of his own. In addition, all construction sites, no matter how small, were found to be vulnerable to overtures from local foot patrolmen.*

In a small job like the renovation of a brownstone, the general contractor was likely to pay the police between $50 and $150 a month, and the fee ascended sharply for larger jobs. An excavator on a small job paid $50 to $100 a week for the duration of excavation to avoid summonses for dirt spillage, flying dust, double-parked dump trucks, or for running vehicles over the sidewalk without a permit. A concrete company pouring a foundation paid another $50 to $100 a week to avoid summonses for double-parking its trucks or for running them across a sidewalk without a curb cut. (Concrete contractors are especially vulnerable, as it is essential that foundation-pouring be carried on continuously. This means that one or more trucks must be kept standing by while one is actually pouring.) Steel erectors paid a weekly fee to keep steel delivery trucks standing by; masons paid; the crane company paid. In addition, all construction sites were approached by police for contributions at Christmas, and a significant number paid extra for additional police patrols in the hope of obtaining protection from vandalism of building materials and equipment.

In small contracting companies, payments were generally negotiated and made by the owner; larger firms often had an employee whose sole job was to handle negotiations with agencies which regulate construction. This man, called an expeditor, negotiated and made all such payments, both to the police and to inspectors and permit-granting personnel from other agencies. In either case, when work was started on a new site, arrangements were made with the local police.

One contractor, whose experiences were fairly typical, spoke at length with Commission investigators and later—with promise of anonymity—testified before the Commission in executive session. He was a small general contractor who worked on jobs of less than one million dollars. He started his own company in the early sixties with a contract for a small job in Brooklyn. During the first week of construction, a sector car pulled up to the construction site and a patrolman came onto the site, asking to see the permits for demolition, sidewalk construction, etc. He looked over the various permits and left. The following day, another sector car came by, and one of the patrolmen issued a summons for obstruction of the sidewalk. The contractor protested that he had the necessary permit and was in no way violating the law. "If we don't work together," the patrolman told him, "there will be a ticket every day." When the contractor asked how much "working together"

---

*One small contractor told how it's done: "Put a five dollar bill in one pocket, a ten in the other. Fold it up real small. Size up the situation and pay accordingly. You can pass it in a handshake if necessary. It really isn't. You know the touch is on as soon as he . . . walks on the job to see your permit and questions it."

would cost, he was told, "$50 a week." The contractor testified that he balked at this, claiming that his was a small operation and that he couldn't afford such payments. He said he would prefer to operate within the limitations of his permits and go to court to answer any summonses he might receive.

The following day, the contractor received another summons for $100. Two days later, he was approached again and told that it would be cheaper to pay off the police than to accumulate summonses. "We decided for our own good to make that $50 payment and not maintain our hero status," he said. He continued to make payments of $50 a week to a patrolman from the sector car for the duration of the construction work, which lasted about one year. His site was never again inspected by the police and he received no more summonses.

This contractor further testified that he was approached by the police, and paid them, on all the jobs he did in various City precincts. On none of these was he ever served with a summons. On his last job, in 1970, when he was in financial difficulties which eventually led to bankruptcy proceedings, he was, as usual, approached by the police for payoffs. Pleading insolvency, he refused to pay and used various ruses to avoid payment. He again began receiving summonses for violations—the first that had been served on him since he started paying the police.

This contractor stated that in addition to paying the police he has also made payments to personnel from the Department of Buildings, other divisions of the Housing and Development Administration, the Department of Highways, and such federal agencies as the Department of Housing and Urban Affairs and the Federal Housing Administration.

Another builder, the owner of a medium-sized contracting company which does work for such clients as Consolidated Edison, the New York Telephone Company and the Catholic Dioceses of New York and Brooklyn, told Commission investigators that his company had paid off the police on every construction job it had done in the City, including the six or eight jobs in progress at the time of the interview. He told the Commission that he paid the police from $50 to $100 a week for each job he had in progress, and that payments were made by his expeditor, whose job it was to obtain permits and pay off police and others. He went on to say that his company frequently negotiated the amount of payment with the precinct commander either at the building site or at the local precinct.

A reliable informant who was intimately connected with this builder told the Commission that the builder's payoffs were in fact much larger than the $50 to $100 he claimed. The informant also reported that the expeditor handled all negotiations for payoffs, then reported to officers of the company, who gave him the appropriate amount out of petty cash. At a later date, the expeditor submitted covering expense vouchers indicating travel or entertainment expenses. During the time this informant was giving information to the Commission, he observed a sergeant approach a foreman at one of the company's construction sites in Queens and threaten to write out a summons for burning refuse. The foreman then told the sergeant that he couldn't see going to court over it and would give him $20 to forget about it. The sergeant said he would have to discuss it with his boss and left the site. That afternoon, the sergeant returned to the construction site with his precinct captain, who advised the foreman that there were "a lot of violations around." He said he wanted to speak to someone about "taking care of it" (a clear reference to the expeditor), and would return on the Tuesday afternoon following. At this point, the informant's role was discovered and the Commission was not able to find out how big a payoff the captain had in mind, although a three installment $2,500 payoff which the informant said was arranged with a building inspector a few days earlier indicates that it would have been sizable.

Comments

The current system of laws and ordinances relevant to construction is badly in need of overhaul. Many ordinances now on the books make construction unduly difficult and create bountiful opportunities for graft. The needed review should preferably be undertaken by members both of the industry and of regulatory agencies.

A start has been made in this direction. In June, 1972, *The New York Times* ran a series of investigative articles which described in detail corrupt practices in the construction industry in the City. In response to the newspaper's allegations, a State Senate committee chaired by Senator Roy Goodman held six days of hearings, which resulted in a plan to have industry leaders, legislators, and the appropriate City commissioners review the tangle of City and state laws governing construction, with a view to eliminating those laws which are unrealistic or unnecessary and which lead to corruption. Industry groups have studies the laws and are expected soon to submit recommendations to the appropriate City commissioners.

One other important reform is needed. Builders in special situations may have a legitimate reason for violating ordinances. However, there is currently no procedure whereby such relief may be afforded. A publicly-recognized means for waiving regulations where necessary and appropriate should be established.

As outlined earlier, the Department has curtailed police enforcement of ordinances relating to construction. The Commission favors this step and feels that, insofar as possible, police officers should be relieved of responsibility for enforcing laws in any area under the jurisdiction of regulatory agencies—in this case, the Department of Buildings, other divisions of the Housing and Development Administration, and the Department of Highways, among others.

We recognize that this approach will not in itself eliminate corruption but may simply transfer it from the police to other agencies. But we believe that corruption in other agencies—undesirable as it is—has far less impact upon the body politic than corruption among the police.

The progression found again and again in the course of our investigation, from the acceptance by a police officer of petty graft to more serious corruption, makes it desirable to remove as many sources of such petty graft as possible. By eliminating the opportunity for petty graft, the Department can perhaps change the current attitude that such graft is an accepted part of the police job—an attitude which makes it easier for a police officer to accept or solicit graft of a more serious nature when the opportunity presents itself. Moreover, policemen are more likely to pursue vigorously a corrupt public official who is not one of their own.

Moreover, as a simple matter of efficiency there is no justification for using the police, with all their powers and prerogatives, in the enforcement of many minor regulations.

A promising method of curtailing construction graft which the Department has yet to use on a broad scale, would be a campaign to arrest contractors who offer bribes to policemen. The recent use in the Bronx of police undercover agents posing as regular policemen has led to the arrests of such would-be bribers. Carrying this technique one step further, Department anti-corruption personnel could, without advance warning, require a police officer to don a concealed transmitter and, under surveillance, give a summons to a construction foreman in his area of patrol with whom he may or may not have had corrupt dealings.

HUD's bonanza
for suburbia

Al Hirshen / Richard T. Le Gates

The Housing and Community Development Act of 1974, signed by President Ford last August, will divert Federal housing money away from most of the big cities, with their rapidly deteriorating inner cores, increasingly minority populations, and pre-dominantly Democratic electorates, to Republican, largely surburban, Middle America. While the funding formula is complex and allegedly "neutral," analysis of where the money will go and its probable use confirms that the measure is another instance of Republican welfare for the rich.

Had it not been for the downfall of Richard M. Nixon, it is likely that suburban Middle American cities would now be receiving a large chunk of "community development" money *automatically.* No forms, no proposal writers, no trips to Washington, no nothing—just money. It is known as "revenue sharing." The

From *The Progressive*, April 1975. Reprinted by permission from *The Progressive*, 408 West Gorham Street, Madison, Wisconsin 53703. Copyright © 1975, *The Progressive*, Inc.

pure Nixonian form of community development revenue sharing languished for four years and finally died, a victim of Congressional jealousy over any threat to its supervisory prerogatives. The 1974 Housing Act represents a compromise between the Johnson Administration's categorical grant programs, which earmarked funds for specific projects, and straight revenue sharing, but it still pulls the money from the Newarks and the Garys and shifts it to Des Moines and Grosse Pointe.

One virtue of the "categorical" programs was that their very "narrowness" made them visible. If funds for a park were given to a city and no park materialized, there were grounds for suspicion. The application and reporting paperwork (while often ridiculously excessive) provided the basic public record for review and control of the programs. Public hearing requirements and, increasingly, "citizen participation" requirements, strengthened the hand of intended program beneficiaries to influence the expenditure of funds.

The generality of fundable activities under the new Housing and Community Development Act, the looseness of application provisions, the nearly automatic nature of the entitlements, and the absence of detailed periodic reporting make visibility and control of the new money difficult and provide almost limitless opportunities for patronage, self-dealing, or graft.

Cities' entitlements under the 1974 Act are calculated by a formula which compares their population, extent of poverty, and extent of overcrowding to national norms. While the Secretary of Housing and Urban Development is empowered to recognize regional or area variations in income and cost of living, HUD regulations state that the Secretary has determined that this is neither feasible nor appropriate. Cities which during the past have received more money than their formula entitlement are protected from any funding cut for three years and then fall to their formula level during a transition period of two years. By 1980 all cities will receive funds on a pure formula basis. This "neutral" formula for a more "rational" and "equitable" distribution of Federal urban development monies is disguised political dynamite. Everything will be fine for three years until the "grandfather clause" runs out. Then the true nature of the legislation will become clear.

What will happen to cities in the San Francisco Bay area is illustrative. The largest cities, with severe urban problems, are in trouble. San Francisco will continue to receive $28.6 million a year for three years (comparable to annual receipts under the categorical housing and urban development programs in recent years), but at the end of that period its entitlement under the neutral formula will drop dramatically to $22 million in 1978, $16 million in 1979, and $12 million in 1980. Oakland will experience a comparable drop, from $12 million to $7 million. The truly depressed cities in the region, with minorities already a majority of the population, will suffer even more. Richmond, with a black/Latino majority and a black mayor, will experience a drop from $3 million to $1.3 million when the grace period runs out; and the extremely depressed black enclave of Pittsburg will see its entitlement drop from $3 million to nothing at all. (With a population less than 50,000, it has no entitlement after the grace period runs out.)

The large middle-class, white-collar suburbs which have grown up elsewhere in the Bay area—physically well-off, overwhelmingly white, and politically conservative—are in an altogether different position. Concord, for example, will be entitled to $229,000 in the first year of special revenue sharing—more than nine times the amount it has received in recent years; within five years that figure will nearly triple. Fremont's share will shoot up from $269,000 in 1975 to more than $1 million by 1980. And this pattern will be repeated nationally.

Newark, New Jersey, will have its funds cut in half between 1975 and 1980—from $20.5 million to $10 million. Gary, Indiana, will have its entitlement cut during the same period from $6,950,000 to $3,773,000. Only a few problem cities with large populations, notably New York and Los Angeles, stand to gain.

Under the 1974 Act many cities have an *automatic claim* to more money than they have ever thought of using for community development activities. And they can spend the money on almost any activity involving physical construction, and they can forget about meeting meddlesome Washington guidelines concerning poverty and race. The new handbooks on the Act will not be regulations but simple "how to do it" guides, according to HUD.

The location, character, and size of the communities which will benefit are significant. Until now, urban development funds have gone to cities with severe physical and social problems which have learned to play the grantsmanship game. The older industrial cities of the eastern and Great Lakes regions have received the most. Those in the Midwest and West with less marked physical deterioration have received less. In conservative states (notably the South), cities have often chosen not to vie for such funds, either because they do not see themselves as having urban problems or because they are philosophically opposed to Federal strings which might ease the plight of poor and minorities.

Relatively well-off cities will benefit from the fact that one of the standards chosen to measure their physical housing needs is overcrowding, not the real condition of their houses. A well-preserved midwestern city with the same total population, comparable overcrowding, and one-half the total poverty of one of the smaller, badly distressed East Coast cities—Camden, New Jersey, for example—would be entitled to 75 per cent of the amount of money Camden would receive. This would be true even if only 3 per cent of its housing could be characterized as deteriorated, as compared to 50 per cent of Camden's.

The HUD programs which already exist in large cities will also change under the new law. Poor and "blighted" neighborhoods in these cities received grants under Great Society categorical programs such as Urban Renewal, Model Cities, and Federally Assisted Code Enforcement. All of these programs tied Federal funding to specific poor and physically deteriorated *neighborhoods*. The 1974 Act funds may be spent *anywhere* in the city. A provision in the Senate bill which would have provided that no more than 20 per cent of an applicant community's funds could be used for activities which do not directly and significantly benefit low and moderate income families or blighted areas was dropped. Where the funds go within the community may be determined solely at the whim of local government.

Some groups are likely to see the subsidy potential for their pet development interests. The Chamber of Commerce has always wanted someone other than itself to pay for some form of central business district renewal—from a mall with concrete planters to a convention center/sports arena/parking garage/shopping complex. Pressure on the administrators of the old categorical Urban Renewal program was to fund more and more of these Central Business District (CBD) projects, rather than those which would rehabilitate or reconstruct poor neighborhoods. The Urban Renewal Administration frequently caved in to these pressures, but exerted some influence to keep small poverty projects going as well (often as the trade-off for funds the city really desired). With local officials fully in the saddle, even this weak barrier no longer exists.

The suburban developers also have a concrete agenda for 1974 Act money: They want sewers and water pipes. HUD sewer and water grants have been the fastest growing category of sought-after money of the last half decade, and most of it goes into tract developments on the urban fringe. In the contest between the Chamber of Commerce and developers on one side and the Model Cities citizen participation component, the Project Area Committees, and the tenant unions on the other, it is clear which side the city council will favor.

If disguised tax relief, cosmetic capital improvements, Central Business District projects, and sewer and water installations are in, what categories of urban development activities are out? Most of the programs targeted at poverty problems have been unpopular with conservative local governments. Virtually none would have been undertaken by local governments with local money. Many cities refused to undertake them even with "free" Federal funds, and others grudgingly undertook them because it was the price of admission to HUD money for the CBD and sewer and water grants. Public housing construction, rehabilitation of deteriorating units, "software" social programs (construction job training, home ownership counseling, health and educational activities) will starve.

HUD cannot be relied on to check those tendencies. By the late 1960s HUD staffing was a mixed bag—aging New Dealers who had come in with the Public Housing Program worked with conservative mortgage bankers who had filtered into the Department through FHA mortgage insurance programs, and more energetic, active, and liberal staff attracted to the Johnson programs (such as Model Cities). Six years of conservative government has demoralized the younger and more liberal staff, many of whom have resigned, been laid off, or transferred (whole wings of the Washington HUD building are empty while the Anchorage HUD area office has grown). The Administration vested greater program control in local area offices which are now largely headed by local personnel from FHA insuring offices—hardly a dynamic set of civil servants. The unlikelihood that this type of HUD official will exert much influence on local jurisdictions to initiate more socially responsive programs is compounded by the legislation. The 1974 Act *requires* the HUD Secretary to approve applications unless in extreme instances he finds that they are severely defective.

Since neither HUD nor local governments could be greatly relied upon to protect the interests of low income and minority persons, a major thrust of the urban legislation of the 1960s was to strengthen "citizen participation" in urban development programs. To a greater extent than anyone ever anticipated, this strategy worked. The Nixon Administration's antagonism toward community participation was rooted in this fear of its success. Perhaps the most bizarre compromise in the new legislation involved the citizen participation requirements. The Senate would have required applicant cities to involve residents in community development activites and to provide adequate resources for their participation. The Act as adopted makes this provision *entirely discretionary.*

In the name of grassroots democracy, equity, and efficiency, the Housing and Community Development Act of 1974 will take funds from the most needy urban areas and give them to the less needy, redistribute wealth and power from Democratic and liberal areas to ones which are predominantly Republican and conservative, and establish a framework in which cosmetic projects and patronage will win over projects desperately needed by the poor.

23

Lethal smokescreen

Dan Berger

On January 30, 1974, Pan American World Airways Boeing 707, Flight 806, from Auckland, New Zealand, approached Pago Pago International Airport in a vicious rain squall. The jet, carrying 101 persons, came in too low, the crew failing to notice the steep descent of the craft. The plane made contact with the ground 3,865 feet short of the runway, shearing off the tops of palm trees as it dove to the soggy earth. After a rolling, bucking 800-foot ride through the jungle, the jet came to rest against a three-foot-high lava rock wall. When the plane was at last still, the cabin was intact and not one passenger had suffered a traumatic injury.

But within a few minutes, 97 of them were dead. Investigators later said all died of smoke inhalation from the fire that engulfed the craft. A shock, then, to families of the victims when

An abridged version of this article appeared in *New Times,* August 8, 1975. This expanded version was prepared especially for this volume. Reprinted by permission of the author.

they read the opening statement in the National Transportation Safety Board's report on the accident: "This was a survivable accident."

Four people got out of the plane alive—attorney Roger Cann of Auckland, N.Z.; his wife, Heather; Charles Culberson, an oceanographic researcher from Oregon; and Dick Smith of Scottsdale, Ariz. All escaped from an overwing exit in spite of thick and deadly smoke.

Smith, perhaps the first passenger to realize the plane was crashing, had spent 33 years in the Air Force and had gone through various survival schools. He was head coach of the United States Olympic diving team and head diving coach at Arizona State University and, at age 58, was in remarkable physical condition.

When the plane jolted to a stop, Smith unbuckled and headed for the nearest exit. He moved to the right overwing exit, grabbed the handle and ripped it open. "I told myself I wasn't going to panic like those others—all running to the front of the plane. But a blast of flame hit me in the face when I opened that door and I knew that was no way out, so I closed the door and looked for another one."

Then Smith took a deep breath and was knocked to his knees. "Never in my life . . . whatever it was, those fumes of smoke hit me. Well, I could have quit like those other people because it was one of the most tremendous, powerful feelings I've ever had in my life for being grabbed like that. I got down low and took another breath and that time I was determined to hold it three or four minutes if I had to. I'm in pretty good shape and I can hold my breath for a long time."

The 5 foot 6 Smith crawled a few feet, made his way across the aisle and opened the left overwing exit. His face was singed by flame but Smith didn't hesitate. He leaped forward with both hands out in front, like a bad belly flop, and landed on the red-hot wing. Seconds later he was crawling through the wet jungle to the safety of a palm tree, to be joined moments later by the Canns and Culberson.

More than 90 of the 97 who died were found near the front and rear door exits that didn't open. They had no time to reach the overwing exits because of the choking smoke and scorching flames. The flames must have terrified them, but it was the smoke that posed the greater danger. Since 1961, when the first of the major survivable crashes were investigated, more than 300 persons have lost their lives as a direct or indirect result of breathing deadly fumes.

Last month's brutal Eastern Airlines crash at Kennedy International Airport revived another long-standing controversy about airplane safety: cabin seats that face the rear of the plane. In this case, according to New York's Deputy Chief Medical Examiner Michael Braden, the velocity of the jet at impact killed most of the 110 people who died in the crash. If the passengers had been facing the rear, they would not have been so violently thrust forward—thereby avoiding such fatal injuries as internal bleeding, skull fractures and broken necks—and more lives might have been saved. Seconds later, however, the craft caught fire and poisonous smoke poured out. Whoever had survived the enormous shock of impact might well have been done in by the lethal fumes anyway.

The first major crash that brought smoke deaths to the attention of the public occurred November 11, 1965, when a United Air Lines Boeing 727 crash-landed at Salt Lake City and remained intact. The carbon monoxide and hydrogen cyanide gas produced by the burning of the cabin interior caused the deaths of 43 of the 91 passengers. The industry and federal officials were upset and pressured by the news media as well as by numerous lawsuits. A series of investigations ensued into cabin interiors, design, the search for new types of polymers and better escape systems.

But in the intervening years, no substantive moves have been taken to solve the problem. Indeed, the type of smoke now produced by burning airplane interiors may be even more noxious than that which was produced by the burning United jet at Salt Lake City.

When the Federal Aviation Administration, the National Transportation Safety Board (NTSB) and airplane manufacturers started investigating the problems of smoke in the mid-1960s, their first thoughts were on flame: stop the flame and you stop the smoke, they reasoned. So a great deal of time and money was spent producing chemical additives that would make the polymers used for carpets, drapes and seat cushions flame-resistant. It all worked quite well in the controlled conditions of the laboratory; when a match was applied to the treated materials, the flame resistant chemicals did not burn. Most would smolder or melt and then help to extinguish the flames.

But a new problem arose: materials treated with flame-retardant chemicals produced more copious and more noxious smoke and fumes than if the material hadn't been treated at all.

Dr. Irwin Einhorn, a researcher working under a federal grant at the University of Utah, concluded in 1969, "To date, the major concern of those engaged in the development of fire-retardant materials has been the reduction of the ignition tendency and flame propagation. Thus, it has been possible to meet code and regulatory requirements regarding flame spread, but in the opinion of the author, the total hazard resulting from incomplete combustion has been increased."

That report, authorized and paid for by the federal government and printed with taxpayers' money, is still available for a couple of dollars. But in the five and one-half years since it has been published, little has been done to set smoke-emission guidelines. The report urged the setting of federal standards for smoke-emission and toxicity levels and in the *Federal Register* of July 30, 1969, the FAA said it was "considering rule-making to establish standards governing the smoke-emission characteristics of aircraft interior materials." Nothing was ever done to set those standards.

A few weeks before this study was published in *New Times,* the FAA apparently heard an investigation in this area was underway. A low-level FAA executive mentioned being interviewed by *New Times.* Within two weeks, on December 30, 1974, the FAA published the following in the *Federal Register:* "The FAA is considering rule-making to establish standards governing the toxic gas-emission characteristics of compartment interior materials used in transport category airplanes when subjected to fire conditions." Apparently the FAA is still "considering rule-making" in this area.

The foot-dragging of the Federal Aviation Association in this matter has been attacked by such governmental agencies as the National Transportation Safety Board and by the Aviation Consumer Action Project, a Ralph Nader-sponsored group. It's not that the FAA is unaware of the problem: The FAA's own Civil Aeromedical Institute in Oklahoma City has been investigating smoke-caused deaths since 1966. But major changes in airplane design, both inside and out, rarely happen rapidly, a fact perhaps best explained by an attorney who has handled a number of air-related accident cases: "Hell, the FAA and the industry are in bed with each other. No one's going to do anything drastic—anything that'll cost too much money."

In an interview with then-FAA Administrator Alexander Butterfield, he was asked about adding a particular safety device to airplanes: Shouldn't it be made mandatory by the FAA? His response: ". . . in promulgating a rule which is going to affect everyone, that's going to force everyone to buy . . . a relatively expensive instrument—although that instrument is probably going to save some lives—I just have to say we have to be very careful about our evaluation." Foot dragging some call it; others call it conflict of interest.

Cost and safety appear to be the least compatible words in industry's vocabulary. Many opponents of the airlines say they can make a perfectly

The Big Seven

Here are the seven major survivable crashes of commercial planes which have killed people not by traumatic injury but by smoke and fire:

July 11, 1961—Denver, United DC-8; 25 of 122 persons on board died.
Nov. 23, 1964—Rome, TWA Boeing 707; 48 of 73 died.
Nov. 11, 1965—Salt Lake City, United B-727; 43 of 91 died.
Nov. 27, 1970—Anchorage, Capital International DC-8; 47 of 229 died.
Dec. 8, 1972—Chicago, United B-737; 43 of 61 died.
Dec. 20, 1972—Chicago, North Central DC-9; 10 of 45 died.
Jan. 30, 1974—Pago Pago, American Samoa, Pan Am B-707; 97 of 101 died.

In each crash the cause of death of all passengers was given as effects of smoke and fire. Authorities began improving the fire-resistant properties of cabin interiors about 1966. But Dr. Irwin Einhorn of the University of Utah hasn't been satisfied with the work done and has worked on the project ever since the Salt Lake City crash.

When the Pan Am jet crashed in Pago Pago, the NTSB's on-site investigation was completed within a few weeks. Then the plane's wreckage was buried, with no independent fire investigator asked to view the vital cabin interior.

safe plane, which does not burst into flames in case of a crash, one which protects passengers much better than at present. But the cost would be excessive. A case in point is in the area of fuel-inerting.

The industry has long realized that the liquid fuel carried on the massive jets produces incredible problems in crashes. The fuel is volatile. It can spill all over creation if a tank ruptures, and the presence of fumes inside the tank also creates hazards. The military realized that a helicopter shot down in Vietnam would surely explode when it hit the ground, because of the volatility of the fuel. Thus, with the aid of NASA, the military developed a fuel tank bladder which is surrounded by a thick layer of foam. In case of a rupture, the bladder often didn't burst and even if it did split, the foam sopped up the liquid fuel before it could ignite.

This, and two other types of fuel-inerting systems, was suggested to a Pan American spokesman. He said all were fine ideas, but "These planes already cost $2 million and up and the safety record is awfully good. What you're talking about makes sense from a safety standpoint, but the cost is so excessive." An FAA executive, told of the systems, said, "Yes, they'd be fine solutions, but they'd cost a fortune and the airlines would take the extra cost out of the customers' hides. . ."

One additional problem was manifest in the Pago Pago crash: an overabundance of jet fuel. Flight 806 was carrying 37,900 pounds of extra fuel as cargo—fuel that would never be used in flight—including 27,540 pounds in a center storage tank. A Pan Am spokesman admitted passengers were not told—nor are they ever told—that a particular passenger plane is also being used to carry fuel from one spot to another. "It's standard practice to carry fuel to places that need it," he said. "Right then we were in the fuel shortage business and we were taking fuel from here to there routinely."

All of this makes the airlines look bad, but in fact the commercial airline industry has a fine record of safety. It's excellent because of the hard work of people like Charles O. Miller, formerly with the National Transportation Safety Board, and others like him, who have dedicated their lives to safety. Even Max Karant, senior vice-president of the Aircraft Owners and Pilots Association, agrees that commercial aviation has a good safety record, far ahead of general aviation—private ownership of planes. Karant is a feisty opponent of waste in the FAA and has been critical of the FAA for years.

Chuck Miller, however, found he couldn't do his job properly and was forced to leave. For the last few years, the FAA and the NTSB have been carrying on an embarrassing feud: the NTSB, attempting to gain more independence, made a number of recommendations to the FAA, asking for Airworthiness Directives to be issued regarding a number of major defects on airliners. The bureaucracy that pervades the federal government, and the "gentlemen's agreements" that are made, produced not a few public battles between the two agencies. Miller was then the main splinter in the FAA's finger.

"While I was at the safety board, we were pretty much on the record over the years," said Miller. "We thought more could be done in the prevention of fires (in survivable crashes). Fuel system integrity is the biggest area . . . that hasn't been exploited. Like detail design of fuel tank fittings, making the tanks themselves more resistible to crashes. I mean, the technology is there and it hasn't been exploited. Like applying the work the Army did for the helicopter in this area. Oh, I know it's not the same in a 'copter as it is in a 747, obviously, but I think that if people put their minds to something, they can do it. If I were to reflect back on the last ten years, I just have not seen what I would call a high-priority project to get at the crash-fire problem in all aircraft."

Cost is a major factor in determining what the industry does voluntarily in the area of safety but expense is apparently not the only criteria the FAA has used in determining that safety equipment should not be carried aboard commercial aircraft. A variety of smoke hoods, bag-type gadgets that passengers could place on their heads in case of smoke, have been tested; all are rather easy to use, not expensive and seem to work. On January 11, 1969, the FAA published a Notice of Proposed Rule Making, saying it was "considering amending . . . Federal Aviation Regulations to require that protective smoke hoods be carried on all [commercial] airplanes. . . ." The FAA's Civil Aero-medical Institute had done an intense investigation into the smoke hood in 1967. It had determined that the smoke hoods were of great value and could be employed on aircraft as standard equipment similar to oxygen masks.

But on August 18, 1970, the FAA withdrew its notice of proposed rule making. The new statement said, "The FAA believes that the use of currently designed smoke hoods might delay emergency evacuation to an unacceptable degree. In addition, in the light of many comments received from representatives of the aviation industry, and other interested persons who support this view, the FAA has concluded that the proposed regulatory action is not justified at this time."

Chuck Miller, former head of the Bureau of Aviation Safety for the NTSB, said he remembers the controversy that surrounded the proposal of smoke hood legislation. He said the FAA had a number of people in favor of it and an almost equal number opposed, and he implied that the airlines put fierce pressure on the FAA to reject the plan. Their rationale: Having a smoke hood on board is an admission to the passenger that a crash is possible.

Not everyone has stood idly by as the FAA has seemingly pandered to the airlines' interests in the toxic smoke controversy. The NTSB, an independent agency with no authority to make regulations, has constantly prodded the FAA to act on its recommendations. Charles Miller, who headed the NTSB's bureau of aviation safety until he took "early retirement" last September 4, made fire and smoke research his pet project. "We thought more could be done in the prevention of fires," he says. "The technology is there and it hasn't been exploited."

The airline industry, which contributed heavily to the Nixon presidential campaigns, made sure that troublemakers like Miller stayed in their place. More than two years ago, Miller says, the White House began to politicize the NTSB. "I just got damn sick and tired of the efforts of the Nixon crew . . . and it became a conflict between myself and what I call the White House Mafia, the guys who were put in these agencies to get rid of people like me, who weren't going to sit back and say what they were told to say." Miller blames a man named Richard L. Spears, a former public relations man with little aviation safety background, for emasculating the NTSB when he became its general manager. Spears directed the board to put on a back burner follow-up studies keeping tabs on the FAA.

"When Spears came in, he took over line management of the Bureau of Aviation Safety. And I objected to this vigorously, and to congressional committees, in every way I knew.

"They (Spears and his bosses) had a basic policy that there would be no public airing of disagreements between parts of the government and the executive branch. And we used to get into some pretty good flaps with the FAA, as you can well imagine.

"Well, I was told in the spring of 1972—two years before the public got tied up with Watergate or anything else—I was told by this guy Spears that the orders were coming from Haldeman. I asked him who the hell was giving you the orders to come in and assume control of the boards? And he named Haldeman. I'd never heard of the guy before. I asked him why, and he said the administration's policy is not to have public controversies.

"One of the fundamental bitches I had at this guy the White House sent over was that he put tremendous pressure and effort on priority work—just getting the reports out. We have 20 fewer air safety investigators today than we had in 1963. Couple those two factors and you'll find out why the recommendations aren't being put out. You'll find out why people aren't making studies and why they're not pursuing the recommendations that have already been made. I am personally totally disgusted with the reaction of the Congress and other people who have permitted this sort of thing to continue. I thought it would change when Nixon resigned, but you've still got the same people who were there during the Nixon administration who issued the orders about emphasis on reports. The recommendations can take a secondary position and nobody's going to do a damn thing to get those people out of there."

Miller has long felt that passengers aren't told enough when they buy their tickets about what they should do in the case of a survivable accident. It's the FAA's fault for not making rules which require the airlines to make this information more available than it now is, says Miller.

"There's a difference between preventing a fire and getting you some time to get out," he said. "What you're trying to buy is time. Given that, I think you're going to get the people out who are going to get out . . . if they know what they're supposed to do. Of course, if you have a material that's going to cook off in 20 or 30 seconds, forget it. And in this area, I think there's some justifiable criticism of the system—and I don't want to point the finger purely at the FAA or purely at the manufacturers or the airlines. All of them are to blame. People just haven't knuckled down and said, 'By damn, we want this and we're gonna get it.' They've got to provide an atmosphere to get these people out and that includes information on how to get out."

At present, passengers may look in the pocket on the seat in front of them for an information card. The card speaks in euphemisms, is usually well-worn and is, one airline official admitted, one of the least looked-at items in the pouch. Miller was asked if it would help to hand each passenger a card as he or she checked in, or perhaps to bolt the directions on the back of each seat, so those still awake could be confronted with the information, whether they liked it or not.

"Those are good suggestions, but I think there is a more fundamental one, though," said Miller. "This has been proposed from time to time and I think it would be the most important piece of education someone could do. That's a program in the terminals or the waiting rooms where you could—without scaring the people—get the message across as to what the emergency evacuations are all about in a medium other than a card or printed instructions. I'm thinking of a slide show or film, and I can understand there is some reluctance on the part of the airlines to go this way for fear of not being able to come up with a non-scary approach. But I think it can be done. It takes somebody to make that first step."

A spokesman for Pan American admitted that "people just aren't supposed to talk about crashes. I mean, flying is still a very frightening experience for most people, no matter how calm they appear in the terminal. Most people don't want to think about the possibility of crashing, so they don't read that emergency card that's in the pouch in front of them" Asked why the airlines didn't provide specific instead of general information, that is, provide each passenger with directions appropriate for his seat location, he said: "It's really a matter of logistics. At each stop, you'd have to make sure every pouch had the right card when a flight lands. For example, if a flight lands in Denver heading for San Francisco, the flight attendants would have to clean up. They have 45 minutes to go through it and make sure there are fresh pillows in the racks, clean out the ashtrays and there's no way to ensure that seat 28 J has a different card than seat 28 K. Besides, you still can't force people to read them." He admitted that a film in the terminals might be a good idea, but he noted that it's not a very good means of advertising flight as a means of travel.

One reason the airlines are not forced to educate the public better is the lack of action in this and other areas by federal agencies. The NTSB has no regulatory powers. It can only investigate and recommend. And over the years the board has made virtually every recommendation needed for the safety of passengers under existing circumstances. That is, the airlines haven't been chided for building airplanes; the board has simply told the FAA to ensure that the airlines "clean up their act."

The problem has existed in the bureaucratic system. The FAA is, some say, unwieldy. The 1974–75 budget for the FAA was $1.76 billion. The FAA has on payroll 55,334 employees, scattered through every part of the United States. Max Karant of the AOPA did a survey in mid-1974 that showed the FAA spent an average of $11,650.85 for every active plane in the United States. The survey noted that there were 2.7 FAA employees for every pilot and 15.37 employees for every plane. Karant and others have charged that the FAA and industry are too closely tied together, and in fact there is a great case for conflict of interest. Karant chides Congress for not stepping in, but admits "they are conceding the problem as they have had it described to them."

The way things are supposed to work after an air crash is that the NTSB begins its investigation. It gathers pieces of the plane, retrieves the plane's flight recorder and other instruments, sifts through debris and tries to reconstruct the crash. This takes time. After a year, in most cases, the NTSB makes its final report on the probable cause of the crash and then its recommendations as to how to prevent future crashes.

The recommendations are passed along to the FAA, the regulatory agency which has the power to pass regulations with teeth. They come in the form of Airworthiness Directives, a dreaded word in the vocabulary of pilots and airplane owners. (There are other methods of enforcement, but Airworthiness Directives carry the worst penalty.)

ADs, as they are called, are the strongest demands the FAA can place on aircraft. When as AD "comes down"—as the pilots say—it means, "Act, and act now." It means that a specific repair or check is to be made immediately, and often ADs cost owners of planes a lot of money, occasionally a small fortune. For this reason, the FAA must be certain it is making the right decision when an AD is issued. A classic example of an FAA error cost 346 lives.

The FAA issued an AD in 1972, requiring McDonnell Douglas to make important changes in the cargo door's locking mechanism of its DC-10s. The AD was issued after a ground pressure test and then, nearly two years later, an inflight near-tragedy over Detroit startled the NTSB. The NTSB demanded and got an AD, but then-FAA Administrator John Shaffer, for reasons only he knows, downgraded the AD regarding that vital change. He told the company it could issue a Service Bulletin, which lacks the same urgency an an AD to its maintenance crews. Congress held hearings after a Turkish DC-10 slammed into a forest near Paris, killing 346 persons, and it heard Shaffer's arrangement with McDonnell Douglas termed a "gentlemen's agreement."

"That was an unfortunate thing," said Max Karant. "I feel sorry for Jack (Shaffer) and I feel sorry for those people on that airplane and I . . . guess I feel sorry for McDonnell Douglas. But those bastards could have done something about that if they had enough push behind them. If an AD had come down, they'd have done it, right now. In fact, you just pick up the phone and say, 'All those airplanes are grounded,' that's all the administrator'd have to say. . . ."

The DC-10 Paris crash can't be blamed entirely on the FAA, however, because hearings held in Washington and Los Angeles later showed that paperwork turned in by McDonnell Douglas "proved" that the cargo door which collapsed had been modified. The NTSB investigation showed it had not. And so perhaps the FAA's error was not in the way it had the problem corrected, but in failing to check that all DC-10s had been properly fixed. The FAA, when it asked last year for a budget of $2.1 billion (which was later cut), said it needed more money to hire more investigators to check on the airline companies, to make sure they follow orders.

The main problem with finding solutions to saving people in the so-called survivable accident is that often people with good suggestions are dead. The FAA has been investigating the smoke-death problem for at least nine years, but back in 1965 a man maned R. H. Dawson wrote the Civil Aeronautics Board with some ideas. The CAB was then doing the same work now being done by the NTSB, and Dawson was one of the survivors of the Salt Lake City crash. Dawson had then worked 19 years for DuPont's Explosives Department.

He was never interviewed by the CAB. His long and carefully prepared letter to Charles Murphy, then CAB chairman, included a number of logical suggestions. He suggested more and better-designed exits, a better emergency lighting system so people can see the exits (since in the Salt Lake City crash "smoke was so thick and traveled so fast with flames spreading closely behind that victims suffocated before they could reach the exits.") He suggested a battery-operated automatic beeping system so passengers could find exits in dense smoke. He suggested more frequent testing of emergency doors and standardization of handles.

"I suggest a dry (empty) sprinkler system be incorporated into every fuselage," Dawson wrote. "The foam hoses could be quickly attached from the fire trucks as they arrive at the crash to flood the inside. . . ." He suggested a better pre-flight education using mock-up emergency doors and windows.

George S. Moore, director of flight standards for the FAA, replied to Dawson, acknowledging that some of his suggestions were good and would be looked into. Yet today, the design of the B-727 is nearly the same as it was then. Moore's reply also contained the phrase, ". . . retrofitting of existing aircraft could cause an extreme economic burden."

To which Dawson replied in a later letter: "How many additional exits could the industry have, compared with the insurance settlements on 58 deaths in Cincinnati, and 43 deaths in Salt Lake City?" In his first letter, Dawson had suggested an unblocking of exits; the suggestion was met with a simple sentence about how the seat in front of an exit folds over to permit easy access. Dawson's reply: "Has anyone tried to fold one over with a person in one?"

As if it weren't enough to be embroiled in public linen washings with the NTSB, the FAA has recently found a new foe: the press. Virtually every agency that either prints or speaks the language has taken a closer look into the workings of the FAA and the NTSB and has found some interesting facts. It leaped onto newspaper front pages in early 1975 when, unexpectedly, the NTSB issued a report critical of airline escape systems. In that report, the NTSB claimed the FAA had refused to act on a number of potential dangers identified during investigations.

In late December 1975, the FAA had announced it would form an independent panel to review safety recommendations made by the House Subcommittee on Investigations. That congressional body had severely criticised the FAA for actions on air safety and said the agency had a record of inaction and delay that "may actually endanger human life."

The main conclusion of the House report was that too often the FAA, despite its billion-dollar budget and 55,000 employees, had permitted the industry to regulate itself. It seemed a rather strong indictment of the FAA, but its origins were not out of the blue. Earlier in the month, a Trans World Airlines B-727 had crashed at Washington's own Dulles International Airport, the same one used by many congressmen. This was hitting too close to home; something now had to be done.

There followed the NTSB's stinging rebuke, perhaps on the theory that, if you kick a man when he's down, you hurt him more. FAA's administrator, Alexander Porter Butterfield, had not come across very well on a recent television program on air safety and there were rumors he was about to be fired. This, combined with the House investigation, made the NTSB's time ripe and the criticism came flowing.

Perhaps the man who saw some of the boat-rocking coming was Claude S. Brinegar, the secretary of the Department of Transportation. Early on he asked President Ford if he could resign. Ford accepted the resignation, effective February 1. Being then a lame duck, Brinegar became more public. He and Butterfield had been at odds for some time and when a three-man panel was created by the FAA to look at the House Subcommittee's air safety recommendations, Brinegar became upset.

Then on January 17, Butterfield—the man who revealed the infamous White House taping system during the Watergate hearings—revealed that his three-man panel had resigned because DOT had cut back its authority. Brinegar gave no reason for cutting back the authority of the panel, but he later announced he was establishing his own panel to study the same areas, 29 recommendations having already been made by the House Subcommittee. Then came published reports that Brinegar was trying to have Butterfield fired, but Ron Nessen, Ford's press aide, scotched that rumor by saying that if Ford had wanted to remove Butterfield, he would have done so himself.

All this public controversy is fairly recent. Mostly what has happened in the past with such government agencies as the FAA and the NTSB is that they went about their business without public exposure. Perhaps the disclosures about the CIA, Watergate, and the FBI prompted reporters to delve into normally placid waters. Perhaps we are just more aware of these problems now.

But back in the dark days of 1972, when the NTSB was being radically changed by internal moves, the public was basically unaware of what was going on.

The apparent gutting of the NTSB came at about the time Dr. Irwin Einhorn of the University of Utah and others were reporting on studies that showed just how great a danger was posed by the fumes: Einhorn's research showed that polymers treated to resist fire produced more carbon monoxide and hydrogen cyanide gases than nontreated materials. Other studies proved that a single deep breath of that sort of mixture could kill; at best, it would incapacitate and disorient a passenger, making his head swim, his eyes function poorly and his arms and legs become hopelessly wobbly.

The airlines now say they are testing new materials even more flame-resistant than those used at present. There is only one thing wrong with that: The new materials will produce more dangerous smoke than ever.

Dr. Einhorn notes that on a recent American Airlines flight, he saw floor carpeting being used on the interior walls of the cabin as a decorative material. Carpeting, although quite resistant to flame when lying on the floor, burns rapidly when in a vertical position.

Safer, alternative materials do exist: the so-called space-age plastics. They are all reputed to be immune to flame and to produce little if any smoke when flame is applied to them. Their names—Tedlar, Durette, Nomex, PBI Foam, Kerimid Glass, Kevlar, and Refset. Some have been around since the mid-1960s. In fact, NASA used Refset in Apollo 11. Yet none of the materials has been used by any major airline. It appears that cost is the reason.

So for the moment, airline passengers concerned with their safety can only continue to do what they have always done: sit near an exit, read the directions in the pocket in front of them, not drink or smoke and pray. The laws that will protect them have not yet been passed.

part VII

Police corruption and usurpations of power

Earlier sociological theories of deviance assumed that it resulted from certain defects in the individuals involved or from defects in their society. The first theory attributed deviance to defects in moral character, psychological makeup or predisposition, individual pathology, or family background and early socialization patterns. The other theory attributed deviance to those features which were considered definitive of a given society. In both cases, investigating the actions of the lawful agents of social control was neglected by sociologists, since that was considered unimportant to understanding the nature of social deviance. The situation has changed greatly since the advent of the "labeling approach" to the study of deviance. The labeling approach contends that attributions to deviance arise from the interactional process between those individuals engaged in some kind of activity and those others who perceive, define, classify, stigmatize, or, in some other manner, respond to these acts. This means that perceptions of deviance are reflexively tied to the standards of those who are judging, or, in the case of legally defined acts, such as crimes, to the social power of certain groups to enforce their own concepts. Furthermore, the labeling approach holds that deviance is contingent on concrete situations. Thus, the development of the sociological labeling theory has led to a new scientific interest in the actions of official agents of control, especially the nature of their relationships with their target populations. These continually developing ideas have generated many excellent studies of official control agents during the past decade, and our sociological understanding of the operations of police officials has been enhanced accordingly.

Part VII opens with an excerpt from the President's Crime Commission Report. "Police Integrity" begins by listing the more common forms of police deviance which were observed by the commission investigators during their field inquiries, continues to an examination of the background and bases for these actions, and concludes with some recommendations to eliminate or reduce official corruption. Although this excerpt is, in many ways, a compe- tent overview of police corruption, our earlier readings have led us to be skeptical of proposals to reduce corruption by the introduction of further formal bureaucratic rules. As we have seen so often, making new rules to correct other rule violations only creates new opportunities for rule viola- tions, albeit ones which may differ from the original ones. Chapter 25, "Police Corruption in New York City," presents some of the Knapp Com- mission findings about widespread police deviance and corruption. Unlike the members of the President's Crime Commission, the Knapp Commission contends that we cannot reach a very good or realistic understanding of police corruption by insisting that it results from a failure of either police integrity or ethical conduct. This "rotten apple" theory has been a great hindrance to our understanding as well as a great obstacle to our reform efforts, according to the Knapp Commission report. This argument receives support in "Invitational Edges of Corruption," (Chapter 26) in which sociol- ogists Peter Manning and Lawrence Redlinger argue that the pervasive cor- ruption of narcotics law enforcement is intimately tied to the goal of con- trolling illicit markets. Similar points are made by William Chambliss in Chap- ter 27, "Vice, Corruption, Bureaucracy, and Power," an excellent sociological analysis of the many complexities of the official corruption found in all of our large cities. These chapters show us that certain forms of police deviance almost invariably result when we ask the police to enforce moralistic laws whose interpretations differ among the diverse groups of our society. It re- mains to be seen how many of our middle-class citizens will come to under- stand this, and the social costs involved, and will demand a cessation of these tyrannical impositions of middle-class standards on the rest of the citizenry. At this time, the prognosis is not a promising one.

Police
integrity

The Need for Ethical Conduct

Exacting ethical standards and a high degree of honesty are perhaps more essential for the police than for any other group in society. Because the police are entrusted with the enforcement of the fundamental rules that guide society's conduct, a policeman's violation of the law or his corrupt failure to enforce it dishonors the law and the authority he represents. Dishonesty within a police agency can, almost overnight, destroy respect and trust that has been built up over a period of years by honest local government and police officials. Nothing undermines public confidence in the police and the process of criminal justice more than the illegal acts of officers. Support for the police in their work, and the bringing about of crucial changes such as those recommended by the Commission to strengthen the police, can easily

From President's Commission on Law Enforcement and the Administration of Justice, *The Challenge of Crime in a Free Society.* Washington: Government Printing Office, 1967.

be impaired by a belief that the police themselves are not taking every possible measure to eradicate corruption and unethical conduct.

As this chapter will point out, the dishonest policeman is, in many cases, strongly influenced by the corruption of others—politicians, businessmen, and private citizens. Although he is inherently no more resistant to temptation than anyone else, his position exposes him to extraordinary pressures. In many cases practices that are accepted in other fields and occupations—such as tipping and doing favors—are particularly difficult to avoid in police work. Conflicting pressures are often placed upon the police. For example, police are required to enforce parking and gambling laws, though most of the community might prefer them not to. Public resistance to the enforcement of such laws greatly increases the temptation to accept favors, gratuities or bribes, or simply to ignore violations. Police dishonesty is, of course, a series of private tragedies for the officers who become involved. It also affects the morale of thousands of honest policemen who suffer from popular identification with those involved in corruption or misconduct. When the "dishonest cop" headline appears, honest police officers throughout the country are adversely affected, "the feeling of pride slips and * * * a hint of shame takes hold."[1]

Field studies undertaken by the Commission and the work of its consultants have revealed that at least in some cities a significant number of officers engage in varying forms of criminal and unethical conduct. The Commission's limited studies afford no basis for general conclusions as to the exact extent of police dishonesty or the degree to which political corruption affects police service today. But these studies have shown that even in some of the departments where the integrity of top administrators is unquestioned, instances of illegal and unethical conduct are a continuing problem—particularly in slum areas, where the most incompetent officers tend to be assigned in some cities. Administrators with whom the Commission has consulted acknowledge that dishonesty is a problem that must be frankly confronted if their objective of eradicating such misconduct is to be achieved.

Patterns of Dishonesty

The violations in which police are involved vary widely in character. The most common are improper political influence; acceptance of gratuities or bribes in exchange for nonenforcement of laws, particularly those relating to gambling, prostitution, and liquor offenses, which are often extensively interconnected with organized crime; the "fixing" of traffic tickets; minor thefts; and occasional burglaries. The Commission's work also revealed some instances of police officers in high-crime neighborhoods engaging in such prac-

1. Mort Stern, "What Makes a Policeman Go Wrong," Denver Post, Oct. 8, 1961, sec. A, p. 1, col. 1.

tices as rolling drunks and shakedowns of money and merchandise in the very places where respect for law is so badly needed.

Political Corruption

Government corruption in the United States has troubled historians, political reformers, and the general public since the middle of the 19th century.[2] Metropolitan police forces—most of which developed during the late 1800's when government corruption was most prevalent—have often been deeply involved in corruption.[3] The police are particularly susceptible to the forms of corruption that have attracted widest attention—those that involve tolerance or support of organized crime activities. But the police, as one of the largest and most strategic groups in metropolitan government, are also likely targets for political patronage, favoritism, and other kinds of influence that have pervaded local governments dominated by political machines. Against both forms of corruption, responsible police leaders have fought a continuing battle—one that appears to be steadily gaining.[4]

The remnants of corrupt political control allied with organized crime and vice operations have, however, continued to plague some cities—as evidenced by widely publicized incidents during the past 10 years, particularly concerning organized crime activities. In Newport, Ky., for example, city officials and police were indicted in 1963 for permitting organized vice and gambling activities to flourish.[5] In 1961, corruption in Boston was exposed through a nationwide television documentary which showed 10 policemen entering and leaving a bookmaking establishment in a locksmith's shop. Prior to release of the film, the Internal Revenue Service, acting upon complaints originating from the New England Citizens Crime Commission, raided the shop; but when State police raided the shop 4 weeks later it was again operating openly. As a result of this scandal, a survey of the department was ordered, and the police commissioner was replaced.[6]

In May 1961, a raid by agents of the Internal Revenue Service on a gambling establishment in New Kensington, Pa., uncovered corruption there. The subsequent election of a reform mayor and the appointment of an honest

2. See e.g., Lincoln Steffens, "The Shame of the Cities" (New York: McClure, Phillips, 1904), 306 p.

3. Charles Reith, "The Blind Eye of History" (London: Faber & Faber Ltd., 1952), p. 83.

4. Ralph Lee Smith, "The Tarnished Badge" (New York: Thomas Y. Crowell Co., 1965), p. 230.

5. "Challenge to Morality," Christian Science Monitor (Boston), Jan. 9, 1963, p. 9, col. 3.

6. Ibid. Also, see Dwight S. Strong, "New England: The Refined Yankee in Organized Crime," The Annals, 247:40–50, 48 (May 1963).

chief of police ended a regime that "was so closely controlled by organized crime that the community seemed helpless in its grip."[7]

Perhaps the most notorious such incident was the gangland-type murder of State Attorney General-elect Albert L. Patterson, resulting in a cleanup of Phenix City, Ala., in 1955. Both the sheriff and the mayor resigned their offices, were charged, and paid fines for wilfully neglecting their duties. Scores of gamblers went to prison.[8]

Another form of political corruption—where police appointments are considered a reward for political favors and police officials are consequently responsive primarily to the local political machine—is still a fairly open and tacitly accepted practice in many small cities and counties. It recurs too, from time to time, in larger cities, though generally in less conspicuous form.

Even in some cities where reforms have ended open political control of the police, policemen who make trouble for businessmen with strong political influence may still be transferred to punishment beats, and traffic tickets may still be fixed in some places through political connections. Honest and conscientious police chiefs often have an extremely difficult time eliminating these practices.

Such assignment practices may be present in the lower ranks of individual precincts or bureaus, and, if detected, are often difficult to prove with the certainty needed to take action under cumbersome civil service regulations. Appeal to a mayor, city council, or prosecutor may of course be fruitless, since they themselves may be involved in or condone such practices. The general public often accepts this style of city government as simply "the way things are," and the policeman who tries to buck such a system is likely to be ostracized by his companions and lose any chance he may have had to advance in his career. Political corruption in police personnel practices, although rarely dramatic enough to make headlines, can in itself destroy the morale of the honest and conscientious officer, and deter able men from careers in law enforcement.

Nonenforcement of the Law

Chapter 2 has discussed the problems that confront the police when they are faced with enforcement of laws in such areas as gambling, prostitution, liquor, and traffic. In many cases there are strong community pressures against enforcement of such laws. In others neither the police nor the rest of the criminal justice system have the resources or ability to attempt full enforcement and in these cases a pattern of selective nonenforcement prevails. Some prosecutors and judges react to selective enforcement problems by dropping cases or imposing fines low enough to be accepted as part of the

7. Supra, note 5 at col. 2.
8. Supra, note 5 at col. 1.

overhead of illegal business. This can create an environment in which dishonesty thrives.

Sometimes enforcement policies are decided openly and rationally by such means as chapter 2 suggests; in such instances selective enforcement is properly regulated. But in others, nonenforcement may become the occasion for bribery or other corruption. Thus, in the prohibition era, millions of people sought and found ways to disregard the ban on liquor, and police attempts at enforcement were met with citizen condemnation and offers of payment for tolerance of community norms.

While the wholesale corruption of prohibition days has passed, illegitimate nonenforcement remains a problem. One west coast police official described in this fashion how a bookie once attempted to influence him:

These people really work on you. They make it seem so logical—like you are the one that is out of step. This bookie gave me this kind of a line: "It's legal at the tracks, isn't it? So why isn't it legal here? It's because of these crooks at the Capitol. They're gettin' plenty—all drivin' Cads. Look at my customers, some of the biggest guys in town—they don't want you to close me down. If you do they'll just transfer you. Like that last jerk. And even the Judge, what did he do?: Fined me a hundred and suspended fifty. Hell, he knows Joe citizen wants me here, so get smart, be one of the boys, be part of the system. It's a way of life in this town and you're not gonna change it. Tell you what I'll do. I won't give you a nickel; just call in a free bet in the first race every day and you can win or lose, how about it?"[9]

The corrupt offer may come from the law-violator, as in the previous example. But initiation of such offers is not confined to people so clearly involved in illicit enterprises. A patrol division commander in one city described another common situation:

This fellow was president of his local service club and he was always shoving something into the officer's hand saying, "here's a little trinket for the wife!" He did the same thing with delivery men and others in return for small favors. In our case it was in appreciation for the officer not tagging overparked or double-parked customers' vehicles in front of the shop. He really didn't see any harm in what he was doing.[10]

In another city it was common practice for a detective to provide a list of names of selected police officers to leading law firms and large hotels for distribution of liquor at Christmas time. In the same city it was customary for

9. This example was one of many provided to the staff of the Commission by police officials from various cities in the United States.
10. Ibid.

detectives assigned to the pawn shop detail to receive special Christmas gitfs from each of the downtown pawnbrokers.[11]

These practices may be little different in kind from exchanges that commonly occur in the business world, but they have a far more ominous implication when they involve public officials. And they may lead to far more serious misconduct.

Certain traffic accidents provide the setting for another form of mutual consent bribery:

In an accident situation where the officer can cite either party, he may stall, maybe give a slight hint—or the citizen may take the initiative. The citizen generally tells the officer a sad story, walks over to the officer's car and leans over the front door. This is the cue. What actually happens is that money is dropped onto the floor of the car. The officer then decides not to issue any citation and leaves in his car—after he has also secretly collected a reward from the tow-car operator. When he "discovers" the money on the floor of his car he now has money from two sources. These cases are very difficult for internal investigations units to make, but it can be done if enough manpower is made available.[12]

In some cities corruption has been so highly organized within a precinct or department that there are regular fees for permitting various activities, collected at set intervals by a "lieutenant's man." In one large eastern city, for example, contractors who wished to unload materials at curbside had to pay a given per diem to the precinct captain—ostensibly to cover the cost of a patrolman to supervise traffic, though in fact there was no basis for such a charge for police services, and no special assistance was given. In another city, workmen at construction sites have been known to line up during their morning coffee break each day to pay a dollar to the beat patrolman for not ticketing their illegally parked cars.

Theft

The problem of theft by police officers sometimes takes a form less blatant than the occasional, well-publicized burglary such as the Summerdale incident, which resulted in the reorganization of the entire Chicago police department in 1960, and the 1961 apprehension in Denver of a ring of police burglars, which resulted in dismissal of 52 men. In some cities, the Commission determined that some officers kept stolen property recovered by investigation, stole small items from stores when a patrol inspection disclosed an unlocked door, or emptied the pockets of drunks before they were taken to the stationhouse.

11. Ibid.
12. Ibid.

A ranking police official from a southwestern city illustrated the problem with this example:

> One night one of our men discovered an unlocked jewelry store. He flushed out the building for a possible burglar, and when he discovered all was secure he checked the safe. It was also unlocked and contained several trays of diamond and ruby rings. He yielded to temptation and took a ring for his wife. He rationalized by thinking the owner would collect insurance when he discovered the loss and that way nobody would really lose.[13]

A pattern that was described by more than one police official was that of storekeepers who also take the attitude that insurance will cover losses and, as a mark of appreciation when policemen discover an unlocked door or investigate a burglary, invite them to help themselves to merchandise that can be reported as having been stolen.

Some officers have also been known to take building material and actually transport it in police vehicles. In one city officers picked up nails, tools, bundles of shingles, roofing paper and other items from the "midnight supply company" while working their shift. They were remodeling their houses and rationalized their act on the basis of numerous reports of stolen property from building contractors presumably much of it taken by workmen on the job. One of the officers was a former building trade worker and looked upon this form of "toting" as an accepted practice.

Kickbacks

Particularly in the case of traffic offenses there is also an opportunity, which has sometimes resulted in publicized incidents, for policemen to receive payments for referring business to others such as towing companies, ambulance companies, garages, and lawyers who specialize in traffic accident damage suits. In one large city, for example, lawyers' "runners" with radio-equipped cars sometimes showed up at accidents. The result was an automatic $25 for the police officer handling it if the victim could be influenced to accept the attorney. [14] Licensing, inspection, and truck weighing duties also have afforded opportunities for this sort of unethical conduct.

The Background of the Problem

Since such conduct continues to be a problem of concern for police officials, inquiry is required into the underlying factors that contribute to dishonesty and violation of ethics. A number of these are apparent from the incidents used in previous examples.

13. Ibid.
14. Ibid.

Political Domination

The problem of old-style domination of the police by political machines has attracted the most intensive reform efforts from the police themselves. As a result, the effort to establish independent, professional law enforcement has made considerable headway over the past 30 years. This movement has not been without its own problems, however; the tradition of improper political interference is deep-rooted.

Further, civil service regulations in many jurisdictions have sometimes restricted the reform attempts of honest police executives. In many cities, for example, it is extremely difficult to remove officers who have engaged in serious acts of misconduct.

It is obvious that improper political interference contributes to corruption. Patronage appointments lower the quality of personnel and encourage all officers to cooperate with politicians, even in improper circumstances. Although a man might withstand this temptation for himself, it may be impossible or even pointless for him to separate himself from the practices of his superiors or partners.

Dishonest Superiors and Fellow Officers

Not long ago, the police commissioner of a large city expressed publicly his pessimism about the ability of training to protect new recruits from the pressures of improper conduct. He preferred to assign his best young officers to a tactical force that operated as a unit entirely separate and apart from the traditional organization. In that way, he said, it kept them out of "the system," where a new man was sometimes subjected to heavy pressures to conform to unethical practices, such as splitting tow-truck rebates and accepting gifts from merchants.

In many cases, of course, an honest recruit if properly trained and motivated will decide to report a matter to his superiors and assist in prosecuting disciplinary action.

For example, proper action was taken by the officer in the following case:

Nothing is more despised by honest policemen than the corrupt officer who leads the younger men into a pattern of graft. If this kind of an officer is part of a two-man motor patrol, he must convince his partner to go along with the shakedown or he can't operate. This happened to me when I was a young officer. But I avoided involvement. Instead we made a case against him and he was fired. My sergeant backed me all the way.[15]

But this is often not easy. In some cases superiors, too, may be involved in dishonesty. When this is known to the officer he should report the incident to a superior he trusts, even if he must go as high as the chief himself or to an outside agency. To protect the officer supervisors can, in most instances, develop a case without revealing the identity of the reporting officer.

All police officers have taken an oath to uphold the law and to support the regulations of their department. While in some cases proper action may be difficult and require considerable fortitude, the general problem cannot be overcome until there is a strong determination within all law enforcement agencies to rid the profession of the "rotten apples." Failure to do so by withholding information should be cause for severe disciplinary action. This rule is firmly enforced within the Federal Bureau of Investigation and may be one of the strong influencing factors responsible for its outstanding record of integrity.

Whenever a number of dishonest officers are tolerated by other officers within a police organization, an atmosphere of mutual support and protection may develop, and eventually it may taint the entire police system. This was illustrated in the 1961 Denver scandal when it became apparent that there were varying degrees of involvement. The illegal practice centered about a small group of corrupt officers. The majority of the officers involved were passive participants; their grave error was only the failure to recognize a sworn obligation to report the activity to officials who could have taken proper action.

The personal ethical standards of police supervisors and executives exert great influence in establishing an agency's attitude toward dishonest police behavior. If an officer suspects that others support or simply condone dishonesty, his own definition of what comprises proper conduct may shift to accord with his concept of departmental norms.

Supervisors may create an atmosphere that supports corruption if they place popularity among patrolmen above their supervisory responsibilities. Such an official may be willing to excuse infractions of departmental rules. He may keep from the police chief information that an officer accepted a number of small items from a local merchant. He may realize that a patrolman is engaging in misconduct, but to avoid controversy and to maintain what he considers a good working relationship, he may remain silent.

Chiefs of police who are suspected of improper action can exert an even more serious influence. Such men may symbolize to young officers the standard for reaching the top. When the chief is known to be responsive to improper political pressure or even to take orders from criminal elements, corruption can be considered a necessary route to promotion. At the least, the existence of dishonesty at the top levels of command may influence an officer to accept favors.

Public Participation

One major reason why police dishonesty continues is that large sections of the public contribute to it or condone it.

It is not merely the professional gambler offering a patrolman a free bet who promotes corruption, but the motorist, who thinks little of offering a traffic officer $5 to avoid a ticket, or the businessman who presses gifts and gratuities on police in return for indulgences or other favors.

Even where such practices seem relatively harmless in and of themselves, they may easily establish an atmosphere wherein it becomes impossible to resist more serious bribery. More generally, it is unrealistic to expect a police force to maintain absolute integrity in a city where petty corruption and political favoritism are accepted by the public.

The widespread practice among other segments of the community of using positions of authority to elicit small gifts or favors may similarly influence the police. Police executives have often compared a businessman's accepting gifts from manufacturers and salesmen with an officer's accepting gratuities from merchants in his patrol area. While such conduct by the police is clearly unethical, the fact that the practice is accepted in the business world understandably leads some officers to question the harm of accepting small gratuities.

Lack of Enforcement Policy

A considerable number of the most serious and persistent kinds of unethical conduct are connected with failure to enforce laws that are not in accord with community norms. Among these are laws concerning gambling, prostitution, liquor, and traffic. The failure of police administrators and other law enforcement officials—and ultimately of legislators and the general public—to acknowledge frankly the paradoxes confronting enforcement officials, has meant that only rarely have explicit policies and guides to enforcement in these areas been developed and enforced.

Recruitment, Training, and Compensation

The inability to attract and retain men of higher character and the failure to screen applicants carefully enough contribute to the problem of dishonesty. A failure to confront in training the various ethical dilemmas that may be faced by a policeman can compound this situation. Recruits may get the idea that a department's command really does not care about ethics in borderline situations. Or they may simply never realize that some practices constitute ethical violations, especially if they have not been so informed, and if they see other officers engaging in such practices.

Low salaries may also contribute to police dishonesty, both by making it more difficult to recruit able men and by providing a convenient rationale for illegal enrichment.

Isolation

The climate of isolation between police and community that exists in some places, particularly in slum neighborhoods, has a pervasive influence in supporting misconduct. In such neighborhoods a policeman tends to see only the bad and to have contact with residents only when they have committed an offense. He may come to feel that the problems he is to deal with are insoluble and that he has no support or cooperation from the community. It is easy for the man who feels himself to be an outcast to react by disregarding standards of ethics and law.

A dishonest officer in such precincts may also, in fact, be less liable to exposure. In too many such cases there is little formal contact between responsible police officials and residents. The latter may feel with justification that to protest dishonest police behavior is futile.

These neighborhoods are characterized as undesirable assignment districts, and, in fact, many officers have been transferred there because of past misconduct. Often too, these neighborhoods have a history of being ignored not only by the police but by the many agencies of government. Consequently, when a department contains a few dishonest officers, and when the story heard is of police tolerance of misconduct, the slumdweller who wants to rely upon the police for protection and counsel may eventually become seriously disillusioned not only with the police but also with all branches of government. This is one important reason why it is recommended in chapter 5 that the most highly qualified officers be assigned to high crime areas of social unrest.

This same isolation tends also to close off discussion of progressive ideas of law enforcement. Outside surveys and research that would analyze organizational structure, personnel, and other important police matters might also uncover dishonest practice. Therefore, corrupt officers, especially those who might hold supervisory positions, will seek to discourage such research. As a result, lax departments may continue with practices that have been discredited and replaced years before in other cities by responsible police officials.

Maintaining Police Integrity

It is the police themselves, in the vast majority of cases, who are ridding their profession of the unethical and the corrupt. An ever-increasing number of law enforcement leaders are realizing that vigilance against such practices is a continuing part of their responsibilities. For over 40 years Director J. Edgar Hoover and his associates throughout the FBI organization have set an outstanding example of integrity within a law enforcement agency. Through the influence of its special agents throughout the country, working in close contact with local police officers, and through its training programs at the FBI National Academy and local training schools, the FBI has encouraged thousands of police officers to emulate its standards.

National, State, and local police associations have also done a great deal to encourage police integrity. The Law Enforcement Code of Ethics has been adopted by all major police associations and agencies throughout the Nation. In California, for example, State law requires that police ethics be taught and that the code be administered as an oath to all police recruits training in the 45 police academies certified by the State Commission on Peace Officers Standards.[16] In 1955, the International Conference of Police Associations[17] developed a lesson plan for the teaching of ethics within police organizations. The California Peace Officers Association and the Peace Officers Research Association maintain highly active committees on police standards and ethics and are responsible for most of the high ethical standards established throughout the State. And the International Association of Chiefs of Police constantly strives to establish and maintain honest police leadership. Other police consulting firms have made similar recommendations. Through numerous surveys of police departments, it has pointed up the need for maintaining police integrity through the establishment of internal investigation units. The Fraternal Order of Police has stressed the need for attracting high caliber police recruits through adequate salaries, sound retirement systems and other benefits.

Such groups should increase their activity in this field. Local police associations especially must be alert to the problem, recognizing the relationship between maintaining integrity and good conduct and improving the public image of the police. This can lead to more adequate pay and equipment, along with improved working conditions. Associations that come to the aid of dishonest officers render an obvious disservice, not only to themselves, but to the entire police profession.

There are a number of specific directions in which action to ensure integrity should be taken.

Political Accountability

Political accountability of the police should be resolved solely at the executive level. The police chief should be responsible to only one executive, and not to minor officials. These officials should bring their suggestions and questions about law enforcement problems to the attention of the political executive. If he considers the matter appropriate for police action, it should be his responsibility to communicate it to the chief of police. General enforcement policies should be discussed among police, prosecutors, and community groups. These should be approved by the political executive and given full publicity in the community, especially with those directly affected.

Articulation of Policy

Police departments should establish policies that outline in detail proper and improper police practice. As discussed in chapter 2 such policies should

16. Admin. Code of Cal., tit. 2, ch. 2, sec. 1003.
17. Until 1955, known as the National Conference of Police Associations.

LAW ENFORCEMENT CODE OF ETHICS

As a Law Enforcement Officer, my fundamental duty is to serve mankind; to safeguard lives and property; to protect the innocent against deception, the weak against oppression or intimidation, and the peaceful against violence or disorder; and to respect the Constitutional rights of all men to liberty, equality and justice.

I will keep my private life unsullied as an example to all; maintain courageous calm in the face of danger, scorn, or ridicule; develop self-restraint; and be constantly mindful of the welfare of others. Honest in thought and deed in both my personal and official life, I will be exemplary in obeying the laws of the land and the regulations of my department. Whatever I see or hear of a confidential nature or that is confided to me in my official capacity will be kept ever secret unless revelation is necessary in the performance of my duty.

I will never act officiously or permit personal feelings, prejudices, animosities or friendships to influence my decisions. With no compromise for crime and with relentless prosecution of criminals, I will enforce the law courteously and appropriately without fear or favor, malice or ill will, never employing unnecessary force or violence and never accepting gratuities.

I recognize the badge of my office as a symbol of public faith, and I accept it as a public trust to be held so long as I am true to the ethics of the police service. I will constantly strive to achieve these objectives and ideals, dedicating myself before God to my chosen profession . . . law enforcement.

---

be stressed in training, reviewed fully with all officers, and publicized in the community at large. The public should be expressly informed of its duties in helping prevent corruption. It should be stressed that prompt action will be taken against persons who participate in violations. Departments should define as unethical the acceptance of gifts, gratuities and favors by police officers, and should outline the common situations in which temptations to engage in dishonest conduct may arise. And such a rule must be enforced. The Oakland Police Department rules and regulations provide the following:

Section 310.70   Gifts, Gratuities, Fees, Rewards, Loans, etc., and Soliciting
Members and employees shall not under any circumstances solicit any gift, gratuity, loan, or fee where there is any direct or indirect connection between the solicitation and their departmental membership and employment.

Section 310.71   Acceptance of Gifts, Gratuities, Fees, Loans, etc.
Members and employees shall not accept either directly or indirectly any gift, gratuity, loan, fee, or any other thing of value arising from or offered because of police employment or any activity connected with said employment. Members and employees shall not accept any gift, gratuity, loan, fee, or other thing of value the acceptance of which might tend to influence directly or indirectly the actions of said member or employee or

any other member or employee in any matter of police business; or which might tend to cast any adverse reflection on the department or any member or employee thereof. No member or employee of the department shall receive any gift or gratuity from other members or employees junior in rank without the express permission of the chief of police.

Section 310.74   Rewards

Members and employees shall not accept any gift, gratuity, or reward in money or other consideration for services in the line of duty to the community or to any person, business, or agency except lawful salary and that authorized by Section 96.4 of the Charter of the City of Oakland which reads as follows:

"The Board of Trustees may on notice from the chief of police reward any member of the department for conduct which is heroic or meritorious. The sum or amount of such reward shall be discretionary with the Board of Trustees but it shall not exceed in any one instance one month's salary and may be paid only out of funds provided by the Council and the Council may on application of the Board of Trustees provide money for such purposes." (Commission note: No reward has been granted since 1950.)

Section 310.80   Free Admissions and Passes

Members and employees shall not solicit or accept free admissions or passes to theatres and other places of amusement for themselves or others except in the line of duty.[18]

Assignments which represent particular opportunity for extortion or bribery should receive special attention in both written policy and spot checking by an internal investigation unit. Particular attention should be given to department assignments that offer unusual opportunities for dishonesty. Vice or gambling squads are obvious examples. Some of the most routine assignments, such as traffic enforcement and inspection duty, may also contain leverage for extortion.

Reasonably precise procedures should be established to govern individual decisions where the exercise of discretion may be bargained for, such as the policing of bars, the assignment of wrecked or illegally parked automobiles to towing companies and the removal of sick and injured persons by ambulance. Departments should also establish policies and regulations governing situations in which officers may take advantage of their position of authority in nonduty situations such as offduty employment which conflicts with police interests and the acceptance of price concessions from businessmen. And procedures should be formulated which adequately control the care, custody, and

18. Oakland Police Department "Manual of Rules and Regulations," (Oakland, Calif.: Oakland Police Department, 1960).

release of property and evidence held by the police, especially money, liquor, jewelry; and firearms.

Internal Investigation Units

Internal investigation units should be established in all medium-sized and large police departments. These should serve in the dual role of general intelligence and investigation of specific reported cases of police misconduct.

In small departments, the chief, or at least a ranking officer, should be responsible for a planned program to ensure integrity. These units should also give attention to causes and manifestations of misconduct, and they should suggest to the police executive appropriate ways to prevent corruption. Such an internal investigation unit should operate separately from the law enforcement intelligence units, which have been established in many larger departments to provide information for attacks on organized crime. Otherwise, it might be impossible for the intelligence unit to gain the confidence and trust of officers and informants.

By broadening their responsibilities beyond investigating reported cases for prosecution, internal investigation units can keep the police administrator aware of various activities within the department that are most vulnerable or have the potential of becoming vehicles of dishonesty. They may also detect unreported instances of unethical conduct.

The problem of misconduct should not be treated as a series of isolated incidents. As an example, one department may discover officers who accept money or goods from local merchants in exchange for nonenforcement of traffic violations of customers or supply companies. The investigation unit may be able to discover the identity of most of the officers responsible, prove the charge, and have them dismissed from the department and prosecuted. At that point, the case is closed.

To stop here, however, leaves unsolved the question of why these officers become involved and others did not, and why some districts were especially prone to have dishonest officers and others were not. Analysis of the information gathered by the investigation unit may provide a variety of answers. One may be that officers who have turned dishonest have pressing debts, or supervision is lax. Or again, such officers may have remained in one assignment for periods greater than others.

Such information is of obvious value in preventing further dishonesty. Unless the study is carried this far, there is at least some reason to suspect that these contributory factors eventually may bring about a reappearance of dishonest practices.

Where cities do not have the resources to maintain adequate internal investigation units, the chief of police should seek assistance from the State attorney general or the State police in attacking internal integrity problems. State governments should provide the necessary trained investigators to assist local authorities. Chapter 4 suggests that police manpower should be pooled in a metropolitan area or among a cluster of cities, to provide the internal investigation support necessary to maintain police integrity. In some areas where professional police organizations exist at the county level it may be possible to provide an internal investigation unit to serve the entire county. In those States where the attorney general has responsibility to move against police dishonesty at the city and the county level this responsibility should be vigorously carried out by him.

Prosecution in Cases of Dishonesty

Police officials have sometimes argued that instances of police misconduct should be quietly resolved within a department itself. Evidence seems to indicate, however, that a department achieves greater respect from the community when dishonest officers are openly and vigorously prosecuted.

Similarly, private citizens and businessmen who offer bribes should also be prosecuted to discourage people who presently feel that only the most serious corruption is considered important enough to investigate or prosecute.

Personnel Selection

Perhaps the most fundamental method of maintaining integrity in law enforcement is through careful selection of personnel. All of the selection techniques available today must be used, including comprehensive background investigations and reliable tests to determine aptitude and emotional stability. As pointed out in chapter 5, personnel testing experts recognize that it is much more difficult to predict latent dishonesty than to predict some other forms of deviant human behavior. Research in depth is needed to devise adequate testing procedures which will provide the police with more reliable screening techniques than now exist.

Training

Officers should be taught the importance of ethics in law enforcement. Training should fully delineate the pitfalls that an officer will face and explain how he can avoid them.

It should clearly indicate the types of action to be taken by the officer under different circumstances, including, for instance, how he should proceed when he witnesses or learns of dishonest acts on the part of another officer. Training should also cover departmental policies for proper decision-making and should emphasize proper conduct as a factor in maintaining good community relations.

Training should especially emphasize the obligation of all officers to rid the profession of the unethical, and it should instill in the trainee a feeling of pride in his important work. In this regard FBI Director J. Edgar Hoover has stated:[19]

19. J. Edgar Hoover, "Message from the Director." FBI Law Enforcement Bulletin (Washington: U.S. Department of Justice, December 1951).

If every officer and law enforcement agency must suffer in some degree from charges made against other officers, we cannot afford to take a passive view, shrugging the matter off as none of our business.

I believe it is the duty of every officer in every law enforcement agency to take a personal interest in maintaining a high standard of conduct with his organization. To do otherwise invites public disgrace. The traitor to ethical standards of law enforcement will be discovered, but often not until he has brought a great deal of harm to both the public interest and the reputation of his organization and fellow officers. We should separate such elements from the profession at the earliest opportunity.

No matter what laws are passed or rules made, public service still demands the highest in personal integrity. We must demonstrate that the men of law enforcement have it in abundance.

Private Police

Traditional police tasks are not always performed by governmental police agencies alone. In order to reduce the threat of vandalism and theft, for example, industrial plants and department stores, among others, often hire private security agencies to provide protective services above and beyond that provided by a local police department. Although the right of these agencies to arrest, to search, or to question is no different from that given to any private citizen, their presence can serve as an added deterrent to persons who are seeking an opportunity to commit crimes. When someone is caught in the act of violating the law, security personnel typically either release the offender after a warning—if the misconduct is minor—or turn him over to the local police.

Recently the Governor of Florida hired a private security agency for quite a different purpose—to uncover facts about crime conditions and corruption within his State. The agency, which is responsible to the Governor alone, has been soliciting information about organized crime and reviewing books and records of selected public officials. As a result, it has accumulated files on individuals and has made at least one arrest.

Any agency that assumes responsibility for law enforcement must be held to high standards of integrity and respect for individual rights. Since it is not possible to subject private agencies to the necessary controls and safeguards that are imposed upon public police agencies, private police agencies should not be used to perform essential public law enforcement tasks, such as the gathering of criminal intelligence, for any branch or agency of government or for any elected or appointed official.

Police corruption in New York City

by The Knapp Commission

We found corruption to be widespread. It took various forms depending upon the activity involved, appearing at its most sophisticated among plainclothesmen assigned to enforcing gambling laws. In the five plainclothes divisions where our investigations were concentrated we found a strikingly standardized pattern of corruption. Plainclothesmen, participating in what is known in police parlance as a "pad," collected regular bi-weekly or monthly payments amounting to as much as $3,500 from each of the gambling establishments in the area under their jurisdiction, and divided the take in equal shares. The monthly share per man (called the "nut") ranged from $300 and $400 in midtown Manhattan to $1,500 in Harlem. When supervisors were involved they received a share and a half. A newly assigned plainclothesman was not entitled to his share for about two months, while he was

From Commission to Investigate Allegations of Police Corruption and the City's Anti-Corruption Procedures (Knapp Commission), *Commission Report*, pp. 1–7, 65–77.

checked out for reliability, but the earnings lost by the delay were made up to him in the form of two months' severance pay when he left the division.

Evidence before us led us to the conclusion that the same pattern existed in the remaining divisions which we did not investigate in depth. This conclusion was confirmed by events occurring before and after the period of our investigation. Prior to the Commission's existence, exposures by former plainclothesman Frank Serpico had led to indictments or departmental charges against nineteen plainclothesmen in a Bronx division for involvement in a pad where the nut was $800. After our public hearings had been completed, an investigation conducted by the Kings County District Attorney and the Department's Internal Affairs Division—which investigation neither the Commission nor its staff had even known about—resulted in indictments and charges against thirty-seven Brooklyn plainclothesmen who had participated in a pad with a nut of $1,200. The manner of operation of the pad involved in each of these situations was in every detail identical to that described at the Commission hearings, and in each almost every plainclothesman in the division, including supervisory lieutenants, was implicated.

Corruption in narcotics enforcement lacked the organization of the gambling pads, but individual payments—known as "scores"—were commonly received and could be staggering in amount. Our investigation, a concurrent probe by the State Investigation Commission and prosecutions by Federal and local authorities all revealed a pattern whereby corrupt officers customarily collected scores in substantial amounts from narcotics violators. These scores were either kept by the individual officer or shared with a partner and, perhaps, a superior officer. They ranged from minor shakedowns to payments of many thousands of dollars, the largest narcotics payoff uncovered in our investigation having been $80,000. According to information developed by the S.I.C. and in recent Federal investigations, the size of this score was by no means unique.

Corruption among detectives assigned to general investigative duties also took the form of shakedowns of individual targets of opportunity. Although these scores were not in the huge amounts found in narcotics, they not infrequently came to several thousand dollars.

Uniformed patrolmen assigned to street duties were not found to receive money on nearly so grand or organized a scaled, but the large number of small payments they received present an equally serious if less dramatic problem. Uniformed patrolmen, particularly those assigned to radio patrol cars, participated in gambling pads more modest in size than those received by plainclothes units and received regular payments from construction sites, bars, grocery stores and other business establishments. These payments were usually made on a regular basis to sector car patrolmen and on a haphazard basis to others. While individual payments to uniformed men were small, mostly under $20, they were often so numerous as to add substantially to a patrolman's income. Other less regular payments to uniformed patrolmen included those made by after-hours bars, bottle clubs, tow trucks, motorists, cab drivers, parking lots, prostitutes and defendants wanting to fix their cases in court. Another practice found to be widespread was the payment of gratuities by policemen to other policemen to expedite normal police procedures or to gain favorable assignments.

Sergeants and lieutenants who were so inclined participated in the same kind of corruption as the men they supervised. In addition, some sergeants had their own pads from which patrolmen were excluded.

Although the Commission was unable to develop hard evidence establishing that officers above the rank of lieutenant received payoffs, considerable circumstantial evidence and some testimony so indicated. Most often when a superior officer is corrupt, he uses a patrolman as his "bagman" who collects for him and keeps a percentage of the take. Because the bagman may keep money for himself, although he claims to be collecting for his superior, it is extremely difficult to determine with any accuracy when the superior actually is involved.

Of course, not all policemen are corrupt. If we are to exclude such petty infractions as free meals, an appreciable number do not engage in any corrupt activities. Yet, with extremely rare exceptions, even those who themselves engage in no corrupt activities are involved in corruption in the sense that they take no steps to prevent what they know or suspect to be going on about them.

It must be made clear that—in a little over a year with a staff having as few as two and never more than twelve field investigators—we did not examine every precinct in the Department. Our conclusion that corruption is widespread throughout the Department is based on the fact that information supplied to us by hundreds of sources within and without the Department was consistently borne out by specific observations made in areas we were able to investigate in detail.

The Nature and Significance of Police Corruption

Corruption, although widespread, is by no means uniform in degree. Corrupt policemen have been described as falling into two basic categories: "meat-eaters" and "grass-eaters." As the names might suggest, the meat-eaters are those policemen who, like Patrolman William Phillips who testified at our hearings, aggressively misuse their police powers for personal gain. The grass-eaters simply accept the payoffs that the happenstances of police work throw their way. Although the meat-eaters get the huge payoffs that make the headlines, they represent a small percentage of all corrupt policemen. The truth is, the vast majority of policemen on the take don't deal in huge amounts of graft.

And yet, grass-eaters are the heart of the problem. Their great numbers tend to make corruption "respectable." They also tend to encourage the code of silence that brands anyone who exposes corruption a traitor. At the time our investigation began, any policeman violating the code did so at his peril. The result was described in our interim report: "The rookie who comes into the Department is faced with the situation where it is easier for him to become corrupt than to remain honest."

More importantly, although meat-eaters can and have been individually induced to make their peace with society, the grass-eaters may be more easily reformed. We believe that, given proper leadership and support, many police who have slipped into corruption would exchange their illicit income for the satisfaction of belonging to a corruption-free Department in which they could take genuine pride.

The problem of corruption is neither new, nor confined to the police. Reports of prior investigations into police corruption, testimony taken by the Commission, and opinions of informed persons both within and without the Department make it abundantly clear that police corruption has been a problem for many years. Investigations have occurred on the average of once in twenty years since before the turn of the century, and yet conditions exposed by one investigation seem substantially unchanged when the next one makes its report. This doesn't mean that the police have a monopoly on corruption. On the contrary, in every area where police corruption exists it is paralleled by corruption in other agencies of government, in industry and labor, and in the professions.

Our own mandate was limited solely to the police. There are sound reasons for such a special concern with police corruption. The police have a unique place in our society. The policeman is expected to "uphold the law" and "keep the peace." He is charged with everything from traffic control to riot control. He is expected to protect our lives and our property. As a result, society gives him special powers and prerogatives, which include the right and obligation to bear arms, along with the authority to take away our liberty by arresting us.

Symbolically, his role is even greater. For most people, the policeman is the law. To them, the law is administered by the patrolman on the beat and the captain in the station house. Little wonder that the public becomes aroused and alarmed when the police are charged with corruption or are shown to be corrupt.

Departmental Attitudes Towards Police Corruption

Although this special concern is justified, public preoccupation with police corruption as opposed to corruption in other agencies of government inevitably seems unfair to the policeman. He believes that he is unjustly blamed for the results of corruption in other parts of the criminal justice system. This sense of unfairness intensifies the sense of isolation and hostility to which the nature of police work inevitably gives rise.

Feelings of isolation and hostility are experienced by policemen not just in New York, but everywhere. To understand these feelings one must appreciate an important characteristic of any metropolitan police department, namely an extremely intense group loyalty. When properly understood, this group loyalty can be used in the fight against corruption. If misunderstood or ignored, it can undermine anti-corruption activities.

Pressures that give rise to this group loyalty include the danger to which policemen are constantly exposed and the hostility they encounter from society at large. Everyone agrees that a policeman's life is a dangerous one, and that his safety, not to mention his life, can depend on his ability to rely on a fellow officer in a moment of crisis. It is less generally realized that the policeman works in a sea of hostility. This is true, not only in high crime areas, but throughout the City. Nobody, whether a burglar or a Sunday motorist, likes to have his activities interfered with. As a result, most citizens, at one time or another, regard the police with varying degrees of hostility. The policeman feels, and naturally often returns, this hostility.

Two principal characteristics emerge from this group loyalty: suspicion and hostility directed at any outside interference with the Department, and an intense desire to be proud of the Department. This mixture of hostility and pride has created what the Commission has found to be the most serious roadblock to a rational attack upon police corruption: a stubborn refusal at all levels of the Department to acknowledge that a serious problem exists.

The interaction of stubbornness, hostility and pride has given rise to the so-called "rotten-apple" theory. According to this theory, which bordered on official Department doctrine, any policeman found to be corrupt must promptly be denounced as a rotten apple in an otherwise clean barrel. It must never be admitted that his individual corruption may be symptomatic of underlying disease.

This doctrine was bottomed on two basic premises: First, the morale of the Department requires that there be no official recognition of corruption, even though practically all members of the Department know it is in truth extensive; secondly, the Department's public image and effectiveness require official denial of this truth.

The rotten-apple doctrine has in many ways been a basic obstacle to meaningful reform. To begin with, it reinforced and gave respectability to the code of silence. The official view that the Department's image and morale forbade public disclosure of the extent of corruption inhibited any officer who wished to disclose such corruption and justified any who preferred to remain silent. The doctrine also made difficult, if not impossible, any meaningful attempt at managerial reform. A high command unwilling to acknowledge that the problem of corruption is extensive cannot very well argue that drastic changes are necessary to deal with that problem. Thus neither the Mayor's Office nor the Police Department took adequate steps to see that such changes were made when the need for them was indicated by the charges made by Officers Frank Serpico and David Durk in 1968. This was demonstrated in the Commission's second set of public hearings in December 1971.

Finally, the doctrine made impossible the use of one of the most effective techniques for dealing with any entrenched criminal activity, namely persuading a participant to help provide evidence against his partners in crime. If a corrupt policeman is merely an isolated rotten apple, no reason can be given for not exposing him the minute he is discovered. If, on the other hand, it is acknowledged that a corrupt officer is only one part of an apparatus of corruption, common sense dictates that every effort should be made to enlist the offender's aid in providing the evidence to destroy the apparatus.

Grass-Eaters and Meat-Eaters

Corrupt policemen have been informally described as being either "grass-eaters" or "meat-eaters." The overwhelming majority of those who do take payoffs are grass-eaters, who accept gratuities and solicit five- and ten- and twenty-dollar payments from contractors, tow-truck operators, gamblers, and the like, but do not aggressively pursue corruption payments. "Meat-eaters," probably only a small percentage of the force, spend a good deal of their working hours aggressively seeking out situations they can exploit for financial gain, including gambling, narcotics, and other serious offenses which can yield payments of thousands of dollars. Patrolman William Phillips was certainly an example of this latter category.

One strong impetus encouraging grass-eaters to continue to accept relatively petty graft is, ironically, their feeling of loyalty to their fellow officers. Accepting payoff money is one way for an officer to prove that he is one of the boys and that he can be trusted. In the climate which existed in the Department during the Commission's investigation, at least at the precinct level, these numerous but relatively small payoffs were a fact of life, and those officers who made a point of refusing them were not accepted closely into the fellowship of policemen. Corruption among grass-eaters obviously cannot be met by attempting to arrest them all and will probably diminish only if Commissioner Murphy is successful in his efforts to change the rank and file attitude toward corruption.

No change in attitude, however, is likely to affect a meat-eater, whose yearly income in graft amounts to many thousands of dollars and who may take payoffs of $5,000 or even $50,000 in one fell swoop (former Assistant Chief Inspector Sydney Cooper, who had been active in anti-corruption work for years, recently stated that the largest score of which he had heard— although he was unable to verify it—was a narcotics payoff involving $250,000). Such men are willing to take considerable risks as long as the potential profit remains so large. Probably the only way to deal with them will be to ferret them out individually and get them off the force, and, hopefully, into prisons.

Pads, Scores and Gratuities

Corruption payments made to the police may be divided into "pad" payments and "scores," two police slang terms which make an important distinction.

The "pad" refers to regular weekly, biweekly, or monthly payments, usually picked up by a police bagman and divided among fellow officers. Those who make such payments as well as policemen who receive them are referred to as being "on the pad."

A "score" is a one-time payment that an officer might solicit from, for example, a motorist or a narcotics violator. The term is also used as a verb, as in "I scored him for $1,500."

A third category of payments to the police is that of gratuities, which the Commission feels cannot in the strictest sense be considered a matter of police corruption, but which has been included here because it is a related—and ethically borderline—practice, which is prohibited by Department regulations, and which often leads to corruption.

Operations on the pad are generally those which operate illegally in a fixed location day in and day out. Illegal gambling is probably the single largest source of pad payments. The most important legitimate enterprises on the pad at the time of the investigation were those like construction, licensed premises, and businesses employing large numbers of vehicles, all of which operate from fixed locations and are subject to summonses from the police for myriad violations.

Scores, on the other hand, are made whenever the opportunity arises—most often when an officer happens to spot someone engaging in an illegal activity like pushing narcotics, which doesn't involve a fixed location. Those whose activities are generally legal but who break the law occasionally, like motorists or tow-truck operators, are also subject to scores. By far the most lucrative source of scores is the City's multimillion-dollar narcotics business.

Factors Influencing Corruption

There are at least five major factors which influence how much or how little graft an officer receives, and also what his major sources are. The most important of these is, of course, the character of the officer in question, which will determine whether he bucks the system and refuses all corruption money; goes along with the system and accepts what comes his way; or outdoes the system, and aggressively seeks corruption-prone situations and exploits them to the extent that it seriously cuts into the time available for doing his job. His character will also determine what kind of graft he accepts. Some officers, who don't think twice about accepting money from gamblers, refuse to have anything at all to do with narcotics pushers. They make a distinction between what they call "clean money" and "dirty money."

The second factor is the branch of the Department to which an officer is assigned. A plainsclothesman, for example, has more—and different—opportunities than a uniformed patrolman.

The third factor is the area to which an officer is assigned. At the time of the investigation certain precincts in Harlem, for instance, comprised what police officers called "the Gold Coast" because they contained so many payoff-prone activities, numbers and narcotics being the biggest. In contrast, the Twenty-Second Precinct, which is Central Park, has clearly limited payoff opportunities. As Patrolman Phillips remarked, "What can you do, shake down the squirrels?" The area also determines the major sources of corruption payments. For instance, in midtown Manhattan precincts businessmen and motorists were major sources; on the Upper East Side, bars and construction; in the ghetto precincts, narcotics, and numbers.

The fourth factor is the officer's assignment. For uniformed men, a seat in a sector car was considered fairly lucrative in most precincts, while assignment to stand guard duty outside City Hall obviously was not, and assignment to one sector of a precinct could mean lots of payoffs from construction sites while in another sector bar owners were the big givers.

The fifth factor is rank. For those who do receive payoffs, the amount generally ascends with the rank. A bar may give $5 to patrolmen, $10 to sergeants, and considerably more to a captain's bagman. Moreover, corrupt supervisors have the opportunity to cut into much of the graft normally collected by those under them.

Sources of Payoffs

Organized crime is the single biggest source of police corruption, through its control of the City's gambling, narcotics, loansharking, and illegal sex-related enterprises like homosexual afterhours bars and pornography, all of which the Department considers mob-run. These endeavors are so highly lucrative that large payments to the police are considered a good investment if they protect the business from undue police interference.

The next largest source is legitimate business seeking to ease its way through the maze of City ordinances and regulations. Major offenders are construction contractors and subcontractors, liquor licensees, and managers of businesses like trucking firms and parking lots, which are likely to park large numbers of vehicles illegally. If the police were completely honest, it is likely that members of these groups would seek to corrupt them, since most seem to feel that paying off the police is easier and cheaper than obeying the laws or paying fines and answering summonses when they do violate the laws. However, to the extent police resist corruption, business interests will be compelled to use their political muscle to bring about revision of the regulations to make them workable.

Two smaller sources of payments to the police are private citizens, like motorists caught breaking the law, and small-time criminals like gypsy fortune tellers, purse-snatchers, and pickpockets who may attempt to buy their freedom from an arresting officer.

Organization of the Department

To understand police corruption in New York and have some idea of how such corruption involves supervisors and commanders as well as the rank and file, one must first know a little about how the Department is organized. The following brief account is by no means complete, but it should suffice to provide some understanding of the Department's organization.

Patrol Force:

Of the thirty thousand men and women in the New York Police Department, approximately two-thirds are assigned to the Patrol Services Bureau, which is headed by the Chief of Patrol. The patrol force is divided into seven borough commands: Manhattan North, Manhattan South, Brooklyn North, Brooklyn South, Queens, Bronx, and Staten Island. Each borough command supervises several divisions* which are, in turn, subdivided into seventy-four precincts. Most uniformed patrolmen are assigned to the precincts, where they are supervised by sergeants. The sergeants in turn report to lieutenants, and the lieutenants to precinct commanders, who are generally captains although they may be of higher rank.

Plainclothes:

The Department's 450 plainclothesmen are patrolmen, sergeants, lieutenants, and captains who wear civilian clothes and work primarily in the areas of gambling, narcotics, and such vices as prostitution and pornography. At the time the Commission's investigation began, plainclothesmen, like the patrol force, were assigned to precinct, division, and borough commands. However, plainclothes has since been reorganized several times with control now centralized in a special Organized Crime Control Bureau under a deputy commissioner.

Detectives:

The 3,000-man Detective Bureau is headed by the Chief of Detectives who, like the Chief of Patrol, reports to the Chief Inspector who reports to the Police Commissioner. At the time of the Commission's investigation, detective squads were assigned to precinct, division, and borough commands. But the Detective Bureau has since been reorganized, and detectives are now assigned to specialized squads within detective districts, which are coterminous with patrol divisions.

---

*Except in Staten Island, where there is no division. Staten Island Borough Command directly supervises the island's three precincts.

The Commissioner's Office:

At the top of this vast pyramid is the Police Commissioner, who is assisted by seven deputy commissioners. The Commissioner is appointed by the Mayor to a five-year term designed to overlap the four-year term of the Mayor. Of the twelve Commissioners appointed during the last forty years, only two have served the full term to which they were appointed. One of these served for eleven years. The other eleven served an average of twenty-three months each.

Patterns

In its investigation into police corruption, the Commission found that each area under investigation had its own distinctive patterns. Each is therefore discussed in a separate chapter which describes what the Commission investigation found, the reasons for the payoffs, the methods of paying, and, where appropriate, setting forth the Commission's comments.

Gambling

"You can't work numbers in Harlem unless you pay. If you don't pay, you go to jail . . . You go to jail on a frame if you don't pay."—Numbers Operator, Executive Session, January 15, 1971.

Policemen, especially those in plainclothes units, were found to shake down gambling operations throughout the City in a regular, highly systematic basis. The collection of tribute by police from gamblers has traditionally been extremely well organized and has persisted in virtually unchanged form for years despite periodic scandals, departmental reorganizations, massive transfers in and out of the units involved, and the folding of some gambling operations and the establishment of new ones.

The Commission received numerous complaints of illegal gambling operations, most allegedly located in ghetto neighborhoods. In those areas where Commission investigators went to check out these allegations, they found the situation to be just as described, with some neighborhoods having a numbers spot every block or two. Investigators also found numerous bookmaking operations and some high-stakes, organized card and dice games. The operators of these games apparently had little fear of police intervention in their enterprises, and their confidence was well-founded. Payments to police insured that their operations would be protected from police action, except for token arrests made to give an appearance of activity.

Reasons for Gambling Payoffs

In New York State it is perfectly legal to buy a ticket in the state-run lottery or to place a bet on a horse either at the racetrack or at a state-run betting parlor, and other forms of legalized gambling have been proposed. Although gambling was considered morally objectionable at the turn of the century when most laws against it were passed, that attitude has largely evaporated, with most citizens, public officials, and policemen feeling that there is nothing wrong with it. There is, therefore, no public pressure to crack down.

The courts, too, take a lenient view of gambling offenses, dismissing a high percentage of cases and imposing light fines in most others.

A State Commission of Investigation study of eighty-eight gambling arrests made during one year at a Bronx social club revealed that forty-seven of the arrests—slightly over one-half—resulted in conviction, and of these, one resulted in a jail sentence—and then only because the convicted gambler chose to go to jail for five days rather than pay a $50 fine. In the remaining forty-five convictions, the offenders were either given conditional discharges or ordered to pay fines ranging from $25 to $250.

A similar study by the Policy Sciences Center, Inc., came up with comparable figures. This study analyzed 356 numbers bank arrests made in Bedford-Stuyvesant over the past ten years. Such arrests can be assumed to have greater impact on the gambling power structure, because an arrest in a policy bank involves a greater number of slips and larger money volume, yet the courts did not show significantly greater punishments for such offenses. Of the 356 arrests, 198 resulted in dismissals, sixty-three in acquittals, and ninety-five in convictions. Of the ninety-five convictions, twelve resulted in suspended sentences, seventy-seven in a fine/time option, and six in jail sentences. Of the six jail sentences, one was for one year and the other five averaged seventeen days.

Our study of 108 gambling arrests made by the plainclothes squad in one division over a five-month period showed that, of fifty convictions, not one resulted in a jail sentence: two resulted in conditional discharge; forty-seven in fines of under $300; and one in a $500 fine. (Five were pending.)

Police officers, sharing the general attitude that gambling does no harm, themselves regard gambling money as "clean" graft. But, despite the changed attitudes toward gambling, most forms of gambling remain illegal, and corrupt policemen at the time of the investigation considered gamblers fair game.

As for gamblers, they were found to regard payments to the police as a necessary business expense. They often pointed out that a numbers operation couldn't exist unless it was under police auspices. As one gambler told the Commission, the police "are the insurance company, and unless you pay your monthly rent, you can't operate."

Plainclothesmen and Gambling

At the time of the Commission's investigation, plainclothesmen bore primary responsibility for enforcing anti-gambling laws, and it was among plainclothesmen that the Commission found the most pervasive and systematic police corruption, particularly in relation to gambling. The Commission received its information about plainclothes payoffs from gamblers, former and current plainclothesmen, police supervisors and anti-corruption officers;

law enforcement officers outside the Department, and, most significantly, from tape-recorded conversations with plainclothesmen actually going about the business of setting up or receiving payments.

At the start of the Commission's investigation, plainclothes units were assigned to precinct, division and borough commands. By February, 1971, borough and precinct units had been eliminated. Finally, in November, 1971, division plainclothes units were merged with the central Public Morals Division and placed under the new Organized Crime Control Bureau, headed by a deputy commissioner.* Reorganizations have not in the past made any noticeable dent in plainclothes corruption, and it remains to be seen whether the latest attempt will be successful.

The Pad

The heart of the gambling payoff system was found to be the plainclothes "pad." In a highly systemized pattern, described to the Commission by numerous sources and verified during our investigation, plainclothesmen collected regular biweekly or monthly payoffs from gamblers on the first and fifteenth of each month, often at a meeting place some distance from the gambling spot and outside the immediate police precinct or division. The pad money was picked up at designated locations by one or more bagmen who were most often police officers but who occasionally were ex-policemen or civilians. The proceeds were then pooled and divided up among all or virtually all of the division's plainclothesmen, with each plainclothes patrolman receiving an equal share. Supervisory lieutenants who were on the pad customarily received a share and a half and, although the Commission was unable to document particular instances, any commanding officer who participated reportedly received two full shares. In addition, the bagman received a larger cut, often an extra share, to compensate him for the risk involved in making his collections. Some bagmen made extra profits by telling gamblers there were more plainclothesmen in the division than there actually were, collecting shares for these non-existent men and pocketing the proceeds. Division plainclothesmen generally met once a month to divide up the money and to discuss matters concerning the pad—*i.e.*, inviting plainclothesmen newly assigned to the division to join, raising or lowering the amounts paid by various gamblers, and so forth. A man newly assigned to plainclothes duty in a division would be put on the pad after he had been with the division for a specified period, usually two months, during which time the other members would check him out and make sure he was reliable. This loss of revenue was customarily made up to him when he was transferred out of the division at

---

*The Thirteenth Division in Brooklyn, which was at that time the subject of a major anti-corruption investigation, was left intact in order not to jeopardize the investigation. The public explanation for leaving this one division out of the reorganization was that it was to be a "control" against which the performance of the new OCCB could be measured.

which time he would receive severance pay in the form of two months' payments after his transfer. Plainclothesmen who put a new gambling operation on the pad were entitled to keep the entire first month's payment as a finder's fee.

This pattern of collection and distribution appeared to Commission investigators to be quite standardized. It was evident in the four Manhattan divisions and the one Queens division which were the focus of the Commission's investigation. Evidence of the same patterns was also turned up in the other Manhattan division and in one division each in Brooklyn and the Bronx, for a total of eight divisions out of the sixteen divisions and Staten Island.* In addition, the Commission received allegations of similar pads in most of the other divisions in the City.

William Phillips, then recently assigned as a plainclothesman in the division covering lower Manhattan, testified on the basis of his own experiences and conversations with fellow plainclothesmen that the average monthly share per man ranged from $400 to $500 in midtown Manhattan divisions, to $800 on the Upper West Side, $1,100 in lower Manhattan, and $1,500 in Harlem. He stated that the reported "nut" (share per man) in two Queens divisions was $600, that in the three Bronx divisions it was $600, $800, and $900, and that in one Brooklyn division it was $800. These figures corroborated quite precisely those received by the Commission from the many sources willing to talk privately but who did not want to take the risk of public testimony, and further corroboration has come from similar sources since the Commission's hearings.

The pad was a way of life in plainclothes. According to Patrolman Phillips, the pad was openly and endlessly discussed whenever plainclothesmen got together. The Commission found no reason to doubt Phillips' opinion, echoing that held by other knowledgeable police officers and informants: "In every division in every area of plainclothes in the City, the same condition exists. There is a pad in every plainclothes precinct and division in the City of New York."

Revelations made before and after the Commission's investigation bore out the consistent nature of plainclothes gambling pads. Prior to the Commission's existence, Patrolman Frank Serpico told about his experience in a Bronx plainclothes division in 1967 and 1968 and described an almost identical pattern of payoffs. In May, 1972, after the Commission's hearings, Kings County District Attorney Eugene Gold announced the indictment of virtually an entire division plainclothes squad in Brooklyn, which collected payments from gamblers without interruption during the Commission's public hearings in precisely the same fashion being described by Commission witnesses. The indictments and related departmental charges involved a total of thirty-six current and former plainclothesmen, twenty-four of whom were indicted.

*There is no division in Staten Island. The three precincts in that borough report directly to borough command.

According to Mr. Gold, at one time twenty-four of twenty-five plainclothesmen in the division were on the pad. It is highly significant that this investigation was carried out without the Commission's knowledge, and yet, like the information given by Frank Serpico, it revealed a pattern of share payments, severance pay, and bagmen that matched in detail the patterns described by Patrolman Phillips and other Commission witnesses and informants.

The corrupting influence of gambling operations is not limited to plainclothes. Gambling pads of various sorts were also found to exist in the uniformed patrol force.

Generally, where such pads existed among uniformed men, the sector car had its own pad, the sergeant theirs, and the desk lieutenant and precinct commander had their own personal pads if they were so disposed. (Precinct commanders who received graft almost always designated a patrolman, "the captain's man," to make their pickups, and in some instances, when a corrupt captain was transferred out and an honest one took over, the captain's man continued to collect payments "for the captain" and kept the money.)

At the time of the investigation, certain precincts in areas with widespread gambling had special gambling cars (patrol cars with the words "gambling car" painted on them) to which two uniformed patrolmen were assigned with the ostensible mission of harassing gamblers. According to Phillips, these patrolmen were notorious for the extensiveness of their pads.

Different Kinds of Gambling and Different-Sized Payoffs

There are three major forms of illegal gambling in New York: numbers, bookmaking, and card and dice games. The size of a payoff was found to vary considerably according to the nature of the gambling operation, with the most lucrative and conspicuous operations paying the highest monthly tariff. Conspicuousness plays an important role in determining the amount of the payoff because the more overt a gambling operation is, the easier it is for police to make arrests and generally harass employees and players. Also, highly conspicuous operations are more likely to generate citizen complaints, which can put the police in a compromising position. Numbers is by far the most conspicuous of the three, depending as it does on numerous permanent locations, large numbers of players coming and going, and crowds gathering outside to hear results. Bookmakers who operate on street corners or from telephone booths are fairly conspicuous, although bookies who operate from apartments using telephone answering services or elaborate electronic equipment designed to prevent detection often escape police notice and thus the pad. High-stakes card and dice games, which involve many players, were generally found to pay if they stayed in one location, but "floating" games are less conspicuous and often didn't pay.

26

Invitational edges of corruption: some consequences of narcotic law enforcement

Peter K. Manning / Lawrence John Redlinger

Prior to the early years of this century, the nonmedical use of narcotics was largely unregulated and distribution and sales were routinely handled by physicians and pharmacists. However, sparked by international obligations and fervent moral crusaders, a series of legislative acts and court decisions were enacted and enforced. The enforcement of the laws resulted in marked changes in the population of users and drove the trafficking of narcotics underground.* Since the early twenties, then, federal, state and local agents have been engaged in enforcing the law and attempting to eradicate the illicit trafficker and his activities. Even though it can be demonstrated by official statistics that large numbers of users and dealers are arrested and prosecuted

Reprinted from Paul Rock, ed. *Politics and Drugs.* New York: Dutton/ Society Books, 1976. Reprinted by permission.

*Extensive research on the early years has been done by several scholars, and the reader interested in how the drug problem was socially constructed,

each year, narcotic law enforcement problems continue to generate considerable governmental and public concern. Our purposes in this chapter are to examine the dominant or operative mode of enforcement, to point out the particular problems associated with it, and to indicate how these problems are not unique to narcotics enforcement.

The enforcers of the narcotics laws stand on the invitational edge of corruption, and the problems they encounter while regulating and attempting to eradicate illicit trafficking of drugs reveal similarities to regulation of other markets. Study of their problems and of the corruption that can, and does occur, will lead to insight into the structural problems of regulation, and to an understanding of the stress or tension points in regulatory apparatuses of the government.

As Robert Merton has noted, there are many similarities between legitimate and illegitimate businesses. *"Both are in some degree concerned with the provision of goods and services for which there is an economic demand"* (his italics) (Merton, 1957:79). Thomas Schelling (1967) has noted that there must be many similarities between illicit and licit markets, and Redlinger (1969) analyzing heroin markets demonstrated remarkable similarities to licit markets. Likewise, Moore's analysis (1970) indicates that the economics of heroin distribution have similar shapes to those of other consumer products. So the question is, then, what are the similarities and differences, and how do these effect variations in the regulation of the market?

Licit and illicit markets share several structural properties in common.* Both involve willing buyers and sellers. The buyers make demands for goods

---

how legislation was passed, and how initial attempts at regulation gave way to the enforcement mode, should look at such works as Brecher, *et al* (1972; Part one); Lindesmith, 1965; Musto, 1972; and King, 1972. One result, however, deserves mentioning primarily because it set up the now accepted linkage between urban crime, poverty, and narcotics addiction. Whereas, prior to criminalization, narcotics users were mostly women who self-administered the drug for a variety of medicinal reasons, after criminalization males became the primary users. In addition, the social class of the user steadily declined so that in contrast to the late 1800's when use was spread throughout the class structure and even concentrated more in the middle and upper classes, the majority of users are today from the lower classes (this does not, of course, include physician addicts who obtain their drugs in other manners). In addition, prior to criminalization, the average age of a user was between 40 and 50 years of age, whereas today, the user is more likely to be under thirty. Thus, resulting from criminalization and the enforcement of the laws, the patterns of addiction and use changed remarkably. Today addiction is most often associated with poor, young, urban males, usually from one of the other "minorities."

*The literature on "legitimate" versus "illegitimate" markets and their associated regulatory activity is growing. Sociologists have long recognized that police control crime rather than eliminating it. For example, Hughes (1971) has written on "bastard institutions" which provide desired products not otherwise available, and Schur (1966) analyzed some of the consequences of making illegal certain consumatory patterns. N. Davis (1973) has provided an intensive and detailed analysis of the changing patterns of the regulation associated with abortion, and sociologist Gusfield (1963) and political scientists such as Lowi (1969) and Edelman (1962) have examined the symbolic fictions of regulation. In a sense, all regulation is an additional price or value-added cost, and while

and services, and the sellers provide those for some reimbursement. In both licit and illicit markets, the sellers have in mind the making of a profit, and ideally maximizing that profit. Both types of markets are regulated by agencies whose mission is to do so, and both types of markets have sellers within them who seek effective control over the manner and type of regulations that will be applied to them. However, there are some differences and these stem from the moral intention of the regulatory statutes, the loyalties of those applying the regulations, and the nature in which they are applied.

The moral intention of regulatory statutes either legitimizes particular behaviors, goods and services, or it jades them. Some goods and services (e.g., the production, distribution, and possession of alcoholic beverages) become morally transformed; first they are defined one way, and then another. The nature of the definition structures the manner in which regulation is to be accomplished. Where products are determined to have "legitimacy" those who buy and sell them often are *licensed*. The license is part of the regulatory process and identifies dealers. These dealers in turn are regulated by a set of standards that are set by the various jurisdictions: for example, federal, state and local. Consumers are assured, in so far as sellers adhere to the standards, that products are of sufficient quality. The moral intention of the regulation, then, is to insure the adequate *delivery* of goods and services and to insure the delivery of *adequate* goods and services. This is not the case for markets that have been morally transformed into "deviant" markets. Demand for products that are defined as illicit places a stigmata on the consumer; selling such products places the dealer in a criminal and highly sanctionable position; the regulation seeks to collapse distribution channels, reduce supplies, and effectively reduce demand. Markets which are defined as immoral become "legally suppressed" and the regulatory functions become "enforcement" functions rather than compliance functions. Strictly speaking, there is no difference between compliance functions of regulations and enforcement functions because both seek to persuade and coerce sellers to "comply" with the regulations. The difference between the two arises out of the intent of the statute. In legal markets, the actions of distribution, production and consumption are not illegal in themselves, and the persons doing this activity are not subject to criminalization. The regulation seeks to insure the channels of distribution and seeks to insure the quality of the product. Licensing of dealers performs this function, and in addition secures revenue for the licensing agent who in this case is the State.* The revenue provides resources for the licensing and

---

the cost of regulation is passed onto both the seller and buyer, more often than not the seller is able to transfer his costs to the buyer. Thus, the buyer becomes the tax-payer. Corruption is a variant on the cost coming as it does, directly as one resultant of the enterprise of morality regulation.

*Associations such as the American Sociological Association and the American Medical Association, also license practitioners and collect revenues for their agents. The agents through their certification attest to the credibility of the licensed persons' claims to be what they are and to be selling what they claim to be selling.

compliance agents to continue their performances. This is not the case with illicit markets. Regulations do not insure product adequacy, cannot provide revenue intake and thus cannot generate their own resources. Finally, the regulations seek "compliance" only in the sense that they wish *no one* to engage in the activity.

In a similar manner, the loyalties of licit market regulators are focused in a different manner than those agents regulating illicit markets. Very often, the regulators of licit markets are products of those markets. The staffing of regulatory agencies is accomplished by using industry executives who are "experts" in the field. Thus, the loyalties of the people as agents is not wholly to the regulation process. They have an "insider's" view of the marketing structure and are able to consider both the regulations and their effects on the sellers. Obviously, this type of interpenetration between regulators and sellers is not extant for illicit markets. The regulators are never drawn from the ranks of sellers,* and one can imagine why. The sellers of illicit products are typically viewed as unwholesome characters, and the aim of the regulations is to put them permanently out of business.

The ways in which the regulations of licit markets are applied vary considerably from the manner in which illicit markets are regulated. Compliance sections of regulatory agencies frequently warn the seller to correct his practices, or at best take him to court where the process of advocacy litigation is applied. The seller when convicted is often fined or reprimanded. Since the regulators are often drawn from the industries they regulate and since the regulations legitimize, albeit regulate, the market, the same moral stigmata is not applied to violators. Indeed, the violators may not view themselves as having committed a violation (see Sutherland, 1949, on this point). Suppressive enforcement has some similiarities, but is ultimately geared toward bringing about virtual *cessation* of activity. Agents may warn a seller of narcotics whom they cannot arrest, but in general, they seek to catch him in the act (although these patterns vary by size of city and patterns of seller's activities). Once caught, they seek to remove him from the market or immobilize him, since removal and immobilization are the only manners in which he can be forced to comply with regulatory standards. Some of the differences we have been discussing between legally regulated and legally suppressed markets and their relationships to regulatory agencies can be summarized in Figure One.

Variation in moral intention, reflected in legal definition, creates differences in the kinds and types of influence sellers have on regulators and

---

*This can be seen through our later analysis to not always be the case. Numerous examples from nations other than the United States will indicate complicity between those who seek to suppress the illicit marketing of products and the sellers of those products. Given the extremely lucrative nature of illicit narcotics, unscrupulous entrepreneurs and power-driven people, whether in legitimate occupations or illegitimate ones, will be tempted. In a society where money is equated with social respectability and power, lucrative ways to make money become extremely attractive, and constraining themes in morality can be neutralized.

FIGURE ONE
A Comparison of Selected Aspects of Legally Regulated
Versus Legally Suppressed Markets

Legally Regulated Markets	Legally Suppressed Markets
1. Willing buyers and willing sellers	1. Willing buyers and willing sellers
2. Sellers seek to maximize profits	2. Sellers seek to maximize profits
3. Intent of law to set and maintain standards of goods and services	3. Intent of law to suppress all activity
4. Law licenses and legitimates dealers	4. Law stigmatizes and illegitimates dealers
5. Law legitimates use	5. Law stigmatizes use
6. Agents of regulation often drawn from sellers' ranks	6. Regulators never drawn from sellers' ranks
7. Agents seek compliance and seek maintenance of market at established levels	7. Agents seek eradication of market
8. Buyer quality protected	8. Buyer quality unprotected

regulations. As we noted earlier, sellers of a product will seek to maximize their profits and will seek to have effective control over market conditions. Legally regulated markets offer the seller more opportunities for influence than do illicit ones. One reason we have already noted; in licit markets very often the regulators are drawn from the ranks of sellers, and often return to those ranks when they leave the regulatory agency. Secondly, in legally regulated markets, sellers have available other means for political influence. Because their activities are defined as credulous, they can utilize legislative means to attempt effective control. That is, they can attempt to have regulations set, sustained or altered in line with their wishes rather than the wishes of other partisans in the market (e.g., agents and consumers). They can "lobby" and thus attempt to influence the legislative process, and they can appear before congressional committees as "expert witnesses." When they appear, they can produce market data to support their position, and their legal staffs can actively seek changes in the law through aggressive court action. They can engage in negotiation with regulatory agents and attempt to mitigate the regulatory effects, or have them apply only after a certain period that will allow for industry "adjustment." They can engage in reactive challenging of regulations; that is, when they are charged formally and brought into court, they can initiate challenges to the law. They can band together into associations on the basis of common interests and utilize these associations to voice their collective position. Finally, they can resort to bribery, blackmail, extortion, pay-offs, and a variety of other corrupting measures in pursuit of their goal of effective control. These corrupting attempts can be made both at higher official levels (since they have access to the personnel at this level of the regulatory process), and at agent enforcement levels. Thus, legally regulated sellers have *both* licit and illicit means of influence available to them.

Sellers operating in illicit markets do not possess the same credibility of licit sellers and, consequently, they do not have the same types of access to influence over their market.* Regulators usually view the sellers as morally reprehensible, and take a hostile position *vis-à-vis* their activities. As a result of the moral intention of the regulations, then, illicit sellers have limited capacity for legitimate political influence. They do not engage in lobbying in a traditional sense, and they do not actively and voluntarily come forth as "expert witnesses" during drug law hearings. They do not engage legal staffs to construct alternatives to present regulations and to initiate active resistance to present statutes through litigation. To challenge regulations, they usually must wait until the regulation is applied to them, and thus, their posture is defensive. They cannot band together and have an Association represent them and their collective views. Presumably, in the United States, their access to officials higher up in the regulatory apparatus and other government agencies is severely limited, and thus, they have minimal opportunities to corrupt upper echelons of regulatory agencies. *Thus, for sellers in illicit markets, their focal points for effective control of their market must be enforcement agents.* Retail sellers in licit markets, to be sure, concentrate at this level since their span of control and resources warrants attempted intervention only at this level. However, wholesalers and producers are able to intervene successfully at higher levels. In legally suppressed markets, even wholesalers must focus on enforcement levels since influence at higher levels is denied them.**

The *structural constraints* of legally suppressed markets expose the agent to an accumulation of attempted influence. Because sellers want effective control over their markets, they must find ways to neutralize enforcement agents. If they cannot avoid at least arrest and charge, and it is probable that

---

*The foregoing analysis operates with the assumption that illicit sellers of narcotics do not sell licit goods and services. This assumption is, of course, not totally warranted. Licit sellers may be engaged in selling illicit goods, and in fact, at higher dealing echelons, this may be a rule rather than an exception. Thus, licit sellers of one set of goods may be able to indirectly use their political influence through these channels to effect the regulations surrounding their "other business." What the nature and extent of effects seller interpenetration may have is difficult to measure due to the relative paucity of data. However, there are several suggestive remarks one can make. In instances where the interpenetration is political in nature, illicit sellers may have direct and enduring influence in the enforcement of regulations and the nature of these regulations. Where mayors or governors, for example, are also sellers of illicit goods and services through illicit organizations or act as middlemen between illicit producers and regulators, the types and kinds of police enforcement capacity are often affected. In some countries other than the United States, the interpenetration between licit and illicit markets and control may be greater. Percentages of the take may be typically allotted to the political structure so that influence will be exerted and the seller can maintain effective market control. Recent cases in this country of government corruption accent the possibility of greater seller interpenetration than heretofore might have been thought.

**Evidence suggests that in America there are no producers of heroin *per se* (it is smuggled in in a refined form). However, even in cases of producers of other illicit substances, the producers rarely have recourse to influence a higher echelon official unless, as noted in an earlier footnote, this official has "interpenetration" with the illicit market.

eventually they cannot, then they must attempt to gain favorable influence with agents. The differences between legally regulated and legally suppressed markets is summarized in Figure Two.

We want to point out that we are not attempting to explain why individual enforcement officials become corruptible and corrupted, nor are we making comparisons between corrupted agents and those who are credulous. Furthermore, we are not arguing that all enforcement is corrupt or that a sizeable number of agents are corrupt. We are specifying the structural conditions which focus pressure and tension on agents, antecedent to the actual day-to-day occasions of enforcement. Each department of agents makes varying adjustments to these conditions: the department may be cognizant of the pressures, demand high agent accountability, and thus be relatively immune to seller influence; or, individual agents within a department may be either "clean" or "on the take" and the problem is isolatable to individuals; or, the entire department can be involved in aiding seller control of the market; or, finally, the department itself can, or agents within the department can be selling in the market resulting in interpenetration of seller and regulator.*

There are additional structural constraints on agents that promote infractions of other laws in the performance of their assigned duties. Because the narcotics market involves willing buyers and sellers, agents must find ways of obtaining information that are not "victim" centered. That is, agents do not have a victim willing to give information. Thus, they must buy information or attempt to gain information from others within or near to the sellers. Moreover, having once obtained access to information about seller activity, agents must find ways of keeping their channels of information open. The manner in which they do so may involve them in infractions of other laws. As we shall detail later, there are structural pressures on enforcement agents that promote both infractions in enforcement of regulations, and that promote obstructing

---

*It is not our argument that these are the sole features conducive to the patterns of corruption we describe below. There may be others. However, these are the most important. Insofar as the market features distinguishing the legitimate from the illegitimate markets for illicit substances obtain, and the differences in patterns of regulation obtain, we would expect to find analogous patterns of corruption, i.e., agent-focused. Many Anglo-American societies follow the regulatory model we have described, and would be expected to possess similar corruption patterns. For example, Gabor (1973) reports that Melbourne, Australia narcotics squads utilized blank search warrants. The warrants are signed *en masse* by a judge and agents could then search the premises of anyone they chose. During or after the search, a name is placed on the warrant. The practice came to light when "following a raid carried out in the usual manner, drug squad officers left behind a folder of papers. On examination the folder was found to contain, among other things, four blank search warrants—but with the signature of a Melbourne JP already attached." (Gabor, 1973:20). Other features of a society, e.g., high levels of violence such as occur in Latin American countries, obviously contribute to the likelihood of discovering violence in drug enforcement operations.

FIGURE TWO

Indicators of Degree of Access to and Influence Upon Sources of Legitimate Authority
for Sellers in Legally Regulated Versus Legally Suppressed Markets

Legally Regulated Markets	Legally Suppressed Markets
1. Sellers have potential political influence	1. Sellers have limited potential for political influence
2. Sellers can engage in lobbying to change and to maintain laws	2. Sellers cannot, do not lobby
3. Sellers can testify as expert witnesses	3. Sellers do not testify
4. Sellers can engage legal services to actively challenge existing law and to create alternatives	4. Sellers do not actively challenge laws
5. Sellers can engage in negotiation on regulations with officials	5. Sellers cannot engage in negotiation
6. Sellers can engage in reactive challenges to charges under regulations	6. Sellers can engage in reactive challenges to charges under regulations
7. Sellers can form visible voluntary associations that can take collective positions	7. Sellers cannot form visible voluntary associations
8. Sellers can engage in the corruption of officials	8. Sellers cannot engage in corruption of officials
9. Sellers can engage in the corruption of compliance agents	9. Sellers can engage in the corruption of enforcement agents

legal proceedings. All of these considerations gradually lead to a corruption of regulations and negotiated law enforcement practices.*

The focus of strain upon the agent points up a structural problem of regulation in general, and specifically the regulation of lucrative illicit markets. By looking at some of the enduring patterns of corruption, we may be able to locate and sensitize ourselves to more general problems of the structuring of regulation. There is little irony in the generalization made by the Knapp Commission in their report on police corruption when it states that "... a corrupt police officer does not necessarily have to be an ineffective one" (1972:55). Agent corruption is a product of the requirements of narcotic law enforcement and a theme found in the history of the enforcement enterprise.** The structural nature of narcotic law enforcement has histori-

*Sykes, in *Society of Captives* (1958), makes a similar argument concerning prison guards. Caught in the bind of being accountable for maintaining order, yet having to rely on the inmates to maintain order, the guard must make "trade-offs" with the inmates. Redlinger (1970) offers a similar explanation for the negotiation of order in homes for emotionally disturbed children.

**It may be too, that certain individuals are channeled into being agents and that these individuals are more corruptible than some hypothetical average; this we doubt. For one thing, many police departments work their men on a rotation basis and thus narcotics agents are policemen transferred into and out of sections. Secondly, given the nature of regulation, other officers have the opportunity for bribe-taking, extortion, etc. as is

cally created the problem of agent corruption,* and is reflected by the social organization of enforcement agencies.

Organizational Aspects of Drug Enforcement Agencies

Narcotics squads, whether specialized sections within police departments, or subsegments of Vice divisions, are characterized by internally and externally generated pressures to produce visible evidence of their activity and achievements. Because the "products" of such organizations are essentially ineffable and difficult to measure, agencies *reify* specific measures of performance. These measures then become powerful inducements to organizational conformity, for in order to show adequate performance, agents must produce data in conformity with the established measures (Manning, forthcoming). The pressures to produce, and the implied sanctions for failing to produce are the structural mechanisms by which policies of agencies become agent conduct.**

Internal pressures can be analytically separated from those external to the agency. In addition, we can separate pressures in terms of their impact. Some

---

amply documented in the literature on police corruption (Sherman, ed., 1974). Assessment on this proposition would require data most difficult to gather. Among other things one would need detailed life histories of agents that would indicate any and all prior involvement in corruption, and these would necessarily have to be matched against a comparable sample of non-agents. Another way of approaching the problem would be to follow a cohort of "clean" agents through their tenure as police officers noting along the way the temptations to corruption. In either case, the officers, especially those who have something to hide, are not likely to voluntarily subject themselves to close scrutiny.

*King (1972) reports that in 1917, two years after the passage of the Harrison Act criminalizing nonmedical use, "the first narcotic agent was caught and convicted for taking a large bribe." In that same year, Treasury agents, who were held responsible for enforcing the regulations, began seizure activities (previous to this time, agents did not seize large amounts of drugs). As King notes, agents, even in 1917, needed a way to show they were doing their job, and one way they did and do is to account for their activity in terms of the dollar value that can be attached to what they have acquired:

By 1917 increasing numbers of civil leaders and responsible citizens were calling for federal intervention and strict federal controls to stop the drug traffic. In that year the first caches of illegal drugs were seized by Treasury agents (and Treasury then started the deceptive practice, continued ever since by drug-law enforcers, of announcing each seizure in terms of how many millions of dollars the contraband substances might have been worth if they had been sold at maximum prices in the illegal market. (1972:25)

**Regulatory agencies of all kinds reside and act in a competitive symbolic domain that includes other agencies sharing similar goals and clientele. Drug agencies seek not only to control their clientele (dealers and users) but also to maintain an *image* of control *vis-à-vis* their public. The public includes not only the tax-payers external to the government but other agencies and members within the government. Within all organizations, there are pressures to survive as an organization and to satisfy the needs (economic, social, etc.) of the members (Clark and Wilson, 1961). At least one formal defining characteristic of organizations is their public obeisance to a set of formal goals (as associative pressures to achieve at least a semblance of these goals) and mechanisms to systematically evaluate organizational achievements.

pressures induce agents to violate laws to enforce the narcotics law, while others induce agents to obstruct justice. The translation of pressure is very indirect; "varying efforts to enforce these (vice laws) undermines the possibilities for strict supervision because the work obliges the men to engage in illegal and often degrading practices that must be concealed from the public" (Rubinstein, 1973:375). Furthermore, the application of successful techniques on the street (discussed below) produces a continuing ambivalence to law-abiding conduct. As Rubinstein (1973) notes, no department ". . . had found ways of fulfilling its obligation to regulate public morality without resorting to methods that constantly provide policemen with temptation and encourage ambiguous attitudes toward official standards of conduct." That is, narcotic law enforcement is virtually always secretive, duplicitous and quasi-legal, and is extremely difficult to effectively regulate.* Greater pressures lead to, at least, greater encounters with problematic situations containing opportunities for corruption. The more pressure there is to enforce the law, the less opportunity for close supervision, and the greater the opportunities for corruption. Ironically, increasing the effectiveness in vice enforcement brings with it the increasing likelihood of corruption.

Internal pressures for excessive enforcement are created by: (1) aspirations for promotion, salary and "easy numbers" within the unit; (2) quotas for arrests or stops insofar as these are tied to notions of success and enforced on agents;** (3) directives from administrators either in conjunction with "dope drives" (departmental efforts to round up users and pushers) or individual officers' attempts; (4) self-esteem maintenance produced by attempts to achieve success in terms of the conventional markers of arrests and buys; (5) moral-ideological commitments by officers to "protecting the kids" by

---

*Modes of supervision and control of narcotics agents tend to replicate the dissembling, duplicity, lying and threat used by officers *against* drug offenders. The Knapp Commission, for example, "turned" four patrolmen to spy on fellow officers, often leading to massive misunderstandings (because the other Knapp agents were not known to them). Of the four, three had been essentially blackmailed into working for the Commission (arrests for corruption-type offenses led to their being invited to work undercover) and were given consideration for this work in their own charges. Further, the borders of entrapment were always skirted, if not violated (Wainwright, 1972; reprinted in Sherman, ed., 1974; Whittemore, 1973:364–383). This mode of undercover and secretive enforcement of disciplinary rules is typical in large police departments, and it creates an ambiance of doubt and suspicion of colleagues. It is always possible that a fellow officer is working for internal affairs, or will inform to them. This condition furthers the already suspicious frame of mind of the officer, and sets him against the administrative strata in a very profound fashion. Consequently, when the agent wishes to resist the control of superiors, resistance takes the form of either complicity with the targets of control (in this case, users and dealers in narcotics), or work slowdowns (see Manning, *Police Work*, Chapter Six, forthcoming, for a further discussion of the question of internal rule enforcement and its organizational consequences).

**In one department the informal quota rules were summarized by a detective in the rhyme: "Two a day keeps the Sarge away." The Knapp Commission (1972) studied the New York City quota system and for many reasons we cite here recommended that it be abandoned, and as a result the system was phased out formally shortly thereafter.

"locking up the junkies and pushers" and thus, "winning the war against dope" and achieving a final E.N.D. ("Eradicate Narcotics Dealers"—a recent Detroit campaign against dealers).

Pressures to obstruct justice flow from similar sources to those mentioned above insofar as to be successful one must: (1) protect informants who constitute the agent's vital link to the underworld; (2) create informants through threats of prosecution on pending cases if cooperation is not forthcoming, and when they do cooperate persuade officials to drop charges against them; and (3) suppress information on cases pursued by other officers (for example, where one's informant is also responsible for a burglary). The last category of obstruction also occurs when there is interagency competition and federal agents, for example, will suppress their information about the case so that other agents (e.g., State agents) will be unable to "break" the case before them, or even with them and get "credit."

Internal pressures are complemented by external pressures to enforce the law and to obstruct justice. Law enforcement, shading into excess, is facilitated by: (1) political pressures from formally elected or appointed political officials translated through the chain of command to agents; (2) media pressures in the form of editorials, feature stories, comments on the rising crime rate (cf. Davis, 1952; Cohen, 1973); (3) grand jury, prosecutor's office and judicial pressure (which can work in a "negative direction" as in Washington, D.C. where District Prosecutor Silvert urged officers not to bring to him cases of personal possession of marijuana to prosecute); (4) ad hoc community groups and community associations; (5) external funding agencies such as ODALE, DOJ and LEAA which provide money and additional manpower (in the form of strike forces or tactical units).

The obstruction of justice occurs as a result of pressures generated by: (1) bribes to agents from users or dealers either to protect their operations or to avoid a charge once arrested; (2) competition and cooperation between and among agents and agencies (this is especially crucial when informants are needed in cases where both state and federal agents are involved, cf. Daley, 1975); (3) grand juries that encourage the development of "big busts" or big cases to show the public that "something is being done," also encourage the protection of snitches in order to have them work bigger cases, and to protect them in the interim from prosecution on other pending charges.

Each of these pressures, it should be emphasized, is not directly translated into the conduct of agents. The point we wish to underscore is that the organizational ambiance of narcotics law enforcement is such that rather than providing inducement to conformity to the law, it is more likely to underscore the virtues of avoidance of the more obvious requirements of law enforcement. It encourages rather more excess in pursuit of the job and modification of procedural rules to maximize arrests and buys. In the course of so doing, one learns to view with only minimal concern somewhat less obvious consequences of systematic obstruction of justice.

Patterns of Agent Corruption in Narcotics Law Enforcement

Corruption, in the sense that we are using the term, refers to departures from correct procedure in exchange for some goods, services or money. That is, the agent modifies what is expected of him by the nature of his employment and thus affects the outcome of enforcement. The corruption of enforcement can occur in seven principal ways:

1. Taking Bribes

If we eliminate for the moment everyday/anyday favors and gratuities, considerations and presents which are exchanged between police officers and the public, bribe-taking is the most common form of corruption (on this point, see Stoddard in Sherman, ed., 1974). In the area of narcotics enforcement, bribe-taking manifests itself in two ways. First, there is a payoff to officers from dealers for advance-warning information concerning raids, or other such warning information. This type of payoff is made on a regular basis. Secondly, there are payoffs made at the time of a raid or arrest. In the first instance, the bribes are made by a single organization or person, whereas in the second, officers accept bribes from a variety of persons; that is, officers accept the bribe from whomever they are arresting. At the time of the arrest, the individual being arrested will make explicit or implicit remarks concerning money or drugs that he may have available. The officers may take the dealer's stash money and then let him go (see Knapp Commission, 1972:94). If the dealer has no money the officers may confiscate his drugs but this case is not as often occurring as the taking of stash money. However, the opportunities for bribery do not end with the making of the arrest, for the agent or agents still have the option of "making the case" badly. That is, the agent can write the case up in such a manner that it will be thrown out of court. And there are other ways:

... [A] police officer who is skillful or experienced enough can write an affidavit which appears to be very strong, but is still open-ended enough to work in favor of a defendant when coupled with appropriate testimony from the arresting officer. For example, an officer could state in his complaint that the suspect threw the evidence to the ground at the approach of the police. Should that officer later testify that he lost sight of the evidence as it fell, the evidence and the case could well be dismissed. The Commission learned that it was not uncommon for defense attorneys in narcotics cases to pay policemen for such favors as lying under oath and procuring confidential police and judicial records concerning their clients' cases (Knapp Commission, 1972:97).

The Knapp Commission data is substantiated by evidence gathered by other researchers (*cf.* Sherman, ed., 1974). For example, Sanders (1972), studying the court experiences of middle class drug users, was able to show that police officers, working through defense attorneys, were willing to later drop narcotics charges for a fee. The attorney acted as a middleman in the situation. He would take money from his client, take a percentage for his "service" and pass on the remainder to the officer. The money may buy a change in the charge (e.g., a reduction from a felony to a misdemeanor), but more likely the money was in exchange for "sabotaging" the trial. The officer would make errors such as incompetent testimony or not being able to find evidence (see Sanders, 1972:242-243).*

The Knapp Commission also uncovered evidence of bribes in several diverse forms:

... [I]t was quite common for an apprehended suspect to offer to pay his captors for his release and for the right to keep part of his narcotics and cash. This was especially true at higher levels of distribution where the profits to be made and the penalties risked by a dealer were very high. One such case was that of a suspended Narcotics Division detective who was recently indicted in Queens County and charged with taking bribes to overlook narcotics offenses. The indictment alleged that this officer accepted $1,500 on one occasion for not arresting a suspected drug pusher who was apprehended while in possession of $15,000 worth of heroin. There is evidence that on another occasion this detective was paid $4,000 by a different narcotics pusher for agreeing not to confiscate $150,000 worth of heroin. The detective has pleaded guilty to attempting to receive a bribe, and his sentence is pending (1972:96).

2. Using Drugs

Agents have been known to use illicit drugs. For example, Harris (1974), interviewing three ex-narcotics agents, reports the smoking of marijuana by agents as they sat "surveillance." In another case witnessed by one of us, an agent about to participate in a late night raid discussed the fact that he was tired, and promptly produced a nonprescription vial of amphetamines from which he took and swallowed three capsules. Undercover agents, to show

*A vice officer presented these rationales to Sanders concerning the deals that go on behind the scenes:

I'm sure that there are lawyers who are paying off policemen in some cases. You'll always have this. But this is controlled by the police department because you have the IID (Internal Investigation Division) and the policeman now is making $12,000 a year—he's making good money. I've heard a lot of stories about a lot of policemen and I've learned one thing—if you don't have something good to say about someone don't say anything at all. So I don't carry tales. Some cases are dealt with between the lawyer and the police officer or through other channels, but I think this is really good. I think it is beneficial to the individual that gets busted. If he can pay $300 or $400 to get out of it, good, you're out of it. That's the type of society this is. This is what was built by other people. We are going to have to realize that it is a good point. Sure, there are a lot of policemen making money on it through lawyers. The reason is that it is an easy dollar and the chances of getting caught are slim. I really believe it is good for the citizen. It may sound fascist but it is good to have a way out of something. When you get busted you need a way out. This is the game (Sanders, 1972:235).

their loyalties to the people on whom they are doing surveillance, often must "turn-on" (use drugs) with them. In several observed cases, officers went to parties and carried their own stash as evidence that they were users.

3. Buying/Selling Narcotics

Evidence gathered by journalists suggests that many observers believe that dealing in narcotics exists among agents, especially local agents in Los Angeles and New York. *New York Times* reporter David Burnham wrote:

> . . . [S]ome policemen wonder whether the transfer of two hundred plain clothesmen, a highly cynical group of men, to the narcotics beat might not result in a net increase in the flow of narcotics into the city. . . . "The moral jump from making illegal drug deals to getting evidence and dealing in drugs to make money is not as big as it might look to an outsider," one experienced narcotics detective said (Burnham, in Sherman, ed., 1974:309-310).

In Gary, Indiana, near Chicago, seven policemen were convicted in February, 1975, of conspiracy to deal in drugs and of drug trafficking (*Washington Post*, February 9, 1975). In 1974, the same group was convicted on trafficking charges. The Knapp Commission discovered in the testimony of two "ex-addicts" that eleven Harlem policemen would supply them with narcotics in exchange for cigarettes, whiskey, power tools, a mini-bike and stereo equipment. The addicts had collected the goods through burglaries (Daley, 1974:339). Several other variations on this pattern occur: the selling of narcotics to informants for resale to other addicts, and the use of narcotics to pay off informants for information useful in making a buy or buy and bust. Narcotics officers also financed heroin buys for others when the aim was not eventual arrest (Knapp Commission, 1972:91-92); they also accept narcotics as bribes, which in turn they sell. In New York, no informant fees were paid officially: narcotics seized in one arrest can be used to pay off informants (Whittemore, 1973:323) (a case of both arrogation of seized property and dealing illegally in narcotics). A more illusive type of corruption is simple conspiracy to deal, such as introducing potential customers to dealers. Since the latter is a requirement of undercover work for informants, it is hardly surprising that agents might introduce, directly or indirectly, clients to a pusher. Without such introductions, the enforcement of most narcotics dealing laws would be impossible.

4. Arrogation of Seized Property

Since the law in most states requires that any property relevant to the crime must be seized until the trial has been held, large amounts of property, typically automobiles, guns, money and drugs are confiscated as evidence. The control of evidence of this type is extremely difficult as well as expensive for large police departments. [Its legal status is under present review (Technical Papers of National Drug Abuse Commission, Appendix, Vol. III).] A series of scandals in the New York Department in 1973 involved missing or stolen property, including well over one hundred kilos of high-quality heroin taken from the Property section of the New York Police Department (Pileggi, 1973a). Further, the arrest situation often involves large amounts of money involved in the exchange that led to the arrest, as well as other monies which may be a part of the dealer's crib or bank. During the Knapp Commission testimony, Patrolman Phillips (one of the corrupt policemen "turned" by the Commission) testified he saw a plainclothesman leaving the scene of a multimillion dollar drug raid with $80,000 confiscated earlier in the raid. In March, 1975, the officer identified by Phillips was indicted, and charged with stealing more than $1,500 in cash and heroin (the minimum amount for a grand larceny charge) (*New York Times,* March 21, 1975). Although the money used in the actual exchange (used by the informant or the agent to buy the drugs) is marked and the serial numbers registered prior to the buy, other confiscated money becomes the responsibility of the agents to collect, record and to insure its safe deposit with the IRS.

5. Illegal Searches and Seizures

There are several ways in which illegal searches and seizures can be initiated, and each is used at one time or another (see Harris, 1974; Sanders, 1972; Wambaugh, 1973; see also Johnson and Bogomolny, 1973, for a study of reported arrest data). One way illegal searches are conducted is for the narcotics officer to claim there was a "quantity of alleged drugs" in "plain sight" (see Wambaugh, 1973; Sanders, 1972), and then search the house, apartment or vehicle of the person. In the case of a vehicle search, often the outward appearances of the person or the vehicle provide clues to officers that a drug violation *may* be occurring, and, in addition, that a "stop" on the vehicle is warranted (Johnson and Bogomolny, 1973, euphemistically refer to these as "ancillary" or "consumption-related" offenses). The officers then stop the vehicle, "see" contraband in plain sight and initiate a search of the vehicle. Another variant on the vehicular search is to claim, as with marijuana, that "smoke could be smelled" and that the search had "probable cause." "Flaking" is a term referring to the act whereby the officer plants illicit drugs on the person (see Knapp Commission, 1972). When an officer has made an illegal search, he may "find" drugs which have been "flaked." Narcotics officers may possess a "sure bust kit" that contains several types of drugs and allows them to select the appropriate contraband that will justify their illegal search. Reiss (personal communication) indicates that a narcotics officer working the Washington, D.C. area told him that he had never made an arrest *without* flaking the person. Still other officers have reported to us, that "If you're gonna' search 'em, it's wise to come up with sumthin'."

A variation on "flaking" is "dropsey." An officer will report that he came upon the subject just as he was throwing contraband away. The "overt act" of throwing the contraband away allows for the search; however, in the case of "dropsey" the officer actually supplies the contraband. Pileggi (1971) quotes one New York City judge as saying: "Surely, though, not in *every* case was the defendant unlucky enough to drop his narcotics at the feet of a policeman. It follows that in at least some of the cases the police are lying."

"Padding" occurs when the officer adds drugs to the already confiscated evidence either to increase the quality of the substance seized and make the evidence more acceptable in court, or to raise the charge from a misdemeanor to a felony after the arrest had been made (Knapp Commission, 1972: 91ff). In one case, agents seized several ounces of lactose and a dealer, but no narcotics. A Marquis field test was done on the seized lactose and produced negative results. At that point the officers "sweetened" the seizure so that a field test would render it positive. In cases where drugs are added to raise the charge, often the motive is to use the more serious charge as a threat and thereby gain greater leverage over the arrestee. This pressure can be used to "turn" the arrestee into a "confidential informant," or extort money from the arrestee, or to persuade the arrestee to offer bribes or service to the officer (for example, sexual favors).*

6. The Protection of Informants

Informants are the heart of the enforcement of narcotics laws. Detectives either pay their "snitches" out of their own pockets, or the department provides a "confidential informant" fund.** All major federal enforcement agencies allocate money for payment of information (FBI, DEA, etc.), as do most major police departments. At least four consequences issue from the use of informants in narcotics law enforcement. First agencies may have to compete for information, and informants have the option of accepting the best deal. In one instance, a confidential informant who was "working off cases" found that federal agents were willing to pay more and consequently began working for them. In another instance, local agents were unable to get the prosecuting attorney to drop charges against a potential snitch, so the "confidential informant" went to the federal agency and the charges were dropped

---

*One Vermont narc allegedly propositioned a young girl after giving her some cocaine (*Time*, March 10, 1975). When she refused, he busted her two weeks later for selling him drugs. This case of alleged corruption, uncovered in Vermont, was one of some six hundred convictions which resulted in a letter from a County Prosecutor to the Governor asking that all six hundred convictions based on the officer's testimony be pardoned. The officer, in addition to attempted extortion, is suspected of confiscating the drugs he planted on an apparently large number of arrestees, and of converting money assigned for buys to his personal use.

**Robert Daley, former Deputy Commissioner of the New York Police Department, describes the present New York system which replaced the previous informal arrangement whereby detectives paid $5 fees to their informants:

[Informants] are listed with the Police Intelligence Division under a code number and usually a code which they have been obliged to sign onto the equivalent of a bank deposit card. Their verifiable signatures are important, because they must sign receipts for money paid them. Each informant is further classified by speciality, and by the area he knows (Daley, 1975:31).

Of course, as the Knapp Commission pointed out, it is possible to create fictitious informants and for an officer to collect the fees himself.

a short time thereafter. Daley (1975) provides another example: federal agents, in protecting their confidential informant *in cognito* and *in communicado,* inhibited local agents from obtaining necessary information to move on local cases. As noted by Skolnick (1966) and Van Maanen (personal communication), and as we have observed, confidential informants often are protected from prosecution on other charges while they are working. That is, as in one case, the confidential informant was caught breaking and entering a home, but the agents "fixed" the charge with the Prosecuting Attorney's office on the basis that the informant was "one of the best." The officer then added five cases to the informant's caseload. Secondly, informants may be working for several agents or agencies. This occurs more frequently in areas where interagency cooperation is virtually nonexistent. The informant is thus able to receive payment from more than one agency and, in addition, perhaps keep more charges off his back. Even in the instance where the informant is working for only one agency, a third consequence results. Most informants are drug users themselves, and the agents provide money or drugs in payment. Thus, the agents become a link in the marketing of narcotics. The fourth consequence we have already briefly noted: informants are oftentimes protected from prosecution. As Skolnick (1966) suggests, informants in effect reverse the hierarchy of criminal penalties in that they are allowed to work off charges, receive no penalty, and may even be paid for their services. In cases where officers hope to reach "Mr. Big," the costs of protection from prosecution spiral. Each level of the dealing chain must be granted some measure of immunity from prosecution, or some consideration for turning state's evidence. For some of those in the dealing chain, charges will never be filed and thus justice will be obstructed in order that someone deemed higher up can be caught.*

7. Violence

Sometimes the information desired from an informant is not forthcoming and some "physical therapy" is necessary (Redlinger, 1969). The potential for violence in narcotics enforcement is high; often addicts are roughed up in attempts to gain information from them. Moreover, violence can be used to force informants to engage in illegal behavior such as stealing *for narcotics officers* (see Knapp Commission, 1972:92). Agents also have the option of turning the name of the informant over to interested dealers, and can effectively use this threat to gain information. Sometimes, of course, especially on

---

*The informant system facilitates extortion, lying, blackmail and violence. Information sold to an officer, or given during questioning, can be used for the officer's own interests. Likewise, the informant can turn the information to his. By informing a dealer that officers are coming, for example, the informant may be able to avenge some affront. Informants often do turn in people they have quarrels or grudges with, and the informant system allows for the turning of the process around. The informant may be able to "set up" an officer much like he sets up dealers. Too, informant information may be used by an officer who is also dealing to effectively eliminate his competition.

informants who may turn out to be quite unreliable, they do turn the names over. The use of unwarranted violence can also occur during raids. Officers can claim that the dealer "went for his gun" and proceed to blow him away; such a procedure has merits in that the dealer is no longer able to testify otherwise, and in addition the officers make a good case and obtain the rewards. Other features of narcotics enforcement make very likely the unfortunate possibility that agents will shoot other agents in the same agency (e.g., in a shoot-out involving an undercover agent who is indistinguishable from the targets of police bullets), or uniformed officers in another agency may shoot narcotics officers (or vice versa) as occurred in Cali, Colombia in February, 1975, and in West Germany in March, 1975. In both of the last cases, U.S. agents killed foreign police officers in "shoot-outs" touched off by raids.

Violence can be used to restore face after agent errors, as happened in Boise, Idaho:

The narcs hired operatives, at 3 dollars an hour, to make connections with dealers. Near Sun Valley, agents gave one such operative $1,000 and waited outside a bar while he went in, strolled through and left by the back door. Burned on another buy when a dealer passed off powdered aspirin as heroin, agents returned posing as Mafia hoods and retrieved their money at gun point. To support this cover, agents offered to buy guns in the underworld: this sparked a wave of sporting goods-store burglaries around Pocatello. When police figured out what was going and complained, the narcs accused them of being involved in the drug trade (*Newsweek*, January 27, 1975).

Comment

Licit and illicit markets have many features in common, but they differ substantially as a result of the moral intention of regulatory statutes, the loyalties of those applying the statutes, and the manner of application. We have noted that sellers in licit markets have both legitimate and illegitimate means to influence regulatory policies and action. Sellers of illicit goods and services (such as narcotics) have recourse only to illicit means, and moreover, because of the nature of their incredulity, they ordinarily must focus their efforts on enforcement agents. Hypothetically, then, if illicit sellers could effect control over their markets through higher, more powerful channels, they would attempt to do so. It is critical to understand that the structural features of society, and in particular regulatory agencies and the activities they regulate, dispose specific elements to be exposed to corruption. Agents, thus, are more often placed upon an invitational edge of corruption, and are a major point of tension in the regulation of legally suppressed markets.*

Our discussion should not be taken as limited to the dramatic instances of corruption in the narcotics field, but rather should be viewed as pointing out areas of corruption that one might find in other regulatory agencies. Since the structural features of both markets and their regulatory-enforcement agencies are similar, evidences of corruption in one should instruct us to look for such features in other agencies and their personnel. The nature of licit markets allows for that corruption to occur at more varying levels than in legally suppressed markets. That is, the same *forms* of corruption occur and exist, but the structural positions where they can occur appear to be more numerous. In addition, because markets and their goods and services are defined as licit, some areas deemed "corruption" in illicit markets are not seen as such in licit ones, and this bifurcation of vision only serves to point out the structuring features of moral intent.**

Although some of the similarities are quite obvious, we would like to compare types of corruption found in licit and illicit markets. In both markets, *bribery* is to be found. The history of American politics is punctuated with pay-offs, bribes, gifts and the like forwarded by legitimate businessmen to regulatory agents. The *use of the product* is in many instances obvious, and most often is not seen as a case of corruption. That is, members of regulatory agencies such as the F.A.A. often ride in planes; members of the F.C.C. often watch television; members of the F.D.A. often use drugs. We have already noted that in legally regulated markets, it is quite common for sellers to be asked to accept positions in agencies that regulate the very markets they come from. The interpenetration of regulators, sellers and producers is hardly considered remarkable in this country. There is a circulation of elites through, for example, the defense department, military, large armaments, shipbuilding and aircraft manufacturing companies. Furthermore, as Lieberson (1971) indicates, the Senate committees that are supposed to regulate spending and investment in markets are committees composed of senators from the very

---

*While agents regulating licit markets are located in a similar position, there is not as much focus for effective control upon their position. Licit sellers have other potentially more powerful means for effecting control over their markets. Thus, while the potential for corruption of these agents exists, its return in terms of effective market control is not as great. Agents regulating licit markets have relatively little power to change policy, and licit market sellers have access through both legitimate and not so legitimate channels to persons of greater power.

**Space does not permit the outlining of what might be called a phenomenology of corruption. Suffice it to say that elements in such an outline would be the nature of the *relationship* between the *recipient*, the *donor* and the *object* transmitted. The *definitions* given to such transactions, as well as the *structure* of the exchange (tertiary, secondary or primary exchange; short- or long-lag systems, *cf.* Blau, 1964 and Levi-Strauss, 1969) would also have to be taken into account. By holding constant *some* of the structural features of regulatory agencies, and examining what is *defined* as corruption, we are suggesting an analytic strategy which we hope to pursue in subsequent analyses.

states that have vested interests in those areas.* *Buying and selling of products* one is supposed to regulate occurs in both regulatory and enforcement agencies, as does the *arrogation of seized property.* For example, automobiles seized in raids by drug agencies supply vehicles for many enforcement agents at both lower and higher echelons of the agencies, while such arrogation is a common process in bankruptcy proceedings. The use of wiretaps and bugging, *modes of illegal entry and/or surveillance* is common in virtually all federal agencies; recent headlines have revealed the use of spying and taps by the Internal Revenue Service, Department of Defense and other agencies. Moreover, private industrial concerns have utilized taps to illegally spy on their regulators. *Informants* are an inimicable part of all prosecutorial activity and immunity granted to witnesses is common throughout not only courts but congressional hearings. Watergate is only a recent example, but policies regarding immunity are also found in the Internal Revenue Service, the F.A.A., the Armed Services, and in the Department of Justice in civil as well as criminal cases.

References

Blau, P.
   1964 *Exchange and Power in Social Life.* New York: Wiley.
Brecher, H. W. *et al.*
   1972 *Licit and Illicit Drugs.* Boston: Little, Brown.
Clark, P. and J. Q. Wilson
   1961 "Incentive Systems: A Theory of Organizations." *Administrative Science Quarterly* 6 (September):129–66.
Cohen, S.
   1973 *Folk Devils and Moral Panics.* London: Palladin.
Daley, R.
   1973 *Target Blue.* New York: Dell.
   1975 "Inside the Criminal Informant Business." *New York* 8 (March 24):31–35.
Davis, F. J.
   1952 "Crime News in Colorado Newspapers." *American Journal of Sociology* 57 (January): 325–30.
Davis, N. J.
   1973 "The Abortion Market: Transactions in a Risk Commodity." Unpublished Ph.D. Michigan State University.
Edelman, M.
   1962 *The Symbolic Uses of Politics.* Urbana: University of Illinois Press.

*For example, the House Agriculture Subcommittee on Tobacco is a seven member committee that has six members from the tobacco-producing states; the Minerals and Fuels Committee is "loaded with senators from states with relatively large segments of the labor force engaged in these extractive industries" (Lieberson, 1971: 579-580). Likewise, the Senate Armed Services Committee has a disproportionately high membership from states that would stand to lose when arms are cut back, and in contrast, "the small Subcommittee on International Organization and Disarmament Affairs is disproportionately composed of senators from states that stand to gain through a military cutback" (Lieberson, 1971:580–581).

Gabor, I.
    1973 "Drug Squad Inquiry." *Drugs and Society* 3 (November)
Gusfield, J.
    1963 *Symbolic Crusade.* Urbana: University of Illinois Press.
Harris, D.
    1974 "An Inside Look at Federal Narcotics Enforcement: Three Ex-Agents Tell
        their Tales." *Rolling Stone* (December 5).
Hughes, E. C.
    1971 *The Sociological Eye.* Chicago: Aldine.
Johnson, W. and R. Bogomolny
    1973 "Selective Justice: Drug Law Enforcement in Six American Cities." pp.
        498–650 in *Drug Use in America: Problem in Perspective.* Appendix Vol. III.
        *Technical Papers of the Second Report of the National Commission on Mari-
        juana and Drug Abuse.* Washington: U.S. Government Printing Office.
King, R.
    1972 *The Drug Hang-up.* New York: W. W. Norton.
Knapp Commission
    1972 *Report* [on Police Corruption] . New York: George Brazillier.
Levi-Strauss, C.
    1969 *The Elementary Structures of Kinship.* Boston: Beacon Press.
Lieberson, S.
    1971 "An Empirical Study of Military-Industrial Linkages." *American Journal of
        Sociology* 74 (January): 562–84.
Lindesmith, A.
    1965 *The Addict and the Law.* Bloomington: Indiana University Press.
Lowi, T.
    1969 *The End of Liberalism.* New York: W. W. Norton.
Manning, P. K.
    Forth- *Police Work: Essays on the Social Organization of Policing.*
    coming
Merton, R. K.
    1958 *Social Theory and Social Structure.* New York: Free Press.
Moore, M.
    1970 "Economics of Heroin Distribution in New York City." Hudson Institute
        Mimeo Report.
Musto, D. F.
    1972 *The American Disease.* New Haven: Yale University Press.
Pileggi, N.
    1971 "From D.A. to Dope Lawyer." *New York Times Magazine* (May 16):34 ff.
    1973 "How Crooks Buy Their Way Out of Trouble." *New York* (November
        19):45–52.
    1973a "Further Developments in the 'French Connection' Case." *New York*
        (September 24).
Redlinger, L. J.
    1969 "Dealing in Dope." Unpublished Ph.D. Northwestern University.
    1970 "Making Them Normal: Notes on Rehabilitating Emotionally Disturbed Chil-
        dren." *American Behavioral Scientist* 14 (December):237–253.
Rubinstein, J.
    1973 *City Police.* New York: Farrar, Straus and Giroux.
Sanders, C.
    1972 "The High and the Mighty: Middle Class Drug Users and the Legal System."
        Unpublished Ph.D. Northwestern University.
Schelling, T.
    1967 "Economics Analysis and Organized Crime." In *Task Force Report: Organized
        Crime.* President's Crime Commission, Washington: D.C.: U.S. Government
        Printing Office.
Sherman, L. W. (ed.)
    1974 *Police Corruption.* New York: Doubleday Anchor Books.

Schur, E.
   1966   *Crimes Without Victims.* Englewood Cliffs, New Jersey: Prentice-Hall.
Skolnick, J.
   1966   *Justice Without Trial.* New York: Wiley.
   1975   *Justice Without Trial* (second edition). New York: Wiley.
Sutherland, E.C.
   1949   *White Collar Crime.* New York: Dryden Press.
Sykes, G.
   1958   *Society of Captives.* Princeton: Princeton University Press.
Wambaugh, J.
   1973   *The Blue Knight.* New York: Dell.
Whittemore, L. W.
   1973   *Super-Cops.* New York: Bantam Books.

Vice, corruption, bureaucracy, and power[†]

William J. Chambliss[*]

I. Introduction

At the turn of the century Lincoln Steffens made a career and helped elect a president by exposing corruption in American cities.[1] In more recent years the task of exposure has fallen into the generally less daring hands of social scientists who, unlike their journalistic predecessors, have gathered their information from police departments, attorney generals' offices, and grand

From *Wisconsin Law Review*, Vol. 1971, No. 4, pp. 1150–73. Reprinted by permission.

†I am grateful to W. G. O. Carson, Terence Morris, Paul Rock, Charles Michener, Patrick Douglas, Donald Cressey, and Robert Seidman for helpful comments on earlier versions of this paper.

*Assistant Professor of Sociology, University of California–Santa Barbara. Ph.D. 1962, University of Indiana. During 1971 and 1972 the author was a lecturer at: the University of Uppsala (Sweden); London School of Economics; Oxford University; Cambridge University; and Durham University.

1. L. Steffens, *The Shame of the Cities* (1904). See *The Autobiography of Lincoln Steffens* (1931).

jury records.[2] Unfortunately, this difference in source of information has probably distorted the description of organized crime and may well have led to premature acceptance of the Justice Department's long-espoused view regarding the existence of a national criminal organization.[3] It almost certainly has led to an over-emphasis on the *criminal* in organized crime and a corresponding de-emphasis on *corruption* as an institutionalized component of America's legal-political system.[4] Concomitantly, it has obscured perception of the degree to which the structure of America's law and politics creates and perpetuates syndicates that supply the vices in our major cities.

Getting into the bowels of the city, rather than just the records and IBM cards of the bureaucracies, brings the role of corruption into sharp relief. Organized crime becomes not something that exists outside law and government but is instead a creation of them, or perhaps more accurately, a hidden but nonetheless integral part of the governmental structure. The people most likely to be exposed by public inquiries (whether conducted by the FBI, a grand jury, or the Internal Revenue Service) may officially be outside of government, but the cabal of which they are a part is organized around, run by, and created in the interests of economic, legal, and political elites.

Study of Rainfall West (a pseudonym), the focus of this analysis of the relationship between vice and the political and economic system, dramatically illustrates the interdependency. The cabal that manages the vices is composed of important businessmen, law enforcement officers, political leaders, and a member of a major trade union. Working for, and with, this cabal of respectable community members is a staff which coordinates the daily activities of prostitution, gambling, bookmaking, the sale and distribution of drugs, and other vices. Representatives from each of these groups, comprising the political and economic power centers of the community, meet regularly to distribute profits, discuss problems, and make the necessary organizational and policy decisions essential to the maintenance of a profitable, trouble-free business.

2. D. Cressey, *Theft of the Nation* (1969); Gardiner, "Wincanton: The Politics of Corruption," Appendix B of *The President's Commission on Law Enforcement and Administration of Justice, Task Force Report: Organized Crime* (1967); in W. Chambliss, *Crime and the Legal Process* 103 (1969).

3. The view of organized crime as controlled by a national syndicate appears in D. Cressey, *supra* note 2. For a criticism of this view see H. Morris & G. Hawkins, *The Honest Politicians Guide to Crime Control* (1970).

4. Most recent examples of this are D. Cressey, *supra* note 2; H. Morris & G. Hawkins, *supra* note 3; King, *Wild Shots in the War on Crime*, 20 J. Pub. Law 85 (1971); Lynch & Phillips, *Organized Crime-Violence and Corruption*, 20 J. Pub. Law 59 (1971); McKeon, *The Incursion By Organized Crime Into Legitimate Business*, 20 J. Pub. Law 117 (1971); Schelling, *What is the Business of Organized Crime?*, 20 J. Pub. Law 71 (1971); Thrower, *Symposium: Organized Crime, Introduction*, 20 J. Pub. Law 33 (1971); Tyler, *Sociodynamics of Organized Crime*, 20 J. Pub. Law 41 (1971). For a discussion of the importance of studying corruption see W. Chambliss, *supra* note 2, at 89; W. Chambliss & R. Seidman, *Law, Order and Power* (1971); McKitvick, *The Study of Corruption*, 72 Pol. Sci. Q 502 (1957).

A. Data Collection

The data reported in this paper were gathered over a period of seven years, from 1962 to 1969. Most came from interviews with persons who were members of either the vice syndicate, law enforcement agencies, or both. The interviews ranged in intensity from casual conversations to extended interviewing, complete with tape recording, at frequent intervals over the full seven years of the study. In addition, I participated in many, though not all, of the vices that comprise the cornerstone upon which corruption of the law enforcement agencies is laid.

There is, of course, considerable latitude for discretion on my part as to what I believe ultimately characterizes the situation. Obviously not everyone told the same story, nor did I give equal credibility to all information acquired. The story that does emerge, however, most closely coincides with my own observations and with otherwise inexplicable facts. I am confident that the data are accurate, valid, and reliable; but this cannot be demonstrated by pointing to unbiased sampling, objective measures, and the like for, alas, in this type of research such procedures are impossible.

B. The Setting: Rainfall West

Rainfall West is practically indistinguishable from any other city of a million population. The conspicuous bulk of the population—the middle class—shares with its contemporaries everywhere a smug complacency and a firm belief in the intrinsic worth of the area and the city. Their particular smugness may be exaggerated due to relative freedom from the urban blight that is so often the fate of larger cities and to the fact that Rainfall West's natural surroundings attract tourists, thereby providing the citizenry with the confirmation of their faith that this is, indeed, a "chosen land!"[5]

However, an invisible, although fairly large minority of the population, do not believe they live in the promised land. These are the inhabitants of the slums and ghettos that make up the center of the city. Camouflaging the discontent of the center are urban renewal programs which ring the slums with brick buildings and skyscrapers. But satisfaction is illusory; it requires only a slight effort to get past this brick and mortar and into the not-so-enthusiastic city center—a marked contrast to the wildly bubbling civic center located less than a mile away. Despite the ease of access, few of those living in the suburbs and working in the area surrounding the slums take the time to go where the action is. Those who do go for specific reasons: to bet on a

---

5. Thinking of one's own residence as a "chosen land" need not of course be connected with any objectively verifiable evidence. A small Indian farm town where the standard of living is scarcely ever above the poverty level has painted signs on sidewalks which read "Isn't God good to Indians?" Any outside observer knowing something of the hardships and disadvantages that derive from living in this town might well answer an unequivocal "no." Most members of this community nevertheless answer affirmatively.

football game, to find a prostitute, to see a dirty movie, or to obtain a personal loan that would be unavailable from conventional financial institutions.

II. Bureaucratic Corruption and Organized Crime: A Study in Symbiosis

Laws prohibiting gambling, prostitution, pornography, drug use, and high interest rates on personal loans are laws about which there is a conspicuous lack of consensus. Even persons who agree that such behavior is improper and should be controlled by law disagree on the proper legal response. Should persons found guilty of committing such acts be imprisoned, or counselled? Reflecting this dissension, large groups of people, some with considerable political power, insist on their right to enjoy the pleasures of vice without interference from the law.

In Rainfall West, those involved in providing gambling and other vices enjoy pointing out that their services are profitable because of the demand for them by members of the respectable community. Prostitutes work in apartments which are on the fringes of the lower class area of the city, rather than in the heart of the slums, precisely because they must maintain an appearance of ecological respectability so that their clients will not feel contaminated by poverty. While professional pride may stimulate exaggeration on the part of the prostitutes, their verbal reports are always to the effect that "all" their clients are "very important people." My own observations of the comings and goings in several apartment houses where prostitutes work generally verified the girls' claims. Of some fifty persons seen going to prostitutes' rooms in apartment houses, only one was dressed in anything less casual than a business suit.

Observations of panorama—pornographic films shown in the back rooms of restaurants and game rooms—also confirmed the impression that the principal users of vice are middle and upper class clientele. During several weeks of observations, over seventy per cent of the consumers of these pornographic vignettes were well dressed, single-minded visitors to the slums, who came for fifteen or twenty minutes of viewing and left as inconspicuously as possible. The remaining thirty per cent were poorly dressed, older men who lived in the area.

Information on gambling and bookmaking in the permanently established or floating games is less readily available. Bookmakers report that the bulk of their "real business" comes from "doctors, lawyers and dentists" in the city:

It's the big boys—your professionals—who do the betting down here. Of course, they don't come down themselves; they either send someone or they call up. Most of them call up, 'cause I know them or they know Mr. .... [one of the key figures in the gambling operation.]

Q. How 'bout the guys who walk off the street and bet?
A. Yeh; well, they're important. They do place bets and they
sit around here and wait for the results. But that's mostly small
stuff. I'd be out of business if I had to depend on them guys.

The poker and card games held throughout the city are of two types:
1) the small, daily game that caters almost exclusively to local residents of the
area or working-class men who drop in for a hand or two while they are
driving their delivery route or on their lunch hour; 2) and the action game
which takes place twenty-four hours a day, and is located in more obscure
places such as a suite in a downtown hotel. Like the prostitutes, these games
are located on the edges of the lower-class areas. The action games are the
play-ground of well-dressed men who were by manner, finances, and dress
clearly well-to-do businessmen.

Then, of course, there are the games, movies, and gambling nights at
private clubs—country clubs, Elks, Lions, and Masons clubs—where gambling
is a mainstay. Gambling nights at the different clubs vary in frequency. The
largest and most exclusive country club in Rainfall West has a funtime once a
month at which one can find every conceivable variety of gambling and a
limited, but fairly sophisticated, selection of pornography. Although admission is presumably limited to members of the club, it is relatively easy to gain
entrance simply by joining with a temporary membership, paying a two dollar
fee at the door. Other clubs, such as the local fraternal organizations, have
pinball machines present at all times; some also provide slot machines. Many
of these clubs have ongoing poker and other gambling card games, run by
people who work for the crime cabal. In all of these cases, the vices cater
exclusively to middle and upper class clients.

Not all the business and professional men in Rainfall West partake of the
vices. Indeed, some of the leading citizens sincerely oppose the presence of
vice in their city. Even larger members of the middle and working classes are
adamant in their opposition to vice of all kinds. On occasion, they make their
views forcefully known to the politicians and law enforcement officers, thus
requiring these public officials to express their own opposition and appear to
be snuffing out vice by enforcing the law.

The law enforcement system is thus placed squarely in the middle of two
essentially conflicting demands. On the one hand, their job obligates them to
enforce the law, albeit with discretion; at the same time, considerable disagreement rages over whether or not some acts should be subject to legal
sanction. This conflict is heightened by the fact that some influential persons
in the community insist that all laws be rigorously enforced while others
demand that some laws not be enforced, at least not against themselves.

Faced with such a dilemma and such an ambivalent situation, the law
enforcers do what any well managed bureaucracy would do under similar

circumstances—they follow the line of least resistance. Using the discretion inherent in their positions, they resolve the problem by establishing procedures which minimize organizational strains and which provide the greatest promise of rewards for the organization and the individuals involved. Typically, this means that law enforcers adopt a tolerance policy towards the vices, selectively enforcing these laws only when it is to their advantage to do so. Since the persons demanding enforcement are generally middle class persons who rarely venture into the less prosperous sections of the city, the enforcers can control visibility and minimize complaints by merely regulating the ecological location of the vices. Limiting the visibility of such activity as sexual deviance, gambling, and prostitution appeases those persons who demand the enforcement af applicable laws. At the same time, since controlling visibility does not eliminate access for persons sufficiently interested to ferret out the tolerated vice areas, those demanding such services are also satisfied.

This policy is also advantageous because it renders the legal system capable of exercising considerable control over potential sources of real trouble. For example, since gambling and prostitution are profitable, competition among persons desiring to provide these services is likely. Understandably, this competition is prone to become violent. If the legal system cannot control those running these vices, competing groups may well go to war to obtain dominance over the rackets. If, however, the legal system co-operates with one group, there will be a sufficient concentration of power to avoid these uprisings. Similarly, prostitution can be kept clean if the law enforcers co-operate with the prostitutes; the law can thus minimize the chance, for instance, that a prostitute will steal money from a customer. In this and many other ways, the law enforcement system maximizes its visible effectiveness by creating and supporting a shadow government that manages the vices.

Initially this may require bringing in people from other cities to help set up the necessary organizational structure. Or it may mean recruiting and training local talent or simply co-opting, coercing, or purchasing the knowledge and skills of entrepreneurs who are at the moment engaged in vice operations. When made, this move often involves considerable strain, since some of those brought in may be uncooperative. Whatever the particulars, the ultimate result is the same: a syndicate emerges—composed of politicians, law enforcers, and citizens—capable of supplying and controlling the vices in the city. The most efficient cabal is invariably one that contains representatives of all the leading centers of power. Businessmen must be involved because of their political influence and their ability to control the mass media. This prerequisite is illustrated by the case of a fledgling magazine which published an article intimating that several leading politicians were corrupt. Immediately major advertisers canceled their advertisements in the magazine. One large chain store refused to sell that issue of the magazine in any of its stores. And when one of the leading cabal members was accused of accepting bribes, a number of the community's most prominent businessmen sponsored a large advertisement declaring their unfailing support for and confidence in the integrity of this "outstanding public servant."

The cabal must also have the cooperation of businessmen in procuring the loans which enable them individually and collectively to purchase legitimate businesses, as well as to expand the vice enterprises. A member of the banking community is therefore a considerable asset. In Rainfall West the vice president of one of the local banks (who was an investigator for a federal law enforcement agency before he entered banking) is a willing and knowledgeable participant in business relations with cabal members. He not only serves on the board of directors of a loan agency controlled by the cabal, but also advises cabal members on how to keep their earnings a secret. Further he sometimes serves as a go-between, passing investment tips from the cabal onto other businessmen in the community. In this way the cabal serves the economic interests of businessmen indirectly as well as directly.

The political influence of the cabal is more directly obtained. Huge, tax free profits make it possible for the cabal to generously support political candidates of its choice. Often the cabal assists both candidates in an election, thus assuring itself of influence regardless of who wins. While usually there is a favorite, ultra-cooperative candidate who receives the greater proportion of the contributions, everyone is likely to receive something.

III. The Bureaucracy

Contrary to the prevailing myth that universal rules govern bureaucracies, the fact is that in day-to-day operations rules can—and must—be selectively applied. As a consequence, some degree of corruption is not merely a possibility, but rather is a virtual certainty which is built into the very structure of bureaucratic organizations.

The starting point for understanding this structural invitation to corruption is the observation that application of all the rules and procedures comprising the foundation of an organization inevitably admits of a high degree of discretion. Rules can only specify what should be done when the actions being considered fall clearly into unambiguously specifiable categories, about which there can be no reasonable grounds of disagreement or conflicting interpretation. But such categories are a virtual impossibility, given the inherently ambiguous nature of language. Instead, most events fall within the penumbra of the bureaucratic rules where the discretion of officeholders must hold sway.

Since discretionary decisionmaking is recognized as inevitable in effect, all bureaucratic decisions become subject to the discretionary will of the officeholder. Moreover, if one has a reason to look, vagueness and ambiguity can be found in any rule, no matter how carefully stipulated. And if ambiguity and vagueness are not sufficient to justify particularistic criteria being applied, contradictory rules or implications of rules can be readily located which have the same effect of justifying the decisions which, for whatever reason the office-holder wishes, can be used to enforce his position. Finally, since organizations characteristically develop their own set of common practices which take on the status of rules (whether written or unwritten), the entire process of applying rules becomes totally dependent on the discretion of the office-holder. The bureaucracy thus has its own set of precedents which can be invoked in cases where the articulated rules do not provide precisely the decision desired by the office-holder.

Ultimately, the office-holder has license to apply rules derived from a practically bottomless set of choices. Individual self-interest then depends on one's ability to ingratiate himself to office-holders at all levels in order to ensure that the rules most useful to him are applied. The bureaucracy therefore is not a rational institution with universal standards, but is instead, irrational and particularistic. It is a type of organization in which the organization's reason for being is displaced by a set of goals that often conflict with the organization's presumed purposes. This is precisely the consequence of the organizational response to the dilemma created by laws prohibiting the vices. Hence, the bureaucratic nature of law enforcement and political organization makes possible the corruption of the legal-political bureaucracy.

In the case of Rainfall West the goal of maintaining a smooth functioning organization takes precedence over all other institutional goals. Where conflict arises between the long-range goals of the law and the short-range goal of sustaining the organization, the former lose out, even at the expense of undermining the socially agreed-upon purposes for which the organization presumably exists.

Yet, the law-enforcement agency's tendency to follow the line of least resistance of maintaining organizational goals in the face of conflicting demands necessarily embodies a choice as to whose demands will be followed. For bureaucracies are not equally susceptible to all interests in the society. They do not fear the castigation, interference, and disruptive potential of the alcoholics on skid row or the cafe-owners in the slums. In fact, some residents of the black ghetto in Rainfall West and of other lower-class areas of the city have been campaigning for years to rid their communities of the gambling casinos, whore houses, pornography stalls, and bookmaking operations. But these pleas fall on deaf ears. The letters they write and the committees they form receive no publicity and create no stir in the smoothly functioning organizations that occupy the political and legal offices of the city. On the other hand, when the president of a large corporation in the city objected to the "slanderous lies" being spread about one of the leading members of the crime cabal in Rainfall West, the magazine carrying the "lies" was removed from newsstand sale, and the editors lost many of their most profitable advertisers. Similarly, when any question of the honesty or integrity of policemen, prosecuting attorneys, or judges involved in the cabal is raised publicly, it is either squelched before aired (the editor of the leading daily newspaper in Rainfall West is a long-time friend of one of the cabal's leading members) or it arouses the denial of influential members of the banking community (especially those bankers whose institutions loan money to cabal members), as well as leading politicians, law enforcement officers, and the like.

In short, bureaucracies are susceptible to differential influence, according to the economic and political power of the groups attempting to exert influence. Since every facet of politics and the mass media is subject to reprisals by cabal members and friends, exposition of the ongoing relationship between the cabal and the most powerful economic groups in the city is practically impossible.

The fact that the bureaucrats must listen to the economic elites of the city and not the have-nots is then one important element that stimulates the growth and maintenance of a crime cabal. But the links between the elites and the cabal are more than merely spiritual. The economic elite of the city does not simply play golf with the political and legal elite. There are in fact significant economic ties between the two groups.

The most obvious nexus is manifested by the campaign contributions from the economic elite to the political and legal elites. We need not dwell on this observation here; it has been well documented in innumerable other studies.[6] However, what is not well recognized is that the crime cabal is itself an important source of economic revenue for the economic elite. In at least one instance, the leading bankers and industrialists of the city were part of a multi-million dollar stock swindle engineered and manipulated by the crime cabal with the assistance of confidence-men from another state. This entire case was shrouded in such secrecy that eastern newspapers were calling people at the University of Rainfall West to find out why news about the scandal was not forthcoming from local wire services. When the scandal was finally exposed the fact that industrialists and cabal members heavily financed the operation (and correspondingly reaped the profits) was conveniently ignored in the newspapers and the courts; the evil-doers were limited to the outsiders who were in reality the front men for the entire confidence operation.

In a broader sense, key members of the economic elite in the community are also members of the cabal. While the day-to-day, week-to-week operations of the cabal are determined by the criminal-political-legal elite, the economic elite benefits mightily from the cabal. Not surprisingly, any threat to the cabal is quickly squelched by the economic elite under the name of "concerned citizens," which indeed they are.

The crime cabal is thus an inevitable outgrowth of the political economy of American cities. The ruling elites from every sphere benefit economically

6. See generally G. Dornhoff, *Who Rules America?* (1969); Overa, *Presidential Campaign Funds* (1946); J. Shannon, *Money and Politics* (1959); Overa, *Money in Elections* (1932); Bernstein, "Private Wealth and Public Office: The High Cost of Campaigning" 22 *The Nation* 77 (1966).

and socially from the presence of a smoothly running cabal. Law enforcement and government bureaucracies function best when a cabal is part of the governmental structure. And the general public is satisfied when control of the vice gives an appearance of respectability, but a reality of availability.

IV. Vice in Rainfall West

The vices available in Rainfall West are varied and tantalizing. Gambling ranges from bookmaking (at practically every street corner in the center of the city) to open poker games, bingo parlors, off-track betting, casinos, roulette and dice games (concentrated in a few locations and also floating out into the suburban country clubs and fraternal organizations), and innumerable two and five dollar stud-poker games scattered liberally throughout the city.

The most conspicuous card games take place from about ten in the morning—varying slightly from one fun house to the next—until midnight. A number of other twenty-four hour games run constantly. In the more public games, the limit ranges from one to five dollars for each bet; in the more select twenty-four hours a day games, there is a pot limit or no limit rule. These games are reported to have betting as high as twenty and thirty thousand dollars. I saw a bet made and called for a thousand dollars in one of these games. During this game, the highest stakes game I witnessed in the six years of the study, the police lieutenant in charge of the vice squad was called into supervise the game—not, need I add, to break up the game or make any arrests, but only to insure against violence.

Prostitution covers the usual range of ethnic group, age, shape, and size of female. It is found in houses with madams *a la* the New Orleans stereotype, on the street through pimps, or in suburban apartment buildings and hotels. Prices range from five dollars for a short time with a street walker to two hundred dollars for a night with a lady who has her own apartment (which she usually shares with her boyfriend who is discreetly gone during business operations).

High interest loans are easy to arrange through stores that advertise, "your signature is worth $5,000." It is really worth considerably more; it may in fact be worth your life. The interest rates vary from a low of 20 percent for three months to as high as 100 percent for varying periods. Repayment is demanded not through courts, but through the help of "The Gaspipe Gang," who call on recalcitrant debtors and use physical force to bring about payment. "Interest only" repayment is the most popular alternative practiced by borrowers and is preferred by the loan sharks as well. The longer repayment can be prolonged, the more advantageous the loan is to the agent.

Pinball machines are readily available throughout the city, most of them paying off in cash.

The gambling, prostitution, drug distribution, pronography, and usury which flourish in the lower class center of the city do so with the compliance, encouragement, and cooperation of the major political and law enforcement officials in the city. There is in fact a symbiotic relationship between the law enforcement-political organizations of the city and a group of *local*, as distinct from national, men who control the distribution of vices.

V. Corruption in Rainfall West

In the spring of 19— a businessman who I shall call Mr. Van Meter sold his restaurant and began looking for a new investment when he noticed an advertisement in the paper which read:

Excellent investment opportunity for someone with $30,000 cash
to purchase the good will and equipment of a long established
restaurant in down town area . . . .

After making the necessary inquiries, inspecting the business, and evaluating its potential, Mr. Van Meter purchased it. In addition to the restaurant, the business consisted of a card-room which was legally licensed by the city, operating under a publicly acknowledged tolerance policy which allowed card games, including poker, to be played. These games were limited by the tolerance policy to a maximum $1.00 limit for each bet.

Thus, Mr. Van Meter had purchased a restaurant with a built-in criminal enterprise. It was never clear whether he was, at the time of purchasing the business, fully aware of the criminal nature of the card room. Certainly the official tolerance policy was bound to create confusion over the illegality of gambling in the licensed card rooms. The full extent to which this purchase involved Mr. Van Meter in illegal activities crystallized immediately upon purchase of the property.[7]

[W]e had just completed taking the inventory of [the restaurant]. I was then handed the $60,000 keys of the premises by Mr. Bataglia, and he approached me and said, "Up until now, I have never discussed with you the fact that we run a book-making operation here, and that we did not sell this to you; however if you wish to have this operation continue here, you must place another $5,000 to us, and we will count you in. Now, if you do not buy it, we will put out this book-making operation, and you will go broke." "In other words," Mr. Bataglia continued, "we will use you, and you need us." I told Mr. Bataglia that I did not come to this town to bookmake or to operate any form of rackets, and I assumed that I had purchased a legitimate business. Mr. Bataglia said, "You have purchased a legitimate business;

7. All quotations are from taped interviews. The names of persons and places are fictitious.

however, you must have the book-making operation in order to survive." I promptly kicked him out of the place.

The question of how "legitimate" the business Mr. Van Meter had purchased was is not so simple as he thought. It was, to be sure, a licensed operation; there was a license to operate the restaurant, a license to operate the card room attached to the restaurant, and a license to operate the cigar stand (where much of the bookmaking operation had taken place before Mr. Van Meter purchased the place). These licenses, although providing a "legitimate business," also had the effect of making the owner of the business constantly in violation of the law, for the laws were so constructed that no one could possibly operate a "legitimate" business "legally." Thus, anyone operating the business was vulnerable to constant harassment and even closure by the authorities if he failed to cooperate with law enforcement personnel.

The cardroom attached to the business was the most flagrant example of a legitimate enterprise that was necessarily run illegally. The city of Rainfall West had adopted by ordinance a tolerance policy towards gambling. This tolerance policy consisted of permitting cardrooms, which were then licensed by the city, pinball machines that paid off money to winners, and panorama shows. The city ordinance allowed a maximum one dollar bet at the card table in rooms such as those in Mr. Van Meter's restaurant.

This ordinance was in clear and open violation of state law. The State Attorney General had publicly stated that the tolerance policy of the city was illegal and that the only policy for the state was that all gambling was illegal. Despite these rulings from higher state officials, the tolerance policy continued and flourished in the city although it did so illegally.

This general illegality of the card room was not, however, easily enforceable against any one person running a card room without enforcement against all persons running card rooms. There were, however, wrinkles in the tolerance policy ordinance which made it possible discriminately to close down one card room without being forced to take action against all of them. This was accomplished in part by the limit of one dollar on a bet. The card room was allowed to take a certain percentage of the pot from each game, but the number of people playing and the amount of percentage permitted did not allow one to make a profit if the table limit remained at one dollar. Furthermore, since most people gambling wanted to bet more, they would not patronize a card room that insisted on the one dollar limit. Mr. Van Meter, like all other card room operators, allowed a two to five dollar limit. The ordinance was written in such a way that, in reality, everyone would be in violation of it. It was therefore possible for the police to harass or close down whatever card rooms they chose at their own discretion.

The health and fire regulations of the city were also written in such a way that no one could comply with all the ordinances. It was impossible to serve meals and still avoid violation of the health standards required. Thus, when the health or fire department chose to enforce the rules, they could do so selectively against whatever business they chose.

The same set of circumstances governed the cabaret licenses in the city. The city ordinances required that every cabaret have a restaurant attached; the restaurant, the ordinance stated, had to comprise at least seventy five per cent of the total floor space of the cabaret and restaurant combined. Since there was a much higher demand for cabarets than restaurants in the central section of the city, this meant that cabaret owners were bound by law to have restaurants attached some of which would necessarily lose money. Moreover, these restaurants had to be extremely large in order to constitute seventy five per cent of the total floor space. For a one-hundred square foot cabaret, an attached three-hundred square foot restaurant was required. The cabaret owners burden was further increased by an ordinance governing the use of entertainers in the cabaret, requiring that any entertainer be at least twenty five feet from the nearest customer during her act. Plainly, the cabaret had to be absolutely gigantic to accommodate any customers after a twenty five foot buffer zone encircled the entertainer. Combined with the requirement that this now very large cabaret had to have attached to it a restaurant three times as large, the regulatory scheme simply made it impossible to run a cabaret legally.

The effect of such ordinances was to give the police and the prosecuting attorney complete discretion in choosing who should operate gambling rooms, cabarets, and restaurants. This discretion was used to force pay-offs to the police and cooperation with the criminal syndicate.

Mr. Van Meter discovered the pay-off system fairly early in his venture:

I found shortages that were occurring in the bar, and asked an employee to explain them, which he did, in this manner: "The money is saved to pay the 'juice' of the place." I asked him what was the "juice." He said in this city you must "pay to stay." Mr. Davis said, "You pay for the beat-man [from the police department] $250.00 per month. That takes care of the various shifts, and you must pay the upper brass, also $200.00 each month. A beat-man collects around the first of each month, and another man collects for the upper brass. You get the privilege to stay in business." That is true; however, you must remember that it is not what they will do for you, but what they will do *to* you, if you don't make these payoffs as are ordered. "If I refuse, what then?" I asked. "The *least* that could happen to you is you will lose your business."

During the next three months, Mr. Van Meter made the payoffs required. He refused, however, to allow the bookmaking operation back into the building or to hire persons to run the card room and bar whom members of the organized crime syndicate and the police recommended to him for the job.

He also fired one employee whom he found was taking bets while tending bar.

In August of the same year, a man whom Mr. Van Meter had known prior to buying the restaurant met him in his office:

Mr. Danielski met with me in my office and he came prepared to offer me $500 per month—in cash deductions—of my remaining balance of the contract owing against (the restaurant) if I would give him the bookmaking operation, and he would guarantee me another $800 a month more business. He warned that if he wanted to give my establishment trouble, he would go to a certain faction of the police department; if he wanted me open, he would go to another faction. "So do some thinking on the subject, and I will be in on Monday for your answer." Monday, I gave Mr. Danielski his answer. The answer was no.

In June of 19—, a man by the name of Joe Link, who I found later was a second-string gang member of Mr. Bataglia's, made application to me to operate my card room. I did give him the opportunity to operate the card room because I had known him some 20 years ago when he was attending the same high school that I was. After I had refused the offer of Mr. Danielski, Mr. Joe Link had received orders from Mr. Danielski and Mr. Bataglia to run my customers out and in any way he could, cripple my operation to bring me to terms. I terminated Mr. Link on November 6, 19—, and shortly after, after I had removed Mr. Link, Police Officer Herb C. conferred with me in my office, and Officer Herb C. said that I had better re-appoint Mr. Link in my card room; that his superiors were not happy with me. If I did not return Mr. Link to his former position, then it would be necessary to clear anyone that I wanted to replace Mr. Link with. Officer C. felt that no one else would be acceptable. He further stated I had better make a decision soon, because he would not allow the card room to run without an approved boss. I informed Officer C. that I would employ anyone I chose in my card room or in any other department. Officer C. said "Mr. Van Meter, you, I think, do not realize how powerful a force you will be fighting or how deep in City Hall this reaches. Even I am not let known all the bosses or where the money goes." I did not return Mr. Link, as I was ordered by Officer C., and I did select my own card room bosses.

On November 7, 19—, I received a phone call stating that I soon would have a visitor who was going to shoot me between the eyes if I did not comply with the demands to return Mr. Link to his former position.

The crime cabal in Rainfall West (including police officers, politicians and members of the organized criminal syndicate), like the criminal law which underpins it, relies on the threat of coercion to maintain order. That threat, however, is not an empty one. Although Mr. Van Meter was not "shot between the eyes" as threatened, others who defied the cabal were less fortunate. Although it has never been established that any of the suspicious deaths that have taken place involving members of crime cabal were murder, the evidence, nonetheless, points rather strongly in that direction. Eric Tandlin, former county auditor for Rainfall West, is but one of thirteen similar cases which occurred from 1955–1969.

Tandlin had been county auditor for seventeen years. He kept his nose clean, did the bidding of the right politicians, and received a special gift every Christmas for his cooperation. In the course of doing business with the politicians and criminals, he also developed extensive knowledge of the operations. Suddenly, without warning or expectation on his part, Eric was not supported by his party, for re-election as auditor, losing the nomination to the brother-in-law of the chief of police. It was a shock from which Eric did not soon recover. He began drinking heavily and frequenting the gambling houses; he also began talking a great deal. One Friday evening, he made friends with a reporter who promised to put him in touch with someone from the attorney general's office. Saturday night at 6:30, just as the card rooms were being prepared for the evening, word spread through the grapevine along First Street that Eric had been done in: "Danielski took Eric for a walk down by the bay."

The Sunday morning paper carried a small front page story:

Eric Tandlin aged forty seven was found drowned in back bay yesterday at around 5.00 p.m. The Coroner's office listed the cause of death as possible suicide. Friends said Mr. Tandlin who had been county auditor for many years until his defeat in the primaries last fall had been despondent over his failure to be re-elected.

The coroner, who was the brother-in-law of the chief of police, described the probable cause of death as "suicide." The people of Miriam Street knew better. They also knew that this was a warning not to talk to reporters, sociologists, or anyone else "nosing around." In the last few years the cabal has been responsible for the deaths of several of its members. Drowning is a favorite method of eliminating troublemakers, because it is difficult to ascertain whether or not the person fell from a boat by accident, was held under water by someone else, or committed suicide.[8] L.S., who was in charge of a portion of the pinball operations, but who came into disfavor with the cabal,

---

8. According to one informant: "Murder is the easiest crime of all to get away with. There are 101 ways to commit murder that are guaranteed to let you get away with it." He might have added that this was especially true when the coroner, the prosecuting attorney and key policy officials were cooperating with the murderers.

was found drowned at the edge of a lake near his home. J.B., an assistant police chief who had been a minor member of the cabal for years, drowned while on a fishing trip aboard one of the yachts owned by a leading member of the cabal. In both instances the coroner, who was the brother-in-law of one of the leading cabal members, diagnosed the deaths as "accidental drownings." Over the years, he has often made that diagnosis when cabal members or workers in the organization have met with misfortune.

Other deaths have been arranged in more traditional ways. At least one man, for example, was shot in an argument in a bar. The offender was tried before a judge who has consistently shown great compassion for any crimes committed by members of the cabal (although he has compensated for this leniency with cabal members by being unusually harsh in cases against blacks who appear before him), and the case was dismissed for lack of evidence.

However, murder is not the preferred method of handling uncooperative people. Far better, in the strategy of the crime cabal, is the time-honoured technique of blackmail and co-optation. The easiest and safest tactic is to purchase the individual for a reasonable amount, as was attempted with Mr. Van Meter. If this fails, then some form of blackmail or relatively minor coercion may be in order.

For instance, Sheriff McCallister was strongly supported by the cabal in his bid for office. Campaign contributions were generously provided since McCallister was running against a local lawyer who was familiar with the goings-on of the cabal and had vowed to attack its operations. McCallister won the election—cabal candidates almost never lose local elections—but underwent a dramatic change-of-heart shortly thereafter. He announced in no uncertain terms that he would not permit the operation of gambling houses in the county, although he did not intend to do anything about the operations within the city limits since that was not his jurisdiction. Nevertheless the county, he insisted, would be kept clean.

The cabal was as annoyed as it was surprised. The county operations were only a small portion of the total enterprise, but they were nonetheless important, and no one wanted to give up the territory. Further, the prospect of closing down the lay-off center operating in the county was no small matter. The center is crucial to the entire enterprise, because it is here that the results of horse races and other sports events come directly to the book-makers. The center also enables the cabal to protect itself against potential bankruptcy. When the betting is particularly heavy in one direction, bets are laid off by wiring Las Vegas where the national betting pattern always takes care of local variations. Clearly, something had to be done about McCallister.

No man is entirely pure, and McCallister was less pure than many. He had two major weaknesses: gambling and young girls. One weekend shortly after he took office a good friend of his asked if he would like to go to Las Vegas for the weekend. He jumped at the opportunity. While the weekend went well in some respects, McCallister was unlucky at cards. When he flew back to Rainfall West Sunday night, he left $14,000 worth of I.O.U.'s in Las Vegas.

Monday morning one of the cabal chiefs visited McCallister in his office. The conversation went like this:

Say, Mac, I understand you was down in Vegas over the weekend.
 Yeah.
Hear you lost a little bit at the tables, Mac.
 Uuh-huh.
Well the boys wanted me to tell you not to worry about those pieces of paper you left. We got them back for you.
 I don't . . . .
Also, Mac, we thought you might like to have a momento of your trip; so we brought you these pictures . . . .

The "momentos" were pictures of McCallister in a hotel room with several young girls. Thereafter things in the county returned to normal.

Lest one think the cabal exploitative, it should be noted that McCallister was not kept in line by the threat of exposure alone. He was, in fact, subsequently placed on the payroll in the amount of one thousand dollars a month. When his term as sheriff was over, an appointment was arranged for him to the state parole board. He was thus able to continue serving the cabal in a variety of ways for the rest of his life. Cooperation paid off much better than would have exposure.

Threats from outside the organization are more rare than are threats from within. Nevertheless, they occur and must be dealt with in the best possible way. Since no set strategy exists, each incident is handled in its own way. During Robert Kennedy's days as attorney general, the federal attorney for the state began a campaign to rid the state of the members of the cabal. People who held political office were generally immune, but some of the higherups in the operational section of the cabal were indicted. Ultimately five members of the cabal, including a high ranking member of the local Teamsters' Union, were sentenced to prison. The entire affair was scandalous; politicians whose lives depended on the cabal fought the nasty business with all their power. They were able to protect the major leaders of the cabal and to avert exposure of the cabal politicians. However, some blood ran, and it was a sad day for the five sentenced to prison terms. Yet the organization remained intact and, indeed, the five men who went to prison continued to receive their full share of profits from the cabal enterprises. Corruption continued unabated, and the net effect on organized crime in the state was nil.

One reason that Mr. Van Meter was not "shot between the eyes" was that, although not fully cooperative, he was nonetheless paying into the cabal four hundred and fifty dollars a month in "juice." Eventually he cut down on these payments. When this happened Mr. Van Meter became a serious problem for the cabal, and something more than mere threats was necessary:

No extortion was paid by me directly to them, but it involved a third party. Some time shortly after the first of each month, the sum of $250.00 was paid to (the above mentioned) Officer C., which he presumably divided up with other patrolmen on the beat. Two hundred dollars each month was given to (another bagman) for what the boys termed as "It was going to the upper braid." The $200.00 per month was paid each month from June 19— with payment of $200.00 being made in January 19—. After that I refused to make further payments . . . . After some wrangling back and forth, I just told them that I would not pay any more. They said, "Well, we will take $100.00 per month on a temporary basis. I paid $100.00 per month for the next twelve months. Early the next year I had planned to cut off all payments to the patrolmen . . . . About the 8th of July the explosion occurred. Police officers Merrill and Lynch conducted a scare program; jerked patrons off stools, ran others out of my establishment; Patrolman Lynch ordered my card room floorman into the rest room; and ordered my card room closed. When my floorman came out of the rest room, he left white and shaking and never to be seen in the city again.

Following this incident, Mr. Van Meter met with his attorney, the chief of police, and a former mayor. Although the meeting was cordial, he was told they could do nothing unless he could produce affidavits substantiating his claims. He did so, but quickly became enmeshed in requests and demands for more affidavits, while the prosecuting attorney's office resisted cooperating.

The refusal of cooperation from the prosecuting attorney was not surprising. What Mr. Van Meter did not realize was that the prosecuting attorney was the key political figure behind the corruption of the legal and political machinery. He was also the political boss of the county and had great influence on state politics, coming as he did from the most populous area of the state. Over the years his influence had been used to place men in key positions throughout the various government bureaucracies, including the police department, the judiciary, the city council, and relevant governmental agencies such as the tax office and the licensing bureau.

There was, however, a shift in emphasis for a short time in the cabal's dealings with Mr. Van Meter. They offered to buy his business at the price he had paid for it. But when he refused, the pace of harassment increased. Longshoremen came into his restaurant and started fights. Police stood around the card room day and night observing. City health officials would come to inspect the cooking area during mealtimes, thereby delaying the food being served to customers; the fire department made frequent visits to inspect fire precautions. On several occasions, Mr. Van Meter was cited for violating health and safety standards.

Finally, he was called to the city council to answer an adverse police report stating that he allowed drunks and brawling in his establishment. At the hearing, he was warned that he would lose all of his licenses if a drunk were ever again found in his restaurant.

During the next six months, the pressure on Mr. Van Meter continued at an ever increasing rate. Longshoremen came into the restaurant and card room and picked fights with customers, employees, and Mr. Van Meter himself. The health department chose five o'clock in the evening several days running to inspect the health facilities of the establishment. The fire inspector came at the lunch hour to inspect the fire equipment, writing up every minor defect detectable. Toward the end of Mr. Van Meter's attempt to fight the combine of the government, the police force, and the criminal syndicate, he received innumerable threats to his life. Bricks and stones were thrown through the windows of his building. Ultimately, he sold his business back to the man from whom he had purchased it at a loss of thirty thousand dollars and left the city.

The affair caused considerable consternation among the legal-political-criminal cabal which controlled and profited from the rackets in Rainfall West. In the "good old days" the problem would have been quickly solved, one informant remarked, "by a bullet through the fat slob's head." But ready resort to murder as a solution to problems was clearly frowned upon by the powers that operated organized crime in Rainfall West. Although the syndicate had been responsible for many murders over the past ten years, these murders were limited to troublesome persons *within* the syndicate. As nearly as could be determined, no outsider had been murdered for a number of years.

Overall the gambling, book-making, pinball, and usury operations grossed at least twenty five million dollars a year in the city alone. It was literally the case that drunks were arrested on the street for public intoxication while gamblers made thousands of dollars and policemen accepted bribes five feet away.

Payoffs, bribes, and associated corruption were not limited solely to illegal activities. To obtain a license for two-truck operations one had to pay ten thousand dollars to the licensing bureau; a license for a taxi franchise cost fifteen thousand dollars. In addition, taxi drivers who sold bootleg liquor (standard brand liquors sold after hours or on Sunday) or who would steer customers to prostitutes or gambling places, paid the beat policeman and the sergeant of the vice squad. Tow-truck operators also paid the policeman who called the company when an accident occurred.

As one informant commented:

When I would go out on a call from a policeman I would always
carry matchbooks with three dollars tucked behind the covers. I

would hand this to the cops when I came to the scene of an accident.

Q. Did every policeman accept these bribes?

A. No. Once in a while you would run into a cop who would say he wasn't interested. But that was rare. Almost all of them would take it.

Most of the cabarets, topless bars, and taverns were owned either directly or indirectly by members of the organized crime syndicate. Thus, the syndicate not only controlled the gambling enterprises, but also "legitimate" businesses associated with night life as well. In addition, several of the hotels and restaurants were also owned by the syndicate. Ownership of these establishments was disguised in several ways, such as placing them formally in the name of a corporation with a board of directors who were really front-men for the syndicate or placing them in the names of relatives of syndicate members. It should further be underlined that the official ownership by the syndicate must be interpreted to mean by all of the members who were in the political and legal bureaucracies and simultaneously members of the syndicate, as well as those who were solely involved in the day-to-day operations of the vice syndicate.

The governing board of the syndicate consisted of seven men, four of whom held high positions in the government and three of whom were responsible for the operation of the various enterprises. The profits were split among these seven men. We are *not* then talking about a syndicate that paid off officials, but about a syndicate that is part and parcel of the government, although not subject to election.

VI. Conclusion

There is abundant data indicating that what is true in Rainfall West is true in virtually every city in the United States and has been true since at least the early 1900's. Writing at the turn of the century, Lincoln Steffens observed that "the spirit of graft and of lawlessness is the American spirit." He went on to describe the results of his inquiries:

in the very first study—St. Louis—the startling truth lay bare that corruption was not merely political; it was financial, commercial, social; the ramifications of boodle were so complex, various and far-reaching, that our mind could hardly grasp them . . . . St. Louis exemplified boodle; Minneapolis Police graft; Pittsburg a political and Industrial machine; Philadelphia general civil corruption . . . .[9]

In 1931, after completing an inquiry into the police, the National Commission on Law Observance and Enforcement concluded:

9. See L. Steffens, *The Shame of the Cities* 151 (1904).

Nearly all of the large cities suffer from an alliance between politicians and criminals. For example, Los Angeles was controlled by a few gamblers for a number of years. San Francisco suffered similarly some years ago and at one period in its history was so completely dominated by the gamblers that three prominent gamblers who were in control of the politics of the city and who quarrelled about the appointment of the police chief settled their quarrel by shaking dice to determine who would name the chief for the first two years, who for the second two years, and who for the third.

Recently the gamblers were driven out of Detroit by the commissioner. These gamblers were strong enough politically to oust this commissioner from office despite the fact that he was recognized by police chiefs as one of the strongest and ablest police executives in America. For a number of years Kansas City, Mo., was controlled by a vice ring and no interference with their enterprises was tolerated. Chicago, *despite its unenviable reputation,* is but one of numerous cities where the people have frequently been betrayed by their elected officials.[10]

Frank Tannenbaum once noted:

It is clear from the evidence at hand—that a considerable measure of the crime in the community is made possible and perhaps inevitable by the peculiar connection that exists between the political organizations of our large cities and the criminal activities of various gangs that are permitted and even encouraged to operate.[11]

Similarly, the Kefauver Commission summarized the results of its extensive investigation into organized crime in 1951:

(1) There is a nationwide crime syndicate known as the Mafia, whose tentacles are found in many large cities. It has international ramifications which appear most clearly in connection with the narcotics traffic.

(2) Its leaders are usually found in control of the most lucrative rackets in their cities.

(3) There are indications of centralized direction and control of these rackets, but leadership appears to be in a group rather than in a single individual.[12]

And in 1969, Donald R. Cressey, using data gathered from the attorney

10. Garrett & Monroe, "Police Conditions in the United States," 14 *National Commission on Law Observance and Enforcement Report on Police* 45 (1931).

11. F. Tannenbaum, *Crime and the Community* 128 (1938).

12. President's Commission on Law Enforcement and Administration of Justice, *The Challenge of Crime in a Free Society* 7 (1967).

general of the United States and local Crime Commission, capsulized the state of organized crime in the U.S.:

In the United States, criminals have managed to put together an organization which is at once a nationwide illicit cartel and a nationwide confederation. This organization is dedicated to amassing millions of dollars by means of extortion, and from usury, the illicit sale of lottery tickets, chances on the outcome of horse races and athletic events, narcotics and untaxed liquor.[13]

The frequency of major scandals linking organized criminals with leading political and legal figures suggests the same general conclusion. Detroit, Chicago, Denver, Reading, Pennsylvania, Columbus and Cleveland, Ohio, Miami, New York, Boston, and a hoard of other cities have been scandalized and cleansed innumerable times.[14] Yet organized crime persists and, in fact, thrives. Despite periodic forays, exposures, and reform movements prompted by journalists, sociologists, and politicians, organized crime has become an institution in the United States and in many other parts of the world as well.[15]

Once established, the effect of a syndicate on the entire legal and political system is profound. Maintenance of order in such an organization requires the use of extra-legal procedures since, obviously, the law cannot always be relied on to serve the interests of the crime cabal. The law can harass uncooperative people; it can even be used to send persons to prison on real or faked charges. But to make discipline and obedience certain, it is often necessary to enforce the rules of the syndicate in extra-legal ways. To avoid detection of these procedures, the police, prosecuting attorney's office, and judiciary must be organized in ways that make them incapable of discovering events that the cabal does not want disclosed. In actual practice, policemen, prosecutors, and judges who are *not* members of the cabal must not be in a position to investigate those things that the syndicate does not want investigated. The military chain of command of the police is, of course, well-suited to such a purpose. So, in fact, is the availability of such subtle but nonetheless important sanctions as relegating uncooperative policemen to undesirable positions in the department. Conversely, cooperative policemen are rewarded with promotions, prestigious positions on the force, and of course a piece of the action.

Another consequence is widespread acceptance of petty graft. The matchbox fee for accident officers is but one illustration. Free meals and cigarettes, bottles of whiskey at Christmas, and the like are practically universal in the police department. Television sets, cases of expensive whiskey, and on

13. D. Cressey, *supra* note 2. For a discussion of similar phenomena in Great Britain see N. Lucas, *Britain's Gangland* (1969). See also D. Bell, *End of Ideology* (1960).

14. Wilson, "The Police and their Problems: A Theory," 12 *Pub. Policy* 189 (1963).

15. See McMullen, "A Theory of Corruption," 9 *Soc. Rev.* 181 (1961).

occasion new automobiles or inside information on investments are common-place in the prosecuting attorney's office.

Significantly, the symbiotic relationship between organized crime and the legal system not only negates the law enforcement function of the law vis-à-vis these types of crimes but actually increases crime in a number of ways. Perhaps most important, gradual commitment to maintaining the secrecy of the relationship in turn necessitates the commission of crimes other than those involved in the vices per se. At times, it becomes necessary to intimidate through physical punishment and even to murder recalcitrant members of the syndicate. Calculating the extent of such activities is risky business. From 1955 to 1969 in Rainfall West, a conservative estimate of the number of persons killed by the syndicate is fifteen. However, estimates range as high as "hundreds." Although such information is impossible to verify in a manner that creates confidence, it is virtually certain that some murders have been perpetrated by the syndicate in order to protect the secrecy of their operations. It is also certain that the local law enforcement officials, politicians and businessmen involved with the syndicate have cooperated in these murders.

The location of the vices in the ghettos and slums of the city may well contribute to a host of other types of criminality as well. The disdain which ghetto residents have for the law and law enforcers is likely derived from more than simply their own experiences with injustice and police harassment. Their day-to-day observations that criminal syndicates operate openly and freely in their areas with complete immunity from punishment, while persons standing on a corner or playing cards in an apartment are subject to arrest, can not help but affect their perception of the legal system. We do not know that such observations undermine respect for and willingness to comply with the law, but that conclusion would not seem unreasonable.

It is no accident that whenever the presence of vice and organizations that provide the vices is exposed to public view by politicians, exposure is always couched in terms of organized crime. The question of corruption is conveniently left in the shadows. Similarly, it is no accident that organized crime is inevitably seen as consisting of an organization of criminals with names like Valachi, Genovesse and Joe Bonana. Yet the data from the study of Rainfall West, as well as that of earlier studies of vice, makes it abundantly clear that this analysis is fundamentally misleading.

I have argued, and I think the data demonstrate quite convincingly, that the people who run the organizations which supply the vices in American cities are members of the business, political, and law enforcement communities—not simply members of a criminal society. Furthermore, it is also clear from this study that corruption of political-legal organizations is a critical part of the life-blood of the crime cabal. The study of organized crime is thus a misnomer; the study should consider corruption, bureaucracy, and power. By relying on governmental agencies for their information on vice and the rackets, social scientists and lawyers have inadvertently contributed to the miscasting of the issue in terms that are descriptively biased and theoretically sterile. Further, they have been diverted from sociologically interesting and important issues raised by the persistence of crime cabals. As a consequence, the real significance of the existence of syndicates has been overlooked; for instead of seeing these social entities as intimately tied to, and in symbiosis with, the legal and political bureaucracies of the state, they have emphasized the criminality of only a portion of those involved. Such a view contributes little to our knowledge of crime and even less to attempts at crime control.

VIII

Explanations and proposed solutions to the problems of official deviance

For those of us who have followed the reporting in the mass media, as well as the private conversations of our fellow citizens, about Watergate, the recent "sex and payroll" scandals, and other instances of official deviance, it is clear that many Americans consider these deeds to be primarily or solely explainable in terms of individual morality. It is commonly said that Nixon and all the President's men did the things they did because they were "evil" individuals or were in some way personally deficient. Social scientists and the more analytical journalists have almost always found this sort of explanation useless, or at best, useful for understanding only isolated and relatively few instances of official deviance. This is because there are general social patterns of official deviance and of public concern over it. Some of these patterns are seen at all times in the Western world, and others are related to specific circumstances. Many of these patterns are discussed in the concluding chapters of this volume.

For social scientists and other scholars who have studied the processes of governing, there is widespread agreement about the universality of favors, bribes, particularistic and personal uses of rules, appointments, influence, and power. Some say this is inevitably and necessarily so. Walter Lippmann (Chapter 28) discusses these practices and some of the reasons for their universality. Scholars also agree that the emergence of machine politics and bossism in the nineteenth and early twentieth centuries was in some ways related to the demands of citizens on governing officials, which either could not be, or were not, met by more legitimate forms of official action. Furthermore, many social scientists feel that bossism, the spoils system, and other features of machine politics possessed some positive functions; that is, such practices helped and benefited many individuals. It is argued, for example, that the old machine politics provided many short-term services, gains, and benefits; that it helped to integrate the diverse groups within a pluralistic society; that it offered a better alternative to earlier patterns of political violence in the settlement of disputes; that it undercut the intense hatreds and resentments which typically fuel class antagonisms; and that it provided opportunities for upward social mobility for groups which were otherwise restrained by prevailing social institutions and conventions. Robert Merton (Chapter 29) and James Scott (Chapter 30) discuss these issues.

For those of us who seek a better and more realistic understanding of official deviance, in order to take remedial action against some of the threats we face today, it is important to have an historical and analytical background in these diverse phenomena. It is important because it helps us to move beyond moralistic perspectives, whether our own, or others that we are exposed to. The authors of several of the earlier chapters in this volume have discussed the limitations of a moralistic perspective when it is applied to the phenomenon of official deviance (See Chapters 1, 8, 11, 15, 21, 26, and 27). But, bearing this in mind, it is also important to realize how fundamentally different and more dangerous is our present, compared to our past. The recent revelations of official deviance, especially of the usurpations and misuses of power at all levels of government, are not mere extensions of the past, or recurrences of older forms of corruption. The solutions used in the past, and especially those that seemed to work (however temporarily), are not likely to work as well, if at all, to resolve our present problems. Several early chapters mentioned instances of corrupt practices which were at least temporarily resolved by "voting the rascals out of office." For example, in chapter 3, Walter Goodman noted that the conflict of interest corruptions of 1853-64 were temporarily resolved this way; and James Dickenson (Chapter 4) described how this was done in the cases of the Teapot Dome and Crédit Mobilier scandals. Chapter 5 included several examples of how the vote was used in this manner against elected federal officials. In Chapter 6, John Gardiner and David Olson told how the citizens of Wincanton put a temporary stop to some of the more blatant corruption in their community at the ballot box. In Chapter 8, Jack Douglas described how Boss Tweed was voted out of power, adding that this did not change the practical or political situation, which Tweed used for his own ends.

Since relatively few of our modern problems with official deviance stem from deficient, defective, or immoral individuals, there is little hope that they can be resolved at the ballot box, by replacing a Yahoo Democrat with a Yahoo Republican. One reason why the ballot box will be relatively ineffective in resolving problems of official deviance is that the new Welfare State Machine is fundamentally different from the bossism and spoils system of old machine politics. The Welfare State Machine (see Chapters 8 and 9) has effectively used decentralized authority and civil service regulations to put many of our political institutions beyond the control of the voters, and, in some cases, beyond the control of the elected representatives as well. This means that the massive and pervasive law enforcement deviance, the extensive corruption of federal legislators, and the great influence of business and labor union interests on state-level officialdom is unlikely to be resolved at the ballot box. Changes of a more fundamental nature are required. John Gardiner (Chapter 31), Robert Winter-Berger (Chapter 32), and James Q. Wilson (Chapter 33) discuss some of these contemporary problems and make some modest proposals for bringing about change.

However corrupt earlier machine politicians were, with their bossism, spoils, special favors, kickbacks, rake-offs, graft, booty, rigged appointments, and so on, it must be said on their behalf that such practices were usually subjected to and controlled by the existing standards of the communities in which they flourished. But there is little hope that our problems will be similarly controlled if only because today there are few shared conventions to act as restraints. This means that we will have to chart creative alternatives to resolve our problems, in order to protect and extend our freedoms. Jack Douglas (Chapter 34), Amitai Etzioni (Chapter 35), and Henry Steele Commager (Chapter 36) discuss these issues and their implications in the concluding chapters of this book.

A theory
about corruption

Walter Lippmann

It would be impossible for an historian to write a history of
political corruption in America. What he could write is the history of the exposure of corruption. Such a history would show, I
think, that almost every American community governs itself by
fits and starts of unsuspecting complacency and violent suspicion.
There will be long periods when practically nobody except the
professional reformers can be induced to pay attention to the
business of government; then rather suddenly there will come a
period when every act of the administration in power is suspect,
when every agency of investigation is prodded into activity, and
the civic conscience begins to boil.

It is a nice question whether a period of exposure signifies
that politics has recently become unusually scandalous or that an

SOURCE: Walter Lippman, "A Theory about Corruption," *Vanity Fair,*
35:3 (November 1930), pp. 61, 90. By permission of the author and publisher. Reprinted from *Vanity Fair* (now *Vogue* incorporating *Vanity Fair*):
copyright 1930, © 1958 by The Condé Nast Publications, Inc.

unusually efficient prosecutor has appeared on the scene. The current revelations about the Walker-Tammany régime in New York City, for example, relate to events that took place two, three, and four years ago. That they have come at this particular time is due largely to the ingenuity of United States Attorney Tuttle who within the last few months had discovered that a comparison of federal income tax returns with transcripts of bank accounts may provide useful clues to the hidden transactions of politicians. Mr. Tuttle's success in cracking the polished surface of the Walker Administration was due to the invention of a new political weapon. He may not be the original inventor, but he has certainly developed the invention remarkably. As a result, he is the first man in a long time who has penetrated the defenses of Tammany.

The contest against political corruption in America is very much like the competition among designers of naval armaments. At one time the reformers have a gun which can pierce any armor plate; then a defense against that gun is developed. I do not think it is a too cynical view of the facts to say that the traffic in privileges, which is what corruption is, has never long lacked men smart enough to find ways of defeating the ingenuity of the reformers. I do not mean to say that American cities are not better governed today than when Bryce said nearly forty years ago that they were the one conspicuous failure of the United States. They are much better governed. They are governed by men who often take a considerable pride in doing a good job. That is true today in New York City under Tammany.

Nevertheless, the fact remains, I think, that the ultimate power over appointments, nominations and policies is in the hands of professional politicians who in one way or another make the public business more profitable to themselves than any private business in which with their abilities and opportunities, they might engage. I have heard, here and there, of a district leader or even of a boss who remains a poor man, and I am not forgetting men like the late Chief Magistrate McAdoo who, after a lifetime in politics, died in poverty. I am not forgetting rather high officials in Tammany about whose integrity there cannot be the slightest doubt. Yet it cannot be denied, I think, that the mainspring which moves the whole complex human organization behind the public government of New York is private advantage.

It certainly is not undiluted patriotism. District leaders are not primarily interested in the administration of justice when they insist on naming magistrates. They insist on naming magistrates, in some and perhaps in many cases, because the candidate pays for the appointment; in all cases they insist because they wish to control the favors that a magistrate can dispense. The power of the district leader over the voters depends upon his ability to dispense favors. He is recognized as a political leader, not because of his views on public questions, but because he is able concretely to demonstrate day after day that his word is law. Because he controls government, he controls votes and because he controls votes he controls government: because he has power he is cultivated by those who have favors to give, and leaving out all items of bribery, he occupies a place where he has, so to speak, a multitude of business opportunities. If he is a lawyer, he has law cases which require his political influence rather than his legal ability. He is remembered by real estate syndicates and by corporations that are affected by government. In short he capitalizes, most often nowadays, I think, in accordance with the strict letter of the law, the political power he possesses.

The prosecuting agencies, when spasmodically they set to work, can deal only with the crudely overt features of political corruption. Anyone who has observed closely a prosecutor's office on the trail of a political ring knows how enormous is the gap between scandalous political conduct and specifically indictable offenses; in my time I have seen case after case of politicians who could not be indicted, or, if indicted, convicted, though they were guilty as Satan, because the development of conclusive legal proof was lacking. The truth of the matter, I think, is that an entirely objective view of political life at its base where political organization is in direct contact with the population, would show that corruption in some form is endemic. I do not mean that everybody is bribed. I do mean that the exchange of favors is the elemental and essential motive power which operates the semi-private machinery inside the political parties which in their turn operate the official machinery of government. It is, I think, literally true that if the exchange of favors were suddenly and miraculously abolished, there would be a wholesale voluntary retirement of petty politicians to private life, for they would lack then the incentive to stay in politics and the very means by which they maintain their political influence. The best proof of this is that the reformers who operate only with ideals and indignation never really make a party which lasts; they soon discover, when they deign to get down to the base of politics, that the motives they appeal to are unsubstantial.

If it is true that the exchange of favors is an essential element of politics, then the common American assumption about political corruption is naïve and misleading. The assumption, inculcated through patriotic text books, is that in the year 1789 a body of wise men founded a new government in a new world, and that corruption is a lapse from this contract to which all their decedants automatically subscribe. Almost all of us feel, I think, that Tammany, for example, is a kind of disease which has affected the body politic. There it is, to be sure; it has been there a long time, and the counterpart of it is to be found in virtually every American community. Nevertheless, we feel that it is not supposed to be there, and that if only we had a little more courage or sense or something we could cut away the diseased tissue and live happily ever after. The implications of this notion seem to me to be false, and I believe that our political thinking would be immensely more effective if we adopted an entirely opposite theory.

That theory would hold that organizations like Tammany, which bind together masses of people in a complex of favors and coercions, are the

ancient form of human association. They might be called natural governments. Our modern, artificial constitutions were superimposed upon them
partly by coalitions of the stronger factions and partly by compromises of
interest. The natural governments are not abolished when this happens. They
continue to a decisive degree to operate through the artificial government.
When the conflicts between these natural associations become too momentous
the constitutional government breaks down in civil war or it is swept aside, as
it has been in all of Eastern Europe, by a dictatorship of one of these associations. In many countries it is only too plain that the constitutional system is a
mere façade behind which the real exercise of power depends upon the barter
of privileges and the use of violence.

My point is that Tammany is not a disease, but simply the old body
politic in its more or less natural state, and that the American ideal of government as a public trust to be carried on by disinterested men represents not
the actuality but a long step ahead in the evolution of man. The very conception of a public trust has not yet been heard of by the mass of mankind. It
has been a recognized public ideal in Europe even among the most advanced
thinkers for not much more than a few hundred years. It is a very difficult
ideal to attain, and I know of no public man even in America and even in
our time who has felt able to be completely loyal to it. The best test is the
appointment of judges, for surely if there is a public trust more imperative
than any other it is the task of the President or the Governor to insure the
highest possible quality in the courts. Does anybody know a President who
has been guided solely by merit in his selection of judges? I doubt it. The best
of Presidents is as virtuous as he dares to be, but at some point or other he
must for political reasons knowingly violate his conscience.

The difficulties increase as one descends in the political scale. Presidents,
governors, perhaps even mayors, move in a realm where ideal motives may be
effective, for their acts are subject to the verdict of the more sensitive
minority and to the judgment of history. They are likely, moreover, to be
exceptional men who have passed beyond the struggle for existence, to be
educated men, and to appreciate the immaterial glories of the state. But down
among district leaders, and second deputy commissioners, and clerks of
courts, the larger rewards, the larger issues, the intrinsic obligations of power,
simply do not exist. These office holders are recruited from men who have to
struggle to exist, who must hold on grimly to what they can get, who never
have any feeling that they are public men making the history of their time.
Men of genius have risen now and then from such political beginnings, but for
the few who rise there is a multitude who know they never will. What can
public office give to them except a job at a meagre salary, an opportunity to
prosper a little on the side, a sense of importance in their neighborhood, and
the excitement of working for the winning team? At the base of the political
structure there are no adequate motives to give meaning to the conception of
public office as a public trust. It is not surprising that this relatively new and

high conception, which has so little ground in the instinctive life of man, should take hold slowly.

As a matter of historical fact we are justified in going a step farther to say not only that what we call political corruption is the ancient and natural political process, but that corruption in the form of jobbery represents a decisive step upward in political life. I think it could be shown from the history of the Mother of Parliaments itself and demonstrated today in certain politically backward countries that corruption is the practical substitute for factional wars. In the Eighteenth Century the civil wars in England came to an end and the habit of political violence dissolved finally in the organization of a thoroughly corrupt but peaceable parliament. There are places in the world today where corruption is progress. I once heard the President of a Latin-American Republic explain that he was consolidating his régime at home by making ambassadors, with extra large grants for expenses, out of his most dangerous political enemies. It had been the custom to shoot them.

I fear that my theory of corruption will seem fantastic to many and a justification for a lazy tolerance to others. It seems to me the serious truth, and conceivably a useful truth. For if it is true that corruption is not a disease, but on the contrary a natural condition which civilized modern man is seeking to surmount, the knowledge that this is so might very well provide us with a clearer idea of what our periodic scandal-chasing is all about, a better appreciation of the realities with which we are dealing, and even a stronger resolve to keep slogging at it. For we should then know that the campaign against corruption on behalf of the ideal of trust is no mere re-pairing of something perfect that has broken down, but the implanting of a new habit of acting in the ancient consciousness of man.

20

Some functions of the political machine

Robert K. Merton

Without presuming to enter into the variations of detail marking different political machines—a Tweed, Vare, Crump, Flynn, Hague are by no means identical types of bosses—we can briefly examine the functions more or less common to the political machine, as a generic type of social organization. We neither attempt to itemize all the diverse functions of the political machine nor imply that all these functions are similarly fulfilled by each and every machine.

The key structural function of the Boss is to organize, centralize and maintain in good working condition "the scattered fragments of power" which are at present dispersed through our political organization. By this centralized organization of political power, the boss and his apparatus can satisfy the need of diverse subgroups in the larger community which are not adequately satisfied by legally devised and culturally approved social structures.

From Robert K. Merton, *Social Theory and Social Structure.* New York: Free Press, 1957 (Second Edition), pp. 72-82. Reprinted by permission.

To understand the role of bossism and the machine, therefore, we must look at two types of sociological variables: (1) the *structural context* which makes it difficult, if not impossible, for morally approved structures to fulfill essential social functions, thus leaving the door open for political machines (or their structural equivalents) to fulfill these functions and (2) the subgroups whose distinctive needs are left unsatisfied, except for the latent functions which the machine in fact fulfills.[92]

Structural Context

The constitutional framework of American political organization specifically precludes the legal possibility of highly centralized power and, it has been noted, thus "discourages the growth of effective and responsible leadership. The framers of the Constitution, as Woodrow Wilson observed, set up the check and balance system 'to keep government at a sort of mechanical equipoise by means of a standing amicable contest among its several organic parts.' They distrusted power as dangerous to liberty: and therefore they spread it thin and erected barriers against its concentration." This dispersion of power is found not only at the national level but in local areas as well. "As a consequence," Sait goes on to observe, "when *the people or particular groups* among them demanded positive action, no one had adequate authority to act. The machine provided an antidote."[93]

The constitutional dispersion of power not only makes for difficulty of effective decision and action but when action does occur it is defined and hemmed in by legalistic considerations. In consequence, there developed "a much *more human system* of partisan government, whose chief object soon became the circumvention of government by law. . . . The lawlessness of the extra-official democracy was merely the counterpoise of the legalism of the official democracy. The lawyer having been permitted to subordinate democracy to the Law, the Boss had to be called in to extricate the victim, which he did after a fashion and for a consideration."[94]

Officially, political power is dispersed. Various well-known expedients were devised for this manifest objective. Not only was there the familiar separation of powers among the several branches of the government but, in some measure, tenure in each office was limited, rotation in office approved. And the scope of power inherent in each office was severely circumscribed.

92. Again, as with preceding cases, we shall not consider the possible dysfunctions of the political machine.

93. Edward M. Sait, "Machine, Political," *Encyclopedia of the Social Sciences*, IX, 658 b [italics supplied] ; *cf.* A. F. Bentley, *The Process of Government* (Chicago, 1908), Chap. 2.

94. Herbert Croly, *Progressive Democracy*, (New York, 1914), p. 254, cited by Sait, *op. cit.*, 658 b.

Yet, observes Sait in rigorously functional terms, "Leadership is necessary; and *since* it does not develop readily within the constitutional framework, the Boss provides it in a crude and irresponsible form from the outside."[95]

Put in more generalized terms, *the functional deficiencies of the official structure generate an alternative (unofficial) structure to fulfill existing needs somewhat more effectively.* Whatever its specific historical origins, the political machine persists as an apparatus for satisfying otherwise unfulfilled needs of diverse groups in the population. By turning to a few of these subgroups and their characteristic needs, we shall be led at once to a range of latent functions of the political machine.

Functions of the Political Machine for Diverse Subgroups

It is well known that one source of strength of the political machine derives from its roots in the local community and the neighborhood. The political machine does not regard the electorate as an amorphous, undifferentiated mass of voters. With a keen sociological intuition, the machine recognizes that the voter is a person living in a specific neighborhood, with specific personal problems and personal wants. Public issues are abstract and remote; private problems are extremely concrete and immediate. It is not through the generalized appeal to large public concerns that the machine operates, but through the direct, quasi-feudal relationships between local representatives of the machine and voters in their neighborhood. Elections are won in the precinct.

The machine welds its link with ordinary men and women by elaborate networks of personal relations. Politics is transformed into personal ties. The precinct captain "must be a friend to every man, assuming if he does not feel sympathy with the unfortunate, and utilizing in his good works the resources which the boss puts at his disposal."[96] The precinct captain is forever a friend in need. In our prevailingly impersonal society, the machine, through its local agents, fulfills the important social *function of humanizing and personalizing all manner of assistance* to those in need. Foodbaskets and jobs, legal and extra-legal advice, setting to rights minor scrapes with the law, helping the bright poor boy to a political scholarship in a local college, looking after the bereaved—the whole range of crises when a feller needs a friend, and, above all, a friend who knows the score and who can do something about it,—all these find the ever-helpful precinct captain available in the pinch.

To assess this function of the political machine adequately, it is important to note not only that aid *is* provided but *the manner in which it is provided.*

95. Sait, *op. cit.*, 659 a. [italics supplied].
96. *Ibid.*, 659 a.

After all, other agencies do exist for dispensing such assistance. Welfare agencies, settlement houses, legal aid clinics, medical aid in free hospitals, public relief departments, immigration authorities—these and a multitude of other organizations are available to provide the most varied types of assistance. But in contrast to the professional techniques of the welfare worker which may typically represent in the mind of the recipient the cold, bureaucratic dispensation of limited aid following upon detailed investigation of *legal* claims to aid of the "client" are the unprofessional techniques of the precinct captain who asks no questions, exacts no compliance with legal rules of eligibility and does not "snoop" into private affairs.[97]

For many, the loss of "self-respect" is too high a price for legalized assistance. In contrast to the gulf between the settlement house workers who so often come from a different social class, educational background and ethnic group, the precinct worker is "just one of us," who understands what it's all about. The condescending lady bountiful can hardly compete with the understanding friend in need. In *this struggle between alternative structures for fulfilling the nominally same function* of providing aid and support to those who need it, it is clearly the machine politician who is better integrated with the groups which he serves than the impersonal, professionalized, socially distant and legally constrained welfare worker. And since the politician can at times influence and manipulate the official organizations for the dispensation of assistance, whereas the welfare worker has practically no influence on the political machine, this only adds to his greater effectiveness. More colloquially and also, perhaps, more incisively, it was the Boston wardleader, Martin Lomasny, who described this essential function to the curious Lincoln Steffens: "I think," said Lomasny, "that there's got to be in every ward somebody that any bloke can come to—no matter what he's done—and get help. *Help, you understand; none of your law and justice, but help.*"[98]

The "deprived classes," then, constitute one subgroup for whom the political machine satisfies wants not adequately satisfied in the same fashion by the legitimate social structure.

For a second subgroup, that of business (primarily "big" business but also "small"), the political boss serves the function of providing those political

97. Much the same contrast with official welfare policy is found in Harry Hopkins' open-handed and non-political distribution of unemployment relief in New York State under the governorship of Franklin Delano Roosevelt. As Sherwood reports: "Hopkins was harshly criticized for these irregular activities by the established welfare agencies, which claimed it was 'unprofessional conduct' to hand out work tickets without thorough investigation of each applicant, his own or his family's financial resources and probably his religious affiliations. 'Harry told the agency to go to hell,' said [Hopkins' associate, Dr. Jacob A.] Goldberg." Robert E. Sherwood, *Roosevelt and Hopkins, An Intimate History,* (New York: Harper, 1948), 30.

98. *The Autobiography of Lincoln Steffens,* (Chautauqua, New York: Chautauqua Press, 1931), 618. Deriving largely from Steffens, as he says, F. Stuart Chapin sets forth these functions of the political machine with great clarity. See his *Contemporary American Institutions,* (New York: Harper, 1934), 40–54.

privileges which entail immediate economic gains. Business corporations, among which the public utilities (railroads, local transportation and electric light companies, communications corporations) are simply the most conspicuous in this regard, seek special political dispensations which will enable them to stabilize their situation and to near their objective of maximizing profits. Interestingly enough, corporations often want to avoid a chaos of uncontrolled competition. They want the greater security of an economic czar who controls, regulates and organizes competition, providing that this czar is not a public official with his decisions subject to public scrutiny and public control. (The latter would be "government control," and hence taboo). The political boss fulfills these requirements admirably.

Examined for a moment apart from any moral considerations, the political apparatus operated by the Boss is effectively designed to perform these functions with a minimum of inefficiency. Holding the strings of diverse governmental divisions, bureaus and agencies in his competent hands, the Boss rationalizes the relations between public and private business. He serves as the business community's ambassador in the otherwise alien (and sometimes unfriendly) realm of government. And, in strict business-like terms, he is well-paid for his economic services to his respectable business clients. In an article entitled, "An Apology to Graft," Lincoln Steffens suggested that "Our economic system, which held up riches, power and acclaim as prizes to men bold enough and able enough to buy corruptly timber, mines, oil fields and franchises and 'get away with it,' was at fault."[99] And, in a conference with a hundred or so of Los Angeles business leaders, he described a fact well known to all of them: the Boss and his machine were an *integral part* of the organization of the economy. "You cannot build or operate a railroad, or a street railway, gas, water, or power company, develop and operate a mine, or get forests and cut timber on a large scale, or run any privileged business, without corrupting or joining in the corruption of the government. You tell me privately that you must, and here I am telling you semi-publicly that you must. And that is so all over the country. And that means that we have an organization of society in which, *for some reason,* you and your kind, the ablest, most intelligent, most imaginative, daring, and resourceful leaders of society, are and must be against society and its laws and its all-around growth."[100]

Since the demand for the services of special privileges are built into the structure of the society, the Boss fulfills diverse functions for this second subgroup of business-seeking-privilege. These "needs" of business, as presently constituted, are not adequately provided for by conventional and culturally approved social structures; consequently, the extra-legal but more-or-

99. *Autobiography of Lincoln Steffens,* 570.

100. *Ibid.,* 572–3 [italics supplied]. This helps explain, as Steffens noted after Police Commissioner Theodore Roosevelt, "the prominence and respectability of the men and women who intercede for crooks" when these have been apprehended in a periodic effort to "clean up the political machine." *Cf.* Steffens, 371, and *passim.*

less efficient organization of the political machine comes to provide these services. To adopt an *exclusively* moral attitude toward the "corrupt political machine" is to lose sight of the very structural conditions which generate the "evil" that is so bitterly attacked. To adopt a functional outlook is to provide not an apologia for the political machine but a more solid basis for modifying or eliminating the machine, *providing* specific structural arrangements are introduced either for eliminating these effective demands of the business community or, if that is the objective, of satisfying these demands through alternative means.

A third set of distinctive functions fulfilled by the political machine for a special subgroup is that of providing alternative channels of social mobility for those otherwise excluded from the more conventional avenues for personal "advancement." Both the sources of this special "need" (for social mobility) and the respect in which the political machine comes to help satisfy this need can be understood by examining the structure of the larger culture and society. As is well known, the American culture lays enormous emphasis on money and power as a "success" goal legitimate for all members of the society. By no means alone in our inventory of cultural goals, it still remains among the most heavily endowed with positive affect and value. However, certain subgroups and certain ecological areas are notable for the relative absence of opportunity for achieving these (monetary and power) types of success. They constitute, in short, sub-populations where "the cultural emphasis upon pecuniary success has been absorbed, but where there is *little access to conventional and legitimate* means for attaining such success. The conventional occupational opportunities of persons in (such areas) are almost completely limited to manual labor. Given our cultural stigmatization of manual labor,[101] and its correlate, the prestige of white-collar work, it is clear that the result is a tendency to achieve these culturally approved objectives *through whatever means are possible.* These people are on the one hand, "asked to orient their conduct toward the prospect of accumulating wealth

101. See the National Opinion Research Center survey of evaluation of occupations which, firmly documents the general impression that the manual occupations rate very low indeed in the social scale of values, *even among those who are themselves engaged in manual labor.* Consider this latter point in its full implications. In effect, the cultural and social structure exacts the values of pecuniary and power success even among those who find themselves confined to the stigmatized manual occupations. Against this background, consider the powerful motivation for achieving this type of "success" by any means whatsoever. A garbage-collector who joins with other Americans in the view that the garbage-collector is "the lowest of the low" occupations can scarcely have a self-image which is pleasing to him; he is in a "pariah" occupation in the very society where is he assured that "all who have genuine merit can get ahead." Add to this, his occasional recognition that "he didn't have the same chance as others, no matter what they say," and one perceives the enormous psychological pressure upon him for "evening up the score" by finding some means, whether strictly legal or not, for moving ahead. All this provides the structural and derivatively psychological background for the "socially induced need" in some groups to find *some* accessible avenue for social mobility.

[and power] and, on the other, they are largely denied effective opportunities to do so institutionally."

It is within this context of social structure that the political machine fulfills the basic function of providing avenues of social mobility for the otherwise disadvantaged. Within this context, even the corrupt political machine and the racket "represent the triumph of amoral intelligence over morally prescribed 'failure' when the channels of vertical mobility are closed or narrowed *in a society which places a high premium on economic affluence, [power] and social ascent for all its members."*[102] As one sociologist has noted on the basis of several years of close observation in a slum area:

The sociologist who dismisses racket and political organizations as deviations from desirable standards thereby neglects some of the major elements of slum life. . . . *He does not discover the functions they perform for the members* [of the groupings in the slum]. The Irish and later immigrant peoples have had the greatest difficulty in finding places for themselves in our urban social and economic structure. Does anyone believe that the immigrants and their children could have achieved their present degree of social mobility without gaining control of the political organization of some of our largest cities? The same is true of the racket organization. *Politics and the rackets have furnished an important means of social mobility for individuals, who, because of ethnic background and low class position,* are blocked from advancement in the "respectable" channels.[103]

This, then, represents a third type of function performed for a distinctive subgroup. This function, it may be noted in passing, is fulfilled by the *sheer* existence and operation of the political machine, for it is in the machine itself that these individuals and subgroups find their culturally induced needs more or less satisfied. It refers to the services which the political apparatus provides

102. Merton, "Social structure and anomie," chapter IV of this volume.

103. William F. Whyte, "Social organization in the slums," *American Sociological Review*, Feb. 1943, 8, 34–39 (italics supplied). Thus, the political machine and the racket represent a special case of the type of organizational adjustment to the conditions described in chapter IV. It represents, note, an *organizational* adjustment: definite structures arise and operate to reduce somewhat the acute tensions and problems of individuals caught up in the described conflict between the "cultural accent on success-for-all" and the "socially structured fact of unequal opportunities for success." As chapter IV indicates, other types of *individual* "adjustment" are possible: lone-wolf crime, psychopathological states, rebellion, retreat by abandoning the culturally approved goals, etc. Likewise, other types of *organizational adjustment* sometimes occur; the racket or the political machine are not *alone* available as organized means for meeting this socially induced problem. Participation in revolutionary organizations, for example, can be seen within this context, as an alternative mode of organizational adjustment. All this bears theoretic notice here, since we might otherwise overlook the basic functional concepts of functional substitutes and functional equivalents, which are to be discussed at length in a subsequent publication.

for its own personnel. But seen in the wider social context we have set forth, it no longers appears as *merely* a means of self-aggrandizement for profit-hungry and power-hungry *individuals,* but as an organized provision for *sub-groups* otherwise excluded from or handicapped in the race for "getting ahead."

Just as the political machine performs services for "legitimate" business, so it operates to perform not dissimilar services for "illegitimate" business: vice, crime and rackets. Once again, the basic sociological role of the machine in this respect can be more fully appreciated only if one temporarily abandons attitudes of moral indignation, to examine in all moral innocence the actual workings of the organization. In this light, it at once appears that the subgroup of the professional criminal, racketeer or gambler has basic similarities of organization, demands and operation to the subgroup of the industrialist, man of business or speculator. If there is a Lumber King or an Oil King, there is also a Vice King or a Racket King. If expansive legitimate business organizes administrative and financial syndicates to "rationalize" and to "integrate" diverse areas of production and business enterprise, so expansive rackets and crime organize syndicates to bring order to the otherwise chaotic areas of production of illicit goods and services. If legitimate business regards the proliferation of small business enterprises as wasteful and inefficient, substituting, for example, the giant chain stores for hundreds of corner groceries, so illegitimate business adopts the same businesslike attitude and syndicates crime and vice.

Finally, and in many respects, most important, is the basic similarity, if not near-identity, of the economic role of "legitimate" business and of "illegitimate" business. *Both are in some degree concerned with the provision of goods and services for which there is an economic demand.* Morals aside, they are both business, industrial and professional enterprises, dispensing goods and services which some people want, for which there is a market in which goods and services are transformed into commodities. And, in a prevalently market society, we should expect appropriate enterprises to arise whenever there is a market demand for certain goods or services.

As is well known, vice, crime and the rackets *are* "big business." Consider only that there have been estimated to be about 500,000 professional prostitutes in the United States of 1950, and compare this with the approximately 200,000 physicians and 350,000 professional registered nurses. It is difficult to estimate which have the larger clientele: the professional men and women of medicine or the professional men and women of vice. It is, of course, difficult to estimate the economic assets, income, profits and dividends of illicit gambling in this country and to compare it with the economic assets, income, profits and dividends of, say, the shoe industry, but it is altogether possible that the two industries are about on a par. No precise figures exist on the annual expenditures on illicit narcotics, and it is probable that these are less than the expenditures on candy, but it is also probable that they are larger than the expenditure on books.

It takes but a moment's thought to recognize that, *in strictly economic terms,* there is no relevant difference between the provision of licit and of illicit goods and services. The liquor traffic illustrates this perfectly. It would be peculiar to argue that prior to 1920 (when the 18th amendment became effective), the provision of liquor constituted an economic service, that from 1920 to 1933, its production and sale no longer constituted an economic service dispensed in a market, and that from 1934 to the present, it once again took on a serviceable aspect. Or, it would be *economically* (not morally) absurd to suggest that the sale of bootlegged liquor in the dry state of Kansas is less a response to a market demand than the sale of publicly manufactured liquor in the neighboring wet state of Missouri. Examples of this sort can of course be multiplied many times over. Can it be held that in European countries, with registered and legalized prostitution, the prostitute contributes an economic service, whereas in this country, lacking legal sanction, the prostitute provides no such service? Or that the professional abortionist is in the economic market where he has approved legal status and that he is out of the economic market where he is legally taboo? Or that gambling satisfies a specific demand for entertainment in Nevada, where it constitutes the largest business enterprise of the larger cities in the state, but that it differs essentially in this respect from motion pictures in the neighboring state of California?[104]

The failure to recognize that these businesses are only *morally* and not *economically* distinguishable from "legitimate" businesses has led to badly scrambled analysis. Once the economic identity of the two is recognized, we may anticipate that if the political machine performs functions for "legitimate big business" it will be all the more likely to perform not dissimilar functions for "illegitimate big business." And, of course, such is often the case.

The distinctive function of the political machine for their criminal, vice and racket clientele is to enable them to operate in satisfying the economic demands of a large market without due interference from the government. Just as big business may contribute funds to the political party war-chest to ensure a minimum of governmental interference, so with big rackets and big crime. In both instances, the political machine can, in varying degrees, pro-

104. Perhaps the most perceptive statement of this view has been made by Hawkins and Waller. "The prostitute, the pimp, the peddler of dope, the operator of the gambling hall, the vendor of obscene pictures, the bootlegger, the abortionist, all are productive, all produce services or goods which people desire and for which they are willing to pay. It happens that society has put these goods and services under the ban, but people go on producing them and people go on consuming them, and an act of the legislature does not make them any less a part of the economic system." "Critical notes on the cost of crime," *Journal of Criminal Law and Criminology,* 1936, 26, 679–94, at 684.

vide "protection." In both instances, many features of the structural context are identical: (1) market demands for goods and services; (2) the operators' concern with maximizing gains from their enterprises; (3) the need for partial control of government which might otherwise interfere with these activities of businessmen; (4) the need for an efficient, powerful and centralized agency to provide an effective liaison of "business" with government.

Without assuming that the foregoing pages exhaust either the range of functions or the range of subgroups served by the political machine, we can at least see that *it presently fulfills some functions for these diverse subgroups which are not adequately fulfilled by culturally approved or more conventional structures.*

Several additional implications of the functional analysis of the political machine can be mentioned here only in passing, although they obviously require to be developed at length. First, the foregoing analysis has direct implications for *social engineering.* It helps explain why the periodic efforts at "political reform " "turning the rascals out" and "cleaning political house" are typically (though not necessarily) short-lived and ineffectual. It exemplifies a basic theorem: *any attempt to eliminate an existing social structure without providing adequate alternative structures for fulfilling the functions previously fulfilled by the abolished organization is doomed to failure.* (Needless to say, this theorem has much wider bearing than the one instance of the political machine.) When "political reform" confines itself to the manifest task of "turning the rascals out," it is engaging in little more than sociological magic. The reform may for a time bring new figures into the political limelight; it may serve the casual social function of re-assuring the electorate that the moral virtues remain intact and will ultimately triumph; it may actually effect a turnover in the personnel of the political machine; it may even, for a time, so curb the activities of the machine as to leave unsatisfied the many needs it has previously fulfilled. But, inevitably, unless the reform also involves a "re-forming" of the social and political structure such that the existing needs are satisfied by alternative structures or unless it involves a change which eliminates these needs altogether, the political machine will return to its integral place in the social scheme of things. *To seek social change, without due recognition of the manifest and latent functions performed by the social organization undergoing change, is to indulge in social ritual rather than social engineering.* The concepts of manifest and latent functions (or their equivalents) are indispensable elements in the theoretic repertoire of the social engineer. In this crucial sense, these concepts are not "merely" theoretical (in the abusive sense of the term), but are eminently practical. In the deliberate enactment of social change, they can be ignored only at the price of considerably heightening the risk of failure.

A second implication of this analysis of the political machine also has a bearing upon areas wider than the one we have considered. The paradox has often been noted that the supporters of the political machine include both the "respectable" business class elements who are, of course, opposed to the criminal or racketeer and the distinctly "unrespectable" elements of the underworld. And, at first appearance, this is cited as an instance of very strange bedfellows. The learned judge is not infrequently called upon to sentence the very racketeer beside whom he sat the night before at an informal dinner of the political bigwigs. The district attorney jostles the exonerated convict on his way to the back room where the Boss has called a meeting. The big business man may complain almost as bitterly as the big racketeer about the "extortionate" contributions to the party fund demanded by the Boss. Social opposites meet—in the smoke-filled room of the successful politician.

In the light of a functional analysis all this of course no longer seems paradoxical. Since the machine serves both the businessman and the criminal man, the two seemingly antipodal groups intersect. This points to a more general theorem: *the social functions of an organization help determine the structure (including the recruitment of personnel involved in the structure), just as the structure helps determine the effectiveness with which the functions are fulfilled.* In terms of social status, the business group and the criminal group are indeed poles apart. But status does not fully determine behavior and the inter-relations between groups. Functions modify these relations. Given their distinctive needs, the several subgroups in the large society are "integrated," whatever their personal desires or intentions, by the centralizing structure which serves these several needs. In a phrase with many implications which require further study, *structure affects function and function affects structure.*

30

The machine an oligarchic response to democratic pressures

James C. Scott

The growth of machine-style politics often represents a large-scale effort by elite groups to manage the problem of rapidly expanding political participation while at the same time retaining their control over state policy. No such effort was required in early Stuart England or twentieth-century Thailand, where participation was confined to a narrow stratum of the population. In this limited sense, machine politics signifies the democratization of certain forms of corruption; the number of participants has increased, the distribution of rewards must be more extensive, and a more elaborate organizational and financial base is required. Just as in the realm of political violence the shift from palace coups to internal war represents an escalation in participation, so in the realm of corruption the shift from aristocratic-elite-centered venality to machine politics represents an escalation in participation.

A Conservative Response to Change

Thriving in periods of rapid social change and expanding suffrage, machine-style politics nevertheless represents a conservative response to its dynamic environment.[1] Machine politics is conservative in at least these four respects: (1) it represents an alternative to violence in managing conflict; (2) it may well increase the legitimacy of a regime for "transitional" populations; (3) it emphasizes short-run particularistic gains at the expense of broad, long-run transformations; (4) it avoids class issues and fosters interclass collaboration.

It is crucial to specify here that although these effects may flow in part from corrupt practices, they are attributable to machine politics and not to corruption *per se*. The central fact about a political machine is that it aims at the "political consolidation of the beneficiaries" of the patronage and graft system for electoral ends (Key, 1936, p. 394). Whereas nonmachine corruption more often involves purely personal competition for spoils or aims only at the consolidation of narrow elites who control wealth or armed force, the machine must remain popular to survive and consequently must meet demands from a broader stratum of citizens. Not all corruption is machine politics and not all machine politics is corrupt.

Avoiding Violence

The social setting of the machine is ordinarily one where ties to the community as a whole are weak and where the potential for violence is great. The capacity of the machine to organize and provide material inducements (often corruptly) operates as a means of solving, for the time being at least, conflicts of interest that might otherwise generate violence. In order to remain popular and thereby win elections, the machine must continually make a place for new, ambitious leaders who could potentially threaten its control. By coopting new leaders, the machine is responsive to particularistic new demands while simultaneously safeguarding its own future.

Much of the corruption for which big-city machines in the United States were noted represented an informal integration of demands which the formal political system all but excluded from consideration. In return for their support of the machine boss, the newly arrived European immigrants received patronage employment, special attention in court, and loans and welfare payments which were often outside the bounds of strict legality. For most immigrants, the machine's connections, knowledge of the ropes, and *promise* of help in time of need was as effective as the delivery of concrete rewards. Thus groups which might otherwise have become susceptible to more radical,

---

1. The use of the term "conservative" here is not entirely satisfactory in covering the effects described. In any event, each of the separate effects may be considered individually.

not to say revolutionary, doctrines were effectively domesticated and given a stake in the system. Much the same might be said of electoral regimes in many new nations: the villagers who have recently arrived in the cities, the businessmen and shopkeepers from insecure minority groups, have all been attached, in greater or lesser degree, to the informal political system which attempts to meet their needs and demands. Corruption acts on such groups essentially as a conservative force which, by granting many of them concrete rewards, weds them more firmly to the political system and dilutes the impulse toward more radical solutions.

In some settings, then, it may be appropriate to view machine corruption as a sort of half-way house between violence and constitutionality—a means by which some of the demands generated by a vast increase in political participation are nonviolently accommodated within a political system whose formal institutions are as yet inadequate to the task. By increasing the government's *de facto* capacity to meet certain demands and by reducing the likelihood of political violence, the corruption that accompanies machine politics may contribute to the stability both of a particular regime and of the electoral system itself.

The tangible rewards of the machine can also, for a time at least, retard the development of vehement demands for large-scale reforms transcending particularistic interests. A striking example of this is the 1946 presidential election in the Philippines where machine inducements were used to temporarily defuse an economic system highly charged with a potential for violence. Faced with a "rising tide of peasant labor discontent," the main sugar, banking, and commercial interests contributed enormous funds to the Liberals, whose electoral campaign virtually smothered the revolutionary fires with cash (Baterina, 1955, p. 82).

The Philippine case illustrates the *limits* of machine conciliation as well. While developing a great capacity for coopting new leaders and distributing particularistic incentives, parties in the Philippines have been unable either to carry out reforms of the agrarian structure or to meet emerging class or broad policy demands. Consequently the party system lurches from election to election with each side patching together a temporary winning coalition on the basis of patronage, bribes, and pork-barrel. The pattern of net government operating receipts for the past decade shows consistent and increasingly severe deficits in the months before an election as the ruling party deploys all the financial resources it can muster to win reelection (Averich *et al.,* 1970, p. 161). In the meantime agrarian unrest among plantation laborers and tenant farmers has grown ever more explosive in the absence of fundamental reforms. The result may very well be that the Philippine party system has only bought temporary peace—a peace which requires ever larger amounts of cash, patronage, and virtuoso brokerage performances to maintain—while failing to tackle major social problems that will soon threaten the entire system. In the final analysis there are political issues that cannot be disposed of by machine-style bargaining and short-term payoffs—issues that require basic policy choices which the machine is ill-suited to make. Machine-style coordination may thus avoid short-run violence at the cost of maintaining basic structures that increase the long-run potential for revolutionary violence.

Depending as they do on particularistic, material incentives, the Nationalists and the Liberals—like machine parties everywhere—are only as effective as their inducements. For portions of the modern sector where broader class loyalties and civic sentiments have begun to take root, or for the traditional sector where deference and symbolic goals are common, machine blandishments are likely to fall on barren soil. Machines therefore can manage conflict best among "transitional" populations and may be unable to alleviate strife—or may actually exacerbate it—in other social contexts.

Creating Legitimacy

Urban American machines have long been credited with wedding the immigrant to the political system by protecting him, meeting his immediate needs, and offering *personal* (particularistic) service. To the immigrant the machine was legitimate in part because it accorded with his desire for a personal patron, usually from his own ethnic group, who stood ready to assist the humblest voter. But the machine gained legitimacy not only because of its warmth and familiarity; much of its legitimacy derived from its effectiveness in meeting the urgent daily material needs of thousands of clients. If it could no longer bring home the bacon, its electoral chances dimmed.

The new immigrants could be tied to the political system most easily through personal, material inducements, and the machine responded because each immigrant represented a potential vote which it needed. How effective such machine inducements were during the Boss Tweed era in New York City was underscored by what happened in the short reform period that followed his rule. Mandelbaum (1965, p. 106) states that, within only one year, reform mayor Havemeyer "did not have the support of a single mass based political organization." Reform governments, determined to avoid the corrupt practices of the machine, soon discovered that the cost of "clean" government was a marked loss of popular support. If the machine had stretched the city's finances to a point where its municipal bonds were no longer saleable, thereby jeopardizing its distributive capacity, the reform government's emphasis on fiscal austerity and the social distance of its leadership from most citizens quickly robbed it of its legitimacy.

In large multi-ethnic new states the favors a machine party can bring to its clientele may help preserve the territorial integrity of the state. Weiner (1967, pp. 71–72) claims, for example, that in India, where many ethnic groups are geographically concentrated, thus compounding the problem of alienation with that of secession, only machine-style bargaining and benefits, short of coercion, can hold the state together. The Congress Party did, in fact, increasingly distribute both particularistic rewards and pork-barrel projects whenever calls for regional autonomy reached threatening proportions, but the success of such efforts was spotty. Ironically, the desire for regional autonomy was prompted in part by a recognition that more civil service posts, more scholarships, and so forth would be available to the local party if regional autonomy were granted than if it were not.

The machine's latent function of building legitimacy is subject to the same qualification that was made for its capacity to settle conflict peacefully. Machine practices may engender support among those for whom material incentives are effective, but on the other hand they may increase the alienation of the new middle class, military officers, students, and the very traditional. Once again, *the impact of the inducement hinges on the social context.* The support generated by machine rewards, moreover, is based rather tenuously on the continuing distributive capacity of the regime. Lacking either ideological or charismatic foundations, the regime may find its support evaporating once it can no longer deliver the tangible inducements that serves as the party's social adhesive.

Short-Run Goals

In a sense the machine must buy its popularity. To the extent that it faces competition, the cost of popularity is raised and the public treasury may not be sufficient for the demands it must meet. The effect of this "squeeze" in urban America has often forced the machine party not only to raise the city's debt[2] but also to rely increasingly on assistance from businesses that potentially have much to gain or lose from city decisions. This latter strategy was not without its penalties, as licenses and franchises were given to traction and power interests for negligible amounts and the city accepted substandard equipment and materials from influential contractors. *Frequently a three-cornered relationship developed in which the machine politicians could be viewed as brokers who, in return for financial assistance from business elites, promoted their policy interests when in office, while passing along a portion of the gain to a particularistic electorate from whom they "rented" their authority.* The substantial long-run costs to the community as a whole were seldom widely appreciated because the machine controlled an electorate with little sense of broad community interests and a preference for immediate, personal inducements.

Looked at in this way, the machine party facilitates a transaction between the poor and the rich. The poor trade their potential electoral power for wealth or security in the form of employment, help with the police, welfare, and bribes. The patronage and bribes distributed to the unorganized poor represent a "side-payment," moreover, which all but precludes basic struc-

2. Boss Tweed, in four years, raised New York City's indebtedness by a multiple of three while leaving both the tax rate and the assessments untouched. Mandelbaum, 1965, p. 77.

tural change that might improve the *collective* access of the poor to economic opportunities and make those opportunities less ephemeral. Wealth elites, on the other hand, are trading their wealth for a measure of political influence over policy decisions that will, they anticipate, greatly enhance their future profits and commercial security. This transaction is a profoundly conservative one in that it provides the financial backers of the machine with an enormous influence over public policy.

Machines in new nations often have followed a similar pattern. The politicians who run such machines are the brokers in an alliance between commercial wealth on the one hand and a mass (but fragmented) electorate in urban or rural areas whose demands can be met particularistically on the other. Although the private sector occasionally was a less significant resource base than in urban America, the machine frequently developed close and occasionally secretive ties with commercial elites—especially in Southeast Asia and East Africa, where minority groups dominate the private sector. In nations such as Ghana, the party developed its most lucrative connections with large foreign firms rather than with indigenous capital, but the basic nature of the transaction was unchanged. The ruling party received much of its income from the private sector in return for protecting and advancing its patrons' various interests in policy, contracts, administrative decisions, and so forth. Meeting its reciprocal obligations to its financial backers and distributing material incentives for popular support have made the machine's pursuit of longer-run development objectives all but impossible unless its material resources were expanded rapidly. Where revenue was not growing, many leaders dismantled electoral forms and turned to coercion to realize their vision of development. Elsewhere a dangerous running down of foreign exchange reserves or steeply inflationary deficits have been resorted to as fuel for the machine, thus eroding the financial base of the regime and focusing all efforts on short-term survival. Such regimes characteristically have been followed by military governments presiding over austerity programs.

Nonclass Focus

The fact that the machine stresses family and parochial loyalties to the virtual exclusion of ideology and class politics requires little elaboration as it is embedded in the definition of a machine.

So long as the public's interest continues to be centered on the scramble for particular benefits for individuals, overt rivalry will tend to be intraclass rather than interclass [Lande, 1965, p. 48].

While it is true that older, high-status elites typically have looked askance at the possibilities for personal mobility provided to those of humbler origins by the machine, class issues of a collective nature beyond vague populism have been rare. Machines, by the nature of the rewards they offer and the personal ties they build into their organization, may well impede the growth of the class and occupational bonds implied by economic change, and thus may prolong the period during which family and/or ethnic ties are decisive.

An accurate assessment of the conservative effects of machine rule requires that one distinguish between a machine party's social base and the manner in which it aggregates interests. Only by making this distinction is it possible to understand how a regime which often finds its electoral strength among the lower classes can nevertheless pursue a basically conservative policy.

With regard to its social base, the machine party is essentially neutral. It links itself to those elements which can organize and deliver the votes on which it depends for victory. In portions of India, for example, the Congress Party has come to terms with locally powerful rajas and large land-owners whom it had once opposed. In other areas where traditional leadership had eroded, the party based itself among commercialized, independent peasant proprietors or among the newly urbanized lower classes who had been organized by ambitious political brokers. The machine can thus adapt itself with some success to a variety of social strata, some of which are inherently conservative and some of which are potentially radical.

When it comes to the question of how interests are aggregated, however, the machine party is no longer either neutral—or very flexible. What a machine party does is to offer personal mobility (wealth, office) to its brokers who control significant "vote banks" and to provide them with the material resources for maintaining and delivering their votes on behalf of its candidates. The machine does not develop or respond to broad policy demands among its electoral clientele. Rather, it distributes particularistic, short-term rewards to a fragmented electorate so as to win at the polls while at the same time keeping its hands free in most policy matters. If the machine party's broad policy decisions are unaffected by its voting base so long as its capacity for doing favors remains strong, its policy decisions are most decidedly affected by the domestic or foreign commercial interests which provide much of its financial sinews. The social policy of a machine party— beyond the material favors it deploys to win elections—is thus apt to be more reflective of the interests of its financial base than of its electoral base.

It is conceivable that under certain circumstances the interests of the machine's financial patrons are more "progressive" than those of its voters. Early nineteenth-century England, where fairly traditional agrarian elites controlled more votes than the new commercial and industrial elites arising in the cities, might be such a case—as might the more traditional areas of India. For the most part, however, the effect of machine rule under universal suffrage is to submerge growing collective policy demands with immediate payoffs, thereby retarding the development of class-based political interests among the lower strata. The machine's lower-class voters are disaggregated and dealt with particularisticly while its upper-class financial backers and bureaucratic capitalists find their collective interests well cared for.

The Failure of the Machine in New Nations

Looking at politics in the new nations during the early 1960s, the machine model would have seemed an increasingly practical tool of analysis. Regimes that had begun with some popular legitimacy as heirs of the colonial regime and organizers of the nationalist movement were steadily losing much of the passionate, symbolic support they had once evoked. Yet at the same time, electoral forms retained enough vigor to reinforce the efforts of ruling parties to remain genuinely popular. Typically the ranks of the party had been swelled by many new members motivated by an understandable desire to acquire some influence in the new order. Politicization of the colonial bureaucracy was often underway and most parties were becoming adept at building support by distributing patronage, illegal favors, and pork-barrel projects. In spite of these harbingers of machine development, relatively few machine parties actually materialized and those that did were generally short-lived.

The task, therefore, is to explain why machines failed to develop as fully or as often as they did in urban America. The simplest answer, of course, is that embryonic machines in new nations generally were thrown out by military coups. Beyond this elementary truth, however, there are additional reasons why machine parties failed to flourish that relate directly to the social context of new nations and to the dynamics of machine politics itself.

The decline of machine politics in America is of only limited use in accounting for what happened to rudimentary machines in the new states. How, after all, does one compare the demise of two machines, one of which (the American) appears to die a more or less "natural" death, with a machine (that of the new nations) that is "assassinated" by a military coup?

Samuel Hays echoes the opinions of most analysts when he ascribes the atrophy and disappearance of the American urban machine to

certain rather obvious by momentous changes in American life. In the first place, a continually increasing majority of the active American electorate has moved above the poverty line. Most of this electorate is no longer bound to the party through the time-honored links of patronage and the machine. Indeed, for a large number of people, politics appears to have the character of an item of luxury consumption.[3]

The services that tied the client to the machine either were no longer necessary or were performed by other agencies than the machine party. With

3. Samuel Hays, cited in Burnham, 1967, p. 305. To my knowledge, no actual empirical tests of hypotheses advanced for the rise or decline of machine politics have been attempted. It would be instructive, for example, to plot the growth and decline of machine-style politics over time in a number of American cities against possible explanatory variables such as rates of in-migration, changes in per-capita income, changes in income distribution, changes in welfare programs, rates of education, and so forth. I am grateful to Garry Brewer for suggesting this general line of inquiry.

aid to dependent children and old age assistance becoming the formal responsibility of the state and federal governments, "the precinct captain's hod of coal was a joke."[4] The protective and defensive functions of the machine party had simply ceased to be so important as political incentives.

Viewed from another angle, the machine simply destroyed its own social base. It had flourished among those who were, for one reason or another, "civic incompetents"; so when immigration slackened, when the new citizens gained a secure foothold and when they developed wider loyalties, the central prop of machine politics was destroyed. Here and there individual politicians managed to adapt to the new style and incentives, but the machine itself disappeared along with its social context.

The failure of machines in new nations not only differed from the American pattern, but varied somewhat from case to case according to the special circumstances of each nation. Nevertheless, we can discern a number of important factors that seem significant in the demise of many such embryonic machines. These factors related to (1) the stability of electoral forms; (2) the pattern of ethnic cleavage; (3) the economic resources of the party; and (4) the size of the potential machine clientele.

In the first place, the full development of a machine depends on its evolving capacity to create and maintain a large popular following with particularistic inducements. Typically, this capacity has developed best in the context of constant electoral pressures. Elections in American cities were virtually guaranteed by the fact that the city was a unit within a larger political system which sanctioned elections; machines perfected their techniques in the knowledge that they would surely face periodic electoral opposition. Ruling parties in new nations, however, often began with a considerable store of popularity generated in the nationalist period. As this enthusiasm deteriorated, the dominant party did not necessarily have to fall back on material incentives to retain its broad support; it could alternatively abrogate elections and escape the usual machine pressures. A good many nationalist leaders—having goals of transformation in mind—were increasingly discouraged at the growth of the particularistic demands from all quarters that liberal democratic forms seemed to foist upon them. Not having the heart for mediating between a host of what they considered short-sighted parochial demands, many leaders concluded that liberal democracy stood in the way of more vital, long-run, national goals. Both Nkrumah and Sukarno spoke feelingly in this regard, and both consciously chose to eschew elections and machine politics for more grandiose, symbolic goals.[5]

4. Banfield and Wilson, 1965, p. 121. The precinct captain still might be of some help in facilitating an application for welfare with a state agency, but the amount of help he could offer and the numbers of people for whom that assistance was important were both reduced.

5. In an otherwise perceptive article, Edward Feit (1968) characterizes, I think mistakenly, Nkrumah's CPP between 1962 and the military coup as a political machine. He distinguishes between a political party which "aggregates demands and converts them

Another factor that basically altered the character of machines in some cases was the predominant position of a single ethnic group. In urban America it was seldom possible for a machine to rule without being obliged to knit together a broad coalition of ethnic groups. And the excluded groups, in any event, could rely on the protection afforded by stable rules of the game. Where the rules were more ephemeral and where machines could be based on one dominant ethnic group—e.g., pre-Ne Win Burma and, to a lesser extent, Nigeria—the excluded ethnic groups, which were often geographically concentrated, demanded more regional autonomy at the very least and actually launched secessionist revolts in some areas.[6] Not only did minority groups fear permanent exclusion from the benefits that government could confer, but they also feared the capacity of the dominant group to change the constitutional rules in order to destroy them or their culture.

Looking at those nations in which machine politics did develop with some vigor, the importance of the legitimacy of elections and of ethnic balance (or homogeneity) is manifest. Lebanon and India, for example, are sufficiently balanced ethnically so as to require some form of collaborative rule, and the Philippines is relatively homogeneous ethnically. No single group could easily dominate in the first two nations while, in the case of the Philippines, the major ethnic group is so overwhelmingly large that there are only a few minority groups, especially the Moslems, which feel threatened or excluded. All three had retained electoral forms as late as 1971. Beyond these two factors, however, are two broader obstacles to machine politics relating to its resource base and the nature of its clientele.

The resource base of successful machine parties in Asia and Africa became steadily more important after independence. Once the nationalist struggle was won the ruling party's support became ever more contingent upon the patronage it could distribute, the size of the government budget it had to work with, and the contributions it could elicit. A substantial loss of resources probably would entail the defection of some supporters, thereby jeopardizing the ruling party's coalition. Such defections were not so damaging to the party in the early independence period when its majorities were overwhelming, but it became a distinct threat as the nationalist coalition narrowed. William Riker (1962, pp. 39, 66) has attributed this paring down of "oversized coalitions" to the fact that the smaller a winning coalition is, the more spoils its members will share, whereas a huge winning majority may dilute winnings to the point of meaninglessness. Although such narrowing, in

into legislative policy" and a political machine which "exists almost exclusively to stay in power." The problem, of course, is that many regimes are motivated almost solely to stay in power—e.g., the Thai military, Haiti's Duvalier—but the term "machine" should be reserved for civilian regimes which rest on a popular base. The CPP, until about 1960, can profitably be seen a machine party, but thereafter coercion and symbolic goals dominated.

6. For an excellent discussion of ethnic configurations and their political implications, see Geertz, 1963.

principle, would reduce the coalition to a bare majority, the uncertainties of political calculations in the new states prevented the process from extending that far. Some narrowing did occur, however, and its effect was to make the ruling party's majority increasingly vulnerable to the defections that a decline in its material resources might touch off. Whereas the party might earlier have survived such losses, they could well now mean the difference between victory and defeat.

A somewhat analogous process can be seen in the collapse of the Chicago Republican machine in the depression of the 1930s. Accustomed to a relatively abundant supply of material resources, the machine found itself in 1931 with a greatly reduced city treasury and fewer city jobs to dispense, with a huge drop in private contributions from streetcar and utility magnates such as Samuel Insull, and with little patronage at the county or state level to fall back upon (Gosnell, 1968). The central role occupied by material resources in the form of city hall patronage and private-sector kickbacks was made evident to machine leaders who, competing without these advantages for the first time, were soundly beaten in the 1932 elections. Latent class and policy issues that had remained dormant as long as the machine had ample material rewards to distribute had reappeared with decisiveness.

Indications are that machines in new nations, like their American counterparts, require a large and steady *growth* in the volume of resources over time. What is more, as new participants learn of the advantages the government can confer, as the state extends its regulation over the economy, and as automatic loyalties erode, the cost of machine coordination grows. Machines in American cities tended, in fact, to live beyond their means, and the evidence suggests that machine parties in new nations behave similarly.[7] As a form of rule, then, machines are particularly subject to "an inflationary process of demand-formation" (Zolberg, 1966, p. 149) and naturally thrive best in an economy that provides them with a continually expanding store of material incentives to distribute.[8] Unlike American machines for which private-sector funds were often decisive, machines in Africa and Asia typically have been far more dependent on rewards such as patronage and contracts financed out of the national and local treasury. For such machines the volume of central government revenue was a key indicator of the ruling party's capacity to keep its electoral coalition intact without resort to coercion.

It is perhaps no coincidence that the high-water mark of machine politics in the new states occurred in the mid-1950s when Korean War boom prices for primary exports underwrote high rates of growth. In addition, there were a large number of "one-time-only" rewards available to ruling parties after

7. This fact may indicate that machine politics is not a stable form of rule.

8. The very success of machine parties in new nations in centrally distributing rewards and regulating the economy meant that when discontent came it was more likely both to be focused on the central government and to jeopardize the stability of central institutions.

independence: foreign businesses could be nationalized, new franchises and licenses could be let, expatriates and older civil servants could be replaced by loyal party workers. But in the absence of domestic economic expansion, the supply of such material incentives was soon exhausted. Assessing the instability of cabinet rule in Indonesia prior to Guided Democracy, Feith (1962, p. 572) concludes that

perhaps most fundamentally, the weakness of these later cabinets stemmed from their shortage of disposable rewards. . . . Moreover, the number of material rewards and prestige roles which government was expected to provide did not decrease. . . . In sum, then, those cabinets were almost as poorly equipped to reward as to punish.

It is reasonable to suppose that the Indonesian case is not unique. The material rewards were, finally, not sufficient to the task and, amid the ruling party's loss of support, the military—which, if it could not reward, could at least restrain and punish—stepped in.[9]

The collapse of embryonic machines in the late 1950s and early 1960s and their replacement by coercive parties or by the military in the new states can in large part be seen as a consequence of an economic pinch created by a slump in export prices for primary products and abetted by poorly performing local economies. At the time when their purses were contracting, however, many party machines were especially vulnerable. They had lost much of their charismatic authority, their own fiddling with electoral laws and preventive detention had undermined their legal claim to rule, and the idealism which the party's ennobling goals had once elicited was effaced by current stories of corruption by cabinet ministers.[10] The machine had thus become a rather profane institution at this point—one that depended almost exclusively on calculations of material advantage just when the material advantages it controlled were slipping away.

The general line of reasoning developed above suggests that the machine flourishes best at the subnational level, which is where it was confined in the United States. That is, *the durability of this political form is maximized where there is an external guarantor of the electoral process, where the machine is a part of a larger growing economy that can afford its expensive habits, and where its bosses do not have a monopoly of coercive authority.* A large measure of the instability of machines in developing nations may thus derive from their national rather than local character.[11]

9. In a number of cases the military intervened only after the ruling party had itself forsaken electoral forms and had come to rely increasingly on coercion to retain its domination.

10. It was at times like these that the American machine selected a "blue-ribbon" front man for mayor who would restore some legitimacy to the operation while allowing the party to remain in command behind the scenes.

11. I am indebted to Henry Hart for suggesting this.

Finally, in many nations economic pressures and demand inflation were not the only factors serving to weaken political machines; there was also some question of how well suited the social context was to machines. On the one hand, the machine faced opposition from a small but strategically placed upper middle class of civil servants, professionals, students, and, above all, army officers, which was much less amenable to material incentives and was, like its American counterpart, profoundly alienated by machine corruption and patronage.[12] On the other hand, these machines, particularly in Africa, faced large numbers of quite traditional folk for whom religious and cultural issues were still important[13] and whose leaders realized. that the machine threatened the ascriptive basis of their power. As the state had not yet effectively penetrated many of these narrow political communities, their populations remained by and large outside the scope of machine incentives and represented, at a minimum, a latent challenge to the machine's authority. Bastions of tradition were often found in areas of "indirect rule" where colonial social and political change had been less severe. The machine, by contrast, won support especially among urban migrants and in areas (often "directly ruled") where folkways had been more uprooted by colonialism. The *transitional* population on which the machine relied was, in these cases, simply not large enough to sustain this form of government when it was menaced by widespread traditional recalcitrance and by a powerful middle class with military allies. Machines require not only an economy that performs tolerably well, but a social context that corresponds to the inducements it can deliver; only where both conditions have been satisfied have machines managed to survive.

12. The fact that machines were typically of national scope in the new states of course made the army a key factor here.

13. To stretch a point, one might link them with the forces in American politics that felt strongest about Sunday laws, prohibition, and so forth.

31

Law-enforcement corruption: explanations and recommendations

John A. Gardiner

Corruption is . . . limited by the extent to which a sense of outrage is aroused among people who are capable of making corruption more costly than correctness.—Rogow and Lasswell, 1963[1]

"Corruption is a persistent and practically ubiquitous aspect of political society; it is unlikely that any reforms will ever eliminate it completely." Wherever men compete for valuable but limited commodities, whether they are licenses to operate taxicabs, franchises to sell goods to the government, or freedom to operate a numbers game, there will be a temptation to secure

From Chapter 7 of *The Politics of Corruption: Organized Crime in an American City.* by John A. Gardiner. Copyright © 1970 by Russell Sage Foundation, New York. Reprinted by permission.

1. Arnold A. Rogow and Harold D. Lasswell, *Power, Corruption, and Rectitude* (Englewood Cliffs, N.J.: Prentice-Hall, 1963), p. 74.

these commodities through corrupt inducements if other efforts fail. Barring some apocalyptic change in human nature, there will always be people who want to gamble, visit prostitutes, or enrich themselves through illegal deals with the government. And, on the other hand, in any large organization, whether it be a police department, tax-collection agency, labor union, or multimillion-dollar corporation, there will always be individuals who will find the rewards of corruption greater than the satisfactions of legitimate behavior.

If this is correct, then the relevant question becomes one of finding ways to *reduce,* not eliminate, the frequency of corruption—to minimize the situations in which corruption is the rule rather than the exception, situations in which corruption affects not only isolated governmental decisions but also the nature and functioning of the political system. While it might also be desirable to eliminate the petty as well as the most blatant forms of corruption, it would probably be impossible to do this without significantly altering our concepts of civil liberties and of public bureaucracies drawn from and responsive to the general citizenry. Before suggesting a series of actions which might serve to reduce the incidence of widespread corruption, it is necessary to identify precisely those conditions which tend to produce or facilitate it. Some relate more directly to Wincanton and the law-enforcement corruption which has been studied here; others deal more broadly with the general phenomenon of political corruption.

The first precondition for corruption is a substantial conflict over the goals of the legal system. As McMullan notes,

A high level of corruption is the result of a wide divergence between the attitudes, aims, and methods of the government of a country and those of the society in which they operate. . . . Therefore the different levels of corruption in different countries depend on the extent to which government and society are homogeneous.[2]

A major source of this kind of norm conflict in mid-twentieth-century America concerns legislation which attempts to restrict what is regarded as "immoral" behavior—gambling, prostitution, and the use of narcotics. In Chapter Four, for example, it was noted that one-half of the Wincanton survey respondents felt that "most" or "a lot" of local residents liked to gamble (Table 4.3). Furthermore, 55 percent felt that the state should legalize gambling; between one-third and one-half of the respondents in surveys conducted in other areas shared this opinion.[3] (It should be noted at this point that it is *conflict* over legislation rather than lack of support for it which is necessary for corruption. If officials in cities where *everyone* wanted

2. M. McMullan, "A Theory of Corruption," *Sociological Review,* IX (July, 1961), 184–185.

3. See Table 4.8 and the surveys cited in Chapter Four, note 20.

to gamble tried to exact payments for protection, they would be ousted by local voters.)[4] Thus in Wincanton, as in most heterogeneous cities, there are demands for both the enforcement of the state's gambling laws and the toleration of petty gambling activities; those who wish to gamble will support the syndicates, and the moralists will demand that the town be "kept clean."

Assuming that wherever a substantial demand for illegal goods and services is found,[5] someone will be willing to satisfy it, the next precondition for corruption is a willingness on the part of the relevant government governmental agency to tolerate this activity in return for an appropriate payoff. Three factors appear to affect the likelihood that the agency will be so disposed: the internal characteristics of the agency, the characteristics of the political system in which the agency operates (including both the formal governmental institutions and informal groups and processes), and the laws and law-enforcement agencies available for the detection and harassment of corrupt officials and their corrupters.

The internal characteristics of governmental agencies which are most likely to affect their susceptibility to corruption are the strength of organizational leadership, the rewards given for legitimate behavior (pay scales, job security, opportunities for advancement, etc.), and the degree of identification with professional standards and codes of ethics. Where leadership is weak, senior members of the organization will be unable to control members of the organization tempted by bribes. Where rewards given for noncorrupt behavior are low, the relative value of corrupt inducements increases. Where professional identification is low or nonexistent, codes of conduct promulgated by professional organizations will present few psychological barriers to the acceptance of bribes.

On all three counts, the internal characteristics of the Wincanton Police Department have facilitated both toleration of gambling and the acceptance of bribes. (It should be kept in mind, however, that even at the height of the Stern syndicate's activities, probably not more than 10 percent of the force was receiving regular payoffs, although perhaps one-half might have accepted Christmas turkeys or liquor.) Since political involvement in police affairs has been a long-standing tradition in Wincanton—incoming mayors regularly elevate patrolmen to command positions and reduce former chiefs to walking a beat—few police officers have felt free to take full command of their department by harassing lazy or corrupt men on the force. While research was being conducted during the summer of 1966, eighteen months before a new administration would take office, police officers reported that men on the force

---

4. See James Q. Wilson, *Varieties of Police Behavior: The Management of Law and Order in Eight Communities* (Cambridge: Harvard University Press, 1968), pp. 148–149.

5. National Crime Commission estimates of the volume of illegal gambling suggest that crime syndicates probably have gross revenues from gambling up to $50 billion, with net revenues of $6 or $7 billion per year. See President's Commission on Law Enforcement and Administration of Justice, *Task Force Report: Organized Crime* (Washington: Government Printing Office, 1967), pp. 2–5, and Donald R. Cressey, *Theft of the Nation* (New York: Harper & Row, 1969), chap. 5.

were beginning to curry favor with local politicians and that sergeants were becoming unwilling to enforce departmental regulations. "How can I tell someone off?" a captain asked. "If the Democrats take office again, I'll probably be walking a beat and *he* may be my boss!" Given the insecurity of their positions, it is not surprising that few Wincanton police chiefs have been strong leaders; the corrupt ones have been kept busy stealing while they had the chance, and the honest ones have been kept busy trying to hold the force together in the face of persistent political interference and departmental factionalism.

From the point of view of patrolmen on the Wincanton police force, neither the city nor the department have offered high rewards for noncorrupt behavior. During the 1950s, Wincanton police salaries were in the lowest quartile of middle-sized cities in the nation, well below the city's median family income ($5,453); in the 1960s, the salary for patrolmen rose to $5,400, still well below the national average. While the state civil service law guarantees that policemen may not be discharged from the force without cause, only friends of politicians seem to get promotions and desirable duties. Until reform mayor Ed Whitton instituted a series of competitive examinations in 1964, there was little incentive for patrolmen to "hustle." Hustlers were only rewarded if they also had political connections, and those who made enemies (of politicians or of policemen or city officials on Stern's payroll) were likely to find themselves transferred to "Siberia"—dragging drunks out of bars or patrolling the riverfront on the midnight shift.[6] Thus the reward system of the Wincanton Police Department not only offered few incentives for legitimate behavior but also worked against those who refused to "mind their own business." Even for men not on Irv Stern's payroll, "looking the other way" was a clearly advantageous policy.

Finally, there is the matter of "professionalism"—that combination of special training and education which gives men unique competence, adherence to a clear code of ethics, and supervision by a professional association. As has been noted by Wilson, Niederhoffer, and Banton, few policemen in America meet these tests; they learn most of their skills on the job, have few clear standards specifying appropriate behavior, and act collectively through union-like bargaining groups, not professional accrediting associations.[7] Even when compared with this low national standard of professionalism, Wincanton police perform poorly. Until reformer Whitton took office in 1964, no member of the force had attended the F.B.I. National

6. Lincoln Steffens observed a similar phenomenon within the New York Police Department while Theodore Roosevelt served as Police Commissioner. Even the policemen who shared his reform values were afraid to act, fearing retaliation when Tammany Hall returned to power. *Autobiography* (New York: Harcourt, Brace, 1931), pp. 275–281.

7. See J. Q. Wilson, *Varieties of Police Behavior*, pp. 29–30; Arthur Niederhoffer, *Behind the Shield: The Police in Urban Society* (Garden City, N.Y.: Doubleday, 1967), chap. 1; and Michael Banton, *The Policeman in the Community* (London: Tavistock, 1964), pp. 105–110.

Academy; formal training was limited to a few weeks of classes conducted by senior members of the force. Until Whitton instituted competitive promotional examinations, advancement was based more on friendship with officers and politicians than on abstract skill or merit. Finally, because of repeated political meddling in departmental affairs and public assumptions of police misconduct (only 11 percent of the survey respondents felt that no policemen would take a bribe), departmental morale and *esprit de corps* have been low.[8] A committee of experts asked by the Wincanton government in 1967 to evaluate the department concluded that it represented the "residual remains of temerity, habit, and limited imagination or fear. . . . Their general morale is low, and their pride, if any exists, is well hidden." Under these conditions, it is not surprising that professionalism has not served as a significant barrier to corruption within the Wincanton police department.

The second broad set of factors which will influence the likelihood that a governmental agency will be corrupt, beyond the internal characteristics of the agency itself, is the nature of the political system in which it operates: the interests and values of the citizenry, the structure of governmental agencies, the activities of political parties and interest groups, and so forth. If most residents are unaware of governmental policies or positively desire illegal goods and services, then the agency will be free to adopt tolerant or corrupt policies. If neither government officials nor private organizations have the ability or desire to demand official morality, then the agencies will be free to act as they please. If, on the other hand, officials, political parties, or private elites are capable of establishing control over the political process, governmental agencies will more likely be forced to accede to their demands. (That an official is powerful does not, of course, necessarily mean that he will be honest or interested in strict law enforcement. Only powerful men, however, will be *able* to supervise bureaucratic activities and, to the extent that they view entreaties from corrupters as threats to their own control over their organizations, they will be likely to want to end corruption or centralize it under themselves.)[9]

Chapters Four and Six suggested a number of ways in which the attitudes of Wincanton residents have facilitated the growth of corruption in law-enforcement agencies. In addition to being sharply divided over the value of antigambling legislation, the survey respondents had little interest in city politics and were poorly informed about the government and its law enforcement agencies. As one real estate broker put it, "Walasek stole darn near everything he could put his hands on. It was made easy for him because most

---

8. See also James Q. Wilson, "Police Morale, Reform, and Citizen Respect: The Chicago Case," in David J. Bordua, ed., *The Police: Six Sociological Essays* (New York: Wiley, 1967), pp. 137–162.

9. See Daniel P. Moynihan, "The Private Government of Crime," *The Reporter*, XXV (July 6, 1961), 14–20; James Q. Wilson: "Corruption Is Not Always Scandalous," *New York Times Magazine*, April 28, 1968; and *Varieties of Police Behavior*, pp. 148–149.

of the city residents didn't pay attention and just went along with it." Even though they were cynical about politicians and were hostile to corruption, the survey respondents were slow to assume that corruption might be involved in city affairs or that corruption might soon return to the city. When asked in 1966 what issues would be important in the 1967 local elections, only nine of the 180 respondents felt that "clean government" or keeping out vice and gambling might be an issue (55 percent had no opinion, 15 percent felt that the recent ban on bingo might be an issue, and 12 percent cited urban renewal, a subject frequently mentioned in the papers in the months preceding the survey). Since, under Ed Whitton, the city was being honestly run and was free from gambling and prostitution, there was no "problem" to worry about. To the extent that they were interested in local politics, it was in terms of issues which affected them personally ("The Republicans increased my property assessment"; "My wife can't play bingo now"; "We need a new playground in the neighborhood"); to the extent that they were interested in the activities of the police department, it was in terms of protection against violence, not the enforcement of morals legislation.

To what extent are the public institutions and private political groups of Wincanton capable of dealing with threats of subversion by crime syndicates? In Chapters Two and Six, it was noted that the formal governmental structure of the city is exceedingly fragmented. Although he can name the officers of the police department, the mayor has little control over either city councilmen and their departments or the independently elected district attorney who handles all criminal prosecutions. The county's political parties, as noted in Chapter Five, are also fragmented organizations which exercise little or no control over city officials; candidates for local office develop their own *ad hominem* coalitions. The city's business community, while probably influential in many recent urban renewal and economic development decisions, has been unable to dominate other aspects of city politics, including the selection of city officials, for at least forty years.[10] While the Wincanton newspapers regularly attacked organized crime, they were never able by themselves to provoke voter rebellions against official corruption; until state and federal investigators provided proof of the corruption underlying local gambling, the papers were forced to concentrate on the gambling itself, hardly a startling or offensive subject for most Wincantonites. As a result of this fragmentation of the formal and informal political processes of Wincanton, it might be said that the city knew a "power vacuum," a situation in which *no one* was able to dominate local politics or to control the Stern syndicates and its corrupt officials. Unlike the old-time bosses who were powerful enough to keep gamblers and prostitutes within limits, Wincanton officials usually took orders from the Stern syndicate. With no one dominating the city's political

10. For discussions of historical changes in the role of economic dominants in urban politics, see the works cited in Chapter Two, note 9.

system, it was easy for Stern to name his own terms, fearing only the inter-vention of state or federal investigators.[11]

The final factor which affects the likelihood that corruption will develop within a political system concerns the laws and the law-enforcement agencies which are available for the investigation and harassment of corrupt officials. In many areas of American politics, the laws defining corrupt behavior are quite ambiguous: campaign contributions by government contractors are per-missible, but *quid pro quo* payments to secure a particular contract are not; contributions to legislators prior to the adoption of a law are frequently legitimate, but contributions to the policemen who administer the law never are.[12] In general, however, the kinds of cash transactions seen in Wincanton which were payments to secure a contract or protection from the police are clear violations of state and local laws, although this may be difficult to prove in court. There are greater variations among cities and among states in the level of investigations and prosecution of official corruption. In some areas, city, state, and federal agencies are constantly scrutinizing official behavior, either in conjunction with an interest in specific programs (e.g., a road-build-ing program or the collection of taxes) or as part of an interest in official morality for its own sake. Wincanton presents a rather mixed picture: federal investigators, particularly from the Internal Revenue Service and the Depart-ment of Justice, have been very interested in organized crime in Wincanton but have been only peripherally interested in official corruption; state agents, on the other hand, have stayed out of the city unless officially invited to act. District attorneys and county judges have taken a similarly passive stance, processing those cases which the police have brought to them, but only rarely (twice during the Donnelly-Walasek era) initiating independent investigations. Apart from federal agents, therefore, Irv Stern had little to fear so long as he could buy protection from Wincanton officials and policemen. If other agen-cies had taken a more independent view of their role in law enforcement, Stern's tenure in Wincanton would have been of much shorter duration.

Proposals for Change

Can anything be done to minimize widespread corruption? The feasibility of change depends on the extent to which reforms would require the acquies-cence of large numbers of people who are committed to the present state of affairs. Edelman and Fleming, after studying European programs to preserve wage-price stability, concluded that indirect actions (changing bank interest

11. That corruption is most likely to develop in political systems which are unable to handle current societal problems is suggested by James C. Scott, "An Essay on the Political Functions of Corruption," *Asian Studies*, v (December, 1967), 501–523; and Samuel P. Huntington, "Political Development and Political Decay," *World Politics*, XVII (April, 1965), 386–430.

12. See Scott, *op. cit.*, and Herbert E. Alexander and Laura L. Denny, *Regulation of Political Finance* (Berkeley: Institute of Governmental Studies, and Princeton: Citizens' Research Foundation, 1966).

rates, reserve requirements, or currency values) were more successful than actions requiring changes in public attitudes or habits: "No democratic government can for long enforce behavior which is strongly resisted by the public, so that when the pressure of public opinion is lacking, enforcement is likely to be absent too, regardless of formal law or declared public policy."[13] If this is correct, then the only feasible paths for reducing corruption are changes which are consistent with existing public attitudes or changes which will work primarily through government officials and law-enforcement agencies without requiring changes in mass behavior patterns. Nothing will significantly reduce popular desires to gamble or make corrupt deals, but the following suggestions may reduce the attractiveness of corruption by increasing the capacity of government to deal with it.

First, law-enforcement corruption might be reduced by improving the internal structure of law-enforcement agencies. While it may be desirable, if difficult, to improve police efficiency through the recruitment of better officers and the expansion of training programs,[14] the primary changes needed in cities like Wincanton concern job security and protection against "political interference." With higher salaries, promotions through competitive examinations, and civil service protection for ranking officers, a police department could both increase loyalty to the organization (offering psychological defenses against the temptations of corruption) and reduce the ability of corrupt politicians to arrange police toleration of organized crime. It is unlikely that even the most drastic increases in salaries or job security will *eliminate* the sense of isolation and frustration felt by American police,[15] but changes in this direction might produce a greater sense of professionalism and freedom from local politicians. Although such changes would also, of course, reduce the ability of honest and progressive local officials to alter police policies, they may be necessary to strengthen those agencies which have the greater exposure to corruption.

The second step for increasing resistance to corruption concerns the role of state and federal enforcement agencies. As has been seen in Wincanton, some state police units take a hands-off attitude toward local crime and corruption problems, while others conserve limited resources by concentrating only on selected target areas. While they have steadily escalated the scope of their attack on gambling, narcotics, and the other business activities of the syndicates, federal agents have seldom been able to act against official corruption, since bribery and extortion involving local officials (unless they

13. Murray Edelman and R. W. Fleming, *The Politics of Wage-Price Decisions: A Four-Country Analysis* (Urbana: University of Illinois Press, 1965), pp. 317–318.

14. See, generally, the recommendations of the President's Commission on Law Enforcement and Administration of Justice, *Task Force Report: The Police* (Washington: Government Printing Office, 1967).

15. See, for example, James Q. Wilson: "The Police and their Problems: A Theory," *Public Policy*, XII (1963), 189–216; and "Police Morale . . . ."

affect interstate commerce) are not federal offenses.[16] In many cases, law-enforcement agencies are so suspicious of each other (often correctly assuming that some agents in other organizations are on the payroll of the syndicates) and jealous of their agency's prestige (wanting to reserve the "big pinch" for themselves) that they refuse to cooperate with each other. The results of this conflict have been a fragmentation of the skills devoted to the problem of organized crime and the reduction of that check on corruption which would result from separate organizations looking for syndicate collusion with police and city officials.[17]

The recommendations which have been made thus far are designed to increase the scope and efficiency of official actions against organized crime and to create incentives within police departments to avoid corruption. As indicated earlier, corruption can also be facilitated by certain weaknesses of local political systems—mass apathy or contempt for the government, the inability of local officials to control enforcement agencies, and the absence of private organizations (political parties, interest groups, citizen associations) which could structure the political process and fill the "power vacuum" which allows a crime syndicate to become the most active force. How might this be accomplished? The most likely source of such a strengthening of the local political system would be an expansion of the powers of the mayor. If Wincanton, for example, adopted a mayor-council structure to replace the commission form of government, more qualified (and publicly attractive) men might find the office worth seeking, and the mayor would have greater ability to oversee the police department and to institute programs which might restore citizen interest in local government and support for its programs.[18] To increase the tax resources for such programs and the involvement of enforcement- and program-oriented middle classes in city affairs, some

16. In a message to Congress in 1969, President Nixon proposed laws making the corruption of local officials and policemen a federal offense, subjecting both corrupters and corruptees to fines and jail sentences. See *New York Times,* April 24, 1969.

17. To overcome the inertia caused by corrupt local police and to remedy other problems in the prosecution of syndicate members, the National Crime Commission recommended the annual impaneling of investigative grand juries with special prosecuting and investigative staffs, provision for the granting of immunity to witnesses, and the power to impose extended sentences on syndicate leaders. Furthermore, the commission called for the formation or expansion of special organized crime units in federal, state, and local law-enforcement agencies, and the development of information-sharing facilities. See *Task Force Report: Organized Crime,* pp. 16–22.

18. That mayors with greater formal authority and party support are more capable of implementing unpopular decisions is argued by Robert L. Crain, Elihu Katz, and Donald B. Rosenthal. See *The Politics of Community Conflict: The Fluoridation Decision* (Indianapolis: Bobbs-Merrill, 1969). See also J. David Greenstone and Paul E. Peterson, "Reformers, Machines, and the War on Poverty," in James Q. Wilson, ed., *City Politics and Public Policy* (New York: Wiley, 1968), pp. 267–292; Robert L. Crain and James J. Vanecko, "Elite Influence in School Desegregation," in Wilson, *City Politics and Public Policy,* pp. 127–148; Edward C. Banfield and James Q. Wilson, *City Politics* (Cambridge: Harvard University Press, 1963), chaps. 8 and 11.

form of metropolitan area-wide government may be necessary.[19] Many of the most exciting and interest-attracting programs for the cities are, of course, financed by federal grants; to reward local officials who reduce corruption, and to convince voters that reform officials can provide more than their own honesty, federal officials might consider a policy of giving urban renewal and Model Cities grants to cities which have successfully reformed. If the legitimate rewards of public office increased (both through increases in salaries and powers and through the satisfactions of major improvements in declining cities), energetic men might be more willing to seek public office, and the focus of political discourse might shift from the issue of corruption to more pressing urban issues. If local government became a more promising vehicle for local action (and less tainted by corruption), it is likely that private interest groups and political organizations would increase their interest in municipal affairs. As the visibility of governmental activities increased, citizen support might increase, and suspicious official behavior would be more quickly noticed. Citizen crime councils, so long as they did not simply harass policemen and reduce morale, might serve as an appropriate vehicle for public interest in crime and law-enforcement problems. Improvement of the activities of local political parties would require an increase in the availability of legitimate funds,[20] but it might be hoped that an improvement in governmental performance would increase mass willingness to contribute time and money to the parties and to run for local office.

Finally, corruption might be minimized by a reduction in the conflict between popular values and formal legislation. In recent years, two broad strategies have been proposed to meet this problem. One calls for an increase in law-enforcement activity, coupled with an educational campaign designed to inform the public of the relationship between consumption of illicit goods and services and the growth of organized crime and corruption.[21] The other strategy assumes that an irreducible mass desire to gamble should be accommodated through the legalization of gambling and/or the operation of gam-

19. For a comprehensive review of various forms of metropolitan government, see John C. Bollens and Henry J. Schmandt, *The Metropolis: Its People, Politics, and Economic Life* (New York: Harper & Row, 1965).

20. See Edward C. Banfield, *Political Influence: A New Theory of Urban Politics* (New York: Free Press, 1961), pp. 256–257; Moynihan, *op. cit.*

21. See Virgil W. Peterson, *Barbarians in Our Midst: A History of Chicago Crime and Politics* (Boston: Little, Brown, 1952), pp. 331–333; Morris Ploscowe, "New Approaches to the Control of Organized Crime," *Annals of the American Academy of Political and Social Science,* CCCXLVII (May, 1963), 74–81; Eliot H. Lumbard, "Local and State Action Against Organized Crime," *Annals of the American Academy of Political and Social Science,* CCCXLVII (May, 1963), 82–92. The role of the syndicates in operating gambling casinos in Nevada is discussed in Wallace Turner, *Gamblers' Money: The New Force in American Life* (Boston: Houghton Mifflin, 1965).

bling activities by the government.[22] Both proposals agree that the public is inadequately aware of the problems of organized crime and corruption, and that popular apathy and desire to gamble have encouraged the growth of corruption. Both probably would agree on the need for a uniform set of policies on a statewide or, optimally, nationwide basis. Where gambling is legal in some areas but illegal in others, it is easy for the syndicates to use the former locations as bases for operations in the latter.[23] They disagree, however, on the consequences of legalization. The proponents argue that once gambling was legalized, police corruption would cease. The opponents argue that legalization would increase the number of gamblers and would simply deflect the syndicates into other areas of illegal activity in which they would be equally corruptive; because of the skills required to operate large-scale gambling activities, syndicate leaders would quickly take control of legalized gambling unless it was operated directly by the government. Criminologist Donald R. Cressey has argued that the insatiable greed of the syndicates demands some form of calculated appeasement, such as negotiations leading to syndicate control of gambling in return for an end to syndicate violence, corruption, and other unlawful activities.[24]

This study has offered but little information on which to base a choice between these proposals. Surveys show a substantial popular desire to gamble, one which might be reduced (but scarcely eliminated) by a strict enforcement policy or increased by easily available legitimate gambling opportunities. Many Americans have an equally intense belief that gambling is wasteful or sinful; they regard proposals to legalize gambling as a threat to government's symbolic role as the protector of public morality.[25] It is true that intermittent reform movements in Wincanton have been able to reduce greatly the level of gambling and corruption in the city. On the other hand, legalization would reduce the incentive to corruption, freeing police resources for other purposes and giving the police a more popularly accepted set of laws to enforce. Would the syndicates simply move into other equally illegal and

22. Among those endorsing the legalization of gambling, with or without government operation, are Jerome H. Skolnick, "Coercion to Virtue," *Southern California Law Review*, XLI (1968), 588–641; John M. Murtagh, "Gambling and Police Corruption," *Atlantic Monthly*, CCVI (November, 1960), 49–53; Sanford H. Kadish, "The Crisis of Overcriminalization," *Annals of the American Academy of Political and Social Science* CCCLXXIV (November, 1967), 157–170; National Council on Crime and Delinquency, *Goals and Recommendations: A Response to "The Challenge of Crime in a Free Society"* (New York: National Council on Crime and Delinquency, 1967); Robert K. Woetzel, "An Overview of Organized Crime: Mores versus Morality," *Annals of the American Academy of Political and Social Science*, CCCXLVII (May, 1963), 1–11.

23. See *Task Force Report: Organized Crime*, p. 11.

24. Cressey, *Theft of the Nation*, chap. 12.

25. Edelman and Fleming, *op. cit.*,; Murray Edelman, *The Symbolic Uses of Politics*. (Urbana: University of Illinois Press, 1964).

equally corrupting activities? I don't know. To the extent that there is greater (but hardly unanimous) public support for police action against the kinds of activities to which the syndicates might turn (e.g., the sale of narcotics, loan-sharking, labor racketeering), the dangers of corruption would be less than in the case of gambling. It is clear, however, that the situation in cities like Wincanton, where long periods of massive corruption are only inter-mittently disturbed by short periods of honest but otherwise ineffectual re-form, is intolerable.

Ending the Washington pay-off

Robert N. Winter-Berger

In his State of the Union address to the Ninety-second Congress on January 22, 1971, President Nixon tried to convince the members to support his various programs by throwing a challenge at them. He said:

What this Congress can be rembered for is opening the way to a new American Revolution—a peaceful revolution in which power was turned back to the people—in which government at all levels was refreshed and renewed, and made truly responsive. This can be a revolution as profound, as far-reaching, as exciting as that first revolution almost 200 years ago—and it can mean that just five years from now America will enter its third century as a young nation new in spirit, with all the vigor and freshness with which it began its first century.

For me, the irony was in knowing that if there was one man

From pp 315–28 of *The Washington Pay-Off* by Robert N. Winter-Berger. Copyright © 1973 by Lyle Stuart Publishing Co., Secaucus, N.J. Reprinted by permission.

in the country who was fully aware that this "challenge" was an infantile daydream, that man had to be Richard M. Nixon. Nixon had been in politics for most of his adult life. He know all the ins and the outs of it. He knew its rottenness. And he could not have been unaware that, among the members of the Congress seated in front of him that night, there were several who should have been behind bars. Nixon himself has never had the reputation of being the boy scout of Washington politics. Fourteen of the persons he named ambassadors were listed by the Citizens' Research Foundation as among the heaviest contributors to his campaign—that is, they were pure political appointees. And if Nixon had no idea that Waller Taylor was running around the country, both before and after the election, picking up contributions, then maybe Nixon needed another long session with Hutschie.

In any case, the President stood there and told the members of Congress that he expected them, perhaps by some miraculous baptism, to abandon their old ways of pay-offs, double-dealing, kickbacks, favoritism, and vested interests, and come out of it all looking like an interfaith College of Cardinals. Immediately after the speech, radio and television news commentators generally agreed that Nixon's "driving dream" was impossible, and that Nixon had merely been laying the groundwork for his re-election. If the country was still a mess late in 1972, Nixon would at least have a potential scapegoat: the Congress.

As I watched Nixon's speech on television that night, I recognized in his audience a number of Senators and Congressmen with whom I had worked during my five years in Washington as a lobbyist, and I found myself wondering whether there were any truly free men in the room. It costs money to run for public office—the higher the office, the higher the cost. And it costs money to remain in public office. Unless an elected official is independently wealthy—and few of them are—he is bound to incur a variety of indebtedness the longer he stays in office, in terms of money, favors, and support, and his best means of liquidating these debts is to use his office—that is, his influence—to pay them off. Besides the money needed to pay off his own debts, the Congressman is expected to raise money for the national committee of his political party. He does this in the same way: by using his influence. Every member of the Congress is appointed to several committess which supervise the operations of federal agencies, federal programs, and federal policies. The more important the man—sometimes in seniority, sometimes in connections, sometimes in experience—the more important his appointments and the greater his influence. Similarly, as the man's influence increases, so does that of his staff members who can speak and act in his name. And yet every time a member of Congress pays a debt he creates a new one, sinking deeper into the bottomless pit of political vulnerability.

A man needs connections in Washington to get certain things done, not done, or undone. All that has been said about Washington bureaucratic red tape is true, and the important man and his vested-interest group will not waste time with it. They know that the members of Congress, usually through committees, control the budgets for all federal departments and agencies. They also know that one telephone call by the member of Congress, particularly if he is on the right committee, gets things done—or undone—a lot faster in the federal departments and agencies than going through the endless governmental red tape, the way ordinary mortals do. They know this is going to cost them something, and they are ready and willing to pay in order to save time and get results. And if for any reason they cannot make direct contact with the member of Congress whose influence they need, they hire someone who can. They hire a lobbyist.

The upshot of all this is that the government of the United States, which is supposed to be of the people, by the people, and for the people, has become a government of the rich and the powerful. This may not be news. But unless something is done about it, unless a serious effort is made to return to the spirit of Lincoln's dictum, it seems questionable to me that the country can long endure.

The biggest business in the world is the United States government, and part of every Congressman's job is to try to get some of that business into his district. This means jobs for the people back home, better living standards and, presumably, higher profits for local companies. If the Congressman is personally successful, his constituents are happy and he gets re-elected. All this is normal and proper. What is improper—and far too often the case—is the methods by which Congressmen get the government's business into their districts. They use back-scratching: you vote for my bill, and I'll vote for yours. They use political debts. They use political pressure. And if they are powerful enough, they use self-help.

In most cases, the political skullduggery is not that obvious. Punishable crimes are committed, sometimes involving the underworld, sometimes bordering on treason, always violating the codes of ethics which both the Senate and the House have composed for themselves but have very rarely enforced. Only the greenest members of the Congress are unaware of the wheeling and dealing going on around them. And they tend to become enlightened as soon as they have a little influence. As long as they can keep their noses clean and their names out of the gossip columns, they are safe. The real crime in Washington, then, is not doing something wrong; it is getting caught.

There is a group in Washington for whom friendship is a tool of their business. They are the lobbyists. In one area, lobbying is a good thing. Across the country there are numerous special-interest groups—in business, in industry, in unions, in farm organizations, in the sciences—and often the ground rules by which these groups operate are determined by federal ligislation. When legislation affecting any of these organizations comes before a Congressional committee, the organization can and should be represented by an expert who can express its views and wishes. This is lobbying in its purest form. It is also lobbying in its rarest form. At its best, lobbying is the voice of the people, aimed directly at elected representatives. Proper lobbying helps to accomplish the following:

1. Inform the public and the Congress on various issues so that both are well aware of the facts before legislative action is taken.
2. Ventilate sore spots in legislation.
3. Stimulate public debate.
4. Forecast how a particular piece of legislation will probably work in practice.

The First Amendment to the Constitution guarantees the right of the people to petition the government for redress of grievances—which includes the right to lobby. If you have ever written a letter to your Congressman expressing your opinion on any given subject, you have lobbied. Sometimes a group of people of similar mind may decide they can get a better hearing in Washington if they hire an expert to speak for them to Congressional hearings, and this too is good and proper lobbying. It is important for a Congressman to know how his constituents feel about a specific issue; and if their feelings are strong enough, he may find the courage to stand up against his party if its policy and his constituents' feelings differ. For example, both Democrats and Republicans in the Congress finally found the courage to stand up against first a Democratic and then a Republican administration on the handling of the Vietnam War—after enough of their constituents voiced their opinion on the matter. This has never happened before in the history of the country. It shows that power can truly be the people's when they demand it.

Unfortunately, this form of lobbying is the exception rather than the rule in Washington. For the most part, Washington lobbying today is on a man-to-man basis—the lobbyist on the one hand and the Representative or the Senator or the appointed functionary on the other. The lobbyist is the only one without any responsibility to the general public. The Senate would never think of approving a Presidential appointment without a thorough investigation of that person's background. And yet the Secretary of the Senate and the Clerk of the House will register a lobbyist without the slightest check into his background or connections. Moreover, the lobbyist need not register at all these days, as long as he can operate under the protective cloak of some political bigwig, such as Nathan Voloshen and others did out of Speaker McCormack's office, as Eddie Adams did out of President Johnson's office, or as Waller Taylor is doing out of Richard Nixon's office. In some cases, it isn't really lobbying but influence peddling. The distinction is more than a matter of semantics.

Influence peddling generally occurs when some matter is too pressing to proceed through so-called normal channels. If the Congressman concerned cuts through red tape and acts on the matter, there is usually a pay-off, whatever its disguise. It may be a donation to the Congressman's campaign fund or a donation in his name to his national committee; it may also be stock in a corporation, often issued in the name of a relative. Or perhaps a relative gets a good job in the company involved; perhaps the Congressman's house gets a new paint job or a new car in the garage. Maybe his family gets an unexpected trip to Europe, or the Congressman happily finds himself booked on a lucrative speaking tour. But in one form or another, there is a pay-off.

On September 8, 1970, Mrs. Helen Delich Bentley, chairman of the Federal Maritime Commission, attended a conference in the Manhattan offices of the late Spyros Skouras, who was then board chairman of the Prudential-Grace Lines, Inc. The purpose of the meeting was to raise funds for the campaign of Republican C. Stanley Blair for the governorship of Maryland. The meeting had been suggested by Vice-President Spiro Agnew. Blair had been an aide to Agnew. No shipping executive with any sense would have turned down an appeal from her for a political contribution. Even so, Blair lost to Democrat Marvin Mandel.

What was significant about the episode was the fact that men and women in public office, including the Vice President, deliberately set out to get political contributions from a highly specialized area of business which depends greatly on the federal government for subsidies.

In 1970, the chairman of the House Committee on Merchant Marine and Fisheries was Representative Edward A. Garmatz of Maryland. Although a Democrat, Garmatz was an old crony of both Agnew and Mrs. Bentley, and he had been playing both sides of the political fence in Maryland and Washington for years. In January of that year Garmatz hired as special counsel to the committee Ralph E. Casey, completely ignoring the fact that Casey had been a registered lobbyist for the American Institute of Merchant Shipping only a year before, and had also been its executive vice president. This was like inviting the Trojan horse into your home. It certainly limited the chances of the American people for a fair shake on how their tax money is used. Not surprisingly, Congressman Garmatz turned out to be one of a number of Congressmen who had accepted illegal campaign contributions from shipping companies. In September 1970, Justice Department files showed that Garmatz had received $1,500 of the $6,000 which the American President Lines, Ltd. and the Pacific Far East Line had made in illegal campaign contributions during the previous year. Named as the recipient of $1,000 was Senator Warren G. Magnuson, Washington Democrat and chairman of the Senate Commerce Committee. The Garmatz and Magnuson committees approved subsidy programs for these companies, but the vote that actually issued the money for the two companies was taken by the House Appropriations Subcommittee, headed by John Rooney of Brooklyn. Further checks from the shippers went not only to the top four members of this committee, but also to other Congressional leaders such as House Minority Leader Gerald Ford and House Majority Leader Hale Boggs.

Over the years, I came to the conclusion that the votes of members of Congress are influenced by six different pressure groups, in the following order of importance:

1. Special-interest groups back home.
2. Executive Department persuasions—the President, the Pentagon, State Department, Agriculture, etc.
3. Washington's paid lobbyists.
4. The simple desire to remain in office.
5. Personal economic interests.
6. Dictates of their own conscience.

Ralph Nader has said that if power is to be exercised responsibly, it has to be insecure, that those exercising it have to have something to lose. To paraphrase this, fewer Congressmen would engage in crooked deals with lobbyists if they knew there were a chance the news might leak back to their constituents. Since there is little risk of exposure by their peers and cohorts, many Congressmen feel secure and act irresponsibly. Exposure, then, is essential to reform. Voters have a right to know what their Congressmen are up to. They have a right to know who visited him during the day, and for what. They have a right to know how their Congreeman voted on the hundreds of minor bills that are rushed through Congress every session in a daily atmosphere of a tobacco auction. Many of these bills are lobbyist-instigated, giving tax breaks, contracts, or a wide variety of other possible privileges to special interests. These are the bills which the Congressmen back-scratch into law. Any Congressman who has a source of income other than his salary as a Congressman would have difficulty acting as a free man when faced with legislation which might be detrimental to him personally or to the source of his income. Voters therefore have a right to know all the sources of income of their Congressman so that they can clearly determine when he has voted in favor of the public good or in favor of his own interests. There is little chance that this information will be volunteered by Congressmen, but voters have the right to demand all of it.

Another possibility, which I had suggested to Congressman Bennett during our meeting, was that members of Congress should divest themselves of *all* sources of outside income as soon as they were elected.

Bennett frowned and said: "If Congressmen could have no outside incomes, what kind of man do you think we would have in Congress? We would have men from the bottom of the ladder."

Reflecting on his words, I wondered why practically every member of Congress requires a pay-off from a lobbyist before doing what he is already being well paid to do. The Congressman will tell you that he needs money for his campaign funds, and everybody agrees that campaign costs are out of control. The Ninety-first Congress, controlled by Democrats, passed a bill limiting campaign spending, but President Nixon vetoed it. The general assumption around Washington was that since Republicans have less trouble raising money than Democrats, there was no point in giving the Democrats that kind of break. But since I already knew that my own clients had to make donations to the campaign funds of Republicans as well as Democrats, I couldn't go along with that.

But I could and do go along with Nixon's recommendation to the Ninety-second Congress that the members clean up their houses. I fear, however, that it will never be an inside job. The clean up will come only when an aroused people demand it—and before the people can make the demand they must have some idea of what has really been going on.

Here is a basis for such a clean up.

1. There should be no fund-raising by cabinet members or commission heads, so that they will not owe anyone any allegiance in return for a campaign contribution.

2. Former lobbyists, with long-time industry ties, should not be appointed, as a reward for party loyalty, to government posts controlling industries for which they have lobbied in the past.

3. Corporations and unions should not make campaign contributions. All existing loopholes should be plugged, and penalties for circumventing the law as it is rewritten should include jail penalties rather than merely a fine and censure. The giver and the receiver should be equally responsible. Ignorance should be no defense as it ludicrously is now. No one is going to contribute without letting the candidate know what he is doing. This has never happened, and it never will. The law should provide for the recall of an erring legislator and the calling of a new election.

4. In no way should campaign contributions be treated as a tax deduction.

5. The support of the rich should be limited to one party only. Campaign contributions should not be hedged, under penalty of law.

6. The backgrounds of lobbyists should be checked and their actions regulated. There should be no unregistered lobbyists in Washington.

7. Campaign contributions and expenditures should be limited.

8. Under penalty of law, no money in excess of a certain limit should be given or lent to a campaign committee. Ignorance of a contribution should not absolve the candidate. The 1925 Corrupt Practices Act, and the 1946 Legislative Reorganization Act, must be merged and rewritten completely to strengthen and give meaning to the law.

9. The electorate should be taxed from 50 cents to $1 a year for campaign expenses which would be put into a campaign kitty. There must be a campaign financing law which will help all and not just a few, the ceiling being commensurate with the office. But it must be remembered that even if the American people are eventually taxed per capita for a campaign kitty, the money that each candidate derives from this fund *must* be his only source of campaign income. To allow him to go to outside

sources for extra income for a campaign would simply be giving the wealthy and well-connected politician the upper hand, thus reopening the loopholes.

And, most importantly, no matter what campaign reform laws are enacted by the Congress for the public funding of campaigns, they must all include a provision that puts a ceiling on total campaign spending in each category. Unless these two overall limits on total campaign spending are included, the legislation enacted would have little effect on all of the existing abuses.

10. Successful candidates for Congress should, like appointed government officials, divest themselves of all outside business interests, including stockholdings and money-earning real estate.

11. Campaign contributions to any one party and any one candidate should be limited and should, under penalty of law, be strictly enforced. There should be no dodges. "Dummy" fund-raising committees for a candidate must be outlawed.

12. Free television time and advertising space should be made available to all candidates on an equal basis.

13. There should be full disclosure of all political contributions. Stringent laws must insure that all money collected or contributed for a political campaign actually goes to the campaign and does not find its way into a politician's pocket.

14. All government contracts must be made public. No provision for waivers or private funds should remain secret.

15. The decision of all waiver review boards must be made public, together with the reason for the waiver.

16. Limits on expenditures for primary campaigns should be instituted.

Nathan Voloshen was indicted, but the entire system of political influence peddling was also indictable. It was the system that spawned him. Voloshen's misfortune was that he got caught. But he was just a small example of what has been going on in Washington: he was the 1969–70 scapegoat. I would prefer to think that this was not the case. I would prefer to think that Voloshen's indictment was only the beginning of a new era of housecleaning. That is what I am sure Robert Morgenthau intended. He wasn't allowed to go as far as he wanted or planned, but it is encouraging that he was able to go as far as he did. Let us hope that the forces of political reform will continue to prevail, as they did in this case, and not end with the smug satisfaction that "right has been done." It has, but in only this one case. The death of Voloshen in the fall of 1971 should not be the end of it.

I became a lobbyist in 1964 because it seemed to me to be a natural extension of the public-relations work that I was doing in New York, and I quit lobbying in 1969.

In 1970, Jack Anderson, journalistic heir to Drew Pearson, published an account of Voloshen's Washington machinations, involving me in them. Similar accounts appeared in *Life* magazine and *The New York Times*. But, I knew that only a small part of the full story had been told; only the surface had been scratched. There was too much to tell, too much that people had a right to know about in full and candid detail. So, after long and careful thought, I decided to write this book—in the hope that it would bring about substantial changes in our electoral laws.

I still believe in this country. I still believe that the people can save it. But in order to do so they have to be made aware. The cloak of secrecy which shrouds so much of government must be lifted. "Secrecy," once noted former FTC Commissioner Philip Elman, "is the bane, not the lifeblood, of the administrative process." This element of secrecy can be eliminated. But it will not be done until the people demand it. In my opinion, the hour is getting late. It's five minutes to midnight and we don't have much time left . . .

33

Corruption: the shame of the states

James Q. Wilson

The best state legislatures, observed Lord Bryce over half a century ago, are those of the New England states, "particularly Massachusetts." Because of the "venerable traditions surrounding [this] ancient commonwealth" which "sustain the dignity" of its legislature and "induce good men to enter it," this body—called the General Court—is "according to the best authorities, substantially pure." About the time that Bryce was congratulating the representatives in the Massachusetts State House, these men were engaged in a partially successful effort to regulate the government of the city of Boston on the grounds that City Hall was becoming a cesspool of corruption owing, in no small part, to the fact that the Irish, led by Mayor John "Honey Fitz" Fitzgerald, had taken over. The chief instrument of state supervision over the suspect affairs of the city was to be the Boston Finance Commis-

Reprinted with permission of James Q. Wilson from *The Public Interest*, No. 2, Winter, 1966. Copyright © 1966 by National Affairs, Inc.

sion, appointed by the Governor to investigate any and all aspects of municipal affairs in the capital.

Now, a half century later, the tables have been, if not turned, then at least rearranged. While no one would claim that the Boston City Hall is "pure," the mayoralty of John Collins (an Irishman) has aroused the enthusiastic backing of the city's financial and commercial elite. Many leading Brahmins work closely with the mayor, support him politically, and—most importantly—stand behind him in many of his often bitter fights with the governor and the state legislature. In contrast, the legislature has been plagued with endless charges of corruption and incompetence, the most recent of which have emerged from the work of the Massachusetts Crime Commission.

This Commission, created by the (reluctant) legislature in July, 1962 and appointed by Republican Governor John Volpe (who had recommended its formation in the first place), was composed largely of the sort of men who used to be *in* the legislature rather than critics of it. In a state where the principal politicians are Irish and Italian graduates of (if anything) Boston College or the Suffolk Law School, the Commission was woven out of Ivy. The Chairman was Alfred Gardner (Harvard '18), senior partner in the austerely respectable law firm of Palmer, Dodge, Gardner and Bradford. Of the other six members, three were graduates of Harvard, two of Princeton, and another of the Harvard Law School. (Although at least one Irishman got onto the Commission, he was an investment consultant and retired brigadier general, and is probably more Yankee than the Yankees.) The American melting pot has obviously not changed the popular belief that, while the Irish are experts on politics, and the Jews experts on money, the Yankees are experts on morality.

The bad repute of Massachusetts government might seem an exaggeration to the casual reader of the recently published Comprehensive Report of the Commission. Except for a brief section on the Massachusetts Turnpike Authority, there are no juicy stories of boodle and skulduggery, nor any inciting accounts of the testimony. The legislature had taken pains to insure that it would not make the same mistake the United States Senate did when it created the Kefauver Committee. Public hearings were explicitly forbidden. All testimony was taken in secret sessions; as intrepreted by the Commission, this restriction also forbade it from publishing the name of witnesses, direct accounts of their evidence, or details of allegations. If it suspected wrongdoing, the Commission was to turn its information over to regular law-enforcement agencies. And when the life of the Commission expired this year, the legislature made certain that its files were locked away in a vault, secure against further scrutiny.

But if the report is dull, the results were not. Attorney General Edward Brooke, on the basis of information furnished by the Commission, brought indictments against fifty-three individuals and fifteen corporations. About two dozen of the individuals were (or had been) state officials, and they included the former Speaker of the House, a former governor, the public safety director, two present and two former members of the Governor's Council, the chairman of the state housing board, and several former state representatives. One can be reasonably confident that much the same results could be produced by similar commissions in many other states, particularly industrial states of the Northeast such as Pennsylvania, Ohio, and the like. Many of these states would never have been described as "pure" by Lord Bryce at any stage of their history (he singled out New York and Pennsylvania as having legislatures that were "confessedly among the worst"); about all that seems to have happened in the last fifty years is that, on the whole, their governors have become more respectable and their political parties more disorganized, thereby transforming what once was well-organized, machine-like corruption into disorganized, free-lance corruption.

Three Theories of Corruption

Why should so many state governments seem so bad? The Massachusetts Crime Commission did not try to answer that question (it said it did not know whether corruption was worse in its state than in others), nor did it address itself to the more fundamental questions, "What is corruption?" "Why does it occur?" In short, the Commission did not develop a theory of corruption. This is not simply an academic deficiency (I am not trying to grade the Commission's report as if it were a term paper in a political science seminar); rather, it is a practical problem of the greatest importance, for without a theory of corruption there cannot be a remedy for corruption unless by happy accident.

There are at least three major theories of government corruption. The first holds that there is a particular political ethos or style which attaches a relatively low value to probity and impersonal efficiency and relatively high value to favors, personal loyalty, and private gain. Lower-class immigrant voters, faced with the problems of accommodation to an unfamiliar and perhaps hostile environment, are likely to want, in the words of Martin Lomasney, "help, not justice." If such groups come—as have the Irish and the Sicilians—from a culture in which they experienced a long period of domination by foreign rulers the immigrant will already be experienced in the ways of creating an informal and illegal (and therefore "corrupt") covert government as a way of dealing with the—to them—illegitimate formal government. The values of such groups are radically incompatible with the values of (for example) old-stock Anglo-Saxon Protestant Americans, and particularly with those members of the latter culture who serve on crime commissions. Whatever the formal arrangements, the needs and values of those citizens sharing the immigrant ethos will produce irresistible demands for favoritism and thus for corruption.

The second theory is that corruption is the result of ordinary men facing extraordinary temptations. Lincoln Steffens argued that corruption was not the result of any defect in character (or, by implication, in cultural values); rather, it was the inevitable consequence of a social system which holds out to men great prizes—power, wealth, status—if only they are bold enough to seize them. Politicians are corrupt because businessmen bribe them; this, in turn, occurs because businessmen are judged solely in terms of wordly success. The form of government makes little difference; the only way to abolish corruption is to change the economic and social system which rewards it. (Steffens admired Soviet communism because it was a system without privilege: "There was none but petty political corruption in Russia," he wrote after visiting there. "The dictator was never asked to do wrong.") A less Marxist variation of this theory is more familiar: men steal when there is a lot of money lying around loose and no one is watching. Public officials are only human. They will resist minor temptation, particularly if everyone else does and someone is checking up. They are not angels, however, and cannot be expected to be honest when others are stealing (no one wants to be thought a fink) and superiors are indifferent. The Catholic Church, having known this for several centuries, counsels the young in its catechisms to "avoid the occasion of sin." The solution to this sort of corruption is, obviously, to inspect, audit, check, and double-check.

The third theory is more explicitly political and has the advantage of seeking to explain why governmental corruption appears to be more common in America than in Europe. Henry Jones Ford, writing in 1904, observed that in this country, unlike in those whose institutions follow the British or French models, the executive and legislative branches are separated by constitutional checks and balances. What the Founders have put asunder, the politicians must join together if anything is to be accomplished. Because each branch can—and sometimes does—paralyze the other, American government "is so constituted that it cannot be carried on without corruption." The boss, the machine, the political party, the bagmen—all these operate, in Ford's view, to concert the action of legally independent branches of government through the exchange of favors. The solution to corruption, if this is its cause, is to bring these various departments together formally and constitutionally. This, of course, is precisely what the National Civil League and other reform groups have attempted by their espousal of the council manager plan for municipal government, and what advocates of strong and responsible political parties have sought with respect to state and national government. If the chief executive, by virtue of either his constitutional position or his control of a disciplined majority party, is strong enough to rule without the consent of subordinates or the intervention of legislators, then no one will bribe subordinates or legislators—they will have nothing to sell. The leader himself will rarely be bribed, because his power will be sufficiently great that few, if any, groups can afford his price. (This is how Ford explained the lesser incidence of corruption in American national government: the president is strong enough to get his way and visible enough to make bribe-taking too hazardous.)

Crime commissions and reform groups in this country have at one time or another adopted all these theories, but at least one has now become unfashionable. Fifty years ago the Brahmins were quite candid about the defects they found in the Boston Irish politicians. These "newer races," as James Michael Curley called them, were considered to be the carriers of corruption. In 1965, the Massachusetts Crime Commission—perhaps out of politeness as much as conviction—begins its report by finding "no basis for saying the corruption in Massachusetts is the peculiar attribute of any one party or racial or religious group." This commendable tolerance is perhaps a bit premature: it is at least arguable that the various ethnic groups which make up our big cities and industrial states differ with respect to their conceptions of the public interest as much as they continue to differ with respect to style of life, party affiliation, and place of residence. The structure of government in many states of the Northeast is quite similar to that found in the Far West, yet the incidence of corruption appears to be significantly greater in the East. The historical reasons for this may include the differing values of the populations involved. While one can understand the reasons a public body might wish to avoid commenting on this, the result is that one theory of corruption is discarded *a priori* and all reforms are based on the other theories.

What Happened to the Cities?

The curious fact about all theories of corruption, however, is that they could apply equally to American cities as to American states, and yet it is the states (and to a considerable extent the counties) rather than the cities which are notorious for corruption. Although some corruption probably is to be found in almost all cities, and a great deal in a few, the most important fact about American municipal government over the last twenty years has been the dramatic improvement in the standards and honesty of public service. In no large city today is it likely that a known thief could be elected mayor (how many unknown thieves are elected must be a matter of speculation); a few decades ago, it would have been surprising if the mayor were *not* a boodler.

The reasons for this change are thought to be well-known—the reduction in the demand for and tolerance of corruption, owing to the massive entry of voters into the middle class; the nationalization and bureaucratization of welfare programs that once were the province of the machine; the greater scrutiny of local affairs by the press and civil associations; and the rise of forms of government—the council-manager plan and nonpartisanship—which make party domination difficult.

But if these changes in American society have had profound consequences for city politics, why did they appear to have so little effect on state politics? To be sure, known thieves are probably not often elected governor, but few people outside the states of the Far West are under much illusion as to the standards of public morality which prevail in and around state legislatures and cabinets.

There are at least two reasons for the difference. The first is that the degree of public scrutiny of government is not the same at the state as at the city level. Big cities have big newspapers, big civil associations, and big blocs of newspaper-reading, civic-minded voters. State capitals, by contrast, are usually located outside the major metropolitan centers of the state in smaller cities with small-city newspapers, few (and weak) civic associations, and relatively few attentive citizens with high and vocal standards of public morality. The cosmopolitan, in Robert Merton's language, seeks to escape the small city and get to the big city; the locals who remain behind typically place a higher value on personal friendships and good fellowship than on insisting that government be subject to general and impersonal rules. (The Massachusetts state capitol is an obvious and embarrassing exception: it is located in Boston but seems unaffected by that fact. Perhaps this is because Boston newspapers are so poor and its civic life is so weakly organized.)

The other reason is that anyone interested in obtaining favors from government finds the stakes considerably higher at the state level. With the exception of urban renewal and public housing programs, the city government administers services rather than makes investments. These services are often controversial but the controversy is more about who is to manage them, how they are to be financed, and whether they are fairly and adequately administered. Education, public welfare, street cleaning, and police protection are important services but (with the exception of police tolerance of gambling) they are not likely to make many people very rich. States, on the other hand, disburse or regulate big money. They build roads and in so doing spend billions on contractors, land owners, engineers, and "consultants." They regulate truckers, public utilities, insurance companies, banks, small loan firms, and pawnbrokers; they issue paroles and pardons, license drivers, doctors, dentists, liquor stores, barbers, beauticians, teachers, chiropractors, real estate brokers, and scores of other occupations and professions; they control access to natural resources, and supervise industrial safety and workmen's compensation programs. The stakes are enormous.

At one time, the stakes in city politics were also high. In the late nineteenth and early twentieth centuries, big cities were making their major capital improvements—in the form of subways, traction lines, utility systems—and the value of the contracts and franchises was huge. Local government was formally weak—it had been made so deliberately, in order to insure that it would be "democratic"—and thus it was possible (indeed, almost necessary) for a boss or a machine to control it in order to exchange privileges for boodle.

Prohibition, and later organized gambling, extended the rewards of municipal corruption beyond the time when rapid capital formation was at an end. Organized crime remains a legacy of Prohibition which is still very much with us, but on different terms. There are no longer any Al Capones. The gamblers continue to corrupt the police but, except in the smaller towns—Cicero and Calumet City near Chicago, Newport and Covington near Cincinnati—they rarely manage (or even try) to take over the entire political structure of a city. And even these famous "sin towns" are rapidly being closed down. By the time urban renewal came along—a program of capital improvements potentially ripe for corruption—the coalitions of businessmen and mayors which governed most big cities and which were most interested in renewal as a "progressive" program to "save the city" were not inclined to allow the success of the program to be threatened by stealing. More importantly, urban renewal is far smaller in scale than the highway program; the opportunities for "windfall profits" are not vast; the program is surrounded by sufficient public controversy to make it very difficult to transact many deals under the table; and the federal government supervises local renewal much more closely than it supervises highway construction.

Unreconstructed State Government

Ironically, the very things which made matters better in the big cities may have made them worse in the states. The preoccupation with urban affairs and the attendant close scrutiny of the conduct of those affairs has diverted public attention from state affairs. If it was true that state capitols were ignored in the past, it is doubly true today. The civil-minded businessman wants to save the central city; the liberal cosmopolitan wants to improve urban race relations and end urban poverty; the federal government, especially the White House, seeks closer and closer ties with the big cities—in part because that is where the voters are and in part because federal officials are increasingly desirous of establishing direct relations with their city counterparts in order to bypass what they often consider to be the obstructionism of the state bureaucracy.

The various governmental innovations—at-large elections, nonpartisanship, the council-manager form—which have made entry into municipal politics attractive to, and possible for, the non-party civic "statesman" have meant that increasingly the more traditional politician has felt uncomfortable in and disadvantaged by city politics. Elections for state office, which continue to be conducted under party labels in relatively small districts, are a more familiar and congenial experience. Success here can still come to the man with strong neithborhood ties, clubhouse connections, a proven record of party loyalty, and a flair for tuning the car of his ethnic compatriots to the ancestral voices.

In short, if government is more corrupt in the states than in the cities, it is because all three theories of corruption (and perhaps others) apply with greater force to the states. The ethnic style of politics is weakening in the cities but not in the states; more boodle is lying around with no one watching in state capitols than in city halls; and state governments continue to be badly decentralized, with formal authority divided among a host of semi-autonomous boards, commissions, and departments. The states have rarely been subjected to the kinds of reforms which over the years have gradually centralized formal authority in the hands of a professional city manager or a single strong mayor.

The last point deserves emphasis. Governors are not "little Presidents." Their power of appointment and removal is sharply circumscribed. Duane Lockard estimates that only slightly more than half the 730 major administrative posts in state government are filled by gubernatorial appointments; the remainder are filled by election or by appointments made by the legislature or special boards and commissions. Nor does the governor generally have the full power of removal normally assumed to be the prerogative of the President. Only five governors can appoint their own superintendents of education; only half can choose their own men to run state departments of agriculture. Of equal or greater importance is the typical governor's weak position within the party and the interest groups which elect him. A governor who is the principal leader of his party and who has in addition a strong and popular personality may do well with little formal authority; lacking these, all the formal executive authority in the world may not suffice, if for no other reason than that the governor must still deal with an independent legislature.

The Massachusetts Crime Commission was not unaware of such problems but—perhaps because it was a crime commission rather than an "effective government" commission—it did not really come to grips with these issues. It was preoccupied with corruption that, in its view, could be attributed largely to the "occasion of sin" theory of wrongdoing. Dealing with such forms of larceny is relatively easy: employ well-qualified administrators selected on their merits to implement high professional standards. This, supplemented by careful inspection and audit procedures, will reduce or eliminate corruption in the letting of contracts, hiring of consultants, issuance of licenses, and regulation of conduct by such agencies as the Registry of Motor Vehicles, the Department of Public Works, the Massachusetts Turnpike Authority, and the Department of Banking and Insurance.

Recognizing that bookkeeper reforms alone are insufficient because they provide no ultimate checks on the behavior of the bookkeepers, the Commission sought to give elective officials clear authority over the behavior of their subordinates and clear responsibility to the electorate. Thus, many of the Commission's recommendations are designed to strengthen the formal powers of the chief executive—the governor and his principal subordinates—so that someone has the power and responsibility for weeding out corrupt underlings. The Commission follows a well-marked tradition: reformers, at least during this century, have favored strong executive authority. In this, of course, they have sometimes undone themselves: reformers correctly believe that a strong executive is less likely to tolerate or encourage corruption than a weak one, but they often forget that in the United States a strong executive is also likely to pay close attention to the demands of the masses. Legislatures, though more likely to be corrupt, are also more likely to be conservative. Reformers often secure cleanliness at the price of conservatism.

But because no attention is paid to the third cause of corruption—the need to exchange favors to overcome decentralized authority—the sort of executive-strengthening recommended by the Massachusetts Commission, while admirably suited to eliminating the occasion of sin, is not so well suited to dealing with legislatures or other independent bodies. The governor must not only be strong in his own house, but in the legislature's house and the party's house as well. Otherwise, the executive branch may be pure, but only out of impotence.

The Uses of Patronage

Unless we are willing to adopt a parliamentary form of state government (and I take it we are not), then the way in which a governor can get important things done (at least in a state like Massachusetts) is by having·something to bargain with that both the legislature and the party value. There are several such resources: for one, his own popularity with the voters; and for another, favors and patronage. The latter the Commission rejects and, I suspect, ill-advisedly. Certainly, patronage abuses should be curtailed (in large part because, as the Commission notes, such abuses lower the morale of public employees). Furthermore, the cumbersome Massachusetts civil service system in its present form probably serves the interests of neither the reformers nor the politicians. (For example, the legislature frequently passes statutes "freezing" certain employees into their jobs. This not only protects some incompetents, it also makes it impossible for the governor to use these positions for patronage purposes of his own.) But I believe that patronage itself should not be eliminated entirely.

The Commission was of course aware of the fact that patronage is often used to induce legally independent officials to act toward some desirable goal. The Massachusetts Turnpike Authority under the leadership of the late William Callahan raised to a fine art the use of jobs, contracts, and insurance premiums for political purposes—but the Massachusetts Turnpike got built, and on time. The Commission faces the issue squarely:

The methods [the chairman of the Authority] used to get results have had no small part in bringing about the deterioration in the moral climate of our state government. This deterioration in moral climate is of far greater importance to every man, woman and child in Massachusetts than the ease and comfort with which it is now possible to drive the length of the state on a multi-lane highway.

Perhaps. I suspect, however, that this is a question on which the people of Massachusetts might have some differences of opinion. It may well be that a deterioration in the moral climate of government and a concomitant weakening of the respect in which citizens hold their government are serious costs of corruption. But these costs, like all others, are matters of degree; hopefully, ways can be found to reduce them without a more than equivalent reduction in benefits.

What is clear is that the strengthening of the governor cannot be achieved by formal means alone, particularly if Massachusetts, like most states, needs two strong and highly competitive political parites.

If the Commission goes too far in some directions, it does not go far enough in others. The most serious cause of the corruption of law enforcement officials is organized crime; recognizing this, the Commission calls only for stronger laws, stiffer penalties, and a "reorganized" state police. "Bookmakers are not entitled to lenience." But raising the penalties against betting will not necessarily eliminate organized crime; it may only raise the price. Because more will be at stake, the police and the politicians are likely to demand bigger bribes and the criminals will be more disposed to use violence to protect their monopoly profits. At a time when the mayor of New York City is advocating offtrack betting, it would seem that some attention might be given in Massachusetts to lowering, rather than increasing, the incentives gamblers have to corrupt the government. (To be sure, in some states and cities vigorous police action has reduced gambling to a bare minimum, but these are states—like California—with very different histories and populations; unless one is prepared to reject entirely the "ethos" theory of corruption, one should not be too quick to conclude that equally good results can be obtained in any state.)

With respect to campaign contributions, the Commission confesses the limitations of its recommendations, which by and large follow a familiar pattern: better reporting systems, the removal of unrealistic and unenforceable limits on dollar amounts, and so forth. Such methods are not likely to deter the favor-seeking contributor, though they are likely to deter perfectly respectable contributors who feel that reports, inspections, and publicity involve too much trouble and possible embarrassment to justify giving anything at all. The Commission "leaves to others" a study of fundamental changes in methods of campaign finance. Unfortunately, calls for "more research" are likely to go unheeded.

It is, of course, easy to criticize crime commissions and to adopt a faintly patronizing tone toward reformers. This would be a mistake. The Commission has turned a number of highly placed rascals over to the attorney general and the courts; and other, lesser rascals are likely to take heed—for the moment.

But it would also be a mistake to make corruption (defined so broadly as to include "good" as well as "bad" patronage) the central issue. The central issue is that many states—Massachusetts is one—are badly governed in the sense that certain goals that should be sought are not, and others that should not be, are. The central problem is the problem of power—how can it be used responsibly but effectively for socially desirable ends? Power is hard to find and harder to use wisely, in great part because in many states we are destroying its informal bases (favors, patronage, party discipline) faster than we are building up its formal bases (legal authority). The result increasingly is that, with the states unable to act, they are being bypassed by cities (where the most visible problems are to be found) seeking the assistance of the federal government (where the power is). To the extent that recommendations of the Massachusetts Crime Commission and its counterparts elsewhere can strengthen the legal capacity of a state to govern, they will have been worthwhile. To the extent they are used only for piecemeal attacks on the more titillating and exotic forms of public corruption, they may do more harm than good.

34

A sociological theory of official deviance and public concerns with official deviance

Jack D. Douglas

Anyone who has followed trends in the major Western societies in recent years knows that there has been a great upsurge in public concern, and even anger, over official deviance, both material corruption and usurpation of power. Although some such concerns are found in most societies at all times, there is little doubt that there has been a recent upswing. Because public outcry seems to be on the rise, we are probably in for a long period of growing revelations of corruption, followed by denunciations and punishments, and consequent social reforms to deal with official deviance of every kind.

Americans are the most concerned and angry people of all. The outpourings of anger and the calls for basic reform have been so great since the Pandora's Box of Watergate was opened in 1973, that Europeans have voiced concern over the stability of American society and, thus, over the whole future of the Western world. They probably overestimate the concern of the average American because they are using printed and broadcast news as the source of their information, without knowing that American journalists have an even greater tendency to focus on government deviance than their European counterparts, who themselves focus on such evils more than the average citizen does. Nevertheless, concern and anger are evident among all but those people who, as true believers in Richard Nixon and others in his camp, try to deny their wrongdoings.

Italians are also deeply concerned and angry about pervasive government deviance, especially the multifarious forms of material corruption—bribery, kickbacks, payoffs, rake-offs, etc. (Italians do not seem much concerned with usurpations of power, probably because the government's problem is one of weakness, rather than excessive power. Still, there is growing resentment and revolt against taxation, both in its direct forms, and in the more important indirect form of inflation, which is produced by printing money. We shall return to this later.) Government corruption has been a major issue in all recent Italian elections and a major reason for the protest vote for the Communist and Socialist parties.

The British have been famous for the honesty and benignity of their public service ever since they instituted sweeping reforms in the early nineteenth century to end what had been rampant corruption. (For a fine overview of this, see Gwyn, in Heidenheimer, 1970; and Venkatappiah, 1965.) But the British too have become concerned about corruption in high places and the usurpation of power. Even the Bank of England, long a hallowed institution, has been rocked by scandal over revelations that some of its highest officials have been falsifying bank records in order to allow businessmen to "recover" large sums (required for foreign currency transactions) they had never really deposited. Angry statements against politicians are common on the streets and in the households and pubs of Great Britain. As one store worker put it disgustedly, "The bloody politicians! You can't trust anything they say these days."

It is probably most remarkable that attacks on government have increased sharply in the highly homogeneous and heretofore very stable Scandinavian countries. All their governments are now minority governments, even in Sweden, where the Social Democrats had held firm majorities for decades. Sweden's government has been the target of attack by major public figures for "tyranny," and even "fascist tyranny", including one by its most famous citizen, film maker Ingmar Bergman.

Most citizens, and certainly those who so adamantly denounce the "crooks" and "tyrants," explain this great surge in public outcry over political corruption and seizure of power in moralistic terms of the "growing villainy" of officials. They believe it is the officials who have changed and that they have changed individually to become more immoral and, therefore, commit more evil deeds. But, as sociologists and other social scientists have been arguing since the nineteenth century, such a general, perhaps almost universal, outcry over government corruption is part of a highly patterned set of events which cannot be explained by such isolated individual factors alone. There must be some pattern of events to correspond to the patterned reactions of individuals throughout the Western world. Various social thinkers, recognizing the validity of this idea, have argued that there are cases of society's encouraging increases in government corruption.

The most popular, certainly in the United States, has been the puritanical argument: people have lost their traditional religions, thus their consciences, and have become more corrupt in every way. (A closely related concept is that of the decline of the family. Proponents of this theory generally see the decline of traditional religion as the cause of the decline of the family, and this as the direct cause of a general increase in deviance. The two theories suffer from the same weaknesses.) This was one of the most popular explanations of the supposed wave of suicides in nineteenth-century Europe. Masaryk's work is probably the best example of it. Durkheim accepted this idea but generalized it to argue that a general decrease in social integration leads to immoral actions. The decline in religious affiliation is only one part of decreased social integration. The problem with this theory is apparent to anyone familiar with the international history of political corruption.

By modern standards, as well as by the different standards of the day, the British government was highly corrupt in 1800 and is almost puritanical today, in spite of recent revelations. (Chapters 5 and 10 describe the close similarities between the kinds of political machine payoffs in the heyday of boss politics, and modern political payoffs (which are on a much larger scale, both absolutely and proportionately) of welfare state political machines. Still, no one who knows the history of politics in the Gilded Age can believe that politics today is as corrupt as it was then, by their standards or ours. (Political scientists, historians, and journalists who have been involved in these studies have no doubts at all about this. (See, for example, Banfield and Wilson, 1967; Goodman, 1963; and Wilson, Chapter 3.) In fact, religious affiliations, especially the formal ones that so concerned Durkheim and others, have continued to decline over many decades, while, in general, official corruption, decreased at the same time and has only sharply increased in recent years, despite the fact that most high-level officials are really quite secular, and even hedonistic.

Another popular idea is that the foundation of the society causing this presumed increase in corruption is the capitalist mode of production, which supposedly leads to a corruption of human relations. This argument suffers from the same problems as the religious theory. Capitalism, by any criterion, has been declining at the same time as corruption is supposedly increasing. If one believed that corruption were really increasing, it would be reasonable to turn the argument around, and claim that decreasing capitalism causes increasing corruption. Recognizing this, some of the more sophisticated proponents of this idea argue that it is the increase of corporate capitalism that supports the charge of increased political corruption. That there has been an increase in corporatism, or centralized production, is just as obvious as that there has been a decrease in capitalism, so this idea has some merit. Its supporters press their advantage by arguing that recent revelations of multinational bribes of government officials is a major source of corruption.

But there are two overwhelming defects in this idea. First, it is the underdeveloped, capital-starved, highly *un*corporate societies that are the most corrupt. And corporatism has continued to increase in Western societies (largely because of government action), while corruption clearly did decrease for about a century and now appears to be resurging. Second, and more important, only true believers in Communism deny that the Eastern European societies have pervasive official corruption, especially in the form of bribery to secure scarce products that are underpriced by government-set price ceilings. (In other words, a huge black market results from officially setting prices below their demand prices.) Official Soviet publications print many stories about the terrible punishments meted out for all these forms of corruption but they continue nevertheless.

There are many other such popular ideas. One that has some appeal is the "growing greed" theory, or the theory of the revolution of rising expectations. It is obvious that the world is greedier today than it was a while ago—or at least, people are acting more greedily today. But that theory and the others fall victim to the same kind of factual analyses we have been making. One cannot explain long-run trends toward less corruption in Western societies by appealing to long-run trends in other social practices which are supposed to increase corruption; and one cannot explain a long-run trend to a decline in corruption, followed by a surge, by long-run trends in social forms that have not shown corresponding increases.

Before attempting to explain the diverse phenomena called political corruption, we must be very specific about what we are attempting to explain. As Robert Brooks pointed out in 1910, such terms as "political corruption" are wildly bandied about whenever major charges and countercharges are made. Corruption and usurpations of power, the two most important kinds of official deviance, come in very diverse forms, both around the world and within one society. They have different denotative and connotative meanings; and they are used freely in political rhetoric, especially in the United States, where officials have almost no legal recourse to stop the charges. Although I have no intention here of going into the vast array of technicalities involved in such definitions (see Heidenheimer, 1970; and Chapter 2, for a partial consideration), it is important to note the clear distinctions being made in each context. When we talk about public concerns, we must not think we are talking about the real phenomena of corruption and usurpations of power. And we must always keep in mind the fact that, in our pluralistic society, the concerns of one major group are often taken complacently by others.

The facts we are mainly concerned with explaining are the long-run developments, or trends, both in real acts of corruption and usurpations and in public concerns. It is important to remember this, because there are obviously short-run perturbations which should not be confused with trends. This is especially true of public concern. Public concerns, as Walter Lippmann argued so well many years ago (see Chapter 28), are very volatile in all matters concerning corruption and usurpations. One "sex and payroll" scandal, such as the Wayne Hays and Elizabeth Ray brouhaha of 1976, can unleash massive public concern, especially news-mediated concern. Many variables go into making these sharp perturbations. These include such extraneous matters as the public love of scandal (especially a sex scandal); the standard operations of the news media which focus on scandals as a way of selling news; and the private, graft-inspired, public relations work of some of the people involved (such as Elizabeth Ray's book on the affair two weeks after she made her first charges). These things do not much concern us here. But we must bear in mind that a significant part of the public tumult over the Watergate syndrome is a short-run perturbation. It is especially important to note that the Watergate concerns are, partly, short-run effects of all the massive exposures that were unleashed one after the other, because the reaction to the original events led to more investigations, more interbureaucratic fights and political rhetoric, which led in turn to further revelations, often about things that had been standard practice for many years. I have tried to weigh such factors in my analysis, but it would take a lengthy book to show how the complex guesstimating was done.

Briefly, I think the major phenomena that need to be explained are the following. Western governments were generally very corrupt and irresponsive to public rights until some time in the nineteenth or early twentieth century. The nineteenth century was, for many reasons not explored here, the great century of liberal-conservative democracy in most Western nations, especially in the United States. The complex, oppressive, and irresponsible bureaucracies of monarchical government were progressively supplanted by the individual freedoms of libertarian democracy, based on the theories of Adam Smith and John Stuart Mill. They led to progressively greater freedom in both economic and noneconomic behavior. Everywhere, though at different paces and in different ways, government regulations shrank; governments became internally weaker; and officials were placed increasingly under public control. This was primarily a middle-class democratic revolution. Middle-class values began to be applied to government and, under these middle-class standards, government became less corrupt. The public's concern with corruption and usurpation waxed and waned in the short run, but was fairly intense until the early twentieth century, when the first great Age of Reform began to wane. With the exception of short-run events, such as the Palmer raids, and the Teapot Dome scandal, there was little corruption or usurpation, and so, little public concern.

But around the 1930s (earlier in some nations), largely as a response to the Great Depression, Western nations entered what I call the Welfare

State Revolution. The basic idea of this widespread and silent revolution was to diminish the economic freedoms of individuals in order to enhance other freedoms. Regardless of intent, the Welfare State Revolution necessarily led to vastly increased government bureaucracies, recreating the Big Government that had been proportionately dismantled by the earlier democratic revolutions; vastly increased government powers; and vastly increased government regulations. At some point in the 1960s, this vast increase in government led to an acceleration in all the ancient forms—and many new ones—of official corruption and usurpation of power. But public concern, and, consequently, exposure of deviance, languished. Part of the reason for this lapse of public concern was simply the long period of low official deviance, a period when a tiny slush fund or a vicuna coat could become a national scandal. But an important part of the public's lack of interest was due to the changing forms of corruption and usurpation. As I have argued in my essays on the parallels between Boss Tweed's corrupt vote-buying by direct payment and John Lindsay's vote-buying by welfare state measures which make indirect payments to voters, there are often remarkable similarities which are obscured for the general public by the sheer complexities of their operations. The average citizen does not understand the accounting aspects of accrued deficits in pension funds well enough to spot a payoff of huge proportions ($6 billion or more in deficits in New York City, and $4 trillion in deficits for Social Security benefits promised by Congress and the President). He certainly does not have the sophisticated economic knowledge essential for understanding all the concealed taxation of massive proportions that is going on intentionally at all levels of government. Such taxation is engineered by using inflation as an indirect tax on the middle class and by naming such programs as unemployment and Social Security and "insurance" programs (when they had been designed as direct pay-out and even deficit-financed programs); and by allowing real tax rates to soar because of inflated tax brackets and property assessments, even as politicians proclaimed tax cuts to buy more votes. But when the average citizen takes in what the experts tell him, he begins to get suspicious and look behind the scenes. And discovery of minor infractions eventually leads to the exposure of massive, pervasive forms of corruption.

There is a final and crucial part to this argument. In the sections that follow, I shall be arguing that, since the 1960s in the United States, and earlier for most other Western nations, there has been an acceleration of public interest in official deviance that goes beyond short-run concerns. There seems to be growing and pervasive suspicion, distrust, alienation, and even revolt against the Big Governments spawned by the Welfare State Revolution. Much of the succeeding argument is intended to explain this reaction. There is no doubt that inferring this phenomenon from the vast and myriad phenomena we can observe, and some of which we can only guess at, is highly problematic. It is certainly possible that we are observing only short-run perturbations. But these reactions seem to me to be too universal and too prolonged in our welfare states to be short-run perturbations. I believe they are more basic than that, and that it is vital that we understand them and deal with them, for they appear to have dire implications for democratic forms of government.

I believe official deviance and the reactions to it can be explained best in terms of two major factors, one long-term and one shorter-term. The crucial point of both factors is not that there is something out there—something in the social structure or in the souls of politicians—that has been producing basic change, although such things do exist. What has changed more than anything is our standards about corruption and our relationships with government officials.

Political scientists have known for a long time that there is a trend toward "middle-classification" of our lives, especially in our ideas about government. (See the argument by James Q. Wilson in Chapter 3.) This social trend has gone by different names, but "reform politics" is probably the most common. It started in Great Britain in about 1800 and led to the establishment of the modern British civil service. It became dominant in the United States during the latter part of the nineteenth century, but was already apparent in the reform forces that swept Boss Tweed out of office and into prison in 1873. It has been growing ever since, and has eliminated the traditional forms of political machine corruption in every major American city, including Chicago (which still has a modified form of the traditional machine, but a relatively clean one). (See Banfield, 1961.)

Partly as a result of this middle-classification, which is most apparent in the greatly improved education of the population and in its changed life styles, and perhaps also because of changes in the political values of middle-class groups, we have become more rigorous in our standards of government action. We have enforced these standards in everything from civil service regulations to procedures for forcing a presidential resignation. Officials have, at least until recently, become less corrupt at all levels of government, *but not enough to keep up with our escalating standards*. While this trend has been going on for a century or two (varying among nations), it accelerated rapidly only in the postwar period. This was when mass education and middle-class styles of life became dominant with the growth of mass prosperity and the development of massive welfare state programs in every Western nation except for Switzerland. The middle-classification of standards of government developed over the long run in the same direction as growing concern about corruption and decreases in the real rates of it, as judged by any available data. It has emerged at precisely the same time as concern with corruption, and it has direct links with such concerns. Ideas of good government are a basic part of mass education everywhere, and all social movements toward government reform are centered in schools and universities. We have, then, three direct links between changes in our middle-class education and ways of life: ideas and values about government, our labeling of government actions as corrupt, and real official actions.

But there is a second major social change that has developed in the same way as these and which largely underlies them, at least in the postwar period. I have already mentioned that the postwar period, which saw the middle-classification of our societies, was the period of the Welfare State Revolution. In virtually every major Western society, governments have grown massively in the past thirty or forty years. They were already growing in proportion to the private sectors of society before the war, but the Great Depression and war years saw the beginning of a massive acceleration. (There have been great variations among nations. Germany started its welfare state reforms in the late nineteenth century, surged into socialism after the First World War, plunged into National Socialism in 1933, reversed direction after the war, but has been increasing its welfare state programs in recent years. The United States did not begin its Welfare State Revolution until the 1930s and has surged into it only since the early 1960s. In about thirty years, Western governments have increased their control of national wealth (gross national product by 400% or more; and have increased their regulations and enforced plans far more (but not always in countable ways). Transfer payments by government have increased 1,000% or more. In most nations government at all levels now controls 50% or more of the gross national product. This is not yet true of the United States because of its late start, but already, government spends 40% of the gross national product.

The surge toward the welfare state has been one of the biggest silent revolutions in human history. It is the massive size of the revolution that concerns us here, regardless of whether we support or oppose it. The simple fact is that everywhere in the major Western nations (except for Switzerland), government is now far larger than it was thirty years ago. The number of government employees has increased about 1000% in most countries. In the United States, the number of public employees tripled in about a decade. Both absolutely and proportionately, there have been far more officials to commit deviant actions. Even if there had been a real *decrease* in the rates of deviance by these officials, there might still be an increase in the proportion of deviance committed by officials, rather than by individuals in private life. If there were no change at all in the rate of corruption by government officials or in the rates of deviance in the private sector, we would expect that, as government increased its control over the economy by 400%, the government's proportion of the total deviance in the society would increase by 400%. Such a development would itself be sufficient to give the average citizen the impression that there was a veritable plague of government corruption. In societies such as Great Britain and Italy, where government controls up to 60% of the gross national product, and where percentages of government employment have increased at higher proportional rates, the increase in government deviance could easily appear to be a bubonic plague of corruption.

Seen in this perspective, the striking fact is, not that there is so much corruption of government officials, but that there is so little. As governments have "govermentalized" economies, both directly, through the nationaliza- tion of industry, and indirectly through taxation, one would expect them to governmentalize deviance. This has happened, but surely not by 400% or more. The reason is, of course, that we have so greatly raised our standards, both individually and generally by middle-classification, and enforced them on government that there has been a real decline in the rate of government corruption, although perhaps not in usurpation of power. This tends to offset the governmentalization of deviance.

But, of course, this offsetting is only partial. The public's subjective per- ception of the government as more deviant than ever has been strong and has helped to produce a sense of alienation, social fragmentation, and even revolt against the system. *The primary reason why the public is so outraged is precisely because we do have higher standards for government officials. Each act of deviance which has been transferred from the private sphere to the government by the Welfare State Revolution has increased our degree of moral outrage over that one deviant act.* The result is that our overall sense of moral outrage, or of alienation and revolt, increases by the very fact of shifting deviance from the private to the public sphere.

There is, of course, the popular idea that an act of deviance by a govern- ment official is worse than one by a private individual, because government officials have more power. This is the justification frequently given for the forty-year prison sentence (since slightly decreased) received by the chief Watergate conspirator, G. Gordon Liddy, for the minor offense of an attempted burglary. (This conviction would almost certainly have led to a suspended sentence or probation had he been a petty thief.) Yet this thinking is patently absurd. To bug the Democratic candidate is no more dangerous than to bug any other citizen, unless you assume that a politician's privacy is more inherently valuable than that of the rest of us. The argument is based on an implicit premise that political deviance is potentially more dangerous because it could become widespread. Yet, this too is nonsense. Any large group that indulges in such crimes, whether it be a Mafia family, or a city police force, or a presidential administration, is dangerous, by legal definition, only to the extent that it has actually carried them out. To convict someone on the basis of abstractly defined potential for crime is as serious a violation of the rule of law in Western societies as anyone could commit. The only way in which the heavy sentences of the officials in this and other cases makes sense is in terms of the public's moral outrage or sense of threat. We come back to the fact that, if Liddy had committed the same crime in a private capacity, it would have been almost overlooked. To commit it in the public realm, however, causes immense outrage and a profound sense of alienation from government.

The conclusion is now clear and important. Governmentalizing deviance, or transferring it from the private to the public realm *has a multiplier effect on the sense of moral outrage and the sense of threat.* That is, each additional bit of perceived official deviance multiplies the public's outraged response. The governmentalization of deviance thus tends to greatly raise the level of moral outrage over deviance and the feeling of being threatened by it, even when it decreases the real incidence of deviance.

So far I have been arguing that governmentalizing deviance does result in real decreases in its incidence. But I have specifially referred only to *illegal corruption.* More specifically, I believe that instances of *legally definable* theft, fraud, bribery, and any other activities that result in *illegal* exchanges of material goods have decreased for many years. But three forms of official deviance have obviously increased in recent years as the Welfare State Revolutions have been carried out. These have combined with the governmentalization of deviance multiplier effect to create more fragmentation, alienation, and revolt.

The greatly broadened scope of government has led to a vast increase in what George Washington Plunkitt (Riordan, 1963) would have called "honest graft," or official corruption that is not clearly illegal, but is a violation of what major segments of the public believe to be right. Social scientists have long recognized that individuals must carry out practical activities based on the concrete realities of the situation. Even functionalists have recognized that there would inevitably be a gap between the prescriptions of abstract rules (such as "thou shalt not take bribes or show favor") and the practical action required. They also realized that, in any society, there are inevitable conflicts between rules. For example, every Congressman has a duty *to help one's specific constituents, but one also has a duty to place the public interest of the nation before them.* Anyone who thinks that does not produce great conflict in concrete situations is living in Cloudopolis. The functionalists thus argue that there must inevitably be "institutional slippage," or allowable forms of deviance from some rules, if practical action is ever to be taken. In recent years, sociologists have produced massive evidence that in our world of complex rules and realities, rapidly changing rules and realities, and conflicting rules and realities, some bending of rules occurs. Add to this the relatively slow and ponderous lawmaking process, and the rapidly changing and conflicting political demands from an increasingly fragmented and multiple-polarized society, and inevitably, the amount of institutional slippage eclipses the amount of conscious application of rules. Otherwise, social legislation never gets enacted because the lawmakers spend all their time arguing about which rules take precedence. As government regulations increase, the world becomes more morally complex, even in the private realm. Consequently, even private groups have to become more deviant, if not illegal, to achieve practical goals. When functions are transferred, directly or indirectly, to government bureaucracies, this complexity is maximized. The result is a situational interpretation of rules, many of which will be seen as deviant, or worse, by those on the outside. Most common, rule entrepreneurs appear whose function is to expedite the unraveling of governmental, bureaucratic, and regulatory red tape. There is also greater interlocking of government officials with the private individuals whom they are supposed to be regulating. The overall effect is the now-familiar outcry from reformers that the regulators are selling out to those whom they are supposed to regulate. The multiplier effect is in full force, so we have an epidemic of moral outrage and sense of threat over "honest graft"—official deviance that cannot be shown to be illegal.

The second way in which the Welfare State Revolution has produced an upsurgence in official deviance in recent years is obvious, but is almost universally obscured by the failure of people to see the simplest relationship between rules and violations. In 1910, Robert C. Brooks argued, in *Corruption in American Politics and Life*, that the more rules we have for political life, the more corruption we may have, simply because there can be no corruption without rules: Political *duty* must exist or there is no possibility of being corruptly unfaithful to it. This statement may seem a truism, but the logical consequences to be drawn from it are of major importance. Among other things it follows that the more widely political duties are diffused the more widespread are the possibilities of corruption. A government which does not rest upon popular suffrage may be a very bad sort of government in many ways, but it will not suffer from vote-buying. To carry this thought out fully let us assume an absolute despotism in which the arbitrary will of the ruler is the sole source of power.* In such a case it is manifestly impossible to speak of corruption. By hypothesis the despot owes no duty to the state or to his subjects. Philosophers who defend absolute government naturally lay great stress on the monarch's duty to God, but this argument may be read out of court on the basis of Mencius's dictum that Heaven is merely a silent partner in the state. The case is not materially altered when responsibility under natural law is insisted upon instead of to the Deity. Now since an absolute despot is bound to no tangible duty, he cannot be corrupt in any way. If in the conduct of his government he takes account of nothing but the grossest of his physical lusts he is nevertheless not unfaithful to the principles on which that government rests. Viewed from a higher conception of the state his rule may be unspeakably bad, but the accusation of corruption does not and cannot hold against it.

Conversely corruption necessarily finds its richest field in highly organised

---

*Mr. Seeley has shown, of course, that no actual despotism, so-called, really conforms to this conception, but for purposes of argument, at least, the assumption may be permitted to stand.

political communities which have developed most fully the idea of duty and which have intrusted its performance to the largest number of officials and citizens. The modern movement toward democracy and responsible government, beneficent as its results in general have been, has unquestionably opened up greater opportunities for evil of this sort than were ever dreamed of in the ancient and mediaeval world. This same point was later made more systematically by Howard Becker (1963) in his labeling theory of deviance: Without rules, there would be no labeling of actions as deviant; once we make a rule, we create the possibility of deviance, by definition. The point is illustrated strikingly by a recent misadventure in journalism. A reporter happened to come across the booking ledger of a New York City police precinct for 1910. Poring over it, he was astounded to find that there were no bookings for narcotics addition of any kind. Newspapers all over the country published his breathless report that in 1910 there were no drug addicts in New York City, in marked contrast to today, when there are many thousand. Since there was no law against possession of addictive substances in 1910, the discovery is not so astounding. It was the passage of the Harrison Stamp Tax Act, making the nonmedical possession of opiates a crime, which *created* crimes out of actions that had previously been legal.

There is, of course, a crucial intervening variable which is only implicit in Brooks's statement. As Durkheim has already noted, there are always rule violations. Human behavior is so tremendously variable that there is almost always someone who does the most horrendous things imaginable. But the most horrendous things seldom have rules forbidding them, because they happen so rarely. They are simply grouped under the category of universal deviance, or madness. What Durkheim had in mind were more common violations, such as theft and murder. These occur everywhere. Those considered the most horrible, such as murder, are relatively rare occurrences, but they have never been completely eliminated anywhere.

I have already argued that citizens of Western societies see official deviance as more outrageous than private deviance. Because of this, we seem for many decades to have had less deviance, as we shifted activities from the private to the public realm. But the intensity of public outrage has obviously not eliminated it entirely. It seems only to have lessened it. At the same time, however, the Welfare State Revolution, especially in recent years in the United States, has generated vastly more rules, both laws and regulatory agency rules. Though no one has been able to count their number, and it is not clear what such a count would even look like, we might guess that the growth of rules has been exponential in the past decade or two within government agencies themselves, precisely because *our greater concern over official deviance leads to more rules for government activity than for private activity, even when government is being given more and more power*—perhaps precisely because it is being given more power. An extreme example is the jungle of laws and official rules passed to control the dispensation of welfare funds.

California has thousands of pages of such regulations. It is literally impossible for any official to know all of them, and some of them are contradictory. It is inevitable that he will violate some, even many, rules if he tries to do his job according to stated law. But, far more important, we know that there are always intentional violations of even the most simple and unconflicting rules, so we know that we shall be contributing to official deviance by adding to existing laws, and that is what we have been doing on a massive scale in recent years. Consequently, we now have an upward spiraling in the rate of official deviance to feed the moral outrage of citizens.

When we put together the fact of greatly increased government action with the universal finding that there will always be some violations of laws, we get a very different perspective on many forms of deviance in Western societies today. For example, in Great Britain, there would not have been any corruption of the Bank of England officials had there not been a law passed which imposed certain stringent restrictions on buying foreign monies and on investing abroad. Because the state has decided that it has both the right and the power to restrict previously unregulated activities, new forms of official and unofficial deviance are created. Again, there were no invasions of privacy of American citizens by the CIA and the FBI in 1910 because there was no CIA or FBI. Moreover, there could not have been any such activity on such a large scale by government agencies because there were no government agencies big enough to do the job.

There is a clear general principle in this. *The bigger the scale of government, and the more rules it seeks to enforce against its own agents, the more real official deviance there will be—inevitably.* So, it is not surprising to find that citizens see more acts of official usurpations of power. They are inevitably there, and they will continue to grow as government expands and its rules multiply. Since we have reason to believe that the sense of moral outrage about official deviance is greater by some multiplier factor than that of private deviance, we can expect that the sense of moral outrage over increased government deviance, and the resulting sense of alienation and revolt, will accelerate.

The third form of official deviance that has surged in recent years with the acceleration of the Welfare State Revolution is usurpation of power, as defined by important segments of our societies, but not as defined by the government itself. Every new law or regulation is aimed at someone. As we have said, many, perhaps most, are directed at the agents of government itself. But many are directed at the citizens, in order to tax, control, punish, or reward them. Most of the new regulations are directed toward changing the situation of some citizens for the better, and some for what citizens themselves would define as the worse. It is obvious that members of our society weigh their own private losses, brought about by government action, more heavily than they weigh the gains of someone else which result from these losses. Even in those all-too-rare instances in which taxpayers are glad that someone benefits from the increased taxes they pay, their negative feelings still outweigh their positive ones. A businessman may feel glad that society as a whole will benefit from pollution controls, but he regrets that his business is the one being regulated. It has been common belief among political scientists, at least since Walter Lippmann's great work *The Public Philosophy,* that there is no longer (if there ever was) enough identification with the public interest to compensate individuals who are taxed or regulated for the immediate losses to them. Compare this with the feeling parents have about their children. Because they identify with the interests of their children, they gladly give them things. Parents gladly pay to provide benefits to their children, at least up to a point. The same is not true of most people who pay taxes. If a man does not see personal gain in paying taxes, (such as in getting a school for his children), he does not want to pay those taxes. The result is that, as our welfare states have increased the levels of taxation and regulation, they have made more and more individuals feel injured. As people have felt more injured, they have come to doubt the state's legitimacy. *The state's very size and power become the deviance.*

Even in highly homogeneous societies which have a high degree of public spirit (the Scandinavian countries, for example), there are now large factions which see the state as the enemy, and as being deviant in and of itself. Any enlargement of official bodies or their powers then becomes, in itself, an act of deviance. Indeed, at the extreme of polarization, some citizens come to see the whole state as the deviant, the enemy. At the same time, of course there are those who benefit from the state's growth and from its regulations. These people see those who are opposed to the state as the deviants. The growth of the state, with its polarizing tendencies, creates a situation in which some groups come to see the state as more and more deviant, and more and more a usurper of their rights. This growth tends to pit groups against each other, with each labeling the others as deviants. Needless to say, that further erodes a common feeling of public interest, so exacerbating the conflict.

In highly pluralistic societies, especially in the United States, the Welfare State Revolution has already caused great alienation from the government, especially in the highly individualistic South and Southwest, which have always seen the "feds" as the enemy. Their alienation and anger have not yet solidified into formal opposition, and may never do so, simply because the very individuals who are angriest at growing taxes, regulations, and bureaucracy are also the beneficiaries of some of the handouts and tyrannical rules they denounce. But growing anger, both at the government and between different groups, is apparent.

Given all of the factors which lead to greater official deviance and still greater outrage over that deviance, what seems likely to happen in the years ahead? The obvious answer is, more of the same welfare state will produce more of the same official deviance, and more of the same public protest.

There are very powerful political forces in support of an ever-bigger welfare state, but the growth of the welfare state has also produced very powerful political opposition. Will the welfare state in each nation merely advance to the stage where opposition to it prohibits further growth? If this happens, then what will happen to official deviance and our reaction to it? Will we adjust our standards downward, accepting a higher level of official deviance, thereby reducing our outrage, and so, stabilizing government? Possibly, but if we do, then do we not open the door to more official deviance, which, in turn, will increase our outrage? Lowering our standards may well be self-defeating.

Should we then increase our efforts to eradicate official deviance, without raising our standards? I see no reason to think this would be successful. Quite the contrary. We must keep in mind another basic truth about human beings. When a group is attacked, it becomes more united and counterattacks. We must remember that, just as the public becomes alienated from the government, so do government officials under attack become alienated from the public. This was a turning point in the Nixon administration, which seems to have looked at itself as an embattled group fighting against powerful public forces (the news media, Democrats, students, intellectuals, and others). Most public moralists have decided this was caused by Richard Nixon's personal pathology. I suggest these critics have never had bricks thrown at them, or endless news stories printed attacking them. A brick, and certainly a barrage of hostile news stories, can make anyone feel embattled. I suspect government officials feel that way today. In fact, I don't know any who do not. Turning the screw a notch tighter could easily lead to the final state of citizen-government conflict—progressive usurpations of power, then tyranny or revolt.

The third alternative is to cut back the welfare state. But would this actually decrease conflict and alienation? To cut back the welfare state, government officials would have to take away the benefits already enjoyed by certain groups. These groups would then become disgruntled and turn on the government, even as other groups ease up on their attacks. This is to say that achieving any long-lasting consensus on these issues in the coming decades is highly improbable—if not actually impossible.

Only two things seem clear. First, there are no obvious solutions. No amount of abstract social theorizing will yield any practical solutions. Solutions will have to be created politically to fit the evolving situations of each nation at a particular time. Second, we seem to be in for a long period of intense social conflict, great public outrage over official deviance and, consequently, political instability. No one can predict what will happen in such a tumultuous period. But I suspect we shall see a series of great political upheavals throughout the Western world, complete with revolutions and civil wars.

Bibliography

Banfield, Edward
1961   Political Influence. New York: The Free Press.
Banfield, Edward, and James Q. Wilson
1967   City Politics. Cambridge, Mass.: Harvard University Press.
Becker, Howard
1963   Outsiders. New York: The Free Press.
Brooks, Robert C.
1910   Corruption in American Politics and Life. New York: Dodd, Mead & Co.
Goodman, Walter
1963   All Honorable Men: Corruption and Compromise in American Life. Boston: Little, Brown & Co.
Gwyn, W. B.
1970   "The Nature and Decline of Corrupt Election Expenditures in Nineteenth-Century Britain." In Robert Heidenheimer, Political Corruption. New York: Holt, Rinehart & Co.
Heidenheimer, Robert
1970   Political Corruption. New York: Holt, Rinehart & Co.
Riordan, William L.
1963   Plunkitt of Tammany Hall. New York: E. B. Dutton Co.
Venkatappiah, B.
1965   "Office—Misuse of." In The Encyclopedia of the Social Sciences: 272–276. New York: Macmillan & Co.

35

Human beings are not very easy to change after all

An unjoyful message and its implications
for social programs

Amitai Etzioni

A while back there was a severe shortage of electricity in New
York City, and Columbia University tried to help out in two
ways: A card reading "Save a watt" was placed on everyone's
desk, and janitors removed some light bulbs from university corridors. The ways in which this shortage was made up for illustrate
two major approaches to social problem solving. One approach is
based on the assumption that people can be taught to change
their habits, that they can learn to remember to switch off
unused lights. The second approach assumes that people need
not, or will not, change and instead alter their environment so
that, even if they leave light switches on, watts are saved.

The prevalent approach in the treatment of our numerous and
still-multiplying social problems is the first. Imbedded in the programs of the federal, state, and city governments and embraced
almost instinctively by many citizens, especially liberal ones, is

From *Saturday Review*, June 3, 1972, pp. 45–47. Copyright © Saturday
Review, Inc. Reprinted by permission.

the assumption that, if you go out there and get the message across—persuade, propagandize, explain, campaign—people will change, that human beings are, ultimately, quite pliable. Both political leaders and the general public believe that advertising is powerful, that information campaigns work, and that an army of educators, counselors, or rehabilitation workers can achieve almost everything if they are sufficiently numerous, well trained, and richly endowed.

But can they? We have come of late to the realization that the pace of achievement in domestic programs ranges chiefly from the slow to the crablike—two steps backward for every one forward—and the suspicion is growing that there is something basically wrong with most of these programs. A nagging feeling persists that maybe something even more basic than the lack of funds or will is at stake. Consequently, social scientists like myself have begun to re-examine our core assumption that man can be taught almost anything and quite readily. We are now confronting the uncomfortable possibility that human beings are not very easily changed after all.

Take smoking, for instance. Since 1964, when the surgeon general began calling attention to the dangers of cigarettes, a vast and expensive campaign has been waged, involving press releases, lectures, television advertisements, pamphlets, and notations on the cigarette package. The positive result of all this activity, however, has been slight. At first there was no effect at all; actual cigarette smoking continued to rise until 1967. Then it dropped from 11.73 cigarettes per day per person aged eighteen years and over to 10.94 in 1969. More recently the level has risen again.

The moral? If you spend $27 million, you may get enough people to switch from Camels to Kools to make the investment worthwhile for the Kool manufacturers. However, if the same $27 million is used to make nonsmokers out of smokers—that is, to try to change a basic habit—no significant effect is to be expected. Advertising molds or teases our appetites, but it doesn't change basic tastes, values, or preferences. Try to advertise desegregation to racists, world government to chauvinists, temperance to alcoholics, or—as we still do at the cost of $16 million a year—drug abstention to addicts, and see how far you get.

In fact, the mass media in general have proved to be ineffectual as tools for profoundly converting people. Studies have shown that persons are more likely to heed spouses, relatives, friends, and "opinion leaders" than broadcasted or printed words when it comes to deep concerns.

Another area in which efforts to remake people have proved glaringly inefficient is that of the rehabilitation of criminals. We rely heavily on re-educational programs for prisoners. But it is a matter of record that out of every two inmates released, one will be rearrested and returned to prison in short order. Of the 151,355 inmates in state prisons on December 31, 1960, there were 74,138, or 49 per cent, who had been committed at least once to adult penal institutions. Reformatories come off no better. A study of 694 offenders released by one well-known institution reports 58.4 per cent re-turned within five years. The study concludes self-assuringly: "But this is no worse than the national average."

What about longer, more sustained educational efforts? Mature people can be taught many things—speed reading, belly dancing, Serbo-Croatian—usually with much more pain, sweat, cost, time, and energy than most be-ginning pupils suspect. When we turn, though, to the modification of ingrown habits, of basic values, of personality traits, or of other deep-seated matters, the impact is usually much less noticeable.

What is becoming increasingly apparent is that to solve social problems by changing people is more expensive and usually less productive than approaches that accept people as they are and seek to mend not them but the circumstances around them. Just such a conclusion was implicit, for instance, in an important but widely ignored study of automobile safety done by the Department of Health, Education, and Welfare. Applying cost-effectiveness measurements to efforts to cut down the horrendous toll on American highways—59,220 Americans were killed in 1970—the HEW study noted that driver education saves lives at the cost of $88,000 per life. New automobile accessories, as simple as seat belts, proved more than a thousand times as effective; saving a life this way, it was computed, costs a mere $87. Yet we continue to stress driver education as the chief preventive measure; the laws regarding the redesign of autos are moderate in their requirements and are poorly enforced. Similarly, we exhort people not to drive while under the influence of liquor, even not to drink in excess to begin with. But these are rather monumental, perhaps impossible, educational missions. However, a simple device that measures the level of intoxication by breath analysis and that is widely used by highway patrols in Great Britain has tended to scare drunken drivers off the roads in that country. It could be applied to a rapid reduction of traffic fatalities in this country. Educate drinkers later.

The problem of educating against drug addiction in general offers parallel lessons. Acting on the belief that personality predispositions yield fairly rapidly to such approaches, we have tried a variety of informational, per-suasive, personal, and group-therapeutic techniques in the battle against addiction. However, these approaches have rehabilitated only a few addicts. Much more promising are counter-drugs. For example, Antabuse, which if taken makes a person feel quite uncomfortable when he drinks, is more effective than psychotherapy in dealing with alcoholics. It takes so much less effort to decide each day to take medication than to decide, all the time, to refrain from drinking. True, Antabuse so far is a little-known remedy, and many who do know of it are skeptical, because early experiments in which a high dosage was administered seem to have resulted in some fatalities. Now, though, smaller dosages are being given, and Antabuse is slowly regaining serious consideration. ·

The failure of educational and therapeutic approaches to help most heroin addicts has led, finally, to the wide use of a substitute, methadone, which is usually referred to as a blocking drug because it is said to curb the craving for heroin. Let's not ask here if methadone is the most suitable drug for the purpose, to what extent it is different from heroin, or even if it actually blocks out heroin. For our purpose, it is sufficient to say that, unlike the educational and therapeutic approaches to heroin addiction, methadone is effective. That is, people taking methadone work, study, are satisfied, function as human beings and citizens, and have a much lower criminality record. Thus, of a group of 990 men carefully examined, those employed or attending school rose from 27 per cent at admission to the methadone program to 65 per cent after one year on the program, to 77 per cent after two years, and to 92 per cent in the third year. A report by the director of the District of Columbia narcotics treatment division shows that as the number of addicts on methadone increased, the level of crimes that addicts tended to commit fell almost proportionally. Thus, with about 20 per cent of the addicts on such treatments, robberies in Washington, D.C., fell from 12,432 in 1969 to 11,222 in 1971. There is no evidence that any educational program has ever had such an effect.

Though there seem to be no similarly effective drugs to help food addicts (or persons afflicted with obesity), we have recently been informed by medical researchers that serious weight problems seem to arise, *not* from faulty will power, character, or motivation—qualities subject to educability—but from different rates of metabolism and divergent nutritional pathways. These pathways are established early in childhood and may be either set for life or altered by medication, but exhortation or other educational efforts can alter them little.

Again medication has proved to be more promising than education in dealing with mental patients. After year upon year of increase, the number of patients in mental hospitals declined sharply in 1956. This turning point came about, not because therapy was expanded or intensified or a new procedure found, but because tranquilizers were widely introduced. Most of those discharged now live on medications at home.

Technological devices and medication are not the sole approaches we may rely upon more heavily once we understand the limits of adult educability and allow ourselves to see the full extent and implications of these limits. Improved matching of persons and jobs may go a long way toward reducing the need for job training. Here the two alternative assumptions about the pliability and perfectibility of human nature come into sharp focus. Few educators are quite willing to assume, as it was once put rather extremely, that "given time and resources, we can make a piano player out of anybody." Yet whole job-training programs are still based on such an assumption. For instance, the scores of training programs for the unemployed or the to-be-employed that are run or supported by the Department of Labor assume that people can be changed, and quite fundamentally.

The Department of Labor stresses, in its discussion of "social-psychological barriers" to employment, the need to modify "attitudes, aspirations, motivation (especially achievement motivation), ability or willingness to defer gratification, and self-image." And the 1968 Manpower Report suggests "the necessity of direct efforts to modify the attitudes of the disadvantaged before introducing them to job situations." One major training program aims at providing "needed communication skills, grooming and personal hygiene, the standards of behavior and performance generally expected by employers."

In a study I conducted with three of my colleagues for the Center for Policy Research, we found that persons have deep-seated preferences in their work behavior that are very difficult to change, and we concluded that it may be unethical to try to change them. Thus, if a person prefers to engage in nonroutine work of the more creative type, at an irregular pace, training him or her to be a "good" assembly-line worker—which entails teaching not only how to turn bolts but also how to be a more "uptight" person—may be both ineffective and morally dubious, especially if we are correct in suggesting that people's existing preferences can be readily analyzed so that they can be helped to choose jobs compatible with their personalities. It is also much less costly to test and assist people than it is to train and mold them. If we run out of compatible jobs, jobs may be changed to suit people rather than people to suit jobs.

One of the few effective and efficient ways in which people can be basically remade lies in a total and voluntary reconstruction of their social environment. Thus, when students withdraw from the campus into a rural commune, or Jews emigrate from the U.S.S.R. and Eastern Europe to found a new Israeli kibbutz, life can be deeply recast. The creation of a whole new environment for addicts—indeed, a new social community—on a voluntary basis, as achieved by Synanon, is highly effective, and Alcoholics Anonymous seems to provide a cure as effective as or better than Antabuse. Many alcoholics and mental patients who are integrated into therapeutic communities are reported to recover well.

This total-change approach is very appealing to a radical New Left perspective, which suggests that new persons cannot evolve except in a new society and that a new society will emerge only from the deep efforts of people in the crisis of reshaping their world. At the same time one must note that effective total-change groups work only for those who join voluntarily. Most addicts, mental patients, prison inmates, and others in need of change don't volunteer to join. Hence, the total-change approach is considerably less applicable to social problems than some would have it be.

Much of what I have said is primarily concerned with adult educability. It also holds true, albeit to a lesser degree, for children. While children, especially younger ones, are more educable than adults—who must often first be disabused of the education they have acquired as youngsters—most

Americans, both the general public and the policy-makers, still enormously overestimate what the education of children can achieve.

The schools, which are still the main institutions of education for children aged six through eighteen, cannot carry out many of the missions assigned to them. Most schools do not build character, open the mind, implant an appreciation of beauty, or otherwise serve as the greater humanizer or the social equalizer as educators would wish them to do. In desperation it is suggested now that the schools concentrate on teaching the three Rs, and it is common knowledge that they have a hard time doing even that.

Probably the greatest disappointment educators have encountered in recent years, and have not quite come to terms with, is the failure of intensive educational campaigns to help children from disadvantaged backgrounds catch up with their more advantaged peers. As has already been widely reported, virtually all of the 150-odd compensatory education schemes that have been tried either have not worked at all or have worked only marginally or only for a small proportion of the student population. The Coleman Report makes this point, and the same conclusion comes from another source. Professor Jesse Burkhead of Syracuse University found that differences in the achievements of high school students in large-city schools are almost completely conditioned by the students' social backgrounds and environments, including the incomes and occupations of the parents (class), housing conditions, and ethnicity.

The reasons for this inability to bridge the distance between the educational achievements of disadvantaged and better off children are hotly debated. It seems to me that the key reason for the failure of compensatory education lies in the fact that the disadvantaged children are locked into total environments, which include home, neighborhood, parental poverty, discrimination, and inhibiting models of behavior. We cannot hope to change one without changing the others. Education will become more effective when it works together with other societal changes—which, of course, means that, by itself, it is not half so powerful as we often assume.

The contention that personal growth and societal changes are much harder to come by than we had assumed, especially via one version or another of the educationalist-enlightenment approach, is not a joyful message, but one whose full implications we must learn to accept before we can devise more effective social programs. Once we cease turning to ads, leaflets, counselors, or teachers for salvation, we may realize that more can be achieved by engineers, doctors, social movements, and public-interest groups; and the educators will find new and much-needed allies.

"Is freedom dying in America?"

Henry Steele Commager

"Those, who would give up essential liberty to purchase a little temporary safety," said Benjamin Franklin, two centuries ago, "deserve neither liberty nor safety."

Today we are busy doing what Franklin warned us against. Animated by impatience, anger and fear, we are giving up essential liberties, not for safety, but for the appearance of safety. We are corroding due process and the rule of law not for Order, but for the semblance of order. We will find that when we have given up liberty, we will not have safety, and that when we have given up justice, we will not have order.

"We in this nation appear headed for a new period of repression," Mayor John V. Lindsay of New York recently warned us. We are in fact already in it.

Not since the days when Sen. Joseph McCarthy bestrode the political stage, fomenting suspicion and hatred, betraying the Bill

From *Look*, July 14, 1970 Volume 34, No. 14. Copyright © 1970, Cowles Communications, Inc. Reprinted by permission.

of Rights, bringing Congress and the State Department into disrepute, have we experienced anything like the current offensive against the exercise of freedom in America. If repression is not yet as blatant or as flamboyant as it was during the McCarthy years, it is in many respects more pervasive and more formidable. For it comes to us now with official sanction and is imposed upon us by officials sworn to uphold the law: the Attorney General, the FBI, state and local officials, the police, and even judges. In Georgia and California, in Lamar, S.C., and Jackson, Miss., and Kent, Ohio, the attacks are overt and dramatic; on the higher levels of the national administration, it is a process of erosion, the erosion of what Thomas Jefferson called "the sacred soil of liberty." Those in high office do not openly proclaim their disillusionment with the principles of freedom, but they confess it by their conduct, while the people acquiesce in their own disinheritance by abandoning the "eternal vigilance" that is the price of liberty.

There is nothing more ominous than this popular indifference toward the loss of liberty, unless it is the failure to understand what is at stake. Two centuries ago, Edmund Burke said of Americans that they "snuff the approach of tyranny in every tainted breeze." Now, their senses are blunted. The evidence of public-opinion polls is persuasive that a substantial part of the American people no longer know or cherish the Bill of Rights. They are, it appears, quite prepared to silence criticism of governmental policies if such criticism is thought—*by the Government*—damaging to the national interest. They are prepared to censor newspaper and television reporting if such reports are considered—*by the Government*—damaging to the national interest! As those in authority inevitably think whatever policies they pursue, whatever laws they enforce, whatever wars they fight, are in the national interest, this attitude is a formula for the ending of all criticism, which is another way of saying for the ending of democracy.

Corruption of language is often a first sign of a deeper malaise of mind and spirit, and it is ominous that invasions of liberty are carried on, today, in the name of constitutionalism, and the impairment of due process, in the name of Law and Order. Here it takes the form of a challenge to the great principle of the separation of powers, and there to the equally great principle of the superiority of the civil to the military authority. Here it is the intimidation of the press and television by threats both subtle and blatant, there of resort to the odious doctrine of "intent" to punish anti-war demonstrators. Here it is the use of the dangerous weapon of censorship, overt and covert, to silence troublesome criticism, there the abuse of the power of punishment by contempt of court. The thrust is everywhere the same, and so too the animus behind it: to equate dissent with lawlessness and nonconformity with treason. The purpose of those who are prepared to sweep aside our ancient guarantees of freedom is to blot out those great problems that glare upon us from every horizon, and pretend that if we refuse to acknowledge them, they will somehow go away. It is to argue that discontent is not an honest expression of genuine grievances but of willfulness, or perversity, or perhaps of the crime of being young, and that if it can only be stifled, we can restore harmony to our distracted society.

Men like Vice President Spiro T. Agnew simplistically equate opposition to official policies with effete intellectualism, and cater to the sullen suspicion of intellectuals, always latent in any society, to silence that opposition. Frightened people everywhere, alarmed by lawlessness and violence in their communities, and impatient with the notion that we cannot really end violence until we deal with its causes, call loudly for tougher laws, tougher cops and tougher courts or—as in big cities like New York or small towns like Lamar—simply take authority into their own hands and respond with vigilante tactics. Impatient people, persuaded that the law is too slow and too indulgent, and that order is imperiled by judicial insistence on due process, are prepared to sweep aside centuries of progress toward the rule of law in order to punish those they regard as enemies of society. Timid men who have no confidence in the processes of democracy or in the potentialities of education are ready to abandon for a police state the experiment that Lincoln called "the last best hope of earth."

The pattern of repression is, alas, all too familiar. Most ominous is the erosion of due process of law, perhaps the noblest concept in the long history of law and one so important that it can be equated with civilization, for it is the very synonym for justice. It is difficult to remember a period in our own history in which due process has achieved more victories in the courts and suffered more setbacks in the arena of politics and public opinion than in the last decade. While the Warren Court steadily enlarged the scope and strengthened the thrust of this historic concept, to make it an effective instrument for creating a more just society, the political and the law enforcement agencies have displayed mounting antagonism to the principle itself and resistance to its application. The desegregation decision of 1954 has been sabotaged by both the Federal and local governments—a sabotage dramatized by the recent decision of the Justice Department to support tax exemption for private schools organized to frustrate desegregation.

There are many other examples. Pending legislation, including the Organized Crime Control Act of 1969, provides for "preventive detention" in seeming violation of the constitutional guarantee of presumption of innocence; limits the right of the accused to examine evidence illegally obtained; permits police to batter their way into a private house without notice (the no-knock provision); and provides sentences of up to 30 years for "dangerous special offenders." And the government itself, from local police to the Attorney General, persists in what Justice Holmes called the "dirty business" of wiretapping and bugging to obtain evidence for convictions, though this is a clear violation of the right of protection against self-incrimination.

Equally flagrant is the attack on First Amendment freedoms—freedom of speech, press, petition and assembly—an attack that takes the form of intimidation and harassment rather than of overt repudiation. The President and the Vice President have joined in a crusade designed to force great newspapers like the New York *Times* and the Washington *Post* to moderate their criticism of Administration policies, and to frighten the television networks into scaling down their coverage of events that the Government finds embarrassing; a position that rests on the curious principle that the real crime is not official misconduct but the portrayal of that misconduct. Mr. Agnew, indeed, has gone so far as to call on governors to drive the news purveyed by "bizarre extremists" from newspapers and television sets; it is an admonition that, if taken literally, would deny newspaper and TV coverage to Mr. Agnew himself. All this is coupled with widespread harassment of the young, directed superficially at little more than hairstyle, dress or manners—but directed in fact to their opinions, or perhaps to their youthfulness. And throughout the country, government officials are busy compiling dossiers on almost all citizens prominent enough to come to their attention.

Government itself is engaged increasingly in violating what President Dwight D. Eisenhower chose as the motto for the Columbia University bicentenary: "Man's right to knowledge and the free use thereof." The USIA proscribes books that criticize American foreign policy at the same time that it launches a positive program of celebrating the Nixon Administration and the conduct of the Vietnam war through films and a library of "safe" books selected by well-vetted experts. The Federal Government spends millions of dollars presenting its version of history and politics to the American people. The Pentagon alone spends $47 million a year on public relations and maintains hundreds of lobbyists to deal with Congress, and the Defense Department floods schools and clubs and veterans organizations with films designed to win support for the war.

Meantime, the growing arrogance of the military and its eager intervention in areas long supposed to be exclusively civilian gravely threaten the principle of the superiority of the civil to the military power. Military considerations are advanced to justify the revival of the shabby practices of the McCarthy era—security clearances for civilians working in all establishments that have contracts with Defense—a category that includes laboratories, educational institutions and research organizations. What the standards are that may be expected to dictate security "clearance" is suggested by Vice President Agnew's proposal to "separate the [protest leaders] from our society—with no more regret than we should feel over discarding rotten apples from a barrel." That is, of course, precisely the philosophy that animated the Nazis. Military considerations, too, are permitted to dictate policies of secrecy that extend even to censorship of the *Congressional Record*, thus denying to congressmen, as to the American people, information they need to make decisions on foreign policy. Secrecy embraces, not unnaturally, facts about the conduct of the war; Attorney General Mitchell, it was reported, hoped to keep the Cambodian caper secret from Congress and the people until it was a *fait accompli.* So, too, the CIA, in theory merely an information-gathering agency, covers its far-flung operations in some 60 countries with a cloak of secrecy so thick that even Congress cannot penetrate it. The Army itself, entering the civilian arena, further endangers freedom of assembly and of speech by employing something like a thousand agents to mingle in student and other assemblies and report to the Army what they see and hear. This is, however, merely a tiny part of the some $3 billion that our Government spends every year in various types of espionage—more every year than the total cost of the Federal Government from its foundation in 1789 to the beginning of the Civil War in 1861!

It would be an exaggeration to say that the United States is a garrison state, but none to say that it is in danger of becoming one.

The purpose of this broad attack on American freedoms is to silence criticism of Government and of the war, and to encourage the attitude that the Government knows best and must be allowed a free hand, an attitude Americans have thought odious ever since the days of George III. It is to brand the universities as a fountainhead of subversion and thus weaken them as a force in public life. It is to restore "balance" to the judiciary and thereby reverse some of the great achievements of the 16 years of the Warren Court and to reassure the Bourbons, North and South, who are alarmed at the spectacle of judicial liberalism. It is to return to a "strict" interpretation of the power of states over racial relations and civil liberties—a euphemism for the nullification of those liberties.

The philosophy behind all this, doubtless unconscious, is that government belongs to the President and the Vice President; that they are the masters, and the people, the subjects. A century ago, Walt Whitman warned of "the never-ending audacity of elected persons"; what would he say if he were living today? Do we need to proclaim once more the most elementary principle of our constitutional system: that in the United States, the people are the masters and all officials are servants—officials in the White House, in the Cabinet, in the Congress, in the state executive and legislative chambers; officials, too, in uniform, whether of the national guard or of the police?

Those who are responsible for the campaign to restrict freedom and hamstring the Bill of Rights delude themselves that if they can but have their way, they will return the country to stability and order. They are mistaken. They are mistaken not merely because they are in fact hostile to freedom, but because they don't understand the relation of freedom to the things they prize most—to security, to order, to law.

What is that relationship?

For 2,500 years, civilized men have yearned and struggled for freedom from tyranny—the tyranny of despotic government and superstition and ignorance. What explains this long devotion to the idea and practice of freedom? How does it happen that all Western societies so exalt freedom that they have come to equate it with civilization itself?

Freedom has won its exalted place in philosophy and policy quite simply because, over the centuries, we have come to see that it is a necessity; a necessity for justice, a necessity for progress, a necessity for survival.

How familiar the argument that we must learn to reconcile the rival claims of freedom and order. But they do not really need to be reconciled; they were never at odds. They are not alternatives, they are two sides to the same coin, indissolubly welded together. The community—society or nation—has an interest in the rights of the individual because without the exercise of those rights, the community itself will decay and collapse. The individual has an interest in the stability of the community of which he is a part because without security, his rights are useless. No community can long prosper without nourishing the exercise of individual liberties for, as John Stuart Mill wrote a century ago, "A State which dwarfs its men, in order that they may be more docile instruments in its hands . . . will find that with small men no great thing can really be accomplished." And no individual can fulfill his genius without supporting the just authority of the state, for in a condition of anarchy, neither dignity nor freedom can prosper.

The function of freedom is not merely to protect and exalt the individual, vital as that is to the health of society. Put quite simply, we foster freedom in order to avoid error and discover truth; so far, we have found no other way to achieve this objective. So, too, with dissent. We do not indulge dissent for sentimental reasons; we encourage it because we have learned that we cannot live without it. A nation that silences dissent, whether by force, intimidation, the withholding of information or a foggy intellectual climate, invites disaster. A nation that penalizes criticism is left with passive acquiescence in error. A nation that discourages originality is left with minds that are unimaginative and dull. And with stunted minds, as with stunted men, no great thing can be accomplished.

It is for this reason that history celebrates not the victors who successfully silenced dissent but their victims who fought to speak the truth as they saw it. It is the bust of Socrates that stands in the schoolroom, not the busts of those who condemned him to death for "corrupting the youth." It is Savonarola we honor, not the Pope who had him burned there in the great Piazza in Florence. It is Tom Paine we honor, not the English judge who outlawed him for writing the *Rights of Man*.

Our own history, too, is one of rebellion against authority. We remember Roger Williams, who championed toleration, not John Cotton, who drove him from the Bay Colony; we celebrate Thomas Jefferson, whose motto was "Rebellion to tyrants is obedience to God," not Lord North; we read Henry Thoreau on civil disobedience, rather than those messages of President Polk that earned him the title "Polk the Mendacious"; it is John Brown's soul that goes marching on, not that of the judge who condemned him to death at Charles Town.

Why is this? It is not merely because of the nobility of character of these martyrs. Some were not particularly noble. It is because we can see now that they gave their lives to defend the interests of humanity, and that they, not those who punished them, were the true benefactors of humanity.

But it is not just the past that needed freedom for critics, nonconformists and dissenters. We, too, are assailed by problems that seem insoluble; we, too, need new ideas. Happily, ours is not a closed system—not yet, anyway. We have a long history of experimentation in politics, social relations and science. We experiment in astrophysics because we want to land on the moon; we experiment in biology because we want to find the secret of life; we experiment in medicine because we want to cure cancer; and in all of these areas, and a hundred others, we make progress. If we are to survive and flourish, we must approach politics, law and social institutions in the same spirit that we approach science. We know that we have not found final truth in physics or biology. Why do we suppose that we have found final truth in politics or law? And just as scientists welcome new truth wherever they find it, even in the most disreputable places, so statesmen, jurists and educators must be prepared to welcome new ideas and new truths from whatever sources they come, however alien their appearance, however revolutionary their implications.

"There can *be* no difference anywhere," said the philosopher William James, "that doesn't make a difference elsewhere—no difference in abstract truth that doesn't express itself in a difference in concrete fact. . . ."

Let us turn then to practical and particular issues and ask, in each case, what are and will be the consequences of policies that repress freedom, discourage independence, and impair justice in American society, and what are, and will be, the consequences of applying to politics and society those standards and habits of free inquiry that we apply as a matter of course to scientific inquiry?

Consider the erosion of due process of law—that complex of rules and safeguards built up over the centuries to make sure that every man will have a fair trial. Remember that it is designed not only for the protection of desperate characters charged with monstrous crimes; it is designed for every litigant. Nor is due process merely for the benefit of the accused. As Justice Robert H. Jackson said, "It is the best insurance for the Government itself against those blunders which leave lasting stains on a system of justice. . . ."

And why is it necessary to guarantee a fair trial for all; for those accused of treason, for those who champion the popular causes in a disorderly fashion, for those who assign their social and political rights against community prejudices, as well as for corporations, labor unions and churches? It is, of course, necessary so that justice will be done. Justice is the end, the aim, of government. It is implicitly the end of all governments; it is quite explicitly the end of the United States Government, for it was "in order to establish justice" that the Constitution was ordained.

Trials are held not in order to obtain convictions; they are held to find justice. And over the centuries, we have learned by experience that unless we conduct trials by jury and suffuse them with the spirit of fair play, justice will not be done. The argument that the scrupulous observance of technicalities of due process slows up or frustrates speedy convictions is, of course, correct, if all you want is convictions. But why not go all the way and restore the use of torture? That got confessions and convictions! Every argument in favor of abating due process in order to get convictions applies with equal force to the use of the third degree and the restoration of torture. It is important to remember that nation after nation abandoned torture (the Americans never had it), not merely because it was barbarous, but because, though it wrung confessions from its victims, it did not get justice. It implicated the innocent with the guilty and outraged the moral sense of the community. Due process proved both more humane and infinitely more efficient.

Or consider the problem of wiretapping. That in many cases wiretapping "works" is clear enough, but so do many things prohibited by civilized society, such as torture and invasion of the home. But "electronic surveillance," said Justice William J. Brennan, Jr., "strikes deeper than at the ancient feeling that a man's home is his castle; it strikes at freedom of communication, a postulate of our kind of society. . . . Freedom of speech is undermined where people fear to speak unconstrainedly in what they suppose to be the privacy of home or office."

Perhaps the most odious violation of justice is the maintenance of a double standard: one justice for blacks and another for whites, one for the rich and another for the poor, one for those who hold "radical" ideas, and another for those who are conservative and respectable. Yet we have daily before our eyes just such a double standard of justice. The "Chicago Seven," who crossed state lines with "intent" to stir up a riot, have received heavy jail sentences, but no convictions have been returned against the Chicago police who participated in that riot. Black Panthers are on trial for their lives for alleged murders, but policemen involved in wantonly attacking a Black Panther headquarters and killing two blacks have been punished by demotion.

Turn to the role and function of freedom in our society—freedom of speech and of the press—and the consequences of laying restrictions upon these freedoms. The consequence is, of course, that society will be deprived of the inestimable advantage of inquiry, criticism, exposure and dissent. If the press is not permitted to perform its traditional function of presenting the whole news, the American people will go uninformed. If television is dissuaded from showing controversial films, the people will be denied the opportunity to know what is going on. If teachers and scholars are discouraged from inquiring into the truth of history or politics or anthropology, future generations may never acquire those habits of intellectual independence essential to the working of democracy. An enlightened citizenry is necessary for self-government. If facts are withheld, or distorted, how can the people be enlightened, how can self-government work?

The real question in all this is what kind of society do we want? Do we want a police society where none are free of surveillance by their government? Or do we want a society where ordinary people can go about their business without the eye of Big Brother upon them?

The Founding Fathers feared secrecy in government not merely because it was a vote of no-confidence in the intelligence and virtue of the people but on the practical ground that all governments conceal their mistakes behind the shield of secrecy; that if they are permitted to get away with this in little things, they will do it in big things—like the Bay of Pigs or the invasion of Cambodia.

And if you interfere with academic freedom in order to silence criticism, or critics, you do not rid the university of subversion. It is not ideas that are subversive, it is the lack of ideas. What you do is to silence or get rid of those men who have ideas, leaving the institution to those who have no ideas, or have not the courage to express those that they have. Are such men as these what we want to direct the education of the young and advance the cause of learning?

The conclusive argument against secrecy in scientific research is that it will in the end give us bad science. First-rate scientists will not so gravely violate their integrity as to confine their findings to one government or one society, for the first loyalty of science is to scientific truth. "The Sciences," said Edward Jenner of smallpox fame, "are never at war." We have only to consider the implications of secrecy in the realm of medicine: What would we think of doctors favoring secrecy in cancer research on the grounds of "national interest"?

The argument against proscribing books, which might normally be in our overseas libraries, because they are critical of Administration policies is not that it will hurt authors or publishers. No. It is quite simply that if the kind of people who believe in proscription are allowed to control our libraries, these will cease to be centers of learning and become the instruments of party. The argument against withholding visas from foreign scholars whose ideas may be considered subversive is not that this will inconvenience them. It is that we deny ourselves the benefit of what they have to say. Suppose President Andrew Jackson had denied entry to Alexis de Tocqueville on the ground that he was an aristocrat and might therefore be a subversive influence on our democracy? We would have lost the greatest book ever written about America.

There is one final consideration. Government, as Justice Louis D. Brandeis observed half a century ago, "is the potent, the omnipresent teacher. For good or for ill, it teaches the whole people by its example." If government tries to solve its problems by resort to large-scale violence, its citizens will assume that violence is the normal way to solve problems. If government itself violates the law, it brings the law into contempt, and breeds anarchy. If government masks its operations, foreign and domestic, in a cloak of secrecy, it encourages the creation of a closed, not an open, society. If government shows itself impatient with due process, it must expect that its people will come to scorn the slow procedures of orderly debate and negotiation and turn to the easy solutions of force. If government embraces the principle that the end justifies the means, it radiates approval of a doctrine so odious that it will in the end destroy the whole of society. If government shows, by its habitual conduct, that it rejects the claims of freedom and of justice, freedom and justice will cease to be the ends of our society.

Eighty years ago, Lord Bryce wrote of the American people that "the masses of the people are wiser, fairer and more temperate in any matter to which they can be induced to bend their minds, than most European philosophers have believed possible for the masses of the people to be."

Is this still true? If the American people can indeed be persuaded to "bend their minds" to the great questions of the preservation of freedom, it may still prove true. If they cannot, we may be witnessing, even now, a dissolution of the fabric of freedom that may portend the dissolution of the Republic.